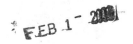
Transnational Criminal Organizations, Cybercrime, and Money Laundering

A Handbook for Law Enforcement Officers, Auditors, and Financial Investigators

James R. Richards

CRC Press
Boca Raton   London   New York   Washington, D.C.

Acquiring Editor: Harvey Kane
Project Editor: Sylvia Wood
Marketing Manager   Becky McEldowney
Cover design: Dawn Boyd

Library of Congress Cataloging-in-Publication Data

Richards, James R., 1960–
     Transnational criminal organizations, cybercrime & money
laundering : a handbook for law enforcement officers, auditors, and
financial investigators / James R. Richards
          p.   cm.
     Includes bibliographical references and index.
     ISBN 0-8493-2806-3 (alk. paper)
     1. Money laundering.   2. Money laundering investigation.
3. Organized crime.   4. Computer crimes.   5. Transnational crime.
I. Title.
HV6768.R53   1998
364.16′8—DC21   98-8240
                                                                   CIP

Introduction

Criminals and criminal groups have long been associated with their particular law-enforcement counterparts: in the 1930s, Al Capone and his Treasury nemesis Eliot Ness; the French Connection and Interpol in the 1960s; and the Colombian drug cartels' "kingpins" and the special agents of the DEA in the 1980s. In addition, these criminals and criminal groups have traditionally been indentified with specific cities or countries: the Sicilian Mafia with Palermo; the American Mafia families with New York (the Genovese and Bonnano families), Chicago (Al Capone), and Las Vegas (Bugsy Siegel); the Chinese Triads and Japanese Yakuza with Hong Kong and Tokyo, respectively. And their law-enforcement counterparts have shared the same local or national character.

But no longer. The 1990s have seen the local character of these criminal groups and their law-enforcement counterparts changed to an international, or transnational, character, replete with regional and global alliances. They have gone global.

What has brought about this change from local or national crime to international crime? A number of landmark events have coincided with this shift: the creation of free-trade blocks such as the European Union and the 1986 North American Free Trade Agreement (NAFTA); the advent of the World Wide Web beginning in 1990; the collapse of the Soviet Union in 1991; and the commercialization of China (including the hand-over of Hong Kong on July 1, 1997). These events have combined with other lesser happenings to foster a new species of international or transnational criminal organization.

As the activities and interests of these organizations have become more global, they have begun to enter into strategic alliances with other criminal groups to gain access to new markets, and to take advantage of their brethren's unique criminal skills. As their activities become more sophisticated and more profitable, the means they use to launder money also become more polished. Add the recent phenomenon of cyberbanking to the factors previously mentioned, and it becomes clear that these "bad guys" and their criminal activities and money-laundering methods remain a step ahead of the "good guys" and the legal tools at their disposal.

Recognizing this gap, authors have been diligently adding to the library of books and articles on how to combat the criminals and their efforts. Hundreds of treatises on the various international criminal organizations have been written *by* the law-enforcement community *for* the law-enforcement community; hundreds more have been written by government regulators for banking and other compliance officers on the subject of money laundering; and hundreds more have been written by computer "geeks" (my apologies to those esteemed writers of computerese — I won't use the term twice) on computer crimes, wire transfers, and such obtuse topics as clipper chip technology. What has been lacking, however, is reference books that combine all three subjects — criminal organizations, cyberbanking, and money laundering — in a style that can be understood by those who need the information most: financial investigators, law-enforcement personnel, and auditors.

Thus, this book. It is intended to give the reader a quick, but thorough, understanding of the basic histories and interrelationships of and between the various international criminal organizations (ICOs) or transnational criminal organizations (TCOs); money-laundering concepts, terms and phrases; the background and makeup of the various state, federal, and law-enforcement and regulatory agencies involved in the local, national, and international fight against ICOs in general and money laundering in particular; the laws and treaties available to these agencies; and the mechanics of wire transfers and cyberbanking, and their corollary, cybercrime. The book's intended audience includes local, state, and federal law-enforcement personnel, bank compliance officers, financial investigators, criminal defense attorneys, and all others who are interested in becoming familiar with the basic concepts of international crime and money laundering. In addition to these basic concepts — the three stages of money laundering, some of the legislation in place, an overview of the relevant federal agencies, the various transnational criminal organizations, and the basic investigatory techniques — this book also lends some insight into otherwise horrendously complicated topics such as wire transfers, cyberbanking and the BCCI Affair. It is not intended to be a legal treatise or law-review-style work.

With these concepts in mind, I organized this book into five sections: Part I, The Bad Guys, describes what I have termed the "big six" international criminal organizations, and, to a lesser degree, terrorist organizations and strategic alliances among these groups. Part II, Money-Laundering Techniques, describes the mechanics of money laundering, cybercrime and cyberbanking, and the various financial institutions — categorized as banks and non-bank financial institutions — that criminals use to launder the profits of their illegal activity. Part III, The Good Guys, describes the various federal law-enforcement and regulatory agencies that are charged with ending these activities. Part IV, Anti-Money-Laundering Tools, describes the various statutes, forms, and practices in place to combat money laundering, as well as investigatory techniques and examples of law-enforcement efforts, including asset forfeiture. Finally, Part V, The World Stage, aims to offer some insight into the major international law-enforcement agencies as well as 55 of the main countries of the world that are involved in international crime and money laundering, either positively or negatively. They are organized into three groups: the Pan-American countries of Canada, Mexico, Panama, and Colombia; Russia and the former Soviet Union nations; and 50 others.

To the best of my ability, the research is current through Friday, March 13, 1998. Most of it was done online. All information was either taken directly from government or public sources, or has been confirmed through those sources. Perhaps the best origins of information have been transcripts of testimony before the various House and Senate committees and subcommittees. Other principal sources include the web sites for the various Treasury Department bureaus and offices, the State Department, a number of congressional sites, including "Thomas," and sites for various senators or congressmen. I have tried, where possible, to identify these government web sites, and I encourage the reader to explore them also. I have also relied heavily on cases reported in the various federal law reports series, notably federal cases recorded in the Federal Reporter or Supreme Court Reports. Case citations reflect these sources. I have also used a great number of Canadian government sources, including those of the Royal Canadian Mounted Police.

I have tried, wherever possible, and with due diligence, to identify all sources. Where I have failed to do so, these were either primary sources or government materials within the public domain.

To satisfy certain obligations, please note that this work represents the opinions and conclusions of its author, and not necessarily those of any law-enforcement or prosecutorial office with which the author is, or has been, associated.

James R. Richards
Milton, Massachusetts
March 30, 1998

Acknowledgments

Thank you to Senator John Kerry (Dem., Mass.) for his work in the BCCI Affair and his encouraging reply to one of my earliest inquiries regarding this work. The senator and I share a common background with the Middlesex County District Attorney's Office in Cambridge, Massachusetts. Another "thank you" is owed to Tom Hoopes of Boston, who is living proof that being a gentleman and a criminal-defense attorney are not mutually exclusive. Tom offered some insightful tips on what was lacking in an early draft. Others who gave their time and advice include Carlton Fitzpatrick, Supervising Criminal Investigator, Financial Fraud Institute, Federal Law Enforcement Training Center (FLETC), Glynco, Georgia; Michael Eid, of the Treasury Department's Financial Crimes Enforcement Network (FinCEN) in Vienna, Virginia; and John Moynihan, of BERG Associates, Washington, D.C. and Boston, whose enthusiasm for this field is contagious. Special thanks to Sylvia Wood, my editor at CRC, for her valiant efforts at turning a sow's ear into a silk purse. Thanks, too, to Sergeant Ron Halverson, my former C.O. from Invermere Detachment, "E" Division, Royal Canadian Mounted Police, who taught me more in a few months about "the law" than I learned in three years of law school.

Finally, saving the best for last, my gratitude to my wife, Johanne, for putting up with my nightly forays into the Internet and the constant clacking of the computer keyboard. Also, I would be remiss not to mention the arrival, in the midst of my writings, of our fourth, Matthew Jonathan, born September 18, 1997. Law-enforcement agencies worldwide could learn from young Matthew — be able to fall asleep in the back seat of a moving car but never sleep more than two hours at a time, and always have at least two changes of clothes wherever you go. Mention of our fourth requires naming the first, second, and third: Stephanie, at nine already smarter than her old man; Nicolas, whose first-ever goal in ice hockey was the family's other major event of 1997; and Michael, the four-year-old master of erasing computer files. I love you all, but four is enough, thank you.

The Author

James Richards is Director of the Asset Forfeiture Group, Special Investigations Unit, of the Middlesex District Attorney's Office in Cambridge, Massachusetts. In addition to his duties supervising and prosecuting more than 1,000 forfeiture cases annually, he prosecutes white-collar crimes, including attorney embezzlement, public corruption, and gaming. In 1997, he investigated and prosecuted the "Boston College Gambling Case." Investigators from the Massachusetts State Police, New York State Police Organized Crime Unit, the F.B.I., and the N.C.A.A., joined in the investigation, which led to the indictment of the six key figures in three organized gambling rings operating on two different college campuses. All six eventually pled guilty.

Born and raised in Canada, James Richards obtained his Bachelor of Commerce and Bachelor of Laws degrees at the University of British Columbia in Vancouver. After six years as a barrister in Ontario, Mr. Richards emigrated to Boston. Three years at a major law firm there preceded his tenure as an Assistant District Attorney. Squeezed into this "multinational" or "transnational" experience was a stint as a Special Constable with the Royal Canadian Mounted Police.

James Richards has lectured extensively in the areas of Asset Forfeiture, Money Laundering, and the Fifth Amendment. His audiences are diverse — from street-level law-enforcement officers to prosecutors to college and university students. He also has acted as a trial and moot-court advisor for Harvard Law School and Boston College Law School. He is licensed to practice law in Canada, Massachusetts, and in the United States Federal Court (First Circuit). In his free time, he enjoys his four children, coaching youth soccer and hockey, and playing tennis with his wife. But he has yet to get around to fixing the broken steps.

Table of Contents

8 Regulatory (Anti-Money-Laundering) Forms 179

9 Asset Forfeiture 191

13 The Pan American Countries: Canada, Mexico, Panama, and Colombia 243

14 Russia and the Former Soviet Union Nations ... 259

Part I
The Bad Guys

International Criminal Organizations

1

Organized crime is nothing less than a massive attack on the fabric of society affecting practically all of its components at the individual, collective and institutional levels ... organized crime threatens some of the most basic elements of our democratic order.

— **Secretary-General of the United Nations**
Report on the Impact of Organized Criminal Activities at Large, April 1993

I.   Introduction

Where criminals and criminal organizations are limited only by their imagination, local and national law-enforcement agencies have always been limited to combating crime by the confines of the law and their particular geographic jurisdiction. At best, local agencies may have worked together on a regional basis, or with federal authorities to fight crime within the national jurisdiction.

It follows, then, that where jurisdiction is limited, perspective is equally limited. Thus, organized crime has traditionally been viewed as a local or national issue — the Mafia in Italy and the United States, the Yakuza in Japan, etc. However, in the last 10 years, there has been a growing recognition that crime and criminal organizations have crossed jurisdictional boundaries and gone global. This change has coincided with — has, in fact, been caused by — the collapse of the Soviet Union, the growth of capitalism in China, the enactment of the North American Free Trade Agreement, and the lowering of European customs, currency, passport controls, and other lesser events. Now, Colombian drug cartels are operating in Western Europe; Russian gangsters are operating in Eastern Europe, the United States, and Asia; the Chinese Triads dominate Asia and the west coast of the United States; and the Mexican criminal organizations dominate the world methamphetamine trade. Not only are these organizations operating globally, they are forming strategic alliances with each other, with rogue governments, and with terrorist organizations. These international criminal organizations (ICOs, also known as transnational criminal organizations, or TCOs) and their strategic alliances are the dominant problem facing local, national, and international law enforcement today.

Canada's Royal Canadian Mounted Police's Criminal Intelligence Directorate has identified 14 characteristics shared by organized crime groups or criminal organizations.

1. Corruption: the use of illicit influence, exploitation of weaknesses, and the blackmail of public and prominent figures.
2. Discipline: the enforcement of obedience to the organization through fear and violence.
3. Infiltration: continued effort to gain a foothold in legitimate institutions to further profit or gain a level of protection from detection.
4. Insulation: protection of the organization's leaders by separating them from the soldiers, cell from cell, and function from function.
5. Monopoly: control over certain criminal activities within a geographic area with no tolerence for competition.
6. Motivation: sole motivation is power and influence resulting from the accumulation of wealth (this motivation separates organized criminal groups from terrorists, who are motivated by political or social gains).
7. Subversion: of society's institutions and legal and moral value systems.
8. History: has allowed entrenchment and refinement of criminal activities and practices.
9. Violence: used without hesitation to further the criminal aims of the organization.
10. Sophistication: in the use of advanced communication systems, financial controls, and operations.
11. Continuity: like a corporation, the organization survives the individuals who created and run it.
12. Diversity: in illicit activities, to further insulate the organization from dependence on one criminal activity.
13. Bonding: individual to individual, and individual to organization, for solidarity and protection, often through complex initiation rites.
14. Mobility: a disregard for national and jurisdictional boundaries.

There are three main types or groups of global or transnational criminal organizations. First, there are the traditional Big Five transnational criminal organizations: the Italian Criminal Enterprises (including the Sicilian and American Mafia families), the Russian Mafiya, the Japanese Yakuza, the Chinese Triads, and the Colombian Cartels. To round out this group, now making it the "Big Six," can be added the five Mexican drug cartels known as the Mexican Federation. The second tier of criminal organizations is the smaller, yet highly organized, groups with certain criminal specialties that work with and for the Big Six in much the same way as a franchisee would work for its parent company. This tier includes groups based in Nigeria, Panama, Jamaica, Puerto Rico, and the Dominican Republic. Third, there are the terrorist groups, which deal in contraband, narcotics, smuggling, etc., simply as a means to finance their political objectives. These groups include, among others, Japan's Red Army, Peru's Shining Path, Colombia's FARC (Revolutionary Armed Forces of Colombia), and the People's Irish Republican Army.

II.   The Big Six International Criminal Organizations

A.   Italian Criminal Enterprises

Italian organized crime is commonly thought of as the Mafia. However, the Mafia is but one of four distinct criminal groups operating from Italy: the other three are the Camorra, the 'Ndrangheta, and the Sacra Corona Unita, or Sacred Crown. These organizations are generally organized on family or clan affiliations, and have existed for centuries through a system of power known as the *sistema del potere*. Although this system has allowed the various clans to co-exist for centuries, it has broken down in the last few years as the groups expand their empires from Italy and form alliances with other transnational criminal organizations.

1.   *The Mafia*

The Sicilian Mafia, or *Cosa Nostra* (literally, "our affairs") is the most famous organized-crime group in the world. Worldwide, the Mafia is controlled from its historic home of Palermo. It operates in more than 40 countries, including the heroin-producing nations of the Far East (one estimate has $750 million in Southeast Asian heroin going to New York each year through Mafia-controlled distribution networks).

The Mafia consists of approximately 180 families with 5,000 members. Since the term "mafia" means "refuge" in Arabic, it is believed by some scholars that the Mafia's origins date back to the 9th century, when Sicily was occupied by Arabic-speaking invaders. The local Sicilians banded together to seek refuge from the invaders.

Mafia members are bound by an oath of five basic principles: (1) *omerta*, or code of silence, a vow never to reveal any Mafia secrets or members' names under threat of torture and death; (2) total obedience to the "don" or boss; (3) assistance to any befriended Mafia faction, no questions asked; (4) to avenge any attack on members of the family; and (5) to avoid any and all contact with law-enforcement authorities.

From its traditional base of Palermo, the Sicilian Mafia controls criminal groups and crime throughout the world: France's Foreign Intelligence Service estimates that as much as $20 billion in laundered criminal profits returns each year to Palermo, a city that ranks 80th among Italian cities in reported per-capita income but fifth in consumer spending.

The Mafia is the most established and geographically diverse organized-crime group in the world, and often uses this stature to act as intermediary between other groups. The Mafia and the Russian Mafiya have recently undertaken some joint efforts in drug and human smuggling, using Russian transportation and the Italian know-how (rumor has it that Mikhail Gorbachev's many vacations to Sicily in the 1970s were spent as a guest of one of the bosses sitting on the Mafia's "Commission," or ruling body).

In the United States, the Mafia (known by the FBI as Italian Organized Crime or IOC) is a criminal alliance of ten major "families" or *brugads*, each having control of various criminal and legitimate enterprises in recognized distinct geographic areas of the United States and Canada. From its origins in Sicily, the Mafia emigrated to the United States with the Italian/Sicilian immigrants in the late 1800s, and originally took hold in New Orleans. By the early 1900s, every major U.S. city had a Mafia chapter. Their activities were originally limited to extortion; but by the early 1920s, the local "dons," or bosses, had moved into prostitution and gambling.

The Mafia really began to flourish with prohibition in the 1920. Al Capone in Chicago and Salvatore "Lucky" Luciano in New York turned bootlegging, gambling, rackets, and prostitution into millions of dollars and virtual control of their cities. However, the fortunes to be made at that time resulted in hundreds of deaths as rival gangs sought control of the streets. In 1931, after a bloody struggle for national dominance between rival groups, the various gangs, led by Lucky Luciano, Meyer Lansky (credited by many as the first to master the concept of laundering money), and Bugsy Seigel (the first to build a major casino in Las Vegas) worked out a system of arbitration through a council and divided the country into 10 regions, each controlled by one of the original 10 families.

Although the structure, makeup, membership, and even the existence of the Mafia families are constantly changing, there have been, historically, 10 major and another 15 (or so) minor families. The five largest East Coast families are based out of New York City, and are named after their present or former boss: the families of Vito Genovese, Carlo Gambino (who succeeded Lucky Luciano; Gambino in turn was succeeded by John "the Teflon Don" Gotti, until Gotti's under-boss, Salvatore "Sammy the Bull" Gravano, ratted Gotti out in 1994), Gaetano Lucchese, Guiseppe Magliocco, and Joseph Bonanno. The other five families are known by their city or regional affiliations — families from Buffalo, Rhode Island and Boston, Tampa, Detroit, and Chicago.

The U.S. Mafia's main activities include drug trafficking, union control and corruption, loan sharking, illegal gambling, stock market manipulation, and the takeover of legitimate businesses. Recently, the five New York families have been working with, or receiving tribute payments from, the Russian crime groups operating out of Brighton Beach in the oil and gas tax scams (see the section on the Russian Mafiya).

Through a sustained effort by U.S. and Canadian law-enforcement agencies, the U.S. Mafia has been hit hard in recent years. As a result of a number of "made" members becoming informants — including Peter Savino of the Gambino family in the mid-1980s and Sammy "the Bull" Gravano of the Gambino family in the early 1990s — more than 1,300 Mafia members and associates have been imprisoned. In addition to these setbacks, the monopolies the Mafia historically had enjoyed have been threatened by the Russian Mafiya, the Colombian Cartels, and the East Asian tongs or triads. However, the New York crime families remain strong, particularly the Genovese family, which has an estimated 1,500 made members.

The Sicilian Mafia has also been hit hard. On August 27, 1997, one of the Italian Mafia's most senior dons, Mario Fabbrocino, was arrested in Argentina on suspicion of drug trafficking, murder, and other charges. He was on Italy's 10 most-wanted list, and had been on the run for nearly a decade. The future of the Sicilian Mafia is uncertain; on September 26, 1997, 31 of the highest-ranking members of the Mafia were convicted of murder in the 1992 highway bombing of Italy's top anti-Mafia prosecutor, Giovanni Falcone: 26 received life sentences. Among those convicted was Salvatore "Toto" Riina, the Mafia's reputed "boss of bosses."

2. The Camorra

The Camorra, based in Naples, Italy, is made up of 30 clans with approximately 6,000 members. U.S. law-enforcement agencies consider the Camorra to be the "up and coming" criminal enterprise, often trumping the Sicilian Mafia in its ability to adapt to new trends and form new alliances. For example, the Camorra is known to have strong ties with the Russian Mafiya; in 1995, the Camorra and the Mafiya had an arrangement whereby the Camorra would bleach out U.S. $1.00 bills and reprint them as $100, then ship them to the Mafiya for distribution in 29 eastern bloc and FSU (former Soviet Union) countries (it is estimated that there are more U.S. dollars in circulation in the FSU countries than in the United States itself). In exchange, the Russians paid the Camorra with property (including a Russian bank) and FSU arms, smuggled into eastern Europe and Italy.

Suffering the same fate as their Mafia counterparts, the Camorra was hit hard on August 8, 1997, when the Italian "anti-Mafia police" seized approximately U.S. $285 million in assets belonging to the powerful Caserta clan of the Camorra. The assets included over 200 buildings, 49 land holdings, 26 companies, and race horses, cars, stocks, and bonds.

3. 'Ndrangheta

The 'Ndrangheta is the third of the four Italian criminal enterprises. It consists of approximately 140 cells with perhaps 5,300 members, and is based out of Calabria. This group has been particularly active in heroin trafficking. A U.S. federal investigation that concluded in 1989 found that 'Ndrangheta members used pizza shops in major East Coast cities as fronts for heroin trafficking (they used a New York travel agency to launder their money). A 1997 operation, code-named Operation Cat's Eye, uncovered an extensive 'Ndrangheta heroin trafficking ring operating from Toronto, Canada, and Tampa, Florida (see Chapter 10).

4. Sacra Corona Unita (Sacred Crown)

This relatively new group, founded in the 1970, consists of 20 clans with approximately 1,400 members. It is concentrated in Puglia, Italy.

B. The Russian Mafiya

In size, resources, brutality, and growth, the Russian Mafiya is becoming the world's dominant criminal organization. The Mafiya is known in Russia as the *reketiry,* or racketeers; in the U.S., it is known by many names, both formal (the ROC, or Russian Organized Crime) and colloquial (Redfellas). Regardless of the moniker, the Russian Mafiya consists of approximately 100,000 members organized into as many as 300 identifiable, structured groups. Of these, three are dominant: the Brigade of the Sun, the Odessa Mafia, and the Armenian Organized Crime Groups. Yuri Ivanovich Esin, the leader of one of these organizations (Brigade of the Sun), was arrested in Italy on March 17, 1997, while attending a meeting between the Mafiya and the Camorra.

Although the Russian criminal class has a history reaching back centuries, Russian organized crime, as we know it today, was essentially born on the day the former Soviet Union collapsed (December 25, 1991). The end of the old Soviet regime unleashed a wave of criminality unparalleled in modern days. For example, world opium-based production has doubled in that period.

The Russian Mafiya includes much of the ruling class from the old KGB. It is dominant in currency and arms smuggling, prostitution, racketeering, and narcotics trafficking. It has developed a sophisticated heroin pipeline from Burma (now Myanmar) across Asia Minor to the Balkans, to Germany and/or Nigeria for distribution in Europe and the U.S. Like the Chinese Triads, who use "Chinatowns" as their bases of operation, the Russian Mafiya has looked to pockets of expatriate Russians in American cities for establishing their footing: the Odessa Mafiya in Brighton Beach (New York) and Revere (Boston), and the Armenians in Los Angeles are two such examples.

Worldwide, the Mafiya is involved in slavery and human smuggling, car theft (thefts of luxury automobiles in Germany have increased exponentially in the last five years), extortion, arms smuggling (including nuclear arms smuggling), murder for hire, credit theft, forgery, design and production of designer drugs, illegal export of raw materials (as much as $40 billion per year, a figure that does not include the smuggling of Russia's most lucrative export, diamonds), and, of course, money laundering. It is estimated that the control of over 400 Russian banks by the Mafiya allows it to launder an estimated $250 billion per year in its own, and others' (principally the Italian Mafia's), international drug profits. The U.S. federal government's Foreign Broadcast Information Service (FBIS) reports that the Mafiya controls 85% of the voting stock of Russian corporations and 50% to 80% of all Russian banks (the former director of the CIA, John Deutch, disputes these figures: see Chapter 14).

The Mafiya is bound by an 18-part "Thieves' Code," or *vorovskoy zakon*. A typical Mafiya organized-crime group is led by a boss, or *pakhan*, controlling criminal cells through an intermediary called a "brigadier." Each of the group's cells has a specialty, such as drugs, prostitution, political contacts, enforcement, smuggling, rackets, protection.*

The Mafiya is particularly skilled in gasoline theft and fraud, both in Russia and the U.S. In Russia, the Mafiya's scheme is a simple smuggling operation. First, they buy tanker trucks of gasoline at state-subsidized prices of about $.60 per gallon. Using various networks of bribed officials, they then ship the gasoline through the FSU satellite countries and into Germany, where they sell it on the black market for about $4.00 per gallon — still well under the market rate of about $5.25 per gallon. Payment for the gasoline is often made in the form of stolen luxury vehicles, liquor, cigarettes, and consumer products, which are then smuggled back into Russia. Most cash payments are deposited in various European banking havens.

The Mafiya is active in most American cities. Brighton Beach, New York, has been the traditional base since the mid-1970s, and other cities include Boston (the Revere Beach area), Chicago, Miami, Cleveland, Philadelphia, Seattle, Los Angeles, San Francisco, and San Diego. Its growth in the U.S. has been incredible — in 1993, the FBI put the number of Mafiya groups operating in the United States at 15. By 1996 (according to FBI Director Louis

* The Office of the Attorney General of California, California Department of Justice, Report on Russian Organized Crime, available at *www.sgrm.com/Russian.html*.

Freeh), the number had risen to over 200, all with ties to parent organizations in Russia. The rise in prominence of the Mafiya is reflected in the FBI's establishment of a Moscow office (in July, 1994, the FBI opened an office in Moscow and entered into a cooperation agreement, or protocol, with their Russian counterparts, the FSB, or Federal Security Service, and the Russian Interior Ministry), and their addition to the Department of Justice's priority-target list. The Mafiya's rise also corresponds with the increase in the number of Russians and FSU nationals emigrating to the United States; in the 25 years prior to the collapse of the Soviet Union, approximately 200,000 Soviet citizens emigrated to the U.S. The enactment of the Lautenberg Amendment in November, 1989, allowed for a quota of up to 50,000 Soviet refugees to enter the U.S. That quota has been filled every year. In addition, since May, 1991, Russia has granted its citizens the right to emigrate and travel freely.

The Mafiya has imported its old Soviet-style gas frauds into the U.S. These fuel frauds — mostly in New York and Los Angeles — result in an estimated loss of over $2 billion in federal and state gasoline taxes each year. The Mafiya's scam of choice is the daisy-chain scheme. Here, they falsify state and federal tax forms and use fictitious companies to avoid paying tax on gasoline. Only the consumer actually pays gasoline tax; those in the distribution chain pay the tax but then receive a credit once the gas is passed on in the distribution chain. The Russian and Armenian Mafiya create a string of companies, known as "burn" companies, so that by the time federal and state auditors can determine which company in the long string of companies that have purchased, then sold, the gasoline is ultimately responsible to pay the roughly $0.50 per gallon tax, that company — and its owners — have disappeared.

Other gas tax schemes include extending fuel by adding tax-free additives, rigging fuel pumps, and manipulating dyed agricultural fuels (which are not taxed) and selling them as regular gasoline (the Mikaelian Organization, a group of Armenian Mafiya, was indicted in 1995 for various racketeering and money-laundering offenses arising from their scheme of using falsified wholesale permits to purchase tax-free diesel fuel, which was then diverted and sold at various independent, Russian-controlled gas stations). Russians are also known for selling low-grade fuel as premium-grade.

The Russian Mafiya are also in the toxic waste disposal business. They are paid by producers to haul away the waste, where it will ostensibly be refined or burned at great cost to the disposal company, leaving a small but reasonable profit. However, the criminals are incurring no costs to dispose of .the waste; instead, they are dumping it into tanker trucks of gasoline, where it mixes with the gas and is eventually burned in cars.

In many instances, where there are profits to be made from crime, there seems to be a Russian or Mafiya presence. In July, 1997, two Russian gangsters (nicknamed Redfellas) were apprehended trying to deliver tactical nuclear weapons and surface-to-air missiles to buyers in the U.S.* A second scheme, uncovered through Operation Odessa, a task force tracking Russian organized crime in South Florida, involved the potential sale of a Russian Tango-class diesel submarine to Colombian drug traffickers. Posing as a geological company looking to map the Caribbean floor, the Redfellas were negotiating the purchase of this Russian submarine, complete with an 18-man crew, when they were caught in a sting operation.

Other areas of crime the American branches of the Mafiya are involved in include telecommunications fraud (the cloning of cellular phones is a favorite of the American-based Mafiya); loan sharking; murder for hire; and medical and insurance fraud, including staged auto accidents and false billing schemes. In one infamous case, a $1 billion false medical-billing scheme by two brothers, Russian emigrés with ties to Russian organized crime, was uncovered by the U.S. Attorneys Office in Los Angeles in 1991. In this scheme, the perpetrators set up mobile medical laboratories that conducted false tests on patients; fraudulent and inflated bills were then sent to insurance companies. In 1994, one brother turned against the other and testified for the government; the other brother was sentenced to 21 years in prison, ordered to forfeit $50 million in assets, and pay more than $43 million in fines and restitution. Medical-insurance fraud seems to be a common Russian scheme. From 1992 to 1994, Russian-born Igor Borisovich Razvitnov managed a Pittsburgh medical clinic owned by Russian Mafiya. During that period, he paid Russian emigrés to fake accidents and injuries and file fraudulent claims worth over $5 million. Razvitnov and three co-conspirators were indicted. Razvitnov skipped bail, and the others are serving federal prison sentences.

Of great significance to law-enforcement personnel is the practice of Russian (and former Soviet) criminals to receive tattoos for various crimes they had committed and time they had served in prison. Essentially, a Russian criminal's tattoos are a pictorial history of his or her life in crime. According to Russian criminologist Arkady G. Bronnikov, who has studied Russian inmates' tattoos and lifestyles for years, "tattoos are like a passport, a biography, a uniform with medals. They reflect the convict's interests, his outlook on life, his world view."**

C. Japanese Yakuza

The Boryokudon, known in the West as the Yakuza, is Japan's answer to the Mafia. The Yakuza's roots can be traced back to the early 1600s, when roving

* *Time Magazine* (July 14, 1997, Canadian edition, p. 37.)
** See also *Natural History Magazine,* November, 1993, "Telltale Tattoos in Russian Prisons."

bands of eccentric samurai, known as *kabuki-mono* (literally, "crazy ones") terrorized villages, defended by the *machi-yokko* ("servants of the town"). The Yakuza as an organized group did not begin to flourish until the later 1700s, when bands of *bakuto* (gamblers), *tekiya* (street peddlers), and *gurentai* (general hoodlums) began to form into loose groups (these terms are still used to describe Yakuza members today). The word *Yakuza* comes from a hand in a blackjack-like card game played by the *bakuto*. In this game, a hand of 20, the worst score, results in a score of zero: one such losing combination is 8-9-3, pronounced ya-ku-sa. The *bakuto* also contributed the practice of cutting off the top joint of the little finger as a sign of fealty to the *oyabun*, or leader (practically, the severing of this joint made it difficult for a gambler to hold his cards). Tattooing is also a common practice of the Yakuza; from the 1600s through the 1800s, criminals were often "branded" as such by the use of tattoos — one black ring tattooed around an arm for each offense committed. Later, tattoos became a symbol of virility or strength, with complete back tattoos considered the peak of symbolic strength.

The Yakuza's numbers and power really began to grow during the Allied Occupation after World War II. By 1963, there were more than 184,000 Yakuza members, organized into some 5,200 gangs. Bloody and violent inter-gang wars reduced their numbers, so that today the Yakuza's ranks now number in excess of 60,000 (making it the second largest, behind the Chinese Triads, of the original Big Five organized crime groups), loosely organized into families. These families are led by the *oyabun*, or father: the under-boss, officers, enlisted men, and apprentices all serve the *oyabun*.

The man who brought the Yakuza to its present prominence in Japan's legal and illegal economies was Kazuo Taoka, the leader of the Yamaguchi-gumi faction from the mid-1940s until his death in 1981. At his death, the Yamaguchi-gumi controlled over 2,500 illegal and legal businesses, including sports and entertainment businesses, which grossed almost $500 million per year. The faction was headed up by approximately 100 bosses controlling over 500 street-level gangs.

With Taoka's death, the Yakuza again entered a dark age of bloody gang wars. Finally, in March, 1992, the Japanese government passed the Act for Prevention of Unlawful Activities by *boryokudon* (Yakuza or criminal gang) members. The act mainly prohibits the *boryokudon* from realizing profits made from forms of extortion, gambling, etc. However, their criminal activities continue; the Yakuza remain involved in every aspect of Japan's economy, both legitimate and illegitimate, with emphasis on the production and distribution of amphetamines, as well as control of casinos, brothels, loan sharking, and protection and extortion rackets focusing in large corporations and banks. Hard-core pornography, illegal in Japan, is another big business for the Yakuza. They also operate satellite gangs around the world, with major bases in South Korea, Australia, Costa Rica, Brazil, Hawaii, and all of the major cities on the West Coast of the U.S.

The Yakuza have entered alliances with Taiwanese-based Triads — notably, the Bamboo Union — for the distribution of methamphetamine, the drug of choice for Japanese addicts. The drug is produced in Taiwan by the Bamboo Union, and smuggled to Japan by the Yakuza through Kaohsiung, Taiwan's largest port (and the world's third busiest for container traffic, behind Hong Kong and Singapore).

The economic boom years of the 1980s saw a meteoric rise in Yakuza activity and prominence. The Yakuza were used to forcibly evict tenants from their homes to pave the way for new construction and to keep corporate meetings short and quiet.

The Yakuza's influence in Japan may have far-reaching and devastating effects on Japan's economy. Japan's Finance Ministry suggests that as much as US$300 billion to $600 billion in bad debts is owed to Japan's banks from the boom-to-bust real estate of the 1980s, that most of it is owed to Yakuza-affiliated real estate speculators, and that the banks are afraid to liquidate or collect.

D.   The Chinese Triads

1.   Background

The Six Great Triads, as well as smaller satellite groups, form the world's largest criminal association, with over 100,000 members scattered throughout the world. Five of these Triads are centered in Hong Kong and Taiwan, and have recently formed an alliance with the Great Circle Triad in Shanghai. The largest and most powerful of the Triads is the Hong Kong-based Sun Yee On ("new righteousness and peace") Triad, a 56,000-strong, tightly structured organization involved in all aspects of criminal activity, including extortion, heroin trafficking, and alien smuggling in Canada, Australia, Thailand, and Central America. The Sun Yee On has close ties with the Communist government in Beijing, as well as extensive holdings in the Shenzen Special Economic Zone in southern Canton (now Guangdong) province.* How the Triads develop over the next few years is tied to mainland China's use and treatment of Hong Kong. To date, the emergence of capitalism in Mainland China and the takeover of Hong Kong have greatly enhanced the power of the Triads and have led them to form new global alliances with each other and with other international criminal organizations.

Structured like corporations, the Chinese Triads (the name comes from one of the Chinese characters, shaped like a triangle) are the world's oldest criminal organizations, with roots back thousands of years. Like their

---

* The Sun Yee On Triad and the Wo Hop To Triad are the two dominant American-based triads.

counterparts in the Mafiya and Yakuza, the Triads have employed their ethnic communities in North America as their bases of operations. The Triads are particularly strong in the Pacific Rim — Hawaii, Seattle, Vancouver (particularly with Hong Kong going back to the Chinese on July 1, 1997), and San Francisco — as well as the eastern centers of Toronto, Boston, and New York.

The Triads control the eastern Asian heroin trade, with annual profits in excess of $200 billion. Smuggling weapons accounts for about $3 billion per year; smuggling cars, boats, and electronic equipment adds about $4 billion per year; and the "importation" of illegal aliens into North America and Europe brings in about $3.5 billion per year. This last enterprise has a double benefit: not only do the Triads charge as much as $30,000 to smuggle someone into the U.S., that person is essentially sold as an indentured slave to brokers, who assimilate him or her into the various Chinatowns, where he or she work for years to pay off fee by manning the Triads' brothels, sweatshops, and drug businesses.

Triads are also known in North America as "Tongs." However, the word *tong* actually means "meeting hall," and many Chinese Tongs are, in fact, legitimate business associations. It is extremely difficult to differentiate between legitimate and illegal tongs and triads. One of the first Triad members to publicize the life of the Triads was a witness, known as Mr. Ma, who testified before a Congressional Committee in August, 1992. Mr. Ma described the hierarchy of the Triads: a typical Triad is led by a "dragonhead," administration by a "white paper fan," recruitment by an "incense master," inter-gang liaison by "straw sandals," and enforcement by "red poles." Mr. Ma also described his life as a member of the 14K Triad, from recruitment at age 14 through his career as a member of the Hong Kong police, where he ran a protection racket, to his role running prostitution and gambling rings, to smuggling heroin into the U.S. via corrupt Nicaraguan diplomats and bulk-container shipments into New York.

Almost all of the heroin flowing through China and Hong Kong — and thus through the Triads — originates in the jungles of the "Golden Triangle" of Thailand, Myanmar, and Laos. For more than 30 years, until 1996, this opium production was controlled by one man, Khun Sa (see below). Since the late 1980s, the Chinese have dominated the world's heroin market, which has seen a huge increase in the number of addicts, while the price of heroin has plummeted. The introduction of "China White" — a very pure form of heroin that can be snorted or smoked — has led to greater acceptance and use among the middle class.

2.   Recent Operations Against the Chinese Triads

The FBI's Operation Whitemare illustrates the extent and sophistication of the Triads' efforts to move their heroin profits from Canada and the U.S. to

Hong Kong. These methods include a vast legion of couriers, the use of wire transfers, and mailing bank drafts and money orders through the postal systems.* In addition, the Asian groups use a scheme that is now well known to law enforcement. It involves shipping goods to a non-existent business at a particular address, where the goods are removed and replaced with cash of the same weight. The packages are then resealed and returned to the postal or courier service as undeliverable or rejected, where they are shipped back to the original sender in Hong Kong. More often than not, Canadian/U.S./Hong Kong Customs officials do not inspect these returned packages, as they seem never to have been actually delivered.

In 1992, the Wo Hop To Triad was targeted by federal authorities. In this case, Peter Chong, the leader of the Triad's San Francisco, Los Angeles, New York, and Boston cells, as well as a number of his associates, were indicted for several offenses, including the illegal importation of automatic weapons (AK-47 assault rifles), conspiracy to import heroin, murder-for-hire, gambling, loansharking, and money laundering.

E.   Colombian Drug Cartels

The international drug syndicates operating throughout our hemisphere are resourceful, adaptable, and extremely powerful. These syndicates have an unprecedented level of sophistication, and they are far more powerful and influential than any organized crime enterprise preceding them.

— **Donnie Marshall, Deputy Director of the Drug Enforcement Agency**
Testimony to the House Government Reform and Oversight Committee's National Security, International Affairs and Criminal Justice Subcommittee, March 12, 1998.

Virtually all of the world's coca leaves and cocaine base are grown and produced in the three Andean countries of Peru and Bolivia (70%) and Colombia (30%). From this base, the traffickers manufacture cocaine hydrochloride. The DEA's Operation Breakthrough, a scientific research project designed to assess the amount of cocaine produced in South America, estimates production of cocaine to be approximately 715 metric tons (1995 figures). Historically, almost all of this supply has been distributed by traffickers operating out of Medellín and Cali, Colombia — the two most notorious Colombian drug cartels. Two new cartels — the Cartel de la Costa and the so-called Northern Valle del Cauca drug traffickers from the northern

---

* Unlike their American and Mexican counterparts, the Asian criminal organizations seem to know that the U.S. and Canadian postal services require search warrants to open and inspect packages, while the private "mail" services, such as UPS and Federal Express, do not.

Caribbean coastal area, including Cartagena — have gained prominence since the 1995–1997 arrests of the Cali and Medellín Cartel kingpins.

Closely allied with the Colombian drug cartels are the coca producers of Peru and Bolivia, led by Waldo Simeon Vargas Arias (aka "El Minestro"), who, until his arrest in 1997, was responsible for supplying more than one-half the cocaine base refined by the Colombian cartels.

In addition to producing almost all of the cocaine used in the U.S., the Colombian cartels are now producing and/or distributing over one-half of the heroin used in the United States.

1.   The Medellín Cartel

Prior to its collapse in the late 1980s, drug kingpins operating from Medellín, Colombia, controlled the world's cocaine trade. They have been replaced, for the most part, by the Cali Cartel. The most infamous of the Medellín kingpins was Pablo Escobar Gaviria, who controlled the cartel from the mid-1980s until his death in 1993. Another Medellín kingpin, Juan David Ochoa-Vasquez, imprisoned at Envigado in 1990 and released in 1995, still controls the Ochoa family drug business, which remains one of the most powerful of the Colombian drug organizations. Other Medellín bosses included Gustavo de Jesus Gaviria Rivero, Escobar's cousin and right-hand man; and Jose Gonzalo Rodriguez Gacha, aka "El Mexicano," reputed to be the most violent of them all.

Pablo Escobar Gaviria (1944–1993) was the leading drug figure of the Medellín Cartel until his death during a rooftop shootout with Colombian National Police and army commandos on December 2, 1993. In 1982, Escobar Gaviria had formally joined with the Ochoa family — brothers Jorge Luis Ochoa Vasquez, Juan David Ochoa Vasquez, and Jorge's son Fabio "Fabito" Ochoa Restrepo — and Carlos Lehder Rivas into a cartel to squeeze out any remaining competition and to gain better control of their production, smuggling, distribution, and money-laundering operations. Escobar Gaviria was given control of U.S. distribution and transportation; the Ochoas provided the bribes and (the corollary to bribes) murder, extortion, and general "enforcement." To lend surface credibility to his operations, Escobar Gaviria arranged to be elected to the Colombian Congress as an alternate, which had the side effect of affording him immunity from arrest. By 1984, the Medellín Cartel controlled 80% of the U.S. cocaine market, and Escobar Gaviria was worth more than $2 billion.

The Medellín Cartel was at its peak between 1984 and 1987. During this period, it solidified its cultivation (in Bolivia and Peru), production (drug labs in Colombia, Nicaragua, and Panama), and smuggling operations (in the Bahamas, Turks and Caicos, and later in Mexico). It was responsible for the assassination of at least 15 Colombian judges and a number of U.S. law-enforcement (DEA) informants. In November, 1986, Escobar Gaviria was indicted in Miami on racketeering and drug charges relating to the smuggling of over 60 tons of cocaine; however, Colombian judges, after receiving death threats, refused to extradite him. The charges were dismissed.

In the early and mid-1970s, Escobar Gaviria rose in the ranks of the Colombian drug world to become a major player. In 1976, he was arrested and charged with possession of almost 18 kilos of cocaine. He was never tried. The arresting officer was killed, nine judges refused to hear his case, and all official records and exhibits simply disappeared from the court files. Escobar Gaviria's almost-mythical reputation grew from there. Soon, he was one of the undisputed leaders of the emerging Medellín Cartel, joining Jorge Luis Ochoa Vasquez and Carlos Lehder Rivas to gain a virtual monopoly of the North American cocaine trade. Escobar Gaviria also gained a great deal of his power by his largesse with the masses, building low-cost housing, hospitals, and soccer fields.

Beginning in the late 1980s, the Medellín Cartel was decimated by arrests and the efforts by American officials to shut down the Caribbean/Florida entry of cocaine. In 1989, Medellín drug kingpin Jose "the Mexican" Gonzalo Rodriguez Gacha was killed in a shootout with Colombian National Police in Cartagena (documents seized from his various lairs showed that he had almost $300 million stashed away — about $140 million in various banks around the world ($22 million in Panama, $42 million in Colombia, $40 million in Luxembourg, $10 million in Switzerland, $6 million in Austria, $2 million in the U.S.), and about $150 million actually buried in various locations in Colombia. Gacha's death, combined with other incidents, made way for the Cali Cartel to begin a rise to prominence, and by the time Escobar Gaviria died in 1993, the Medellín Cartel was but a shadow of its former self.

2.   The Cali Cartel

a.   Introduction.   The Cali Cartel is now responsible for 80% of the world's cocaine supply — over 600 metric tons per year. During the late 1980s, groups from Cali assumed effective control of the Peru–Bolivia–Colombia cocaine production and distribution trade, supplanting the Medellín Cartel. Where the Medellín Cartel was overtly violent, the Cali Cartel members learned to be more circumspect (although their restraint was more public relations than fact). In addition, the cartel's rise to prominence was based on the use of sound business practices: Colombian police officers refer to *los caballeros* (the gentlemen) of Cali in contrast to *los hampones* (the hoodlums) of Medellín.

Initially, the Cali Cartel used the Caribbean for its transportation routes of drugs to, and money from, the United States. With successful interdiction by U.S. authorities resulting in huge losses, it has shifted to Mexico, contracting with Mexican drug organizations for their smuggling through the southwest border with the U.S. At first, the cartel paid the Mexicans $1,000 to $2,000 per kilo. As it became more dependent on the Mexican corridor, and the Mexicans became more sophisticated, this arrangement changed so that now Mexican smugglers are paid in product — between 40 and 50% of the drugs themselves. However, the cartel's profits remain incredible: the DEA, in Congressional testimony, estimates that the Cali Cartel kingpins' profits were more than U.S. $8 billion for 1995 alone. To put that amount in perspective, the annual revenues from Colombia's largest legal export, oil, were approximately $1.5 billion in 1995; the DEA's annual budget reached $1 billion for the first time in 1997; Coca-Cola's total sales were approximately $8 billion (with profits of $120 million); and General Motors and Wal-Mart's *combined* profits were just less than $8 billion. If the Cali Cartel were a corporation, it would rank number one in gross profits, beating out Exxon ($7.5 billion), General Electric ($7.3 billion), Philip Morris ($6.3 billion), and IBM ($5.4 billion).*

Whereas the Medellín Cartel relied primarily on violence and corruption to smuggle drugs into the U.S., the Cali Cartel uses deception and guile. For example, U.S. Customs and DEA agents have uncovered cocaine hidden inside hollowed-out cedar boards (in 1988, U.S. Customs agents seized 3,270 kilos of cocaine hidden in 700 of 9,000 boards shipped from Ecuador), encased in chocolate blocks (also in 1988, Customs agents found 2,270 kilos of cocaine wrapped in lead and encased in 1,200 blocks of chocolate shipped from Ecuador), and hidden in drums of toxic chemicals (in 1989, agents out of New York found almost 5,000 kilos of cocaine inside 250 drums of highly toxic lye). The Cali Cartel's schemes are endless.

The Cali Cartel has been led by four major crime figures — Gilberto and Miguel Rodriguez-Orejuela, Jose Santacruz Londono, and Pacho Herrera. However, all four were arrested in 1995, and Londono was killed after escaping prison in 1996. In addition, all four were the principal, specially designated narcotics traffickers (or SDNTs) sanctioned by President Clinton in October, 1995, along with 355 other related individuals and business entities they owned or controlled.** The names of the major SDNTs are listed at the end of this chapter in Appendix 1.1.

In addition to the three Cali kingpins, five other major Cali Cartel drug leaders were arrested and incarcerated in 1995. During these arrests, thousands of key documents depicting the cartel's vast financial empires were seized. These documents formed the evidentiary basis for instituting the PDD 42 sanctions. In all, 1995 saw the arrests of the following Cali kingpins:

---

* Figures courtesy of *The Wall Street Journal Almanac 1998*, (Random House 1997).
** See Chapter 7, the International Emergency Economic Powers Act, or IEEPA, and Presidential Directive Decision 42, which prohibited any American company or individual from doing business with Colombian drug traffickers.

- June 5th: the arrest of Cachique Rivera, the cartel's top Peruvian supplier of cocaine base, captured during a police raid in Bogotá and extradited to Peru
- June 9th: the arrest of Gilberto Rodriguez-Orejuela, the top Cali boss, captured during a police raid in Cali
- June 19th: the arrest of Henry Loaiza, reputed head of the cartel's "military" operations, when he surrendered to the Colombian army in Bogotá
- June 24th: the arrest of Victor Patino, the cartel's reputed expert in maritime smuggling, when he surrendered to military police in Bogotá
- July 4th: the arrest of Jose Santacruz Londono, one of the cartel's bosses (along with the Rodriguez-Orejuela brothers), captured by police in a Bogotá restaurant
- July 7th: the arrest of Julian Marcillo, one of the cartel's leading financial experts, captured by police while at his girlfriend's apartment in Bogotá
- July 8th: the arrest of Phanor Arizabaleta, the cartel's chief money launderer and supplier of the chemicals used to make cocaine, when he surrendered to national security forces in Bogotá
- August 6th: the arrest of Miguel Rodriguez-Orejuela, the number two cartel leader, captured during a police raid in Cali

b. The Leaders of the Cali Cartel

i. The Rodriguez-Orejuela Family. Gilberto and Miguel Rodriguez-Orejuela, arrested on June 9, 1995 and August 6, 1995, respectively, by the Colombian National Police (CNP), controlled one of the largest and most sophisticated criminal organizations in history, an "immense monolithic network of compartmentalized cells of smugglers, transporters, distributors, and money launderers," according to the DEA. Gilberto was known as the strategic planner for the Rodriguez-Orejuela organization. Known as "the chess player," or "Lucas," he was indicted in Miami in June 1995, (when he was arrested in Colombia) for illegal importation of 200,000 kilos (200 metric tons) of cocaine over the previous 10 years. His brother Miguel Angel (whose aliases include El Señor, Patricia, Patricio, Patty, Pat, Manuel, Manolo, Mike, Mauro, Doctor MRO) is known as the transportation specialist for the Rodriguez-Orejuela organization and is (note the present tense — he still maintains control while in prison) responsible for the day-to-day operations, assisted by his son William Rodriguez-Abadabia. On January 17, 1997, Miguel and Gilberto received nine-year (later increased to 23) and $10^{1}/_{2}$-year sentences, respectively, for various drug-trafficking offenses.

The Rodriguez-Orejuela organization is allied with the Amado Carrillo-Fuentes organization of the Mexican Federation. However, since the incarceration of the Rodriguez-Orejuela brothers, splinter groups of once-loyal lieutenants have broken off, led by the Urdinola-Grajales and Henao-Montoya families. In addition, in May 1996, the organization's U.S. infrastructure was severely compromised as a result of Operation Zorro II (see Chapter 10).

ii.   Jose Santacruz Londono.   Prior to his July 4, 1995, arrest in Bogotá, Jose Santacruz Londono (aka Chepe, Don Chepe, El Gordo Chepe, the Fat Man, or "07") was the third-ranking of the four Cali kingpins. He was imprisoned in Bogotá's infamous La Picota prison until his escape in January 1996, which was aided by his own jailers, who reportedly had been bought off. He was later killed in a shootout with the CNP. During his regime, he controlled much of the U.S. cocaine trade, with major centers including the traditional drug centers of New York, Miami, Los Angeles, San Francisco, and Houston, as well as Las Vegas and Chicago. He was considered one of the most violent of the Cali kingpins, and a money-laundering expert.

iii.   Pacho Herrera Buitrago.   The fourth of the major Cali kingpins, Helmer "Pacho" Herrera Buitrago (aka "H7") surrendered to authorities on September 1, 1996. He was known to operate one of the Cali Cartel's most sophisticated and profitable money-laundering operations from a base in New York. Herrera Buitrago's entire known organization — 57 individuals and 21 businesses — was the subject of the recent PDD 42 sanction, issued January 15, 1997.

3.   Cartel de la Costa

The Cartel de la Costa is one of the two new and prominent Colombian drug-trafficking organizations to emerge following the 1995 through 1997 arrests of most of the major bosses of the Medellín and Cali cartels. This group has returned to using the traditional Colombian smuggling routes through the Caribbean corridor, avoiding the Mexican distributors (who now charge as much as 50% of the product shipped, compared with the 20 to 33% charged by Puerto Rican and Dominican distributors).

The Cartel de la Costa distributes as much cocaine in Europe as in the U.S. Its future is in doubt, however, as three of the top four leaders have been arrested. According to the DEA, on March 6, 1998, Colombian authorities arrested Julio Cesar Antichario (the fourth-highest-ranking figure in the cartel) and his lieutenant, William Moises Nader. Antichario is wanted in Florida, while Nader is wanted in Texas. The U.S. is intending to seek extradition of both men. These could be the cases that test Colombia's new extradition laws (see Chapter 13). These arrests followed the late-February 1998 arrest of the cartel's second-in-command, Roger Eliecer Pombo. Only the leader of the cartel, Alberto Orlandez Gamboa, remains at large.

4. Northern Valle del Cauca Traffickers

Like their counterparts of the Cartel de la Costa, the new kingpins of the Northern Valle del Cauca have risen to power following the arrests of the leaders of the Cali and Medellín cartels. These new, independent traffickers share many of the characteristics of the early Medellín kingpins — running smaller, extremely aggressive and violent groups — rather than the highly structured, centrally controlled, and businesslike Cali organizations.

These traffickers have also shifted to the Caribbean corridor. However, unlike the Cartel de la Costa, these traffickers are responsible for huge volumes of both cocaine and heroin. The new bosses include brothers Jairo Ivan and Julio Fabio Urdinola Grajales, brothers Arcangel de Jesus and Jose Orlando Henao Montoya (thought by many law-enforcement agencies to be the most powerful of the various independent traffickers in the Northern Valle syndicates), and Diego Montoya Sanchez.

5. Recent Operations Against the Cartels

1995 and 1996 saw the death, arrest, or surrender of seven of the eight leading cartel kingpins, as well as operations against the Peru–Colombian "Air Bridge," the cartels' aerial supply route for cocaine base. The losses, however, have not slowed down the supply of cocaine; rather, there has been a shift in supply routes (to Mexico, Venezuela, and the eastern Caribbean), a shift in production to places such as Brazil, and the rise of a new generation of young traffickers based out of Colombia's northern coast and northern Valle del Cauca (look for the Henao Montoya brothers to rise in power). In addition, the DEA has identified a decentralization of the "Cali-centric" cocaine trade to independent trafficking groups in Peru, Bolivia, Mexico, and the Southern Cone countries of Argentina, Chile, Paraguay, and Uruguay.*

F. Mexican Criminal Organizations: The Mexican Federation

There are four major groups from Mexico under the umbrella of the Mexican Federation — the Gulf, Juarez, Sonora, and Tijuana Cartels — that control the majority of the heroin, cocaine, and marijuana production, smuggling, and distribution in Mexico and the western U.S. Each of these cartels operates within a distinct geographic area along the Mexico/U.S. border. A fifth group, the Amezqua Organization, dominates the methamphetamine trade. The Mexican Federation launders over $7 billion annually, equivalent to about 2.5% of the Mexican economy's value.

---

* For a detailed review of this issue, see the June 1996 report prepared by the Latin American Unit of the Strategic Intelligence Section of the DEA, entitled "The South American Cocaine Trade: An Industry in Transition."

Although the cartels of the Mexican Federation have enjoyed an incredible rise in "business" over the last 10 years, 1997 was not particularly prosperous. The Juarez Cartel lost its boss, Amado Carrillo-Fuentes, and the Gulf Cartel lost its operations manager.

1.   Gulf Cartel

This group was headed by Juan Garcia Abrego until his arrest on January 14, 1996, as one of the FBI's 10 most-wanted fugitives. After his arrest, Mexican authorities expelled him to the U.S. (there is no extradition between the two countries), where he awaits (in Houston) charges for conspiracy to import cocaine, and various continuing criminal enterprise and money-laundering offenses. Other top lieutenants of the Gulf Group have been arrested recently, including Juan's brother Humberto Garcia Abrego (although he was mysteriously "released" from Mexican prison in late February 1997), Adolfo de la Garza-Robles (believed to be the main contact with the Colombians), Jose Luis Sosa Mayorga (responsible for the Colombia-to-Mexico smuggling route), the interim leader Oscar Malherbe de Leon (one of Abrego's top lieutenants, money launderers), and his operations manager.

2.   Juarez Cartel

Until his death in early July 1997 (from complications arising from liposuction surgery), Amado Carrillo-Fuentes ran the Juarez Cartel, which was considered the most powerful of the four major drug-trafficking organizations in Mexico and the *de facto* leader of the Mexican Federation. Amado Carrillo-Fuentes was allied with the most powerful of the Cali Cartel organizations, the Rodriguez-Orejuela family, as well as the Ochoa brothers of the Medellín Cartel. It is the Juarez Cartel that has taken over much of the lucrative New York cocaine market from the Cali Cartels, which appear to be shifting their attention to Europe (allied with the Sicilian Mafia) and the former Soviet Union nations (allied with the Russian Mafiya).

Carrillo-Fuentes was known to forward $20 to $30 million to Colombia for each major operation, and from these he generated tens of millions of dollars in cash each week, a large part of which is known to have been repatriated to the U.S. and invested in real estate. Carrillo-Fuentes pioneered the use of large aircraft, thus has moniker "Lord of the Skies."

Since Carrillo's death, there has been a bloody struggle for control of the Juarez Cartel, both within the cartel itself and (it is suspected) by members of the Arellano Felix organization looking to wrest control of the lucrative New York market from the Juarez Cartel. The day after Carrillo died, his top money launderer, Tomas Colsa McGregor, was dragged from his home, tortured, and shot in the head. Within two weeks of Carrillo's death, five more mid-level cartel members were gunned down in Juarez, including Carrillo confidant Juan Eugenio Rosales (aka "the Genius"). Although there is no clear-cut successor, it appears that, as of August 1997, Carrillo's top three lieutenants were sharing power. These men have been identified as Juan Jose "Blue" Esparragoza, Vicente Carrillo (Amado's younger brother), and Hector "the Blond" Palma. In addition, Eduardo Gonzalez Quirarte has gained some prominence; Gonzalez is believed to be the liaison between the Juarez Cartel and once-General Jesus Gutierrez Rebello, the former anti-drug chief now imprisoned on charges he accepted bribes from the drug traffickers. Authorities are particularly concerned about Palma, who is considered the most violent of the four. Palma has a long-standing feud with the Arellano Felix brothers, dating back to 1989 when they sent Rafael Clavel Moreno to infiltrate Palma's group. Clavel seduced Palma's wife, had her turn over $7 million of Palma's money, then beheaded her and sent her head to Palma. Clavel later kidnapped and killed Palma's two children.

In mid-September, 1997, U.S. authorities froze $26 million in a Citibank account held by Alejandro Ventura Cohen. Ventura's brother Jaime was arrested (and released for lack of evidence) in Chile in August, 1997 as part of a Chilean investigation into Carrillo's drug operations in Chile. The U.S. authorities have alleged that the Citibank monies belong to Carrillo's Organization.

3. Sonora Cartel

Also known as the Caro-Quintero Organization, the Sonora Cartel is headed by Miguel Caro-Quintero, notwithstanding his incarceration in Mexico since 1989. With the assistance of his two brothers Jorge and Genaro, Miguel remains the effective leader of the Sonora Cartel. This group focuses on the transshipment of cocaine for the Cali Cartel, cultivation and distribution of marijuana, and some transportation and distribution of methamphetamine. Another brother, Rafael, is in prison for his role in the assassination of DEA Special Agent Enrique "Kiki" Camarena. Miguel himself is the subject of several indictments and provisional arrest warrants in the U.S.

4. Tijuana Cartel

Led by Alberto Benjamin Arellano-Felix and based out of Tijuana, Mexico, this group (also known as the AFO) is considered the most violent of the Mexican cartels. Alberto's lieutenants include his six brothers and four sisters; they all "inherited" the business from Miguel Angel Felix Gallardo upon his incarceration in 1989 for complicity in the assassination of DEA Special Agent Kiki Camarena in 1985. In May 1996, the Tijuana and Sonora cartels' U.S. infrastructure was severely compromised as a result of Operation Zorro II.

The "protection" for the Tijuana Cartel is controlled by Ramon Eduardo Arellano-Felix. He controls a San Diego-based security/execution group called the "Logan Heights Calle 30," which has been responsible for multiple murders in southern California. In February 1998, a federal grand jury in San Diego indicted 10 members of the Logan Heights gangs on charges of serving as paid killers for the Arellano-Felix family. The indictments charge that the gang members participated in "missions to eliminate rivals of the Arellano-Felix organization's control over drug trafficking along the California–Mexico border."

In addition to their extensive use of force, the Tijuana Cartel reportedly pays more than $1 million per week in bribes to Mexican judges, prosecutors, law enforcement, army, and customs officials. The Mexican Attorney General has filed papers in a U.S. court case (seeking extradition of a cartel member) admitting that 90% of Tijuana judges and prosecutors are on the cartel's payroll. The Tijuana Cartel is responsible for transportation, importation, and distribution of the big-four drugs — heroin, cocaine, marijuana, and methamphetamine. With the death of Carrillo Fuentes, leader of the Juarez Cartel, it is expected that the Tijuana Cartel will try to move into the southwest (Texas) border area, challenging the Juarez Cartel.

5.   *Amezqua Organization*

Although not considered one of the four groups of the Mexican Federation, the Amezqua Organization is nonetheless a major force in narcotics trafficking, effectively controlling the Mexican methamphetamine trade. Led by the Amezqua-Contreras brothers (Jesus, Adan, and Luis) and operating out of Guadalajara, this group controls the production, transportation, and distribution of methamphetamine in Mexico and the U.S. and is the world's largest smuggler of ephedrine, the precursor chemical, using contacts in Thailand and India.

The Amezqua Organization is growing in size, stature, and power because the methamphetamine trade is the Mexican traffickers' most profitable business; unlike the cocaine and heroin business, where the Mexicans are but one link in the drug-distribution chain, the Amezquas control the methamphetamine trade from beginning to end, from smuggling of ephedrine and pseudoephedrines from all over the world (principally from southeast Asia), to the production of the methamphetamines (known in the 1960s as speed or "bennies") in clandestine labs, or "kitchens," to distribution in Canada, the U.S., Mexico, and now even to Europe. The Amezquas also work with local gangs in producing and distributing methamphetamine. This was best evidenced by the massive DEA-led investigation that ran from February 1997 to December 1997, and led to the arrests of more than 100 people in an Amezqua-run methamphetamine ring on December 5, 1997.

Using wiretaps and other investigative techniques, the DEA (and 42 other local, state, and federal agencies) uncovered a network capable of supplying the majority of the United States. Precursor chemicals were smuggled from Colina, Mexico (on the Pacific coast, west of Mexico City), through Tijuana, to drug labs in greater Los Angeles. These labs were generally controlled by a second drug family, the Anguianos. After processing in Los Angeles, the finished methamphetamine was transported to a third gang family located in Dallas, headed by Daniel Virgen. The Virgen group then distributed the drugs throughout the East Coast and Southeast from Dallas. The arrests included Daniel Virgen himself, Rafael Anguiano-Chavez, the head of the Los Angeles gang, and others in the Mexico–Los Angeles–Dallas–North Carolina chain. In addition, authorities seized 133 pounds of methamphetamines, enough solution to create as much as 500 pounds of methamphetamines, 1,100 kilograms of cocaine, 1,300 pounds of marijuana, and $2 million cash.

The methamphetamine trade is growing exponentially, as are the seizures and "shuttering" of clandestine methamphetamine labs (over 1,100 labs were closed between September 1996 and September 1997). Another barometer of the scope of the methamphetamine trade is the number and scope of seizures of precursor chemicals; in August, 1996, Mexican customs officials seized nearly three tons of ephedrine, worth an estimated $10 million on the U.S. black market, which had been smuggled inside air conditioners shipped from Hong Kong via Los Angeles. In spite of this and other seizures, the trade continues to grow; in late 1996, local, state, and federal authorities in Southern California uncovered a ring of drug stores that had sold 41 tons of Sudafed tablets to Amezqua-related drug dealers — the active ingredient in Sudafed, and many other over-the-counter cold medications, is pseudoephedrine.

III. Other International Criminals and Criminal Organizations

A. Nigerian Criminal Organizations

Nigerian criminal gangs are the drug-smuggling specialists used by the Big Six criminal organizations. The U.S. State Department estimates that as much as 40% of all heroin being smuggled into the U.S. is brought in by Nigerians working for the Russian Mafiya, Colombian Cartels, Chinese Triads, or the various Italian Criminal Enterprises. In 1994, Interpol found that Nigerians were the third-largest ethnic drug-smuggling group (and perhaps the least successful — there are more Nigerian nationals imprisoned around the world for drug offenses than any other nationality).

The Nigerians' money-laundering efforts involve standard techniques (smuggling, the use of money-exchange houses, etc.) but with a uniquely African twist. Commonly, they purchase heroin from source countries such as Myanmar, Pakistan, and Afghanistan, paying for their product in U.S.

currency. They then smuggle the drugs to the U.S. and Europe. After selling the drugs, the proceeds are used to buy (conspicuous) consumer goods (luxury cars, electronic goods, and watches are favorites) for shipment to Nigeria, where they are sold in a very lucrative black market. If the Nigerian drug trafficker wishes to convert proceeds, now in the form of Nigerian "naira," into dollars or any other currency for use overseas or to purchase more product, he must proceed with the next step in the laundering cycle: converting the naira into American dollars, since it is only illegal to export naira, not other currencies.

To convert their naira into American dollars, the Nigerian traffickers/money launderers arrange for the naira to be delivered to one of the large cities along the Nigeria, Chad, and Camaroon border. These three African neighbors share a common currency, the Communité Financiere Africaine (CFA) franc, a currency created and secured by France to promote trade with its former colonial holdings. The Nigerians exchange their naira for CFA francs through "friendly" money exchanges, which provide the receipts and other documents needed by the Nigerians to deposit their proceeds in various Lagos banks for later wire-transfer to English banks. Once in accounts in England, the CFA francs are converted to U.S. dollars. Eventually, the dollars are used to finance the next heroin deals or to maintain the drug traffickers' lavish lifestyles.

In addition to their drug-smuggling activities, Nigerians are known for credit-card scams, "advance-fee fraud" (where the criminals lure greedy businessmen into advancing either cash or account information with promises of incredible profits yet to come. In fact, of course, they never arrive). (For background on Nigeria, see Chapter 15)

B. Khun Sa

Khun Sa has long been touted as the world's most notorious heroin trafficker, responsible for as much as 60% of the heroin on the streets of the U.S. Prior to his 1996 "surrender" to DEA Bangkok and Royal Thai Police in Operation Tiger Trap, Khun Sa led his own army, the Shan United Army (SUA) in cultivating, smuggling, and selling most of the world's heroin from his bases in the jungle highlands of the Golden Triangle of Myanmar, Laos, and Thailand. His surrender came about, in part, because of mutinies by his army of 20,000, who realized that Khun Sa was more interested in drug production and smuggling as the end, rather than the means to the end (independence for the Shan state). His army has continued its fight against the government of Myanmar.

For more than 30 years, Khun Sa controlled the production of the opium that fed the Chinese heroin pipeline. He began his career as a former nationalist general under Chiang Kai-shek, fleeing to Burma in 1949 after the

Communist revolution. It is reported that he got into the opium business with the help of the CIA, who wanted Khun Sa's anti-Communists funded and armed but could not otherwise provide the money. Within a few years, he was the *de facto* ruler of the Shan state, virtually enslaving the highland poppy farmers. Since his 1996 surrender, he has been living in an opulent villa in Rangoon. The government has not only pardoned him for the crimes for which he was arrested, but has refused to extradite him to the U.S. to face narcotics trafficking and conspiracy charges.

C. Manuel Noriega

General Manuel Antonio Noriega was Panama's dictator until his capture after the Panama invasion of 1988 and later indictment and conviction in Miami on various drug-smuggling and money-laundering charges. Among other exploits, Noriega was a CIA informant in the early 1960s, and became head of Panamanian military intelligence in 1968. Noriega "earned" millions from various drug-smuggling and money-laundering activities. His money-laundering technique was classic and instructive.

Between 1982 and 1986, Noriega opened accounts with BCCI for the "placement of funds of the Panama National Guard," using his own name and signature. By 1986, he had placed over $30 million into the the bank's Panamanian branch for deposit in various other BCCI accounts, using these funds for his personal use and that of his family. In 1986, there was at least $23 million on deposit in BCCI accounts in London and Luxembourg. In July, 1986, he, along with his BCCI contact Z.A. Akbar, began to "layer" the money; they transferred two of Noriega's BCCI Luxembourg accounts, totaling $11.1 million, to the account of the Banco Nationale de Panama at the Union Bank of Switzerland in an account in the name of Finlay International (owned by Noriega and controlled by Akbar); and they transferred over $11.8 million from other Noriega accounts at BCCI London into the account of the Banco Nationale de Panama at a Hamburg, Germany, bank, also in the name of Finlay International. The result was that the entire sum of Noriega's BCCI accounts, held ostensibly for the Panama Defense Forces, was transferred to banks other than BCCI in accounts in the name of an entity other than Noriega. By September, 1988, these two accounts were consolidated into the Banco Nationale de Panama account at the Middle Eastern Bank in London. Later that same month, the Chief of the Private and Investment Banking Division of Banco Nationale de Panama instructed the Middle East Bank to transfer the $23 million from its Banco Nationale de Panama account to the account of Finlay International. At this point, the Panamanian bank is now removed from the picture. Two days later, $20.5 million was transferred to Capcom and credited to two of its customer accounts, where it was traded about on various futures contracts, commissions paid, etc. The remaining $2.5 million was paid to a coded Swiss bank account. The final result was a classic example of placement, layering, and integration of illicit funds.

IV.   International Terrorist Organizations

A.   Introduction

Section 2656f of Title 22 of the United States Code (22 U.S.C. s. 2656f) defines terrorism as "premeditated, politically motivated violence perpetrated against noncombatant targets by subnational groups or clandestine agents, usually intended to influence an audience." The same section defines a terrorist group as "any group practicing, or that has significant subgroups that practice, international terrorism." The FBI defines terrorism as "the unlawful use of force or violence against persons or property to intimidate or coerce a government, the civilian population, or any segment thereof, in furtherance of political or social objectives." In addition, this statute compels the State Department to publish an annual report on terrorism, including a list of terrorism countries. The U.S. State Department's most recent annual report is entitled *1996 Patterns of Global Terrorism Report.**

The Report classifies terrorism as either domestic (common in countries such as Algeria, Sri Lanka, India, and Pakistan) or international (defined in 22 U.S.C. s. 2656f as "terrorism involving citizens or the territory of more than one country"). The Report notes that in 1996, the number of international-terrorist incidents fell to a 25-year low, yet the overall threat of terrorism remained high, as the trend was for more-ruthless attacks on mass civilian targets and the use of more-powerful bombs. In addition to the Report, on October 8, 1997, Secretary of State Madeline Albright designated 30 foreign organizations as terrorist groups. Interestingly, the IRA and the PLO were not included in this list (ostensibly because of their roles in pending peace talks in Northern Ireland and Israel, respectively). The list included 13 Islamic organizations and two far-right Israeli groups.

With the collapse of the Soviet Union and the economic and social upheaval in Iran, Iraq, Libya, Cuba, and other "sponsor" states, traditional terrorist organizations have found themselves without state sponsorship (except for continuing support from Iran), and in need of alternate sources of financial sustenance. Drug trafficking, arms smuggling, kidnapping, extortion, and other illegal activities — the lifeblood of the TCOs (transnational criminal organizations) — were obvious sources. As a result, the distinction

---

* An online version of the Report is available at the State Department's web site at *http://www.state.gov/www/global/terrorism/1996Report.*

between terrorist groups pursuing political objectives and the TCOs pursuing economic objectives has blurred, and they are increasingly forming strategic alliances to further their own goals.

B.   Terrorist Organizations

Appendix B to the Report lists 39 of the major terrorists groups that have been active recently. These include the following:

- Abu Nidal Organization (ANO, or Black September, split from the PLO in 1974)
- Japan's Aum Supreme Truth (Aum Shinrikyo, known for the sarin gas attacks on Tokyo's subway system in 1995)
- Spain's Basque separatists (known as the ETA, a Spanish acronym for Basque Fatherland and Liberty)
- MAMAS (the Islamic Resistance Movement, operating in the West Bank areas of Israel and Jordan and dedicated to the destruction of the State of Israel)
- Hizballah (the Party of God, dedicated also to the destruction of Israel and the establishment of an Iranian-style Islamic republic)
- Sri Lanka's Tamil Tigers (known as drug couriers moving heroin from Asia to western Europe)
- Bolivia's National Liberation Army (ELN, self-styled heirs to Che Guevara's legacy)
- Cambodia's Khmer Rouge (involved in heroin production in the Golden Triangle area of southeast Asia)
- The Popular Front for the Liberation of Palestine.

For a comprehensive review of terrorist groups and terrorism generally, see the Terrorism Research Center's web site at *www.terrorism.com.*

1.   *Peru's Shining Path Terrorist Group*

Peru's Shining Path, or *Sendero Luminoso* (SL), is the larger of the country's two major insurgency groups (the other is the Tupac Amour Revolutionary Movement, which held 72 hostages for more than four months in the Japanese ambassador's residence from December 1996 to March 1997). The SL was founded in the late 1960s by then-university professor Abimael Guzman; the stated goal of the SL is to rid Peru of foreign influence and to destroy existing Peruvian institutions and replace them with a "peasant revolutionary regime." The Shining Path is considered one of the world's most ruthless guerrilla organizations, specializing in indiscriminate car bombings, bombing diplomatic missions, assassinations, and, most recently, kidnapping (according to reports, on August 15, 1997, SL rebels kidnapped 29 oil workers in Peru's central jungles, the first reported kidnapping by the SL).

Since 1992, the Shining Path's effectiveness has been lessened because of Guzman's capture (in September 1992), the arrests of other SL leaders in 1995, defections, and President Fujimori's amnesty program for "repentant" terrorists. However, the SL remains active in the production and distribution of cocaine to fund its operations, and continues its terrorist activities.

2.   Provisional Irish Republican Army (PITA or IRA)

Northern Ireland's IRA, or Provost, is dedicated to uniting Northern Ireland and Ireland by terror. The IRA was formed in 1969 as a clandestine armed wing of Sinn Fein, a legal political party. Prior to and since the 1994–1996 ceasefire, the IRA has conducted bombings, assassinations, kidnappings, and robberies in Northern Ireland, the Irish Republic, and Britain. Much of the IRA's financial aid is thought to come from sympathizers in the U.S. As set out above, the IRA has been removed from the U.S. list of terrorist organizations, ostensibly because of its role in recent peace talks.

3.   Colombian Revolutionary Groups

There are two main revolutionary groups operating in Colombia. The largest, best trained, and best equipped is FARC, or Revolutionary Armed Forces of Colombia. FARC's goal is the overthrow of the Colombian government. It finances its 7,000-man "army" by kidnapping for profit, bank robberies, and drug trafficking. FARC is closely allied with the Colombian drug cartels, and most domestic drug production, smuggling, and transportation are done with the "blessing" of FARC.

The other main guerrilla group is the National Liberation Army, or ELN, a Marxist-Leninist organization operating primarily in the northern and eastern rural areas of Colombia. It is known for its practice of kidnapping foreign employees of large corporations, of disrupting the oil industry, and extracting "protection" money from the small coca and opium farmers.

V.   Strategic Alliances Between the Transnational Criminal Organizations

A.   International Strategic Alliances Generally

A study of how and why multinational corporations form strategic alliances provides the basis for understanding how and why transnational criminal organizations (TCOs) form strategic alliances. Knowing how and why such alliances are formed will enable nations to tailor their intelligence efforts to obtain information on the formation of these alliances, to develop strategies to fight them, and to implement these strategies.

Traditionally, legitimate international businesses form alliances out of mutual need; each has something, or has access to something, that the other wants, such as new markets, a type of specialized service, a supply of raw materials, a proven distribution chain, operating capital, knowledge of the local economy, etc. Once entered into, legitimate strategic alliances face a number of hurdles that might undermine the initial strategy and chemistry. Typically, these hurdles include a clash of cultures, incompatible interests or goals, different operating systems and values, unequal gains or profits from the alliance resulting in distrust and enmity, a failure of the alliance to live up to expectations, or a defection by one partner once its goals have been met (for example, once one partner has gained a foothold in a new market, it may feel it no longer needs its host partner). Like marriages, international alliances are easier to create than to maintain. Add into the mix the fact that criminals are seeking alliances with other criminals with a view to better their illegal activities, hunted all the while by national and international law enforcement, and the chances of success are slim. Although the track records of various TCO strategic alliances has not been good (see below for a discussion of the Medellín and Cali Cartels' alliance in the mid-1980s), the existence of the TCOs themselves is so new that any alliances between them are still in the early stages — whether the alliances survive and mature remains to be seen.

B. The Colombian Cartels: A Strategic Alliance Case Study

In the early 1980s, a number of petty hoodlums and crooks from Medellín began to dominate the North and South American cocaine trade. Recognizing the benefits of cooperation — eliminating their fringe competition, employing economies of scale in production and distribution, and taking advantage of their unique areas of specialization — this handful of traffickers formed a cartel.

A parallel cocaine-trafficking group rose to prominence in Cali. These people, however, were from a social class different from that of their Medellín counterparts; many of them were sophisticated businessmen. The two cartels soon began to share in the production and distribution of cocaine in the U.S. market, which was, at that time, growing exponentially. The Medellín Cartel eventually ceased to exist as an organization, and by the early 1990s, the Cali Cartel controlled the Colombian cocaine trade. The Cali leaders formed strategic alliances with the Mexican Federation for the smuggling and distribution of cocaine through Mexico into the U.S.

However, by the late 1980s, a number of factors led to the deterioration of this strategic alliance between the two cartels. As American and Colombian law-enforcement efforts were stepped up, the risks increased and the profits were reduced, creating tensions between the two groups as to how to respond. For example, profits from the cocaine distribution in the South Florida area (a market given to the Medellín Cartel) dropped precipitously in 1987 and 1988, so the Medellín leaders sought access to the New York area, a Cali market, leading to turf battles and animosity. In addition, the Medellín kingpins, with their criminal backgrounds, solved their domestic problems with terror by killing rivals and assassinating government figures. The Cali leaders preferred an approach of co-opting and corrupting the government, and refused to go along with the Medellín leaders' strategy. In addition, personality clashes between the rival kingpins themselves led to the breakup of the alliances (for example, allegations by Pablo Escobar, the *de facto* leader of the Medellín Cartel, that the Cali leaders had been involved in the killing of Rodriguez Gacha, a Medellín kingpin, is mentioned as the proverbial straw that broke the camel's back).

APPENDIX 1.1

Specially Designated Narcotics Traffickers (SDNTs)

The International Emergency Economic Powers Act, 50 U.S.C. s. 1701, allows the President to issue Executive Orders to sanction terrorists, countries, and narcotics traffickers where their activities constitute *an unusual and extraordinary threat* to the United States' national security and economy. The details of the IEEPA are set out in part B(7) of chapter 8, "Domestic Money Laundering Laws and Statutes."

Beginning in October 1995, President Clinton issued four such orders directed specifically against the Colombian drug cartels. There are currently 359 SDNTs, consisting of four principle individuals, other individuals, and various entities:

Principal Individuals: Name (and alias) — City
Herrera Buitrago, Helmer (aka Pacho, H7) — Cali
Rodriguez Orejuela, Gilberto (the Chess Player, Lucas) — Cali
Rodriguez Orejuelo, Miguel Angel (El Senor, Patricia, Patricio, Manuel, Doctor MRO) — Cali
Santacruz Londono, Jose (Chepe, Don Chepe, El Gordo Chepe) — Cali

Other Individuals: Name (and Alias) — City
Acevedo, Fransisco Luis — Cali
Aguando Ortiz, Luis Jameson- Cali
Aguilera Quijano, Harold — Cali
Alvarez Gaviria, Jaime Antonio — Cali
Amaya Orozco, Luis Alberto — Cali
Amezquita Meneses, Salustio — Cali
Andrade Quintero, Ancizar — Cali
Angulo Orobio, Jose Fransisco — Cali
Arbalaez Alzate, Rafael — Cali
Arbalaez Gallon, Gladys — Cali
Arbelaez Pardo, Amparo (four Colombian passports) — Bogotá
Arboledo, Julio — Cali
Arboledo A., Pedro Nicholas (aka Nicolas) — Bogotá
Arisizabal Atehortua, Jamie Alberto — Cali

Arjona Alvarado, Rafael — Bogotá
Arlone Facelli, Roberto — Bogotá
Avendano Gutierrez, Fransisco Eduardo — Bogotá
Avila de Mondragon, Ana Dolores — Cali
Baeza Molina, Carlos Alberto — Cali
Baron, Carlos — Cali
Bechara Simanca, Salim — Cali
Benitez Castellanos, Cesar Tulio — Cali and Quito, Ecuador
Borrero Q., Hector Fabio — Cali
Buitrago, Sulay (aka Herrera Buitrago, Sulay) — Cali
Buitrago de Herrera, Luz Mery — Cali
Buitrago Marin, Adiela — Cali
Buitrago Marin, Nubia — Cali
Calderon Rodriguez, Solange — Cali
Cardona Ochoa, Carlos Julio — Cali
Carmona, Juan Manual — Cali
Carrillo Silva, Armando — Cali
Casquete Vargas, Orlando — Bogotá
Castano Arango, Fernando — Cali
Castro de Santacruz, Amparo(three Colombian passports) — Cali
Caviedes Cruz, Leonardo (three Colombian passports) — Cali
Chang Barreo, Pedro Antonio — Cali
Cortez, Oliverio Abril — Cali
Cuartes Morales, Juan Carlos — Cali
Daza Quiroa, Hugo Carlos — Bogotá
Daza Rivera, Pablo Emilio — Bogotá, and Quito, Ecuador
Delgado, Jorge Armando — Bogotá
Diaz Sanchez, Alberto — Cali
Dominguez Garibello, Freddy Orlando — Cali
Donneys Gonzalez, Federico — Bogotá
Echeverry Trujillo, Martha Lucia — Cali
Echeverry Trujillo, Oscar Alberto — Cali
Escobar Buitrago, Walter — Cali
Estrada Uribe, Octavio — Cali
Galindo, Gilmer Antonio (aka Guzman Trujillo, Carlos Arturo) — Cali
Galindo Herrera, Diana Paola — Cali
Galindo Herrera, Diego Alexander — Cali
Gallego Berrio, Elizabeth — Cali
Gallego Sossa, Rosa Esperanza — Cali
Garces Vargas, Elmo — Cali
Garcia Montilla, Edgar Alberto — Cali
Garzon Hernandez, Rodrigo — Cali

Garzon Restrepo, Juan Leonardo — Cali and Bogotá
Gaviria Posado, Gilberto — Bogotá
Gil Osorio, Alfonso (four Colombian passports) — Bogotá
Giraldo Arbalaez, Fernando — Cali
Giraldo Jaramillo, Clara Stella — Cali
Giraldo Sarria, Octavio — Cali
Giraldo Sarria, Rosa Amelia — Cali
Gomez, Julio Humberto — Bogotá
Gomez Beltran, Jorge — Bogotá
Gomez Berrio, Olmes (Holmes) de Jesus — Cali
Gomez Galindo, Omaira — Cali
Gomez J., Luis Fernando — Cali
Gomez Lopez, Diego Fernando — Cali
Gomez Mora, Ricardo — Bogotá
Gomez V., Manuel Antonio — Cali
Gonzalez Robledo, Julio Cesar — Bogotá
Gutierres C., Alvaro (aka Gutierrez C., Alvaro) — Bogotá
Gutierrez Ardila, Eduardo — Cali
Gutierrez Cancino, Fernando Antonio — Bogotá
Gutierrez Lozano, Ana Maria — Bogotá
Gutierrez Lozano, Juan Pablo — Bogotá
Henoa Lopez, Alberto — Bogotá
Henoa de Sanchez, Hortensia — Bogotá
Henoa Vda. de Botero, Maria Yolanda — Bogotá
Hernandez C., Hector Fabio — Cali
Herrera Buitrago, Alvaro — Cali
Herrera Buitrago, Stella — Cali
Herrera Infante, Alberto — Cali
Herrera-Ramirez, Giselle — Cali
Herrera Ramirez, Linda Nicolle — Cali
Herrera Tobon, Maria Cecilia — Bogotá
Holguin Sarria, Alvaro — Bogotá, Cali
Ibanez Lopez, Raul Alberto — Cali
Idarraga Ortiz, Jaime — Bogotá, Cali
Izquierdo Orejuela, Patricia — Bogotá
Izquierdo Quintero, Rosalino — Cali
Jaimes Rivera, Jose Isidro — Cali
Larranaga Calvache, Juan Carlos — Cali
Libreros diez, Orlando — Cali
Linares Reyes, Jose Ricardo (aka Llenares Reyes, Ricardo Jose) — Cali
Lindo Hurtado, Edgar — Cali
Lopera Londono, Vicente de Jesus — Cali

Lopez Valencia, Oscar — Cali
Lozano de Gomez, Zilia — Bogotá
Lozano Cancino de Gutierrez (aka Lozano de Gutierrez, Gladys Maria
    Gladys) — Bogotá
Lugo Villafone, Jesus Alberto — Cali
Marmolejo Loaiza, Carlos Julio — Cali
Marmolejo Vaca, Hernan Rodrigo — Cali
Marquez Canovas, Alberto — Cali
Mazuero Erazo, Hugo- Cali
Millan Rubio, Alba Milena — Cali
Mogollon Rueda, Eduardo — Bogotá
Mondragon de Rodriguez, Mariela — Bogotá
Monroy Arcila, Fransisco Jose — Cali
Montano Bermudez, Libardo — Bogotá
Moran Guerrero, Mario Fernando — Bogotá
Mosquera, Juan Carlos — Cali
Munoz Paz, Adriana del Socorro — Cali
Munoz Paz, Joaquin Emilio — Cali
Munoz Rodriguez, Juan Carlos — Bogotá, Cali
Munoz Rodriguez, Soraya — Bogotá
Ortiz Palacios, Willington A. — Cali
Osorio Cadavid, Maria Victoria — Cali
Osorio Pineda, Jorge Ivan — Bogotá
Patino Uribe, Carlos Augusto- Cali
Paz Mahecha, Gonzalo Rodrigo — Cali
Pelaez de Henai, Teresa — Bogotá
Perez Garci, Carlos — Cali
Perez Varela, Jaime Diego — Cali
Pinzon, Marco Antonio — Bogotá
Prado Cuero, Salomon — Cali
Quintero Salazar, Lisimaco — Cali
Ramirez, Julio Cesar — Cali
Ramirez, Manuel Nernan — Cali
Ramirez Cortes, Delia Nhora (Nora) — Cali
Ramirez Libreros, Gladys Miriam — Bogotá
Ramirez M., Oscar — Quito, Ecuador
Ramirez Valenciano, William — Cali
Restrepo Villegas, Camilo — Cali
Ricuarte Florez, Gilma Leonar — Bogotá
Rivera Mosquera, Mauricio Jose — Cali
Rizo, Diego — Cali
Rizo Moreno, Jorge Luis — Cali

Rodriguez, Manuel — Bogotá
Rodriguez Abadia, William — Bogotá
Rodriguez Arbelaez, Carolina- Cali
Rodriguez Arbelaez, Maria Fernanda — Bogotá, Cali
Rodiguez Mondragon, Humberto — Bogotá
Rodriguez Mondragon, Jamie — Bogotá
Rodriguez Mondragon, Maria (aka Rodriguez Mondragon, Alexandra) — Bogotá
Rodriguez Moreno, Juan Pablo — Cali
Rodriguez Moreno, Miguel Andres — Cali
Rodriguez Moreno, Stephane — Cali
Rodriguez Orejuela de Gil, Amparo — Bogotá
Rodriguez Orejuela de Munoz (aka Rodriguez Orejuela de Rojas, Haydee) — Bogotá
Rodriguez Ramirez, Claudia Pilar (three Colombian passports) — Bogotá
Rojas Mejia, Hernan — Cali
Rojas Ortis, Rosa — Cali
Rosales Diaz, Hector Emilio — Cali
Rozo Varon, Luis Carlos — Bogotá
Ruida Fajardo, Herberth Gonzalo — Bogotá
Ruiz Hernandez, Gregorio Rafael — Cali
Saavedra Restrepo, Jesus Maria — Cali
Salcedo R., Nhora Clemencia — Cali
Salcedo Ramirez, Jaime — Cali
Saldarriaga Acevedo, Carlos Omar — Cali
Sanchez de Valencia, Dora Gladys — Cali
Santacruz Castro, Ana Milena (three Colombian passports) — Cali
Santacruz Castro, Sandra (U.S. SSN 090-80-3433) — Cali
Sarria Holguin, Ramiro (Robert) — Cali
Silva Perdomo, Alejandro — Cali
Solaque Sanchez, Alfredo — Bogotá
Torres Cortes, Joselin(three U.S. passports) — Bogotá
Trejos Marquez, Arnulfo — Cali
Triana Tejeda, Luis Humberto — Cali
Trujillo Caicedo, Fransisco Javier — Cali
Uribe Gonzalez, Jose Abelardo — Cali
Valencia, Reynel — Cali
Valencia Arias, Jhon Gavy (John Gaby) — Cali
Valencia Arias, Luis Fernando — Cali
Vargas Garcia, Carlos Alberto — Quito, Ecuador
Victoria, Mercedes — Bogotá
Victoria Potes, Nestor Raul — Cali

Villalobos, Luis E. — Bogotá
Villegas Arias, Maria Deisy (Deicy) — Cali
Villegas Bolanos, Silver Amado — Cali
Zabaleta Sandoval, Nestor (one Colombian, two U.S. passports) — Cali
Zuniga Osorio, Marco Fidel — Bogotá

Entities: Name (Common name or alias) — City
Agricola Humyani Ltda. — Cali
Agropecuaria Betamia Ltda. — Cali
Agropecuaria y Reforest Adora — Cali
Alfa Pharma S.A. — Bogotá
Amparo Rodriguez de Gil y Cia S. En C. — Cali
Andina de Construcciones S.A. — Cali
Asesorias Cosmos Ltda. — Cali
Aspoir del Pacifico y Cia Ltda. — Cali
Aureal Immobiliaria Ltda. — Bogotá
Blanco Pharma S.A. (aka Laboratorios Blanco Pharma S.A.) — Bogotá
Color 89.5 FM Stereo — Cali
Comercializadora de Carnes del Pacifico Ltda. — Cali
Comercializadora Integral Ltda. (aka Cars & Cars Ltda., Proyecto Cars &
    Cars, Centro Comercial del AutomovilCentro Comercial del
    Automovil) — Cali
Comercializador Oroblanco (aka Socir S.A.) — Cali
Compax Ltda. (aka Inversiones y Distribuciones Compax Ltda.) — Cali
Concretos Cali S.A. — Cali
Constructora Dimisa Ltda. — Cali
Constructora Gopeva Ltda. — Cali
Constructora Tremi Ltda. — Cali
Construexito S.A. (aka Cone S.A.) — Cali
Creaciones Deportivas Willington Ltda. — Cali
Deposito Popular de Drogas S.A. — Cali
Derecho Integral y Cia Ltda. — Cali
Distribuidora de Drogas Condor (aka Condor Ltda.) — Bogotá
Distribuidora de Drogas la Drogas la Rebaja (aka Distribuidora de Rebaja
    S.A., Drogas la Rebaja Principal S.A.) — Cali and Bogotá
Distribuidora Migil Ltda. (aka Migil, Distribuidora Migil Cali S.A., fka
    Distribuidora Migil Bogotá Ltda.) — Cali
Distribuidora Myramirez S.A. — Cali, Bogotá
Drogas la Rebaja Barranquilla S.A. — Barranquilla
Drogas la Rebaja Bucaramanga S.A. — Bucaramanga, Cucuta, Valledupar
Drogas la Rebaja Cali S.A. — Cali
Drogas la Rebaja Neiva S.A. — Neiva

Drogas la Rebaja Pasto S.A. — Pasto, Puerto, Asis
Drogas la Rebaja Pereira S.A. — Pereira
Export Cafe Ltda. — Cali
Farallones Stereo 91.5 FM — Cali
Farmatodo S.A. — Bogotá
Ganadera Ltda. (aka Ganaderia) — Cali
Grupo Santa Ltda. — Cali
Hacienda la Novillera (aka Novillera, Novillera Ganadera) — Cali, Valle
  del Cauca
Hacienda Sandrana (aka Sandrana, Sandrana Ganadera) — Cali, Valle
  del Cauca
Haydee de Munoz y Cia S. En. C. — Cali
Industria Avicola Palmaseca S.A. — Cali
Inmobiliaria Aurora Ltda. — Cali
Inmobiliaria Bolivar S.A. (aka Administracion Inmobilaria Bolivar S.A.)
  — Cali
Inmobiliaria Samaria Ltda. — Cali
Inmobiliaria U.M.V. S.A. — Cali
Intercreditos S.A. (aka Intercreditos Bogotá, Intercreditos Cali) — Cali
Inversiones Ara Ltda. — Cali, Jamundi
Inversiones Betania Ltda. — Cali
Inversiones Camino Real S.A. — Cali
Inversiones El Paso Ltda. (aka Inversiones Negoagricola S.A.) — Cali
Inversiones El Penon S.A. — Cali
Inversiones Geele Ltda. — Cali
Inversiones Geminis S.A. — Cali
Inversiones Herrebe Ltda. — Cali
Inversiones Integral y Cia — Cali
Inversiones Invervalle S.A. (aka Invervalle) — Cali
Inversiones La Sexta Ltda. — Cali
Inversiones Miguel Rodriguez e Hijo — Cali
Inversiones Mompax Ltda. (aka Mompax Ltda.) — Cali
Inversiones Rodriguez Arbelaez y Cia S. En. C. — Cali
Inversiones Rodriguez Moreno y Cia S. En. C. — Cali
Inversiones Rodriguez Ramirez y Cia S.C.S.S. — Cali
Inversiones Santa Ltda. (aka Inversiones y Construcciones Santa Limitada)
  — Cali
Inversiones y Construcciones Valle S.A. (aka Incovalle) — Cali
Laboratorios Blaimar de Colombia (Blaimar S.A.) — Bogotá
Laboratorios Genericos Veterinarios de Colombia S.A. — Bogotá
Laboratorios Kressfor de Colombia (aka Kressfor S.A.) — Bogotá
Mariela de Rodriguez y Cia. S. En C. — Cali

Maxitiendas Todo En Uno — Cali
M. Rodriguez O. y Cia. S. En C.S. — Cali
Munoz y Rodriguez y Cia Ltda. — Cali
Penta Pharma de Colombia S.A. — Bogotá
Plasticos Condor Ltda. — Cali
Previa S.A. (aka Prevencion y Analisis de Riesgos) — Cali
Radio Unidas FM S.A. — Cali
Revista del America Ltda. — Cali
Rionap Comercio y Representaciones S.A. — Quito, Ecuador
Samaria Arrendamiento — Cali
Samaria Canas- Cali
Samaria Intereses — Cali
Samaria Ltda. — Cali
Samaria Tierras — Cali
Sandrana Canas — Cali
Servicios Inmobiliarios Ltda. — Cali
Servicios Sociales Ltda. — Barranquilla
Sociedad Constructora la Cascada (aka Constructora Cascada S.A.) — Cali
Socovalle Ltda. (aka Sociedad Constructora y Adminstradora del Valle Ltda)
    — Cali
Supertiendas la Rebaja — Cali
Tobogon — Cali
Valle Comunicaciones Ltda. (aka Vallecom) — Cali
Valores Mobiliarios de Occidente S.A. — Bogotá
Viajes Mercurio Ltda. — Cali
W. Herrera y Cia S. En C. — Cali

Part II
Money-Laundering Techniques

An Introduction to Money Laundering

2

The money laundering problem we are facing today is increasingly international in character. The greater integration of the world economy, and the removal of barriers to the free movement of capital, have combined to create new commercial opportunities. Unfortunately, the same efficiency and convenience that the global economy affords to legitimate commerce also makes easier the job of disposing of criminal proceeds.

— Raymond W. Kelly, Treasury Undersecretary (Enforcement)
Testimony before the House Judiciary Subcommittee on Crime, July 24, 1997

I. Money Laundering: What Is It?

According to West Legal Publications' 1961 edition of *Words and Phrases,* laundering means "to wash, as clothes; to wash and to smooth with a flatiron or mangle; to wash and iron; as to launder shirts."

By the 1989 edition, the definition had been extended to include a quite different meaning. Now it was also "a process by which cash derived from a criminal enterprise may be easily exchanged without a trace of its origin."

Much has changed in the last 30 years. Although criminals have sought to "launder" their criminal profits for years (early money-laundering texts suggested that the term "money laundering" came from the practice of the 1920s Chicago mobsters — Al Capone and the like — of buying and operating local laundries with their gambling, rackets, and liquor profits), the term did not appear in print until 1973 during the Watergate scandal.*

Regardless of when the term first appeared, its use is now commonplace. Like many other technical terms, however, its actual meaning is not so well known. Money laundering has been described or defined a number of different ways: money laundering is the process by which one conceals the existence, illegal source, or illegal application of income, and then disguises

---

* The first reported sighting of the term "money laundering" in a legal context was not until 1984 (see *United States v. $4,255,625.39, et seq.,* 551 F. Supp. 314, SD Fla 1984).

43

that income to make it appear legitimate; or ... money laundering is the process of taking the proceeds of criminal activity and making these proceeds appear legal; or ... money laundering is the act of converting funds derived from illegal activities into a spendable or consumable form.

Perhaps the most encompassing definition of money laundering has been developed by the U.S. Customs Service: "Money laundering is the process whereby proceeds, reasonably believed to have been derived from criminal activity, are transported, transferred, transformed, converted, or intermingled with legitimate funds, for the purpose of concealing or disguising the true nature, source, disposition, movement or ownership of those proceeds. The goal of the money-laundering process is to make funds derived from, or associated with, illicit activity appear legitimate."

Whichever definition of money laundering is used, the purpose of laundering money is to reduce or eliminate the risks of seizure and forfeiture so that the ultimate goal of the underlying criminal activity — to spend and enjoy the profits — can be realized. Obviously, "hiding" dirty money is not the same as "laundering" it; even if a criminal hides his dirty money, he cannot spend it until it is laundered.

The Financial Crimes Enforcement Network (FinCEN) estimates that over $750 billion in illicit funds is laundered worldwide annually, of which $300 billion is laundered in or through the U.S. Compare this figure with the combined gross sales of General Motors and Ford, the world's two largest auto makers, of $301 billion in 1996. In fact, money laundering could now be the world's third-largest "business," trailing only legitimate currency exchange and worldwide automobile production. The greatest source of illicit funds in need of laundering is the illegal narcotics trade — in its Annual Report for 1996–1997, the Financial Action Task Force, or FATF, a 26-nation group formed in 1989 to address money-laundering issues, identified drug trafficking as the single biggest source of illegal proceeds (the illegal arms trade, human smuggling, and terrorism also contribute to the supply of illicit funds for money laundering). The nations used by narcotics money launderers have traditionally been the drug-consumer nations in Europe, the U.S., and Canada; the Caribbean "offshore banking" nations, and the South and Latin American drug-source and transit countries of Mexico, Colombia, and Panama. The FATF now points to Eastern Europe and the Former Soviet Union (FSU) nations as rivaling these traditional centers.

How does money laundering work? Using narcotics traffickers as an example — they account for 60% to 80% of all federal U.S. money-laundering prosecutions — money laundering involves the transportation and conversion of billions of dollars in small-denomination U.S. currency into Colombian or Mexican pesos or Italian lira in the hands of the various drug cartel "kingpins." The process of converting the street-level drug proceeds into cash in the hands of the kingpins generally involves three steps: "placement" of the dirty money into the financial system; "layering," where the dirty money, now in the banking or financial system, is moved through the global financial system to hide its origins or separate it from its illegal source; and "integration," where the illicit funds are blended back into the economy and become indistinguishable from legitimate funds.*

II.   Money Laundering: Why Fight It?

Until the mid- to late-1980s, the traditional emphasis on fighting criminal organizations had been to disrupt the supply of the products (drugs) and to arrest the suppliers — the organizations' leadership, or "kingpins." Since that time, coinciding with the criminalization of money laundering itself, the priority has shifted to target the profits. The logic of this new approach appears sound: the criminal organization's incentive is to make money, so seizing the money removes the incentive to continue the illicit business. And, since the criminal organizations are "laundering" these profits in an effort to evade seizure and forfeiture, the battles are now being fought in the arenas of money laundering — banks, other financial institutions, securities brokers, wire-transfer businesses, money remitters, casinos, etc.

But is money laundering, per se, such a bad thing? Arguably, the existence of offshore-banking industries has transformed the otherwise dormant economies of many Caribbean nations such as Aruba and the Netherlands Antilles, and, as a result, promoted the tourism industry. Clearly, there is a positive multiplier effect in having so much money moving in and through a nation's financial sector. The legions of bankers, lawyers, accountants, and the attendant service industries alone have revitalized many economies. However, money-laundering negatives far outweigh the positives: corruption of the financial-services industry, the government bureaucracy, and all three branches of government are foremost. Therefore, anti-money-laundering efforts, both on a national basis and internationally, have a double benefit: fighting international criminal organizations, arms dealers, and terrorists; and ensuring the integrity of our economic and civil institutions.

To use an analogy, 1997 saw a great uproar over allegations of improper campaign-financing practices by the Democratic National Committee, illustrated in part by the so-called coffee klatsches and Lincoln-bedroom sleepovers. The fear was that those industrialists, financiers, and bankers could buy influence in the executive and legislative branches of the U.S. government. Clearly then, having drug traffickers, arms smugglers, and terrorists

---

* A classic money-laundering scheme is described in United States vs. Saccoccia at the end of this chapter.

using the proceeds of crime — proceeds introduced into the financial system through money laundering — to corrupt and bribe the executive, legislative, and judicial branches of government, and to corrupt the banking, securities, and financial industries, would be catastrophic. The fear of Johnnie Huang's fund-raising efforts involving the Asian-American community and Indonesian corporations, and whether the resulting donations to the Democratic National Committee would corrupt the decision-making process in the Executive level of the U.S. government, pales in comparison with the fear that would exist if Mexican, Colombian, Russian, Chinese, Japanese, and American drug lords and crime bosses controlled political, social, and economic institutions in the U.S.

III. The Mechanics of Money Laundering

After having amassed incredible profits from illegal activities, the typical criminal is faced with several issues: how to convert the mountains of cash into an anonymous and reasonably portable form of cash, currency, or other monetary instrument; how to convert the bulk cash so as to leave no evidentiary trails back to him or his criminal activities; and how to ensure that the criminals he uses to launder his cash don't rip him off or turn him in.

To meet or resolve these needs or problems, money launderers must complete three basic steps to change illicit funds to legitimate funds. As mentioned earlier, these three steps are known as placement, layering, and integration. *Placement* involves changing the bulk cash derived from criminal activities into a more portable and less suspicious form, then getting those proceeds into the mainstream financial system. *Layering* involves the movement of these funds, often mixed with funds of legitimate origins, through the world's financial systems in numerous accounts in an attempt to hide the funds' true origins. *Integration* is the process of reintroducing these layered funds back into the mainstream economy, where they can be invested and spent freely.

For example, drug cash is picked up in various East Coast cities and moved to a counting house. From there, it is broken up into smaller amounts, usually less than $10,000, to avoid the most common reporting regulations, then converted by "smurfs" (a nickname alleged to have been used by investigators in Florida who noticed that the runners looked like the cartoon "smurfs" as they scurried in and out of various banks) into bank checks. These checks are then deposited in small amounts into various local banks. These bank funds are then wire-transferred to an account in Tampa, and then wire-transferred to London via a Federal Reserve bank in New York. In London, those funds are converted to certificates of deposit that are then used as collateral for a bank loan generated in the Bahamas. The loan proceeds are then wire-transferred from the Bahamas to the account in Tampa. From Tampa, these loan proceeds are wire-transferred to Chile, and from there to the trafficker in Colombia.

A real example of money laundering, uncovered in New York in 1994, also illustrates the three steps. This involved a Bulgarian diplomat, one police officer, two lawyers, a fireman, three bankers, and two rabbis (this sounds like the start of a bad joke, but truth really is stranger than fiction). This network used a trucking business and beer distributorship as business covers; a law firm for advice on money-laundering and structuring laws; the diplomat, firefighter, and rabbis as couriers to pick up the drug proceeds; and a Citibank assistant branch manager as the insider accepting the cash. Once the cash was deposited into various accounts (between $70 million and $100 million over two years), it was then wire-transferred to a private Swiss bank. Once there, it was remitted to other accounts controlled by the traffickers.

Regardless of the exact steps taken to launder money, most money-laundering schemes involve some or all of the classic three stages. Every manual on money laundering begins with a description of the three stages, then describes each stage in turn, one following the other, as if placement must be followed by layering, which must in turn be followed by integration. However, this linear thinking can be deceptive. For example, illegal money might be mixed with legitimate money prior to placement into the financial system (for example, with cash-rich businesses such as casinos, restaurants, and bars). In addition, illegal money possibly never enters the mainstream financial system, instead going through various underground banking systems, such as the *Hawala* or *fei chi'en* parallel banking systems in India and China, respectively. However, to completely understand money-laundering basics, it is necessary to understand the basics of most money-laundering schemes: the three stages.

A. The Three Stages of Money Laundering

If a trafficking organization sells $1 billion worth of illicit drugs on the streets of New York, it must contend with more than 256,000 pounds of illicit currency. If we assume a conservative figure of $50 billion for all illicit drugs sold in the United States, the amount of illicit currency produced by those sales weighs almost 13 million pounds.

— **Mary Lee Warren, Deputy Assistant Attorney General, Criminal Division**
Testimony before the House Judiciary Subcommittee on Crime, July 24, 1997

1. Stage 1: Placement

Placement is usually the first of the three steps in laundering illicit funds. Placement involves changing the money derived from criminal activities into a more portable and less suspicious form, then getting those proceeds into the mainstream financial system. It is the most difficult and vulnerable step, simply because most illegal activity generates profits in the form of cash, and cash is bulky, difficult to conceal, and, in large amounts, very noticeable to the average bank teller, casino employee, etc.

Placement requires finding a solution to the problem of how to move the masses of cash generated from illegal activity into a more manageable form for introduction into the financial stream. For example, the Justice Department calculates that 450 paper bills weigh 1 pound, so that $1 million in $5 bills weighs 440 pounds, $1 million in $10 bills weighs 220 pounds, $1 million in $20 bills weighs 110 pounds, and $1 million in $100 bills weighs 22 pounds. Therefore, converting drug cash, usually in the form of $10, $20, or possibly $100 bills into a manageable form is critical to placing those funds into the banking system.

On July 24, 1997, Deputy Assistant Attorney General Mary Lee Warren testified before the House Judiciary Subcommittee on Crime that because banking regulations had made it increasingly difficult for criminals to use the banking systems to move their profits, the best opportunity to target these profits is when the criminals are converting the huge volume of cash — in other words, at the placement stage. Warren testified that "our basic anti-money-laundering objective is currently to identify and prevent the initial placement of the drug proceeds into our financial system." Warren set out various calculations from the Department of Justice comparing the weight of drugs with the weight of the cash proceeds from the drugs: the weight of the cash generated by the street sale of heroin is about 10 times the weight of the drug itself; for cocaine, it is about six times the weight of the drug sold. Therefore, the sale of 10 kilos, or 20 pounds, of heroin and cocaine would produce over 220 pounds and 120 pounds, respectively, of cash in need of laundering.

The methods used to place bulk cash into the system are endless, from simply depositing cash into an account to using front corporations, such as jewelry stores or check-cashing businesses, to converting the cash to negotiable instruments such as cashier's checks, money orders, or traveler's checks.

The particular method used by a criminal organization to place its illicit funds is governed by the organization's level of sophistication and its relative geographical considerations. For example, the Cali Cartel faces more difficulties and vulnerabilities during the initial placement stage than their counterparts in the Mexican Federation because of the greater distances the money must travel. Historically, Colombians have amassed currency in strategic locations for smuggling out of the U.S. by air cargo or outbound freighter. Once out of the U.S., it is easily placed into offshore banking centers, where it is layered and integrated. The Mexican Federation drug organizations do not have the same logistical concerns as their Cali counterparts; they simply smuggle cash out of the U.S. the same way they smuggle drugs into the U.S. DEA's Operation Zorro II (see Chapter 10) identified the typical placement scheme used by the Mexicans.

Both the Mexican and Colombian organizational structures (self-sufficient cells controlled by regional directors reporting to the kingpins) separate the production and distribution of drugs from the laundering of the drug proceeds to insulate them from threats posed by both rival traffickers and law-enforcement agencies. Unnoticed placement of narco-dollars into the U.S. financial system is now extremely unpredictable and risky. The better approach is to smuggle the cash out of the U.S. and into an offshore financial system, where it can be repatriated back to the U.S.

2.   Stage 2: Layering

Layering is the second of the three steps of laundering illicit funds. Layering involves making a series of financial transactions that in their frequency, complexity, and volume often resemble legitimate financial activity. Typically, layering involves the wire transfer or movement of funds placed into a financial or banking system by way of numerous accounts in an attempt to hide the funds' true origins. The most common method of layering is to wire-transfer funds through offshore-banking havens such as the Cayman Islands, Panama, The Bahamas, the Netherlands Antilles, and, increasingly, Pakistan and Chile. Once out of the U.S. and into countries with strong bank-secrecy laws, the funds' origins become even more difficult to trace. To add to the complexity, funds can be routed through shell corporations, or by using counterbalancing loan schemes. The sheer volume of wire transfers adds to the problem of tracking the origins.

Perhaps the key to a successful layering operation is to ensure that the layering transactions cross several national borders — either physically or electronically, or through corporate structures involving entities in a number of different countries. At the least, layering should involve at least two, if not three, jurisdictions.

Typically, traffickers use the services of "controllers" and money brokers to launder their money. A few years ago, these agents were simply recruited from the ranks of the criminal organizations themselves. However, as money-laundering techniques — and the law-enforcement efforts to stop them — have become increasingly sophisticated, criminal organizations have begun to employ specialists recruited from the ranks of professionals — accountants, lawyers, money managers, stock brokers — lured by the incredible profits.

3.   Stage 3: Integration

Integration involves the movement of the layered funds into the global financial world to be mixed with funds of legitimate origin. Once funds are sufficiently layered, they are then integrated into the mainstream financial world by a limitless variety of financial instruments, such as letters of credit, bonds, securities, bank notes, bills of lading, and guarantees. Some of the largest seizures of laundered funds occur where integration fails and the entire account or accounts are seized.*

IV. Money-Laundering Techniques and Tools

A. Smuggling

Money laundering and structuring were criminalized in 1986. Since then, smuggling has been the most common method of beginning the laundering cycle. Smuggling gets the cash out of the U.S., with its strict bank-reporting laws, and into countries with strict bank-secrecy laws. From these offshore-banking havens, the proceeds are layered and repatriated, or smuggled back into the U.S. in the form of non-cash financial instruments.

How does the smuggling process work? A simple smuggling technique involves a manipulation of the cash-reporting regulations at the U.S. border. A launderer smuggles cash from the U.S. to Mexico without declaring the money on a CMIR report. He then turns around and comes back into the U.S., declaring the funds at U.S. Customs as legitimate revenue, backed up with invoices, receipts, etc., derived from phony business dealings in Mexico. Customs then issues the proper form, allowing the smuggler to deposit that cash in any U.S. bank without raising suspicion. Once the cash is in the account, it could then be wire-transferred anywhere, since there are no reporting requirements for wire transfers.

The utility of this smuggling technique is borne out by statistics: A FinCEN study of money declared along the United States–Mexico border between 1988 and 1990 showed that Brownsville, TX, had the most funds declared upon entry to the U.S. — almost $8 billion. Second was the small town of Nogales, AZ, with $5 billion. Both of these figures are disproportionate to the flow of legitimate commerce. The largest population centers along the Mexican border — El Paso and San Diego — placed third and fourth, respectively.

DEA and Customs estimates suggest that as much as $50 billion is smuggled out of the U.S. annually, avoiding the many sophisticated money-laundering reporting and other regulations aimed at financial institutions. This number is only a rough guess, as authorities know only of what they seize, but can only estimate what they do not seize. For example, in the four-year

---

* See, e.g., *United States v. All Monies ($477,048.62)* (in ... *Israel Discount Bank, New York*), 754 F. Supp. 1467 (D. Haw. 1991); and *United States v. Sonny Cook Motors* (819 F. Supp. 1015, ND Ala 1993).

period ending September 1992, the Customs Service had interdicted and seized $171 million in currency and negotiable instruments that were being smuggled out of the U.S. More than $50 million of that total was seized at New York's JFK Airport.*

While the majority of heavy-cargo smuggling occurs at or through the main ports of entry — San Diego, Miami, New York — most individual attempts to smuggle cash and contraband occur along the United States–Mexico border. In fiscal year 1997, Customs inspectors and special agents in west Texas and New Mexico seized more than 150,000 pounds of marijuana (up from 106,000 pounds in 1996), 4,900 pounds of cocaine (up from 4,200 pounds in 1996), and 60 pounds of heroin (down from 66 pounds in 1996).

Why does smuggling cash out of the U.S. appear to be the method of choice? The main reason could be that the primary goal of the U.S. Customs Service is inbound drug (and other contraband) interdiction. However, smuggling drugs and contraband into the U.S. is only one of three types of smuggling used in the drug trafficking/laundering cycle. The other two are outbound cash smuggling and inbound financial-instrument smuggling (or repatriation of the now-laundered drug proceeds). In 1994, for example, only 85 of the 338 Customs ports had staff performing outbound inspections on a full-time basis; this staff totaled only 130 persons, out of 6,228 inspectors in Customs. The sheer volume of traffic between Mexico and the U.S. prohibits effective interdiction. An estimated 5,000 trucks enter the U.S. from Mexico each day, with only 200 of those inspected (1 in 25). The magnitude of Customs' task means that, in an average year, 8 million cargo containers enter the U.S.; an inspection of just one of those containers would take five customs agents three hours to complete; and only 13 of these containers filled with cocaine would need to slip through to satisfy the demand for cocaine in the U.S. for a year.**

Smuggling cash is generally done in one of three ways. First, by shipping bulk cash through the same channels used to bring in the drugs (by container ship, truck, or airplane); second, by hand-carrying cash (by courier); or third, by changing the cash into negotiable instruments (such as money orders or traveler's checks), then mailing these to foreign banks or other foreign destinations.

Smugglers of both cash and contraband seem to have an inexhaustible supply of schemes available to conduct their business. For example, an ingenious scheme was uncovered in January 1994 with the seizure of 52 kilos of

---

* 1994 Report to the Senate Committee on Governmental Affairs, Permanent Subcommittee on Investigations.
** Testimony heard by the House Committee on Foreign Affairs, Subcommittee on International Security, International Organizations and Human Rights on May 11, 1993.

heroin and arrests of four Thais and four Mexicans in Ensenada, Mexico. This trafficking group had infiltrated some postal offices in both Mexico and Thailand and were shipping bath products from Mexico to false addresses in Thailand. There, they were "intercepted" by the cooperating postal workers, opened, stuffed with heroin, resealed, then sent back to Mexico as undeliverable. Because the packages had not originated in Thailand and apparently had not been opened, they were not inspected by Mexican customs agents, and sent back to the original senders in Mexico. Fortunately, or unfortunately for the traffickers, the Mexican authorities stumbled across the scheme before the drugs were smuggled into the U.S.

B.   Structuring

Structuring is the term used to avoid the reporting requirements of the Bank Secrecy Act (BSA) by dividing large deposits of cash into multiple smaller transactions of less than $10,000 each. Structuring transactions to evade the reporting requirements was made a crime in 1986, and is codified at 31 U.S.C. s. 5324(a) — relating to domestic cash transactions — and s. 5324(b) — relating to international monetary-instrument transactions.

The BSA's operative regulations appear in the Code of Federal Regulations at 31 C.F.R. 103. A number of definitions are set out in section 103.11, including a definition for structure or structuring: "a person structures a transaction if that person, acting alone, or in conjunction with or on behalf of, other persons, conducts or attempts to conduct one or more transactions in currency, in any amount, at one or more financial institutions, on one or more days, in any manner, for the purpose of evading the reporting requirements ... ." The term "in any manner" is specifically described as including, but not being limited to "the breaking down of a single sum of currency exceeding $10,000 into smaller sums, including sums at or below $10,000, or the conduct of a transaction, or series of currency transactions, including transactions at or below $10,000. The transaction or transactions need not exceed the $10,000 reporting threshold at any single financial institution on any single day in order to constitute structuring within the meaning of this definition."

Prior to the enactment of the MLCA 1986, the BSA did not specifically prohibit structuring, so that money launderers could structure their activities to avoid the BSA reporting requirements. A money launderer using 10 "smurfs," each depositing $9,900 in 10 banks each day for one business week can place almost $4.5 million into the banking system, reducing it from bulky cash to easily smuggled money orders. The most notorious case of structuring or smurfing was the Grandma Mafia Case where a 60-year-old grandmother led a group of middle-aged women in making structured deposits of over $25 million in Florida drug money at various California banks.

Prior to 1994, the government had to prove that the alleged structurer "willfully violated" the anti-structuring requirements. The anti-structuring penalty section, 31 U.S.C. s. 5322(a), provided penalties for anyone "willfully violating" the structuring requirements of section 5324. The Money Laundering Suppression Act of 1994 excluded section 5324 structuring offenses from the 5322(a) penalty subsection, and added penalties directly to subsection 5324(c)(1) without the "willfully violating" language. This change was made in response to the Supreme Court's interpretation of the "willfully violating" language of subsection 5322(a) in *Ratzlaf v. United States* (510 U.S. 135, 146, 114 S.Ct. 655, 661-61, 1994). In *Ratzlaf*, the defendant ran up a large debt at a casino. A few days later, he returned to the casino with $100,000 in cash, ready to pay the debt. The casino informed him that all transactions over $10,000 had to be reported to federal authorities, but that it would accept a cashier's check for the full amount without triggering any reporting requirement. The casino then packed Ratzlaf into a limousine and sent him around to various banks in the area. Informed that banks, too, were required to report cash transactions in excess of $10,000, Ratzlaf purchased multiple cashier's checks, each for less than $10,000, and each from a different bank. He then returned to the casino and paid his debt with the 11 cashier's checks. Ratzlaf was convicted of structuring transactions to evade the banks' obligations to file CTRs (currency transaction reports) in violation of 31 USC s. 5322(a) and 5324(3). At trial, the district court judge instructed the jury that while the government had to prove Ratzlaf knew of the banks' reporting requirements, it did not have to prove that he knew that structuring was unlawful. The Supreme Court reversed the conviction, holding that "to give effect to the statutory 'willfulness' specification, the Government had to prove Ratzlaf knew the structuring he undertook was unlawful." The Court took great pains to point out that while ignorance of the law is no defense, it is where Congress uses the phrase "willfully violating." As set out above, in 1994 Congress amended the structuring statute to remove the "willfulness" component. *Ratzlaf* is now moot.

C. The Use of Front Companies

1. *Front Companies in General*

Front companies are used by launderers to place and layer illicit proceeds. Any cash-rich business can be an effective front company — jewelry stores, check-cashing businesses, travel agencies, import/export companies, insurance companies, liquor stores, race tracks, and restaurants are common fronts. In addition, businesses that have inventories of products or materials that are difficult to value, such as precious metals, jewelry, antiques, art, etc., are also common. For example, Cirex International, ostensibly a legitimate precious-metals business, turned out to be a front company used by Colombian drug trafficker Eduardo Orozco-Prada to deposit more than $150 million in cash with various American banks and investment firms over a period of several years in the late 1970s and early 1980s. Orozco-Prada was later prosecuted for CMIR and CTR reporting requirements.

Front companies are also used to conduct fraudulent international commercial trade to layer and integrate illegal proceeds. For example, drug proceeds can be deposited into an American bank and then used to fund letters of credit for the fictitious importation of consumer goods into the U.S. from Colombia or elsewhere. Then, an individual presents a false bill of lading at the appropriate bank in Colombia and collects the proceeds. In 1991, as part of Operation Polar Cap, a Rhode Island precious metals business was used to launder over $100 million in drug money over a five-year period. The store was targeted when several of the over 50 banks it used reported suspicious transactions with the IRS (for a detailed description of Operation Polar Cap, see Chapter 10).

Front companies are effective tools for money laundering for two reasons. First, they do not necessarily require the complicity of their financial institution or any non-bank financial institution in order to operate. Second, they are difficult to detect if they are also conducting legitimate business, particularly businesses exempt from CTR-reporting requirements by banks because of the large volume of cash transactions. Exempt businesses include liquor stores, race tracks, restaurants, and approximately 75 other businesses that banks can unilaterally exempt from CTR-reporting requirements.

2.   *Businesses Commonly Used as Front Companies*

a.   Jewelry stores.   Jewelry stores are convenient fronts for money laundering. In 1989, a Justice investigation into Adonian Brothers Mfg. Co. and Ropex Corporation revealed that operators laundered over $1 billion in cash, ostensibly from the corporations' jewelry stores, by placement of the cash into various Los Angeles banks and then wire-transferring it to South American banks. In 1990, a Manhattan money-laundering ring was broken up when Wells Fargo contacted the FBI to report suspicious cash deliveries from two small jewelry stores to various banks. Although the banks knew that these small stores appeared to be grossing more than Tiffany & Co., it took intervention from Wells Fargo to break up a ring that laundered more than $1 billion (see Chapter 10.III.K).

b.   Money-service businesses (MSBs).   Money-service businesses, or MSBs, include money transmitters, check-cashing businesses, traveler's-check and money-order issuers, currency exchangers, and issuers of stored-value cards. They are notorious as fronts for money laundering (see Chapter 5).

c. Travel agencies. Travel agencies that have the capacity of wiring funds are also attractive as front companies. One New York travel agency serving mainly Colombian clientele laundered over $1 million per month by wire transfers.

d. Import/export companies. Import-export companies are popular as fronts for money laundering. Typically, these operations use three schemes to launder money: under-valuation and over-valuation of goods, double invoicing, and financing exports. This latter scheme might be the most effective, as it is cloaked in otherwise legitimate transactions. For example, Colombian Cartel launderers will contact a Colombian company that imports goods from the U.S. The launderer will offer (perhaps an offer the importer cannot refuse) to pay the American exporter in U.S. dollars for the goods as "agent" for the importing company. In exchange, the importing company pays the launderer in Colombian currency, often receiving a premium on the exchange rate. Schemes such as this, involving goods produced for export by General Electric, Microsoft, Apple Computer, and General Motors (these innocent firms were wrongly reported to have been on the receiving end of these schemes), led to PDD 42, a 1995 Presidential Order that froze the assets of hundreds of Colombian companies operating as fronts for the Cali Cartel.

One of the lamest import/export schemes was offered in defense of the forfeiture of more than $10,400,000 seized from the wire-transfer accounts of various Panamanian front companies owned or controlled by the Jose Santacruz Londono branch of the Cali Cartel. In this case, reported as *United States v. All Funds on Deposit In Any Accounts Maintained at Merrill Lynch, et al.,* 801 Fed. Supp. 984, (E.D. New York 1992), 22 companies ostensibly in the clothing-export business claimed anywhere from $32,000 to $3,400,000 in proceeds located at various Merrill Lynch accounts as legitimate proceeds. The court described their claims as possible, but the jury was justified in dismissing their "implausible stories." Essentially, these companies tried to convince the jury that "massive shipments of manufactured garments were sent abroad from modern plants in Colombia and Panama. They were handed over to ship captains who reportedly toured the Caribbean islands trading the garments for goats and local produce, losing some, having some stolen, and with the remainder disposed of through charity in Colombia and other nontraceable channels ... ." Four of the 22 companies were able to convince the jury of their innocence.

D. The Use of Shell or Nominee Corporations

The synonymous terms "shell corporation," "nominee corporation," or "domiciliary corporation" refer to a corporate structure that provides for anonymous corporate ownership through various combinations of nominee directors and ownership of stock by bearer shares. The FATF defines shell companies as "institutions, corporations, foundations, trusts, etc., that do not conduct any commercial or manufacturing business or any other form of commercial operation in the country where their registered office is located."

Shell corporations are one of the major tools in layering funds. For example, by the early 1980s, as much as 20% of all real property in the Miami area was owned by entities incorporated in the Netherlands Antilles. One piece of property was traced through three levels of Netherlands Antilles shell corporations, with the final "true" owner being a corporation with bearer shares. These offshore corporations were in turn owned or controlled by various drug traffickers.

The rise in the number of shell corporations has been exponential. In the mid-1980s, there were approximately 5,000 shell corporations registered in the British Virgin Islands; in 1994, there were more than 120,000. In 1962, the Cayman Islands had no offshore businesses; by 1995, there were more than 23,500 corporations registered in the Caymans.

The mechanics of setting up and operating a shell corporation are not complex. Typically, a resident lawyer or accountant registers several businesses for a fee, naming himself as nominee chairman. He then sets up a number of corporate bank accounts at various island banks, again naming himself as the nominee signatory. These "shelf" corporations are then kept until needed for immediate availability to foreign clients wishing anonymity.

The creation and use of shell corporations is itself a profitable business. In Grenada, the government collects a $5,000 fee to register an "off-the-shelf" corporation. These are then resold by local lawyers and accountants to foreign clientele — no questions asked — for an average of $30,000.

E. Bank Drafts

Mexican bank drafts are often the instrument of choice used by Mexican money launderers to repatriate dollars back to the U.S. Each year, more than 500,000 bank drafts drawn on Mexican banks enter the U.S. Why so many? Two reasons: first, although large (over $10,000) deposits of U.S. cash require the Mexican equivalent of a CTR (note that prior to November 1996, there was no such requirement), they are seldom reported and there are few effective sanctions against banks for failing to file reports. Once the large deposit is made, the Mexican bank issues a bank draft. Second, through a loophole in the U.S. money-laundering statutes, Mexican bank drafts are not considered to be "negotiable instruments," so it is not necessary to file a CTR or CMIR. Although the Money Laundering Suppression

Act of 1994 attempted to close this loophole, its enabling regulations have not yet been issued.

F.   Counterbalancing Loan Schemes

Counterbalancing loan schemes is another tool used to layer funds. This method involves parking illicit funds in an offshore bank while using the value of the account as collateral for a bank loan in another country. Ironically, launderers using these schemes often gain tax advantages for their apparently legal operations, using the interest expense from the loans as tax deductions. Counterbalancing loans were commonly used by the related companies and banks controlled by the Bank of Commerce and Credit International (BCCI) in its 18-year money-laundering run.

G.   Dollar Discounting

An increasingly popular method of money laundering is dollar discounting, whereby a drug trafficker instructs his accountant, or *comissionista,* to arrange for the cartel's controller to auction or factor the drug proceeds to a broker, or *cambista,* at a discount. The broker then assumes the risk of laundering the money. Essentially, the dealer is simply selling his accounts receivables at a discount. He gets less cash, but he gets it sooner. Discounting drug proceeds may well be the most complex form of international finance. In addition to the standard issues of managing foreign transaction and currency-exchange exposure, a drug trafficker must factor in law-enforcement-intervention risk. But this is really no more than another version of the risk faced by many legitimate businesses, such as spoilage, spillage, theft, or kickbacks. The trafficker simply factors historical law-enforcement seizures into his equation and calculates his receivables accordingly.

For example, after having purchased a block of drug proceeds from a controller, a money broker will then approach a legitimate (or not-so-legitimate) businessman in Colombia or the Panama Free Zone who needs U.S. dollars to buy goods or product in the U.S. The money broker then sells a portion (or all) of the block of proceeds purchased from the controller to the businessman. These proceeds are physically in the U.S., usually having gone through the placement stage, either by the trafficker or the broker himself. The broker sells these funds for a discount, commonly up to 25%. The businessman then deposits the equivalent discounted amount in pesos in the trafficker's account in Colombia (or, if the broker paid for his block of drug proceeds obtained from the controller by depositing pesos in the trafficker's account, the businessman will pay the broker directly). The broker and businessman then arrange for the businessman's agent(s) in the U.S. to obtain the U.S. funds, often using sophisticated schemes involving false bills of lading, receipts, invoices, factor agreements, etc. Typically, a seemingly legitimate business transaction accompanies these funds, but it will be included with $10 items that actually cost $35, or will pay for 100 items when only 20 are shipped, etc.

Dollar discounting is also accomplished through postal money orders. Instead of selling the American money on deposit in the U.S., a blank money order or check is sent directly to either Colombia or the Panama Free Zone. There, the funds can be sold and resold through the network of *casas de cambio*, often going back to Mexican banks for final repatriation in the U.S. with the laundering cycle complete and the money ostensibly clean and untraceable to illicit activity. Throughout this system, the parties create and use fictitious documentation to produce a seemingly legitimate commercial history.

H.   Mirror-Image Trading

Mirror-image trading was the scheme used by subsidiaries of BCCI in the commodities markets to launder huge sums of money for Manuel Noriega, among others. Mirror-image trading involves buying contracts for one account while selling an equal number from another; since both accounts are controlled by the same individual, any profit or loss is effectively netted. The key is to lose these transactions among millions of dollars worth of legitimate transactions.

I.   Reverse Flips

A reverse flip is a real estate ploy whereby a launderer will purchase a property at a documented or reported price well below its market value, paying the balance "under the table" to a willing seller. The launderer then resells the property for its true value, realizing a paper profit, well documented and legal (any capital gains are simply another cost of doing business). For example, the launderer will arrange with a cooperating seller to buy a $500,000 home for $250,000. He will pay 10% or 20% down (say, $50,000) in clean money and take a mortgage on the balance ($200,000). He will then pay the balance of the price under the table with illegal funds. Some months later, he will "flip" the property for its true price of $500,000, paying off the mortgage with his "profit" of $250,000. His profit (the sales price less the cash down payment plus the mortgage) is now laundered, and he has created a trail of paper suggesting that he is a legitimate businessman.

J.   Inflated Prices

Using inflated prices to pay for imported goods is a common laundering technique. Launderers, working through front companies or willing accomplices, simply create false invoices for goods either never actually purchased or purchased at greatly inflated prices. It is estimated that the fraudulent valuation of goods by international traders costs the U.S. as much as $30 billion in unpaid or underpaid taxes per year.*

The ultimate example of this method was uncovered in Customs/DEA's Operation Polar Cap, where it was discovered that U.S.-based precious-metals dealers used as fronts by the Cali Cartel had generated invoices representing the purchase of more than 214,000 troy ounces of gold imported from Bolivia in 1990. At trial, it was proved that this amount of gold represented about 130% of Bolivia's entire gold production for that year. Other examples, based on Customs data on import/export flows, include the importation of raw sugar from Britain at $1,400 per kilogram vs. the going rate of $0.50 per kilogram; the importation of cut emeralds from Panama at $975 per carat vs. the going rate of about $44 per carat; and the importation of razor blades from Colombia at a cost of $900 apiece, vs. the going rate of $0.09 apiece.

K.   The Colombian Black-Market Peso Exchange

The money-laundering cycle commonly used by the Colombian drug syndicates — from smuggling drugs into the U.S. to returning the proceeds to Colombia — is best illustrated by what is known as the the Colombian black-market peso exchange, a money-laundering system estimated to launder as much as 30% to 40% of all U.S. drug proceeds. At its most basic, this black-market exchange system operates to circumvent Colombian restrictions on converting Colombian pesos to U.S. dollars, which are the medium of exchange in the Western Hemisphere. To obtain U.S. currency, an importer must certify that the necessary import permits have been obtained and the requisite duties and import taxes have been paid. By trading in illegal drugs, the Colombian drug kingpins cannot legitimately provide these permits; thus, they cannot obtain U.S. currency, or exchange it for pesos, in the ordinary course of business. Therefore, they have turned to (some people say they created) the Colombian black-market peso exchange.

How does the system work? A detailed description of the system was given to Congress by way of testimony by three Treasury Department agents before the House Subcommittee on General Oversight and Investigations, Committee on Banking and Financial Services, on October 22, 1997. The transcript of the testimony of Special Agent Alvin C. James, Jr., Internal Revenue Service Criminal Investigations; Assistant Director of Investigative Operations Allan J. Doody, U.S. Customs Service; and Special Agent Gregory Passic, FinCEN can be found on the Internet at *www.treas.gov/irs/ci/*congress/blkmart.

---

* Based on a Florida International University analysis of the Commerce Department's database of prices paid for goods in international trade.

The black-market peso exchange evolved so that Colombian importers
— legitimate importers as well as those operating on the fringe and those
operating illegally — could circumvent government taxes and avoid government scrutiny. The exchange consists of two parallel transactions — a
Colombian peso exchange in Colombia, and a U.S. dollar transaction or
series of transactions in the U.S. The Colombian importer will pay the
exchanger with Colombian pesos in Colombia for the U.S. dollars needed
to purchase the products he wants to import. The exchanger then directs
or coordinates the payment of these U.S. dollars to whomever the importer
has specified.

The exchanger now is left with Colombian pesos, but needs to purchase
U.S. dollars outside Colombia. It is important to remember at this point that
the Colombian drug dealer has a great deal of U.S. currency that he needs
to convert to Colombian pesos in Colombia. The exchanger can fulfill the
needs of both the Colombian importer (who has pesos in Colombia but
needs dollars in the U.S.) and the Colombian drug trafficker (who has dollars
in the U.S. but needs pesos in Colombia) by using money launderers or
brokers to place, layer, and integrate the drug cash into the U.S. and international financial systems and economies. From there, the money is funneled
to businesses that eventually sell the products to the Colombian importers.
In many cases, the drug trafficker is also the importer; the trafficker will own
or control, directly or through complex mazes of corporate layering, auto
dealerships, clothing stores, camera stores, etc. — any type of business that
imports goods for sale in Colombia. These businesses are for the most part
perfectly legal and legitimate, except that they are circumventing the normal
or legal currency-exchange channels, and their profits go to their drug-
dealing owners.

This laundering system, called *la vuelta* or the "cycle" or "round," is
extremely complex in its operation but relatively simple in theory and effect.
The basic steps are as follows:

1. A Colombian drug cartel exports cocaine to the U.S.
2. The cocaine is sold for U.S. currency.
3. The cartel sells the cocaine proceeds in lots or blocks to brokers,
   launderers, and/or black-market peso exchangers.
4. The broker or launderer begins the laundering cycle by placing, layering, and integrating the bulk currency into the U.S. financial and
   banking systems.
5. The U.S. dollars are sold to Colombian importers at a rate that reflects
   their savings on import and currency taxes and duties, but includes
   the costs of the illegality of the enterprise.

6. The importers purchase goods from the U.S. or elsewhere, using the U.S. dollars or dollar accounts.
7. The goods are imported to Colombia, where they are sold to Colombians for Colombian pesos.

The result is that the wholesale value of the cocaine returns to Colombia in the form of trade goods (not entirely — as some of the U.S. currency is simply smuggled back to Colombia). The importer obtains dollars at a favorable rate from the exchanger, who has purchased the bulk drug proceeds from the trafficker at a discount. The trafficker will sell his proceeds to the exchanger, broker, or launderer at 70% to 80% of the amount of the bulk cash; the exchanger bears the costs and risks of laundering those proceeds. Typical laundering methods include structuring; using money transmitters or remitter businesses; and smuggling cash to Mexico where it is placed into the Mexican financial system and converted into U.S. currency-denominated financial instruments that are then sold at a discount to the Colombian importers.

One of the most effective tools used by U.S. federal law-enforcement agencies to fight the Colombian black-market peso exchange has been the Numerically Integrated Profiling System (NIPS), a database operated by Customs that identifies trade fraud and anomalies in import and export patterns. The NIPS reveals the types and names of businesses, and the commodities that are being used by these businesses to supply the *contrabandistas* with the merchandise purchased with black-market pesos.

V.   *United States v. Saccoccia:* The Ultimate Example of *La Vuelta*

La Vuelta is the term used by the Cali Cartel to describe the complete cycle of drug cultivation, production, smuggling, and distribution, and the money laundering used to ultimately get the proceeds back into the hands of the drug kingpins. A good example of this cycle involved the investigation (Operation Polar Cap V) and prosecution of a gang of drug dealers and money launderers led by Stephen Saccoccia. From 1986 to 1991, Saccoccia controlled an organization that laundered more than $136,000,000 for two Colombian drug cartels. His scheme was ingenious.

Saccoccia's organization employed almost every imaginable tool to launder money, from smurfing and structuring, the use of front companies, wire transfers, and false invoicing to smuggling. The history of his illegal activities is described in detail in a number of decisions written by judges of the First Circuit Court of Appeals in Massachusetts. The following is a summary of these decisions, principally *United States v. Saccoccia* 58 F.3d 754, (1st Cir. 1995), and *United States v. Hurley, DeMarco, Saccoccia, et al.* (63 F.3d 1, 1st Cir. 1995).

Saccoccia owned and controlled a number of precious-metals businesses, including Saccoccia Coin (located in Cranston, RI), Trend Precious Metals (located in Cranston, and with offices in New York City), and International Metal and Clinton Import/Export (located in Los Angeles). Saccoccia started laundering money with a fellow "metalman," Barry Slomovits, in the mid-1980s. At that time, Slomovits was accepting millions of dollars in small-denomination bills from Duvan Arboleda, who represented the Cali Cartel. At first, Saccoccia simply sold gold to Slomovits, not asking for or receiving any documentation.

By 1987, Saccoccia had proven his ability and trustworthiness, and Arboleda began to deal directly with him. At first, Arboleda and other launderers working for the Cali Cartel (and eventually the Medellín Cartel, also) including Fernando Duenas and Raul Escobar, would arrange for one of Saccoccia's employees (usually it was Richard Gizzarelli, who later turned out to be a valuable government witness) to go to a prearranged location in New York City, often a street corner, to meet another courier to pick up cash. The cash — up to $500,000 per day — was then delivered to the Trend office in New York or to an apartment in New York maintained by Saccoccia, where it was counted.

From there, the money either stayed in New York to be laundered through various gold companies, or was delivered to Saccoccia's businesses in Rhode Island. The New York end of the operation involved Slomovits, who would take the money, buy gold, resell it, and then wire-transfer the proceeds to accounts controlled by Saccoccia (Saccoccia's wife, Donna, organized these wire transfers). A second New York gold dealer, Ahron Sharir, a manufacturer of gold chain, also washed money for Saccoccia. Over the course of three or four years, ending in 1990, Sharir laundered over $35 million for Saccoccia, using methods similar to those of Slomovits.

Most of the drug money — up to $200,000 per day — would be delivered to Saccoccia Coin and Trend in Cranston, either through private armored car services or in the car of a Saccoccia employee. Beginning in 1990, Saccoccia had become so adept (and, in the eyes of his Colombian clients, so trustworthy) that he was invited to bid for opportunities to launder money on behalf of the Colombian cartels (as described above, the traffickers actually auctioned off blocks or lots of drug proceeds to a small cadre of money brokers or launderers — Saccoccia joined this elite group). If his bid was accepted, Saccoccia would receive instructions on when and where to pick up sacks of currency, usually in lots of between $50,000 and $500,000 (one lot or block of money was for $3,000,000).

Once the cash reached Rhode Island, it was counted again and broken down into packets in amounts either greater or less than $10,000. The larger packets were delivered to Saccoccia Coin to be used to purchase gold without documentation; that gold was then resold to legitimate companies in exchange for checks recorded as payments for gold sales. Some of the cash also was laundered through a retail coin shop controlled by Saccoccia.

The packets of cash in amounts less than $10,000 were given to Saccoccia employees with instructions to go to various local banks to purchase cashier's checks payable to Trend. To disguise their efforts — to disguise the structuring or smurfing — they sometimes purchased money orders in amounts greater than $10,000 (triggering the reporting requirements) payable to a number of companies owned by another co-conspirator, Vincent Hurley. This smurfing or structuring was done to avoid, or at least minimize, the filing of accurate CTRs.

Ultimately, the local Rhode Island cashier's checks would be deposited into the Trend account at Citizens Bank in Rhode Island. The Hurley company funds were wired to the same Trend account. From there, Arboleda or Duenas would designate various foreign accounts to which Saccoccia was to wire the Citizens Bank deposits. Between March 1990 and August 1991, more than $97 million was wired from the Citizens account and a further $39 million was wired from a number of other Saccoccia or Hurley accounts to foreign banks, primarily in Colombia. Along the way, Saccoccia would deduct his 10% commission.

Saccoccia's scheme didn't end there. Sometime in mid-1990, Saccoccia began to send the cashier's checks to his offices in California by air courier, hidden inside canisters labeled as containing gold, but that really contained slag or scrap metal so the weight approximated that of gold. Actual gold was also sent from Slomovits and/or Sharir in New York to Los Angeles. In Los Angeles, the gold was resold, and the proceeds wired back to the Trend account at Citizens Bank or one of the other Saccoccia accounts. The cash was used to purchase gold, which was then resold, and these proceeds were also wired back to various Saccoccia accounts.

In August 1991, Saccoccia discovered that he was under investigation. After convening a meeting at his mother's house to caution his associates, he and his wife fled to Switzerland. In short order, he was extradited. In 1992, he and eight others in his organization were tried and convicted. Saccoccia himself received a 660-year sentence; the others, including his wife and brothers, received sentences ranging from six to 18 years. Forfeiture orders were entered against all defendants in amounts ranging from $3,927,357.55 to $136,344,231.86.

Cyberbanking and Wire Transfers

3

I. Cyberbanking

A. Introduction to Cyberbanking

To understand cybercrime, it is first necessary to understand cyberbanking. FinCEN has targeted cyberbanking as one of its highest priorities, creating an E-Money Council to assess the impact of electronic banking and payment systems on regulatory and law-enforcement efforts to combat crime.

Traditional currency — paper and coin — is easy to use, enjoys wide acceptability, and is anonymous. However, its use is generally limited to small amounts ($1 million in $20s weighs approximately 100 pounds) and to the particular country of issuance. Traditional currency, even checks, bank notes, IOUs, or any financial instrument, are eliminated in a cyberbanking or cyberpayment system. Instead of transferring or paying with a financial instrument, these electronic, digital, or cyberpayment systems facilitate the transfer of financial value, either through Internet bank accounts, "smart cards," or the proposed Electronic Benefits Transfer (EBT) cards.

The new cyberpayment systems offer the best attributes of traditional currency — ease of use, wide acceptability, and anonymity — with added features such as unlimited amounts, security, multinational movement, and what is known as "transfer velocity." In other words, cyberbanking allows anyone to move billions of dollars anywhere in the world as fast as the wire transfer and computer banking systems allow. The critical issue is whether cyberbanking should, and will be, absolutely anonymous, and therefore immune to traditional banking regulations and law enforcement.

Some of the world's largest corporations are currently working together to create systems to safely and quickly buy and sell goods and services over the Internet. For example, in June 1997, a consortium led by IBM, Master-Card, Visa, Chase Manhattan Bank, and First Data Corp. introduced the first Secure Electronic Transaction (SET) Initiative, which allows secure credit-card transactions over the Internet. This group is working toward establishing the SET Initiative as the global standard for all future U.S. and international electronic business, or "e-business."*

The "cyberbanks" cropping up on the Internet are not banks at all in the normal sense; they currently do not offer deposit services, but simply act as intermediaries in financial transactions and sales. They are essentially unregulated, and operate in an environment (the Internet) where identities are concealed, without national borders, and with instantaneous transactions. In addition, a cyberbank can operate anywhere in the world, moving digital currency or "e-money" from electronic home to electronic home and using electronic forwarding systems to avoid detection. For example, the European Bank of Antigua was created with a $1 million investment from a Russian bank linked to organized crime. It functioned as a regular offshore bank. When U.S. and Antiguan authorities moved in to investigate, they found that the "bank" was merely a website on the Internet, with its main server plugged into a laptop/cellular telephone system.

The Treasury Department's Office of Thrift Supervision (OTS) is responsible for granting approval to companies looking to offer banking services over the Internet (the OTS is the primary regulator of all federal and many state-chartered thrift institutions, see Chapter 6).

The OTS has granted approval to only two thrift holding companies to offer electronic-banking services (EBS) over the Internet. The first approval was granted on May 10, 1995, when Cardinal Bancshares Inc., a thrift holding company, was approved to offer limited banking services (transferring money between accounts, paying bills, and reconciling statements) through its wholly owned thrift subsidiary, Security First Network Bank, based in Kentucky and operating in Atlanta.

The second grant of approval was given to Atlanta Internet Bank (AIB) on July 14, 1997. AIB is the first approved and regulated all-Internet bank. Among other conditions of approval, AIB is required to adhere to guidelines set out in the June 23, 1997, OTS "Statement on Retail On-Line Personal Computer Banking."

Although the OTS has only approved two on-line banks, most of the major Federal Reserve Board financial institutions have been approved to provide on-line banking services.

B.   Cyberbanking and the Encryption of Data

Banking services are becoming more available on the Internet, and the use of the Internet in general is becoming more common (there were an estimated 25 million American users in 1995, a number expected to triple by

---

* See the group's website at *http://Internet.ibm.com/payment.*

1998 and double again by 2000). Because of this explosive growth, there are some far-reaching issues that must be resolved, such as First Amendment privacy rights, governmental regulation and controls, etc. The critical issue, however, is computer security, which means the ability of a computer system to handle the encryption of data going out, and the subsequent decryption of that data when it reaches its electronic destination. Without access and the ability to use increasingly sophisticated encryption and decryption software, government agencies will be virtually powerless to stop or track these cybertransactions; ironically, the qualities and technology required to make cyberbanking a feasible and secure means of conducting business are the same as those that make it attractive to money launderers.

Essentially, *cyberbanking*, or the use of digital or electronic means of payment, is simply a payment message bearing a digital signature. Each message must go through an encryption process in order to be sent, then through a decryption process to restore the original message once it reaches its electronic destination. The current banking encryption/decryption system, called the Data Encryption Standard, or DES, uses 56-bit encryption keys. In 1993, the federal government established a task force, the National Information Infrastructure Forum, to address the issue of encryption of computer financial transactions on the Internet. Through the work of this task force, the federal government proposed the Clipper Chip, a single, nationwide, 80-bit encryption system for all computer data transmissions, with a single "key" maintained by the federal government. The government's reasoning was that the encryption of computer financial transactions on the Internet was essential to maintain privacy and keep information proprietary, but absolute secrecy would allow hackers (including launderers) to move illicit funds with absolute impunity. Therefore, the need to create a mechanism (a computer chip embedded in every communications and cyberspace device) that would enable the government to have some access to the otherwise impenetrable flow of data. This chip was designed to be tamper-resistant and contained a digital "trapdoor" that would allow the federal government to decode anything sent through the chip.

The original concept proposed that the key would be maintained by two agencies of the federal government — Commerce and Treasury. Each of these agencies would have knowledge of one-half of the computer chip-specific unique key by which to decode the "session" key that encoded a particular transaction or communication passing through that chip. Armed with both halves of this key and a proper federal search warrant, the federal government could decode selected transmissions coming across the Internet. Despite repeated changes to the concept and the technology, including those proposed for Clipper III, the proposal has yet to be adopted (a case of "Big Brother" phobia). Recently, a private encryption system, known as

PGP, for Pretty Good Privacy, which (it is alleged) the government cannot break, has spread worldwide over the Internet. The banking industry is now proposing a triple-DES system that has the security equivalent of 112-bit encryption keys.

On the heels of the rejection of the Clipper Chip proposal, Congress is currently considering various bills addressing the implementation of a national encryption policy. The problem is in balancing the competing interests: privacy, electronic commerce, law enforcement, and national security. Making strong commercial encryption widely available is critical for U.S. software and technology manufacturers to compete globally; businesses and individuals need encrypted products to protect sensitive commercial information and to prevent industrial espionage. However, the increased use of encryption carries a serious risk for law enforcement, so the federal government is now proposing the development of a key-recovery system (key recovery being the technology designed to permit the plain text recovery of encrypted data) through a Department of Commerce public- and private-sector advisory committee, the Technical Advisory Committee to Develop a Federal Information Processing Standard for the Federal Key Management Infrastructure.

The bottom line? Without a government "back door," the technology is so sophisticated that cyberbanking payments could be immune to current anti-money-laundering efforts, resulting in anonymous transactions that are both unlinkable (unable to link two or more payments made by the same person) and untraceable (unable to link a withdrawal at one cyberbank with a deposit at another).*

C. Smart Cards, or Stored-Value Cards

Smart cards, or stored-value cards, are similar to debit cards, except they disburse money that has previously been loaded from the customer's account directly onto the card's microchip through an ATM or a specially adapted telephone. Smart cards are being used more and more, most commonly (in Germany and Ontario, Canada, for example) as "health cards" to store health-care-coverage verification and personal medical history. One estimate suggests that smart-card usage will go from 250 million transactions in 1996 to 10 billion in 2001 and 25 billion in 2005.**

The cash limit downloaded onto any card is potentially limitless, and the use of the card is completely untraceable. For example, armed with two tele-

---

* For a detailed review of these issues, see the Congressional testimony of William Reinsch, Undersecretary of Commerce (3/19–20/97), available at *http://www.fas.org/irp/congress/1997_hr.*

** One smart-card manufacturer, New Jersey-based Schlumberger Smart Cards & Systems, expected to ship 300 million cards in 1997.

phones with the proper software, one located in Medellín and the other in Boston, a launderer can transfer billions of dollars out of the country. Without adequate controls, smart-card technology is ripe for abuse by launderers.

D. Electronic Benefits Transfer Cards (EBT Cards)

A federal task force, led by Vice President Al Gore, has proposed a new nationwide program to deliver more than $110 billion in annual federal benefits by way of an Electronic Benefits Transfer (EBT) card. The EBT card is designed to be the new method of payment for the delivery of recurring government cash-benefit payments to individuals without a bank account. For those with bank accounts, Electronic Funds Transfer (EFT) will continue as the preferred method of making federal benefit payments to those entitled. It is also proposed that the EBT card will be usable to deliver non-cash benefits such as Food Stamps. Acting as an on-line debit system, the cards will be used to retrieve cash from ATM machines or to purchase food and sundries from point-of-sale terminals at grocery stores.

The EBT Task Force has proposed a number of tools, such as biometric identifiers, four-color cards, and holograms, to counter the expected fraudulent use of, or counterfeiting in, EBT cards or the trafficking in non-cash EBT benefits.

II. Cybercrime

A. What is Cybercrime?

Computers are responsible (directly or indirectly) for every aspect of our lives, from the operation of our cars to our personal banking to the flow of data in our businesses. With the exponential rise in the legitimate uses of computers, it follows that there would be an inevitable increase in their illegitimate use.

To answer the simple question of what is computer crime, or computer-related crime, or cybercrime, it is necessary to understand the different types or classifications of crimes that can be linked to computers. For example, hacking into a long-distance telephone service to enjoy free telephone calls is a type of computer-related crime (fraud or theft by computer manipulation), and pirating software is another. The FBI's National Computer Crime Squad (NCCS), one of the leading federal agencies in combating cybercrime,* considers the following to be computer or computer-related crime: violations

---

* Along with the Secret Service's Financial Crimes Division's Electronic Crime Branch, the NCCS is responsible for investigating violations of the Computer Fraud and Abuse Act of 1986, 18 USC s. 1030.

of or into the integrity of the telephone systems (called the "Public Switched Network") such as long-distance-calling schemes, violations of or into the integrity of major computer networks, computer-privacy violations, industrial espionage, pirating of licensed software, and any other crime where a computer is the major factor or tool in committing a criminal offense (such as interstate distribution of child pornography). Other computer crimes now include the emerging crimes of cyberporn, cybertheft, and cyberstalking.

Whatever form computer crimes take, the characteristics that make computer systems, particularly computer banking systems, so attractive for legitimate purposes (security, efficiency, anonymity) make them similarly attractive for illegitimate purposes such as money laundering.

Federal law enforcement and regulatory agencies are particularly concerned about three issues. First, the effectiveness of current reporting requirements against cyberbanking systems. Why? The current regulatory system depends on regulated financial institutions acting as a pass-through or intermediary between two parties, thus facilitating the transaction. The new cyberbanking or cyberpayment systems often eliminate this intermediary and allow what are known as peer-to-peer transactions. The intermediary is simply the Internet.

Second, current investigative techniques such as surveillance and document analysis, and most preventive measures, depend on criminals' physically having to conduct at least some part of a transaction, from actually going to a branch to open an account to depositing cash at a teller's window. An effective know-your-customer program is therefore an integral part of any financial institution's anti-money-laundering program. However, with the advent of home banking, cyberpayment systems, etc., there are fewer face-to-face transactions. Know-your-customer policies are no longer effective.

The third and final issue facing federal law-enforcement and regulatory agencies is the applicability of jurisdictional authority; most cyberbanking and cyberpayment systems operate globally and in multiple currencies. Therefore, traditional physical borders that have determined local, state, or even federal jurisdiction are rendered obsolete by computers.

B.   Justin Peterson: A Cybercriminal's Case History

In 1989, Justin Tanner Peterson, a former concert promoter, sound engineer, and private investigator, gained unauthorized access to (or "hacked" into) the computers of California's Pacific Bell Telephone to intercept and seize the telephone lines to a local FM radio station. He and two friends had developed a computer program that could manipulate or rig promotional radio contests by electronically "seizing" the incoming telephone lines to ensure that they were the only callers able to win contests. Using this program and gaining access to the telephone lines, the three hackers were able to "win" four cash prizes totaling $40,000 and two trips to Hawaii. Peterson's friends also won two Porsche automobiles.

Perhaps jealous of his friends, Peterson stole a Porsche for himself and moved to Texas. While there, he hacked into a national consumer credit-reporting agency and obtained credit information with which he was able to order fraudulent credit cards, which he then used freely.

Peterson was caught and indicted for various violations of the federal Computer Fraud and Abuse Act, including "conspiracy to gain access to a federal interest computer system to carry out a scheme to defraud and to intercept wire and electronic communications." Peterson agreed to enter into a plea agreement requiring his cooperation in apprehending his two partners. While out on bail to assist the FBI, Peterson committed further computer crimes, including credit-card theft, and was rearrested. During a recess in negotiations with federal prosecutors, Peterson fled. While a fugitive, he hacked into the computers of a small bank, Heller Financial, and obtained the codes necessary to effect a wire transfer from that bank to another bank account. After setting up his scheme, Peterson then telephoned a bomb threat to Heller Financial. While the building was being evacuated, Peterson executed a $150,000 wire transfer from Heller Financial to Union Bank, routed through Mellon Bank. Fortunately (for Heller Financial), the transfer was discovered before Peterson could withdraw the money from Union Bank.

In November 1995, Peterson was sentenced to 40 months in federal prison and three years' probation, and was ordered to pay restitution of $40,000. The sentence was upheld on appeal. The full saga is reported as *United States v. Peterson* 98 F.3d 502 (9th Cir., 1996).

C.   Cybercrime Statutes and Laws

Most U.S. federal statutes relating to computer crime are set out in Title 18 of the United States Code. They include fraud and related activity in connection with credit cards and access devices (section 1029) and computers (section 1030), the National Stolen Property Act (section 2314), and the Electronic Communications Privacy Act (section 2701). The U.S. Secret Service has been given the task of investigating violations of sections 1029 and 1030 (see Chapter 6).

The term "access device" in section 1029 means any card, code, account number, or personal identification number (PIN) used in conjunction with a device that can be used to obtain money, goods, services, or any other thing of value, or that can be used to initiate a transfer of funds. A common access device is a credit or debit card.

Section 1029 seeks to prohibit anyone who, knowingly and with intent to defraud, (1) produces, uses, or traffics in counterfeit access devices;

(2) uses an unauthorized access device to obtain goods or services of value aggregating $1,000 or more in any one-year period; (3) possesses 15 or more counterfeit access devices; or (4) possesses equipment to make counterfeit access devices. The penalties range from a fine of twice the value of the goods or services improperly obtained and/or a federal prison sentence of up to 15 years.

Section 1030 describes seven different computer frauds punishable by fines, and up to 20 years in federal prison. These frauds are categorized according to the type of computer or computer system that is hacked into (e.g., computer, nonpublic computer, and protected computer), the nature of the access (e.g., without authorization or exceeding authorized access), and the type of fraud committed (e.g., simply gaining unauthorized access, obtaining financial information such as credit histories of others, obtaining anything of value, intentionally or recklessly causing damage to a computer, supplying a password to an unauthorized person to allow that person to gain access, and others). Protected computers include any computer exclusively for use by a financial institution or the U.S. Government. Therefore, someone who hacks into a credit-card company's database to obtain credit-card numbers and to give himself a positive balance commits at least three offenses: gaining unauthorized access to a protected computer, obtaining financial information without authorization, and obtaining something of value.

III.   Cybersecurity in the Future

> Imagine, if you will … that the power goes out in the Northwest; the 911 system is disrupted in a major city because someone has flooded the phone lines with repeat calls; two bridges across the Mississippi River are destroyed — bridges that not only carry trucks and trains, but also telephone cables — and two Internet-service providers in New York City are out of service. What do we do in such a situation? Who is in charge? Is it merely coincidence? Or a concentrated attack?
>
> — **U.S. Air Force General (Ret.) Robert T. Marsh, Chairman, President's Commission on Critical Infrastructure Protection**
> *National Information Systems Security Conference, October 7, 1997, Baltimore, MD*

The computers of the Department of Defense were the target of approximately 250,000 intrusions in 1996 alone. Ninety-five per cent of all military communications rely on privately owned telecommunications systems. The e-mail system at Langley Air Force Base was rendered inoperative by a targeted attack by e-mail hackers operating in Australia and Estonia, routed through the White House computer system.* To fight threats such as these, on July 15, 1996, the President signed Executive Order 13010, establishing the President's Commission on Critical Infrastructure Protection (PCCIP), to study the issues of computer security and to develop a strategy to thwart attacks on computer systems controlling the various services essential to national security.** The Order reads, in part:

> "Certain national infrastructures are so vital that their incapacity or destruction would have a debilitating impact on the defense or economic security of the United States. These critical infrastructures include telecommunications, electrical power systems, gas and oil storage and transportation, banking and finance, transportation, water supply systems, emergency services (including medical, police, fire, and rescue), and continuity of government. Threats to these critical infrastructures fall into two categories: physical threats to tangible property ("physical threats"), and threats to electronic, radio-frequency, or computer-based attacks on the information or communications components that control critical infrastructures ("cyber threats"). Because many of these critical infrastructures are owned and operated by the private sector, it is essential that the government and private sector work together to develop a strategy for protecting them and assuring their continued operation."

In addition, the Executive Order established an Infrastructure Protection Task Force (IPTF) within the Department of Justice, chaired by the FBI. The IPTF's role is to "identify and coordinate existing expertise and capabilities in the government and private sector as they relate to critical infrastructure protection from both physical threats and cyber threats."***

The Commission is made up of 20 members, 10 each from the public sector**** and private sector.***** It is assisted by an Advisory Committee composed of 15 presidential appointees from the private sector. A Steering Committee made up of Chairman Robert T. Marsh, and four members (including Attorney General Janet Reno) approves the Commission's objectives

---

* Robert T. Marsh, Chairman PCCIP, at Harvard University's John F. Kennedy School of Government, Washington, D.C. Regional Alumni Council Lecture Series, "The Role of Government in the 21st Century," Arlington, VA, September 20, 1997.
** The PCCIP's home page, http://www.pccip.gov, provides that the role of the PCCIP is to "advise and assist the President of the United States by recommending a national strategy for protecting and assuring critical infrastructures from physical and cyber threats."
*** See the ITPF's website at http://www.fbi.gov/program/iptf.
**** Representatives from the departments of Commerce, Defense, Energy, Justice, Treasury, and Transportation, the National Security Administration, the CIA, FEMA, and the FBI.
***** Representatives from banking and financial services, telecommunications, electric power, oil, and gas companies such as AT&T, IBM, Pacific Oil & Gas, and organizations such as Georgetown University, and the National Association of Utility Commissioners.

and reports. These reports are presented to the President through a Principals Committee, made up of Attorney General Janet Reno, the Secretaries of Commerce, Energy, Defense, Transportation, and Treasury, Directors of FEMA, the CIA, and the OMB, the Assistant to the President for National Security Affairs, and the Assistant to the Vice President for National Security Affairs.*

On October 13, 1997, the Commission delivered its final report to the President. The report proposed a number of recommendations designed to protect the nation's infrastructure from physical threats as well as from cyberspace sabotage or computer terrorism. These recommendations were aimed at improving the level of cooperation and coordination between government and private industry for infrastructure protection, and were broken down into six broad categories.

1. Federal government efforts to set and publish standards for information security.
2. The sharing of information about cyber threats between the government and private sector (for example, by providing more information to the private sector about potential threats, as well as allowing the private sector to report cyber threats without fear of retribution, regulation, or adverse publicity).
3. Encouraging education and awareness of the issues, including grants for research in network security and infrastructure protection.
4. Increasing research and development from $250 million per year to $1 billion per year by the year 2002.
5. Revising or creating new federal regulations to support the initiatives.
6. Devising systems to enable the government and private sectors to use these tools and share information, while still allowing the information to be protected (e.g., a credit-card company does not want its competitors to have access to its databases or to take advantage of security problems with its systems).

The Commission also recommended the creation of the National Infrastructure Assurance Council, composed of cabinet-level officials and senior officers from leading companies in each of the eight critical infrastructure areas, which would be supported by an agency within the Department of Commerce. In addition, each critical infrastructure would establish (with the help of designated federal agencies) an information clearing house to identify, collect, desensitize, and disseminate the necessary information to that infrastructure's community. Finally, the Commission recommended the establishment of an Information Warning and Analysis Center, staffed by both

* The Advisory Committee is co-chaired by Senatory Sam Nunn and Ms. Jamie Gorelick, vice chairman of Fannie Mae.

government and industry representatives, that would act as the master clearing house for the various infrastructure clearing houses.

IV. Cyberlaundering: An Example*

A Colombian drug trafficker operating a number of cells in the New York City area has approximately $1 million per week in profits he needs to launder. He hires a computer and banking expert, Pablo Escobar, to wash this dirty money.

Pablo starts the wash cycle by placing the dirty money into the financial system via the tried-and-true method of smurfing, or structuring. Dozens of loyal smurfs open accounts at local branches of small banks, making many small, but regular, deposits of cash in amounts of less than $5,000 using friendly tellers and ATMs. Pablo then arranges for larger withdrawals by way of bank checks, payable to cash. These bank checks are then deposited with various Internet banks that accept electronic cash such as DigiCash, CyberCash, Checkfree, etc.** Once within this virtual world, payments or transfers are essentially untraceable, and the drug trafficker has access to legitimate electronic cash (left out are the various laundering offenses committed by the dealer and Pablo. Left open as well is whether the Internet "bank" to which Pablo has deposited his funds is regulated in any sense, and by what entity).

It should be noted that there appear to be some cyberbanks that are FDIC-regulated institutions, such as the Mark Twain Bank, located on-line at *http://marktwain.com/.* Although the electronic money deposited at these on-line banks is not federally insured (electronic money is not issued by the Federal Reserve, and this private money does not affect the standard monetary supply), these institutions are subject to the Bank Secrecy Act reporting requirements; so long as the transactions are less than $10,000, Pablo's activities would be caught only if the cyberbank chose to file a Suspicious Activity Report.

Once Pablo has deposited his "cash," he can access it from any computer anywhere in the world using commercially available systems such as TelNet to instruct one of his many Internet service providers (America Online,

* This example is borrowed from an article written by R. Mark Bortner entitled "Cyberlaundering: Anonymous Digital Cash and Money Laundering," presented as a final-paper requirement for a seminar at the University of Miami School of Law (1996). Mr. Bortner "grants the right to copy [his] article in its entirety or any portion thereof ..." with the singular request that "such copied material be clearly and correctly cited." I trust that this reference is clear and correct. The example has been cited from its original.
** For a lengthy shopping list of electronic banking and smart-card entities, see the Open Group's website at *http://www.rdg.opengroup.org/public/tech/security.*

Prodigy, and CompuServe are examples of ISPs) to electronically contact the cyberbank to transfer his funds to another bank or to a seller of any product that accepts electronic cash payments. Whether Pablo can avoid law enforcement entirely can be immaterial, so long as he can insulate the transactions enough to make the trail either practically impossible to follow, or so convoluted that law enforcement is always a few steps behind.

Presently, there are few sellers of products on the Internet. Known as cybershops, these entities are not like typical retail vendors that accept credit-card orders over the Internet. They accept electronic money. (For a list of such cybershops, see the Mark Twain Bank home page, above.)

Money Laundering in the Banking Industry

4

Twenty years ago, drug dealers or their associates could simply walk into any bank in this country and deposit satchels of cash, with little fear of detection. Today, through aggressive enforcement of the Bank Secrecy Act regulations, America's banks have virtually been closed as avenues for the wholesale placement of criminal proceeds.

— **Treasury Assistant Under Secretary (Enforcement) James E. Johnson** *testimony before the House Committee on Banking and Financial Services, May 15, 1997*

I.   What is the "Banking Industry?"

The American banking industry is a complex maze of federal, state, and local institutions, regulated by an overlapping web of various federal and state agencies.

The primary banking system in the United States is the Federal Reserve System, known as the Federal Reserve or simply, "the Fed." This is a network of 12 central banks, all regulated by the Federal Reserve Act, 12 U.S.C. ss. 221, *et seq.* and run by a Board of Governors comprising seven individuals appointed by the President for 14-year terms. The System is made up of the Board; the 12 central banks themselves, known as Federal reserve banks, and their branches and facilities; the Federal Advisory council; and the member banks themselves.

A "national" bank must become a member of the Federal Reserve System. National banks are federally incorporated commercial banks, regulated and supervised by the Office of the Comptroller of the Currency pursuant to the National Bank Act, 12 U.S.C. ss. 21, *et seq.* They must contain the word "National" in their name. A state bank or trust company, with the requisite qualifications, can become a member of the System.

In order to promote the stability of, and confidence in, the nation's banking system, Congress passed the Federal Deposit Insurance Act, 12 U.S.C. ss. 1811, *et seq.* The technique used to promote this stability and confidence was to insure all deposits of the member institutions: pursuant to the Act, any "depository institution" that becomes "insured" under the Act is actually insuring each depositor in its institution up to $100,000. Management of the Federal Deposit Insurance Corporation (FDIC) is by a Board of Directors consisting of the Comptroller of the Currency, the Director of the Office of Thrift Supervision, and three others appointed by the President.

Regulatory power over, and supervision of, the various types of banks reside in a number of agencies. The Office of the Comptroller of the Currency regulates and supervises national banks; the Federal Reserve Board regulates and supervises state banks, which are both members of the Federal Reserve System and insured under the FDIC; the FDIC has regulatory and supervisory authority over state banks that are not members of the Federal Reserve System and are not insured; and the Office of Thrift Supervision regulates savings associations and savings-and-loan companies. Other federal agencies that regulate the American banking industry include the Farm Credit Administration and the Federal Housing Finance Board.

For purposes of financial record-keeping and reporting, the Code of Federal Regulations (31 CFR 103) defines "bank" as every branch or office within the U.S. of any entity doing business in one or more listed capacities, including: any state or federal commercial bank or trust company, savings-and-loan association or credit union; a private bank; a savings bank, industrial bank, or other thrift institution; any organization subject to the supervision of a state bank supervisory authority; or any foreign bank operating in the U.S.

II.   Offshore Banking

A.   Introduction

The generic term "offshore banking" refers to both the countries where corporate, banking, securities, and other financial transactions are conducted under strict bank-secrecy laws with minimal, if any, governmental regulation and oversight; and to the products that are offered in those nations.

Countries known as offshore-banking havens include the Cayman Islands (shell corporations), Bermuda (insurance), Luxembourg (banks and banking), the Channel Islands (wire-transfer intermediary), the Netherlands Antilles (shell corporations), and Aruba. About one-half of the recognized offshore-banking centers are members of the Offshore Group of Banking Supervisors (OGBS).

Products and services offered by, and attributes of, most major offshore-banking havens include privacy, little or no currency-exchange restrictions, global market access, confidentiality, ease of cross-border investment, international private and family trusts, offshore investment funds, and "innovative" corporate structures and transactions. (See Chapter 15, "Profiles of Other Countries" for specific attributes that make a country an offshore-banking haven, and for details on 25 of the major money laundering/off-shore-banking nations.)

B. Attributes of Offshore-Banking Havens

In its annual International Narcotics Control Strategy Report, the U.S. Department of State uses certain selection criteria in determining whether a particular nation has a "money-laundering problem." These criteria are a shopping list of attributes that a money launderer would look for in choosing an offshore-banking center from which to ply his trade. They include:

- a limited number of predicate offenses on which prosecutors could base money-laundering prosecution
- a criminal system that has failed to criminalize money laundering or failed to enforce any money-laundering offenses
- rigid bank secrecy laws
- few identification requirements to conduct financial transactions
- ability to use anonymous, nominee, or numbered accounts
- no mandatory disclosure of the beneficial owner of an account
- no mandatory disclosure of the beneficiary of a transaction
- lack of effective monitoring of currency movements
- no recording requirements for large cash or near-cash transactions
- no mandatory reporting of suspicious transactions
- use of bearer monetary instruments
- well-established non-bank financial systems
- ease of incorporation, including the use of shelf corporations, share-holder nominees, and/or bearer shares
- bank regulatory agencies that are understaffed, underskilled, and underpaid, and have limited audit authority over foreign-owned or controlled banks
- domestic banking system that allows foreign banks to control, own, or freely use domestic banks
- law enforcement that has limited asset seizure or confiscation capabilities and/or limited narcotics and money-laundering enforcement capabilities
- access to free-trade zones such as the Colon Free Zone in Panama
- government and civil service that is prone to, or ripe for, official corruption
- ability to use American dollars in the local economy
- a significant trade in gems, particularly diamonds

This list is not exhaustive, but represents a sampling of factors or attributes that, if present, suggest that a particular country could be a target for money launderers.

III.   Underground or Parallel Banking Systems

Because of political and economic uncertainty and a general distrust of banks, a great deal of the world's grassroots banking is done outside of the regulated banking systems and instead is conducted through a parallel, underground banking system. Known as *fei ch'ien* in the Far East (literally, "flying money") or *Hawala* or *hundi* in India and Asia, it is a system based on honor, ethnic ties, and, in the case of collections or bad debts, stunning violence. Although it is not formally regulated, the underground banking systems are a highly efficient means to launder money.

Regardless of whether the system involves Chinese money changers in Hong Kong and the U.S., or Indian money changers in India and Britain, the mechanics are basically the same. For example, a "businessman" can deposit cash with a Hong Kong money exchanger or precious-metals dealer, and receive a chit, note, ticket, or some sort of marker. Often, these pieces of paper or markers appear innocuous, such as a laundry receipt, but are actually coded "bearer notes" that, when presented to a money changer in New York, San Francisco, Paris, London, or anywhere else the *fei ch'ien* or *Hawala* operates, will enable the bearer to the same amount of cash, less a commission (usually 5 to 15% of the amount). One Hong Kong police official reported that a piece of paper seized with the picture of an elephant on it was the collection receipt for $3 million at a Hong Kong gold shop.*

Hawala bankers in London have been connected to terrorists in the Punjab and Kashmir regions of India; *fei ch'ien* bankers in Hong Kong and San Francisco have been linked to heroin traffickers. The underground banking system may be responsible for the transfer of most of the money related to heroin trafficking in Southeast Asia.

IV.   Money-Laundering Techniques Common to the Banking Industry

A.   The Use of Wire Transfers

1.   *How Wire Transfers Work*

Wire transfers have been around as long as the telegraph. Today, a wire transfer is simply the electronic transfer of money from one bank or entity to another. Wire transfers, or electronic funds transfers, are the most common method of moving large amounts of capital around the world, thus, it

---

* The United Nations International Drug Control Program's "Investigators Manual for Financial Investigations and Money Laundering," prepared by Staff Sergeant Robert Preston of the Royal Canadian Mounted Police.

makes sense that they are the most common tool used to "layer" illicit funds. Dirty money, now in the banking or financial system, is wire-transferred throughout the global banking system to hide its origins. They "have become the lifeblood of the international drug trade," according to a 1984 report of the President's Commission on Organized Crime.*

The Uniform Commercial Code defines a wire transfer as "a series of transactions, beginning with the originator's payment order, made for the purpose of making payment to the beneficiary of the order" (U.C.C. Article 4A, Prefatory Note, 1991). The mechanics of wire transfers are quite simple: a customer wishing to transfer money from his account to another bank account simply instructs his bank to wire a certain amount to a specified beneficiary account at another bank. The originating bank sends an electronic "message" to the transfer system's central computer (such as CHIPS or SWIFT, described below), indicating, in electronic format, the sending or originating bank, the amount, the receiving or beneficiary bank, and the specific beneficiary. The transfer system's computer then electronically adjusts the account balances of the originating and beneficiary banks and produces a printout of a debit ticket at the originating bank and a credit ticket at the beneficiary bank. Once the beneficiary bank receives its credit ticket, it notifies the beneficiary of the wire transfer. If the two banks are members of the same wire transfer system (e.g., two CHIPS banks), then they are the only two banks in the wire transfer chain. However, if they are not members of the same system, which is standard for international transfers (e.g., a bank in Colombia and a local bank in Boston), it is necessary to route the transfers through one or more intermediary banks that have "correspondent" relationships with the other banks in the chain. For example, to wire money from a small Boston area bank to a local Colombian bank could require six electronic transactions: the "money" is credited and debited through to a CHIPS member bank, which then "moves" the money to another CHIPS bank that is the correspondent bank for a large Colombian-based bank. That large Colombian bank will then "move" the funds to the small Colombian bank. The local Boston bank is the originating bank, the two CHIPS banks are intermediaries, and the small Colombian bank is the beneficiary.

It is estimated by the banking industry that 80% of all commercial transactions are done on a "straight-through" basis; that is, directly and electronically wired from one customer's account to another account. Wire transfers are the life-blood of the commercial wholesale global economy. Payment orders sent by a bank's customers to their bank generally contain only that information necessary to conduct the transaction. Typically, an individual or corporation gives a payment order to his/its bank. The bank

---

* See also *United States v. Daccarett* 6 F.3d 37, 43 (2nd Cir. 1993).

then formats the order using only sufficient information to allow the receiving bank to conduct and execute the payment appropriately. The original order might not even contain the name of the originator or the person on whose behalf the payment order was made (e.g., one person could pay for goods shipped to a third party). If the payment order is routed through several intermediary banks before it reaches its final destination, the order to the next bank in line is reformatted at each intermediate stop. Again, only sufficient information to allow the next bank to carry out its task appropriately is contained on the order.

In the U.S., there are two main wire transfer systems: the Clearing House Interbank Transfer System (CHIPS) for New York Clearing House banks, and Fedwire, for the Federal Reserve System member banks. A third operator, Brussels-based "SWIFT," operates internationally. Their volume is extraordinary: there are an estimated 700,000 wire transfers each business day, moving well over U.S.$2 trillion (based on statistics provided by the U.S. Office of Technology Assessment). And wire transfers are cheap: the average cost of a wire transfer, regardless of the amount of the money being transferred, is $0.18. In addition, non-bank financial institutions process approximately 13 million wire transfers annually.

Wire-transfers are essentially unregulated, and, through their frequency, volume, or complexity, are almost impossible to detect. In testimony given at the 1993 House Banking Committee Hearings on Money Laundering, Robert Taylor, a former money launderer, recounted the exploits of Ramon Milan Rodriguez (convicted money launderer, serving a 43-year prison term for RICO violations), who wired a total of over $11 billion to various U.S. banks for deposit and for purchases of securities, real estate, certificates of deposit, and other investments. Because the money was received by wire transfer, the banks and brokerage houses were not under any duty to report unless they felt that the transactions were "suspicious." They obviously felt these were not.

The Annunzio-Wylie Act of 1994 sought to regulate wire transfers by regulations taking effect on January 1, 1996. The new regulations are a compromise between law enforcement's tracking needs and the financial world's need to maintain an efficient, low-cost, high-volume payment system. Essentially, they are designed to provide detailed but flexible information at each stage of the wire transfer process: at the originating bank, at the intermediary bank, and at the beneficiary bank. When the originating bank accepts a payment order and subsequently originates a wire transfer, it must verify and retain records of the identity of the individual submitting the payment order. Established customers have a customer account number or name; for new customers, the originating bank must verify identities by an "identification document." If no document is provided, the bank can still process the wire transfer, but must make a "note in the record" that the information was not provided. Likewise, the ultimate beneficiary bank is also under a duty to identify the ultimate beneficiary, to the extent possible, in the records it maintains. Intermediary banks, which receive the transfer order from the originating bank or another intermediary bank, and pass it on to another intermediary bank or to the ultimate beneficiary bank, are required to maintain complete records of the payment orders they receive and to pass them on in their entirety. Intermediary banks have no requirement to verify the records; simply to pass them on in their entirety. The record-keeping and verification requirements for banks and non-bank financial institutions apply only to transmittals of funds equal to or greater than $3,000.

2. *The Major Wire Transfer Systems*

A "clearing house" is an association through which banks exchange checks and drafts drawn on each other, and settle their daily balances. Non-member banks clear their commercial paper through clearing house member banks by agreements with such banks. CHIPS — the Clearing House Interbank Payment System — is the primary site for settlement of all U.S. banking transactions such as international foreign exchange and Eurodollar transactions and all international and domestic trade transactions taking place through the New York-based U.S. banking system. CHIPS' European counterpart, SWIFT — the Society for Worldwide Interbank Financial Telecommunications — operates similarly.

The CHIPS system itself was started in 1970, and is owned by the 10 member banks of the New York Clearing House: the Bank of New York, Chase Manhattan, Citibank, Morgan Guaranty, Bankers Trust, Marine Midland, US Trust, Shawmut Bank (recently merged with Fleet Bank), European American Bank (formerly Franklin National, which went under in 1974), and Republic National Bank of New York. There are approximately 135 banks that participate in CHIPS, but less than 40 (including the 10 New York Clearing House banks) are "settling" banks allowed to make the transfers that settle all net debits or credits in the CHIPS system.

For example, Abe Lincoln writes a $10 check on his Chase account, payable to Jefferson Davis. Jefferson cashes the check at his bank, Morgan Guaranty, which gives Jefferson $10 in cash. Morgan then takes the check over to Chase to get $10 from Chase. Chase hands over $10 to Morgan, then takes $10 from Abe's account. Simple, except that the huge volume of transactions makes it impossible for each bank to deliver each individual check to the other banks that their customers do business with. Therefore, banks devised a system to settle their claims on each other by writing checks, delivered by messenger, to a central location, called the New York Clearing House, for delivery to the payee bank's representative. With the advent of technology, the messengers and representatives were replaced with fiber optic cable and computers and the CHIPS system was born.

CHIPS maintains an escrow account at the New York branch of the Federal Reserve. The key to the day-to-day operation of the CHIPS system is its ability to bring this account to a zero balance at the close of each business day. This account balance increases by those banks making net positive payments (those banks with net transfers out to other banks): the balance is depleted by the banks receiving payments. During the day, the CHIPS computer keeps a running tab of each bank's net position *vis à vis* the other banks. At the end of the day, a single net settlement is made. As set out above, less than 40 of the 135 banks that use the CHIPS system can make these "Fedwire" "settling" transfers: the other 95 or so non-settling banks must settle their net transactions with one of the 40 settling banks. At 4:30 p.m. each day, the system closes and two reports are generated: one for the net debit/credit position of each of the 95 participants; the other showing the net settlement required for each of the 40 settling banks. The net settlement position for each of the 95 non-settling participants is contained in the corresponding report of its settling representative. One hour later, at 5:30 p.m. EST, the settling banks that owe a net payment pay their debt into the CHIPS account, via Fedwire. CHIPS then pays those settling banks with net credit positions, leaving a zero balance in the CHIPS account.

In 1996, the CHIPS system averaged over 200,000 transactions per day, with an average daily dollar volume of over $1.3 trillion. On January 21, 1997, CHIPS cleared almost 420,000 transactions totaling almost $2.2 trillion, a record.

What about wire transfers of foreign currency? Banks have accounts with each other, called Correspondent Accounts, for the purpose of settling international payments. For example, the Royal Bank of Canada (RBC) might sell part of its deutsche mark portfolio to a London bank in exchange for U.S. dollars. Through the CHIPS system's international transactions counterpart, Brussels-based Society for Worldwide Interbank Financial Telecommunications (SWIFT), the RBC will transfer its deutsche marks on deposit with its German bank's correspondent account to the London bank's correspondent account in Germany, and the London bank will transfer the U.S. dollar equivalent on deposit at its New York correspondent account (e.g., at Citibank) to the RBC's New York correspondent account (e.g., at Chase Manhattan). Citibank and Chase will then make the necessary transfers through the Fedwire system into/out of their respective CHIPS accounts. Viola. Finished.

In 1992, the SWIFT board issued a broadcast to its members and participating banks encouraging these users to include full identifying information for originators and beneficiaries of funds transfers. Most countries' banking regulators have imposed corresponding requirements on their members; however, there remain difficulties in identifying the true originating parties in international funds transfers. To correct this problem, SWIFT, working with the FATF, created a new message format, which was to have been implemented after November 1997. This new format has an optional field that will be able to contain more data relating to the identification of the originator and the beneficiary.

Note that SWIFT's computer systems are running on IBM machines using encryption devices by Cylink, a company founded in 1984 to provide secure telecommunication and computer communications for banks, businesses, and utilities. The encryption industry itself is expected to grow from about $1 billion in 1995 to $16 billion (estimated) in the year 2000.

B. The Use of Conduit Accounts

Money launderers establish accounts in various banks throughout the world, using front companies, shell corporations, agents, and third-party nominees, for the sole purpose of acting as intermediaries, or conduits, in wire-transferring money from the originator to the ultimate beneficiary. Often, these agents are individuals whose sole task is to set up an account and to conduct everyday transactions in order to give the account — whether it is a personal or a business account — the air of legitimacy.

Typically, a money launderer will set up as many as 15 or 20 individuals in various cities around the world. These individuals are given a monthly or periodical stipend with which to live and conduct normal, everyday banking transactions: writing checks, using credit cards, debit cards, etc. The purpose is to create a history of normal banking activity. Ultimately, and in conjunction with the others in the "chain," there will be a flurry of wire transfers moving money in and out of the various accounts. By the time regulators and law enforcement are able to recognize the activity for what it is — money laundering — the individuals have moved on to new cities, with new IDs, to operate again. The front, shell, and dummy corporations that received much of the funds are usually not traceable to any identifiable person.

C. The Use of Correspondent Accounts/Due From Accounts

Banks with no branches in a foreign country will establish a "correspondent account" with a foreign bank or a domestic bank with a branch in that foreign country, in order to be able to wire money and conduct (limited) business for its clients with greater ease. The FATF has identified correspondent banking as a serious money laundering concern, principally because it effectively negates a domestic bank's "know your customer" policies. See "Payable-Through Accounts," below.

D.   The Use of Payable-Through Accounts

A type of Correspondent Account, these accounts are maintained at American banks by foreign banks, and are used by the foreign bank to conduct their depositors' U.S. currency transactions. They are, in effect, a master correspondent account of a foreign bank in a U.S. bank through which customers of the foreign bank can transact banking business. Customers of the foreign bank have signature authority in the master payable-through account and are referred to as "sub-account holders."

For example, Banco de Credito Centroamericano (in Nicaragua) and Banco Industrial S.A. (in Medellín, Colombia) may offer their customers U.S. dollar checking accounts. In order to conduct this U.S. currency business, these banks maintain a single account at a U.S. bank (perhaps Barclays Bank in Miami and Bankers Trust Company in New York, respectively). In some cases, the foreign banks are allowing launderers to use their payable-through accounts to conduct personal transactions (laundering), and the American banks are ignorant of the true nature of the transactions.

V.   Preventing Money Laundering in the Banking Industry

A.   Detecting and Preventing Money Laundering Generally

1.   Introduction

Banks and other financial institutions are the front line of defense against money laundering. The federal government's main statutory tool is Title 31, Subtitle B, chapter 1, Part 103 of the Code of Federal Regulations, cited as 31 CFR 103, "Financial record keeping and reporting of currency and foreign transactions." These regulations are a culmination of 26 years of legislative changes from the Bank Secrecy Act of 1970 to the International Crime Control Act of 1996. 31 CFR 103 can be freely copied, as there are no restrictions on the republication of material in the Code of Federal Regulations.*

Banks have long been the target of federal prosecutors looking to enforce the reporting and record keeping laws. The first major case involving a bank's failure to report transactions was the 1985 Bank of Boston case (described in Chapter 8, "Domestic Money Laundering Statutes and Laws," herein). A recent case reported in a FinCEN on-line press release dated July 2, 1997, involved a settlement reached by the Barnett Banks, Inc. to pay a $100,000 civil fine. Although FinCEN determined that criminal proceedings were not warranted, the fine was paid to resolve charges that the Bank improperly

---

* For a statute-by-statute look at the domestic anti-money laundering and banking laws, see Chapter 7, "Domestic Money Laundering Statutes & Laws."

placed two customers on its large currency transaction reporting exemption list (discovered during a routine OCC examination), and that it failed to aggregate a commercial customer's same-day cash withdrawals (discovered during an IRS examination). Authorities indicated that the fine was not higher because of Barnett's otherwise strong record of BSA compliance.

The Office of the Comptroller of the Currency (OCC) has published an excellent booklet entitled "Money Laundering: A Banker's Guide to Avoiding Problems," available at its website, *http://www.occ.treas.gov/launder/orig.htm*. This guide provides a brief review of bankers' obligations under the BSA, a list of indicators of money laundering, and suggestions for preventing money laundering. Some of these obligations and suggestions follow.

2. Basic Steps for Any Bank Compliance Program

All banks are required by law to have an effective written BSA compliance program. Such a program must set out a system of internal controls to assure BSA compliance; provide for the testing of these controls by internal or external auditors; designate a compliance officer; and ensure appropriate training for bank personnel.

In addition, banks are required to establish an effective "Know Your Customer Policy" tailored to their specific operations and customers. The incentives for such a policy are both practical — it is good business to be known as a prudent, safe bank — and commercial — to reduce the risk of the government's seizing and forfeiting a customer's loan collateral when the customer is found to be laundering money through the bank. The OCC has identified certain situations or activities as being indicators of money laundering:

1. activity that is not consistent with the customer's business. Examples of this are: heavy cash activity in a corporate account, cash purchases of money orders, high volume of deposits made by money order and/or wire transfers, large bill transactions in non-business accounts, exchanging small bills for large bills, small business owners making several deposits on the same day at different bank branches, and receipt and sending of wire transfers for no apparent business reason
2. unusual account characteristics or activities, such as customers with addresses outside the bank's normal service area, a loan collateralized by a CD or other investment, frequent safety deposit box access, or accounts opened in the name of a Casa de Cambio.
3. attempts to avoid reporting or record-keeping requirements; such as new business customers asking to be placed on the Exempt Businesses List before their banking history warranted it.

4. certain types of funds transfers, such as wire transfers, and depositing funds into several accounts in amounts below the reportable threshold, then consolidating into a master account

Each of these situations can be avoided by strict compliance with the "Know Your Customer" rules, by continually reviewing and revising the "Exempt Businesses" lists, and by a daily review of five commonly generated bank reports: demand deposit accounts activity report, large transactions report, cash-in/cash-out report, incoming/outgoing wire transfer log, and a $3,000 monetary log.

3.   *"Know Your Customer" Policies*

One effective tool arising from the BSA is a regulation known as the "know your customer" policy, which requires all financial institutions to verify the identity of all customers who open accounts, and verifies the identity of purchasers of negotiable instruments, cashiers checks, and travelers checks in excess of $3,000. To promote these requirements, the regulations provide for statutory immunity from tort litigation for notifying authorities of suspicious activity, and allowing financial institutions to exempt certain businesses or types of businesses from the CTR reporting requirement. The Federal Reserve Board has listed guidelines to assist financial institutions in training personnel in suspicious customer behavior.

The FATF's Forty Recommendations, numbers 10-12, set out the know your customer principles that have been implemented in the BSA. Along with the record-keeping and reporting rules, the know your customer policies are considered by the FATF to be the cornerstone for preventing money laundering in financial institutions.

Banks that focus on implementing an effective KYC program might gain a false sense of security, believing that they are immunizing themselves from all money-laundering activity. In fact, KYC focuses on activity that generally occurs only at the placement stage of the laundering cycle. Most KYC programs do not focus on the movement of funds through a bank's system — the layering of placed funds, or the integration of funds already placed and integrated. Any KYC program must be matched with aggressive suspicious activity monitoring and reporting programs.

4.   *Safe Harbor Provisions*

The 1992 Annunzio-Wylie Money Laundering Act required any financial institution, and its officers, directors, employees, and agents, to report any "suspicious transaction relevant to a possible violation of law or regulation." To encourage such reporting, the regulations included a "safe harbor" provision, protecting those entities and persons from civil liability to their clients and third parties that might otherwise claim to have arisen from the designation of transactions as "suspicious." The actual provisions are contained in 31 CFR 103.21. They protect any "bank and any director, officer, employee, or agent of such bank, that makes a report pursuant to this section [whether such report is required by this section or is made voluntarily] ... from liability for any disclosure contained in, or for failure to disclose the fact of such report, or both, to the full extent provided by *31 USC 5318(g)(3).*"

The safe harbor provisions do not protect banks in every case. In a decision released on November 21, 1997, the Eleventh Circuit Court of Appeals overturned a lower court decision and held that a number of south Florida banks had violated certain of their customers' privacy rights (under the Right to Financial Privacy Act, 12 U.S.C. s. 3401) by releasing wire-transfer information in response to verbal requests from government agents, unaccompanied by a court order or subpoena. In this case, reported as *Lopez v. First Union National Bank* (11th Cir. No. 96-4931 Nov. 21, 1997), several Colombian (drug trafficking) customers whose assets were seized from a number of south Florida banks sued these banks for releasing account and/or wire-transfer information to federal agents.

The Eleventh Circuit found that the banks' actions did not fall within the safe harbor provisions because the federal agents' suspicions regarding the transactions could not be imputed to the banks: the fact that the agents requested information on the transactions and accounts did not render them *per se* suspicious, reported the court.

To understand this ruling, and the extent of the safe harbor provisions, it is important to understand the "suspicious activity" reporting requirement itself. The regulations provide that a bank *shall* file "a report of *any* suspicious transaction relevant to a possible violation of law or regulation" or a report of "*any* suspicious transaction that it believes is relevant to the possible violation of any law or regulation but whose reporting is not required by this section." 31 CFR 103.21(a)(1).

A report is required if it is "conducted or attempted by, at, or through the bank, it involves or aggregates at least $5,000 in funds or other assets, and the bank knows, *suspects, or has reason to suspect that:*" (1) the transaction involves funds derived from illegal activities or is intended to hide or disguise funds or assets derived from illegal activities as part of a plan to violate or evade federal law or to avoid any transaction reporting requirement; or (2) the transaction has "no apparent lawful purpose or is not the sort in which the particular customer would normally be expected to engage, and the bank knows of no reasonable explanation for the transaction after examining the available facts, including the background and possible purpose of the transaction."

Therefore, to gain protection under the safe harbor provisions, the bank must report a suspicious transaction or the information released must relate to a suspicious transaction. If the bank itself has not filed a suspicious activity report or determined on its own that the transaction was suspicious, then it cannot rely on a law enforcement officer's bare request for information on that customer or his/her account or other bank activity.

The corollary of the safe harbor provision is a "Tip Off Provision," which prohibits financial institutions and their officers and employees from "tipping off" customers when a Suspicious Activity Report has been filed. Both the safe harbor and tip off provisions are included in the FATF's Forty Recommendations (numbers 16 and 17, respectively).

5.   Tip Off Provisions

U.S. and Mexican anti-money-laundering banking regulations contain what is known as "no tip off" or "tip off" provisions that prohibit disclosure by financial institutions and their employees of the fact that a Suspicious Activity Report has been filed against a customer. The corollary provision is a Safe Harbor Provision, described above, that protects the financial institutions and their officers and employees from civil liability for reporting suspicious transactions to federal authorities.

6.   Exempt Businesses/Qualified Business Customers

To ease financial institutions' CTR reporting burden, the MLSA 1994 proposed a two-tiered system of exempting certain entities from the CTR reporting requirements (the statute is set out at 31 U.S.C. s. 5313). The first tier was for mandatory exemptions for certain governmental entities and public utilities. The second tier was a "discretionary" one of approximately 75 types of businesses (referred to as "Qualified Business Customers") that were exempt where these businesses' deposits or withdrawals are made from an existing bank account and the business is an established U.S. depositor operating either (1) a "retail" business (exceptions to this exception are auto, plane, and boat dealers); or (2) a sports arena, race track, amusement park, restaurant, hotel, licensed check cashing service, vending machine company, or theater — any business that regularly has large volumes of small cash transactions. Where these businesses are also laundering money, they are almost impossible to detect.

In 1996, the 1994 regulations were revised to reduce the burden imposed on banks, so that currency transactions over $10,000 were no longer required to be automatically reported as such if they involve a bank and (1) another bank in the United States, (2) a federal, state, or local government, (3) a corporation listed on the New York or American Stock Exchange or is designated as a Nasdaq National Market Security, or (4) any subsidiary of such a listed corporation. Any transaction deemed suspicious must still be reported. Because of the risk of abuse, a bank's review of its exempt business lists is critical to proposed BSA compliance.

Notwithstanding these 1996 changes, the exemption criteria were considered to be complicated and confusing. On September 8, 1997, FinCEN announced a final rule and proposed regulation aimed at streamlining the reporting requirements for exempt businesses. In a September 8th press release, FinCEN's DireObtaining, Stanley Morris, stated that the "changes adopted in the final rule are intended to further improve the exemption process. Our goal is to reduce the burden of currency transaction reporting, require reporting only of information that is of value to law enforcement and regulatory authorities, and create an exemption system that is cost-effective and that works."

The "exempt business" regulations are described in detail in Part C of Chapter 7, "Domestic Money Laundering Statutes and Laws."

B. Cash Reserves

The existence of, and patterns in, a federal reserve bank's cash flow has long been considered a major indicator of drug activity in a city. Banks in a normal, growing city have historically run an annual cash deficit that necessitates borrowing from the Federal Deposit Bank. Therefore, large cash surpluses suggest money laundering. For example, leading the "surplus list" for 1993 were Los Angeles ($9.312 billion), Miami ($5.381 billion), Jacksonville ($2.580 billion), San Antonio ($2.434 billion), El Paso ($664 million), Nashville ($365 million), Denver ($223 million), Little Rock ($78 million), Helena ($72 million). The San Antonio Reserve Bank now has a $5 billion cash surplus and was the subject of a Congressional investigation by the Committee on Banking, Finance, and Urban Affairs, U.S. House of Representatives, chaired by Representative Henry B. Gonzalez of Texas.

VI. Money Laundering Through Banks: Case Studies

A. American Express Bank International

A classic case of money laundering through the banking system involved two Beverly Hills, California, bankers at American Express Bank International, Antonio Giraldi and Maria Lourdes Reategui, convicted in 1994 by a Texas jury for laundering $40 million belonging to Mexican drug trafficker Juan Garcia Abrego (leader of the Mexican Federation's Gulf Group).

In this case, Abrego's primary launderer, a Mexican gas station owner named Ricardo Aguirre Villagomez, collected drug proceeds from the southwestern U.S. and smuggled them to Mexico, or wired them from various *casa de cambio,* and on to Switzerland. From there, the proceeds were consolidated and then wired to a Cayman Islands holding company, established for Villagomez by their Amex bankers, Giraldi and Reategui. From there, Giraldi and Reategui invested these moneys in Mexican art, American real estate, and a Blockbuster Video franchise, all with proper loan and collateral documentation. Eventually, Villagomez became the Beverly Hills branch's largest single customer, having posted collateral worth almost $30 million for loans of approximately $20 million.

The laundering came to a close when the U.S. Customs identified and then seized the Cayman Island accounts; Giraldi and Reategui received 10 year and 3^1/$_2$ year sentences, respectively; the bank was fined $7 million, had to forfeit almost $40 million of Villagomez's laundered assets, and was ordered to undergo an employee training program at a cost of approximately $3 million.

B.   Banque Leu

It is not just American banks, or even foreign banks with branches in the U.S., that are the targets; in 1993, the Luxembourg-based Banque Leu was fined for processing transfers of $1.7 million from its accounts to the U.S. In this case, *United States v. Banque Leu* (No. 93-CR-0607, N.D. Cal., Dec., 1993), the bank pled guilty and paid over $3 million in forfeitures and fines where some of its Colombian customers, found to be of "bad repute," had bought various monetary instruments in the U.S. with drug money and deposited these instruments in the Banque Leu in Luxembourg. Bank officials, without having a branch in the U.S. but maintaining a "correspondent account" in the U.S., sent these funds to the U.S. correspondent bank for clearance. The use of the correspondent account, albeit without a physical presence in the U.S., gave the U.S. jurisdiction over Banque Leu.

C.   Bank of Credit and Commerce International (BCCI)*

The most notorious money laundering case of all time, the "BCCI Affair" was an 18-year money-laundering shell game played out in 73 countries, eventually resulting in the loss of over $20 billion from millions of people and hundreds of countries (the true amount will never be known; government officials' illegal deposits — from kickbacks, bribes, skimming, etc. —

---

* An excellent summary of the entire history of the BCCI Affair can be found in Senator John Kerry's 1992 report entitled "The BCCI Affair: Report to the Committee on Foreign Relations." This Senate Report details the origin and early years of the "Bank of Crooks and Criminals International," the relationships between the various governements, auditors, regulators, lawyers, etc., the eventual closure of BCCI on July 5, 1991, and legislative and policy recommendations to prevent another such occurrence. See, *http://www.fas.org/irp/congress/1992_rpt/bcci/01exec.htm.*

will never be claimed; there were billions of dollars on deposit in these "managers' ledger" or "ML" accounts and numbered accounts). The details of BCCI's activities are too great to chronicle here; only the basics will be described. Even the known details are only a fragment of the greater truth. Although there remains almost 100 million BCCI documents in London, over 9,000 boxes of documents containing several million pages of documents, some handwritten in various Arabic dialects in New York and Miami, and even more documents in the Grand Caymans, most of the key documents were either destroyed or shredded, or removed from BCCI's London head office and flown to Abu Dhabi in 1990. In addition, BCCI's founder and mastermind, Agha Hasan Abedi, has suffered a debilitating stroke, and the other key figures are either safely ensconced in Abu Dhabi or in prison.

BCCI has been described as an "impenetrable series of holding companies, affiliates, subsidiaries, banks-within-banks, insider dealings and nominee relationships" operating in 73 countries and free of governmental and regulatory control. It supported terrorism, arms trafficking, and the sale of nuclear technology; it managed prostitution; and it engaged in an elaborate ponzi scheme to defraud its depositors. The key to its success was the establishment of offshore shell corporations established in countries with strict bank secrecy laws, its bribery of Third World politicians in order to secure their countries' Central Bank deposits, handling of foreign currency exchange, and the right to own banks. Another key was BCCI's ability to infiltrate the U.S. market by secretly purchasing U.S. banks while opening BCCI branch offices, then merging these institutions under elaborate shell and nominee corporations and holding companies. The supposedly strict U.S. regulatory scheme only delayed BCCI's illegal entry into the U.S. market; BCCI eventually owned four banks operating in states and the District of Columbia.

1. The Early Years of BCCI

The founder of BCCI was a Pakistani businessman, Agha Hasan Abedi ("Abedi"). In 1972, Pakistan nationalized its banks. One of these was United Bank, whose president was Abedi. Abedi then joined with the Gokal family, Pakistanis who controlled one of the world's largest shipping empires, and Sheik Zayad of Abu Dhabi to found BCCI with an initial capitalization of $2.5 million. The Bank of America was also an initial investor in the bank, in part because of the involvement of various members of the Saudi royal family (Bank of America pulled out in 1980).

To prevent nationalization, BCCI was chartered in Luxembourg. By 1974, BCCI had branches in four Gulf states and in several British cities. In 1975, it split into two separate entities, one remaining in Luxembourg, the other established in the Cayman Islands as a "bank-within-a-bank" of the Luxembourg BCCI (this step was critical as BCCI was able to ensure that neither of its two auditors — one being Price Waterhouse of England — had full access to all of BCCI's operations). The actual operations of both "branches" was moved to London, a critical step in BCCI's step as the Bank of England oversaw its operations and granted it a clean bill of health every year for the next 15 years. By 1977, BCCI was arguably one of the world's fastest growing banks, with over 140 branches in 30 countries and assets of over $2 billion.

2.   BCCI's Move to The Cayman Islands

The Cayman Islands "bank-within-a-bank" was actually a number of legally distinct entities known collectively as ICIC. Using this one abbreviation, Abedi created the following entities: International Credit and Investment Company Overseas, Ltd.; International Credit and Investment Co., Ltd.; International Credit and Commerce (Overseas) Ltd.; ICIC Holdings of Grand Cayman; ICIC Apex Holding Limited; ICIC Overseas, Cayman; ICIC Foundation; the ICIC Staff Benefit Fund; the ICIC Staff Benefit Trust; ICIC Business Promotions; etc. The ultimate ICIC "holding company" was ICIC Apex Holding Limited, incorporated as a charitable trust with the beneficiaries designated as "mankind at large."

Usually, correspondence and transactions involving any of the ICIC entities would refer simply to "ICIC," leaving it to top BCCI officials to determine which of the entities would get credit or be debited for any particular transaction. In addition, the ICIC family was not really a bank at all, but simply a post-office box location in the Grand Caymans available to "book" transactions that were initiated, organized, and approved elsewhere in the upper echelons of the BCCI empire.

3.   BCCI's Move to the United States

a.   Takeover of the National Bank of Georgia.   As set out above, one of the keys to BCCI's success was to infiltrate the U.S. market. Ironically, the techniques used by BCCI so successfully to infiltrate Third World countries — using nominee purchasers, prestigious lawyers, accountants, and public relations firms, and "buying off" politically connected people in order to gain regulatory favor — ultimately proved successful in the tightly regulated U.S. market.

In 1976, BCCI's bid to directly and overtly buy Chelsea National Bank in New York was rejected by state banking regulators. Abedi then turned to a clandestine purchase of Financial General, a Washington D.C.-based bank, that had just been purchased by an investor group which included an Arkansan, Jackson Stephens. Stephens controlled another bank, Worthen National, as well as Stephens, Inc., a large investment bank. Stephens' Naval Academy roommate had been Jimmy Carter; some time in late 1977, Stephens introduced Adebi to Bert Lance, President Carter's Director of the Office of Management and Budget (OMB). Lance had links with Financial General, for it was that bank that had sold to Lance a controlling interest in the National Bank of Georgia in 1975. Abedi, in turn, introduced Lance to Ghaith Pharaon, a Stanford- and Harvard-educated Kuwaiti (Lance had left office). On January 5, 1978, Pharaon acquired Lance's stock in National Bank of Georgia; among other consideration, a loan that Lance had with First National Bank of Chicago for $3.4 million was paid off — by BCCI London.

Pharaon, Lance, Stephens, and Abedi then concentrated on a BCCI takeover of Financial General. As early as 1977, they employed Clark Clifford (former Defense Secretary and lawyer for BCCI) and Robert Altman (Clifford's partner and Lance's attorney) to assist. Also involved was Kamal Adham, a Saudi. In March, 1978, BCCI's application to purchase Financial General was rejected by the SEC and Federal Reserve. Abedi then turned to the bank secrecy haven of the Netherlands Antilles and formed Credit and Commerce American Holdings (CCAH). The largest investor was Kamal Adham. In October 1978, CCAH filed for approval with the Federal Reserve to purchase Financial General. Their application was rejected. Finally, in late 1981, the Federal Reserve approved the purchase of Financial General, despite the Federal Reserve's knowledge of BCCI's involvement and because of false representations by CCAH's shareholders and attorneys (including Clark Clifford and former Federal Reserve counsel Baldwin Tuttle), and favorable reviews by the CIA, the State Department, and other federal agencies. The Federal Reserve allowed a loophole from the commitment that BCCI not be involved in financing or controlling CCAH by permitting BCCI to act as an "investment advisor" and "information conduit" to CCAH's shareholders. When the takeover was completed, in April 1982, BCCI's principals made Clark Clifford chairman and Robert Altman president. The bank was renamed "First American."

b. Establishing a U.S. Commodities Trading Presence.   In addition to its involvement in the U.S. banking industry, BCCI had a "commodities affiliate," Capcom Financial Services, Ltd., based in London, Chicago, and Cairo. Capcom was created, in part, to keep BCCI from financial collapse in 1984 due to losses of over $1 billion in the commodities futures markets by the head of its Treasury Department, a Pakistani national named Syed Ziauddin (Z.A.) Akbar. Akbar incurred these losses on silver futures and long-term government bond futures (actually paying a premium on bond future prices where every other trader in the world was taking them at a discounted rate). To hide the losses, Akbar created, essentially, two sets of books for BCCI: one set for its external auditors, Price Waterhouse LLP, and the other hidden from audit in the name of the various private clients of BCCI. Then, in 1984, Akbar and his co-conspirators decided to further insulate these "Number Two" books by moving them to a new entity, Capcom. Capcom was originally a paper corporation, Hourcharm. Ltd., registered using Akbar's home address in London. He renamed the entity Capital Commodity Dealers, Ltd., and then renamed it again to Capcom Financial Services. Capcom began trading in commodities in London. Within a few months, its customer accounts totaled approximately $160 million, most of it BCCI affiliated (with such terrific business on paper, innocent investors began to pour legitimate capital into the company. By mid-1985, BCCI accounts were ostensibly withdrawn from Capcom to satisfy regulators; however, millions of BCCI-related money continued to come into Capcom in various forms). Capcom moved to the Chicago commodities exchanges in late 1984 as Capcom Futures. It was staffed by former BCCI officials, capitalized almost exclusively by Saudi customers of BCCI, and owned by BCCI, its shareholders, and front-men (including four Americans with no commodities trading experience). Capcom conducted billions of dollars in largely anonymous trades in the U.S., and the extent of its money-laundering activities remains unknown. To further cloud the issue, Akbar himself left BCCI in 1986 and moved to Capcom, taking a controlling interest through his personal corporation, ZASK Trading and Investments, Ltd., a Panamanian-registered, Liechtenstein-operated corporation. Among other things, Akbar directed BCCI's "Number Two Account" Treasury funds, paying himself (through a second Panamanian/Liechtenstein corporation) over $12 million in kickbacks on trades that lost $430 million to Capcom. Through "mirror-image trading," Akbar laundered more than $125 million, including millions for Manuel Noriega. Capcom's activities escaped review when it agreed to cease doing business in the U.S. in 1989. Akbar himself ended up in jail in Britain on drug trafficking charges (see the Epitaph, below).

4.   The Mid-1980s: Something Appears Wrong

By 1985, the Report states that the CIA knew about BCCI's efforts to infiltrate the U.S. banking system, and passed that information along to the U.S. Treasury and the Office of the Comptroller of the Currency. However, neither of these agencies were responsible for the regulation of First American; the CIA should have turned the information over to the Federal Reserve and/or Justice (although Treasury and the OCC did not advise their brethren, either). Regardless, the CIA continued to use the First American Bank, BCCI's secretly held subsidiary, for CIA operations. As a foreign bank whose branches were regulated by state banking officials, BCCI largely escaped federal regulator's review. This regulatory gap has since been corrected by the Foreign Bank Supervision Enhancement Act of 1991.

In 1985, the FDIC approved Ghaith Pharaon's purchase of the Independence Bank, notwithstanding their knowledge that Pharaon was a shareholder of BCCI. The FDIC did not confer with either the Federal Reserve or the OCC.

At about this same time, BCCI began to expand its operations in Latin and South America, adding seven branches in Colombia (five in Medellín alone) with reported assets of $200 million. One of BCCI's largest depositors was Jose Gonzalo Rodriguez Gacha, a known Medellín Cartel kingpin. In 1987, First American bought the National Bank of Georgia, formerly owned by Bert Lance.

5.   1988: Congressional Subcommittees Begin to Look at BCCI

By 1988, BCCI had over 400 branches in 70 countries, with reported assets of $20 billion. In February 1988, Senator Kerry's Subcommittee was authorized to investigate BCCI as a result of information received regarding Manuel Noriega's use of BCCI to launder drug money. Subpoenas for information were delayed because of an ongoing Customs/Justice undercover sting operation, "Operation C-Chase." Subcommittee depositions of various BCCI "players" in early 1989 revealed gross improprieties. Although certain information was turned over to the Justice Department, it appears that there was little interest in continuing the investigation until the same information was turned over to the Manhattan D.A.'s office. By this time, the Subcommittee's mandate had expired. Notwithstanding, Senator Kerry's staff continued to investigate until they received formal authorization to convene another Senate investigation in May 1991, this time headed by Senator Kerry.

6.   1988: BCCI Is Indicted in Federal Court in Tampa, Florida

Meanwhile, in October 1988, BCCI was indicted by a federal grand jury in Tampa, Florida, for conspiring with the Medellín Cartel to launder $32 million in illicit drug profits. The bank hired a Washington public relations firm headed by Robert Gray, who happened to be a director of First American. A January 1990 plea agreement kept BCCI alive; the bank was fined $15 million in 1990 for money-laundering activities in the U.S. and Panama (see *United States v. Awan*, 966 F.2d 1415, 11th Cir. 1992). However, pressure from an investigation by the New York (Manhattan) D.A.'s office, which had begun in 1989, kept the pressure on BCCI and prompted the Federal Reserve to renew its investigation of BCCI's secret ownership of First American, and to ultimately force BCCI out of the U.S. However, the Federal Reserve did not seek a global closure of BCCI, in part from their need to secure the cooperation of BCCI's majority shareholders, the rulers of Abu Dhabi, to provide almost $200 million to prop up First American.

7.   The Late 1980s: The Global Problems of BCCI

On the global scene, the Bank of England had concerns about BCCI as early as the late 1970s. In 1988 and 1989, they learned of BCCI's involvement in the support and financing of terrorism and drug money laundering. In early 1990, the Bank of England, Price Waterhouse, Abu Dhabi, and BCCI conducted "secret" negotiations to attempt to prevent a total collapse of BCCI, with the resulting loss of billions of dollars in deposits held by millions of people as well as hundreds of countries. A proposed reorganization of BCCI into three separate entities based in London, Hong Kong, and Abu Dhabi, in which the government of Abu Dhabi would guarantee the bank's deposits while the nature and extent of BCCI's criminality would be suppressed, was scuttled in great part because of the Manhattan D.A.'s investigation.

8.   1991: The House of Cards Comes Tumbling Down

On June 22, 1991, Price Waterhouse reported to the Bank of England that BCCI was, essentially, a house of cards. Their report, the "Sandstrom Report," chronicled outright fraud beginning as early as 1976. It was the final piece of evidence that led to the global closure of BCCI on July 5, 1991. The investigation into how, why, and where the more than $20 billion in lost deposits (not including the billions in laundered money in the "ML" and numbered accounts) continues today. In addition, questions remain as to the relationship between BCCI and financing of terrorism; the extent of BCCI's involvement in Pakistan's nuclear bomb program; BCCI's ties with the CIA and Manuel Noriega (who had a BCCI Visa card); BCCI's manipulation of European and Canadian commodities and securities markets; the relationship between BCCI and various Iraqi arms dealers, terrorists, and drug dealers; financing Iranian arms deals; and political payoffs and bribes.

9.   Epitaph

The saga of BCCI's former Treasurer, Syed Ziauddin Akbar, sums up the entire BCCI Affair. In 1991, when the scandal was unfolding, Akbar was in a British jail, serving time for drug trafficking. He was paroled and fled to France. In 1992, he was indicted in New York for grand larceny for extorting over $15 million. Meanwhile, he was charged again in Britain for his role in the BCCI Affair, extradited from France, tried, convicted, and given a six-year prison sentence. After serving three years, he was held for extradition to the U.S. However, due to jurisdictional issues raised by his attorneys in France, the extradition proceedings could not be completed, and he was released. He remains a fugitive.

The fallout from the Affair continues to this day. Auditors and forensic accountants are still trying to piece together the documents, many of which were handwritten in Farsi, or downloaded onto impenetrable computer disks, and/or filed and organized without reason in locations all over the world. Various reports, including Lord Justice Bingham's 1992 Report to Parliament entitled "Inquiry into the Supervision of the Bank of Credit and Commerce International," raise more questions than they answer. Prosecutions continue; in May 1994, Swaleh Naqvi (BCCI's number two man) was extradited to the U.S. and later pled guilty to conspiracy, wire fraud, and racketeering and sentenced to 11 years in prison and fined $225 million. In April 1997, Pakistani shipping tycoon Abbas Gokal, one of BCCI's first investors, was convicted in London in the largest fraud case to date tied to BCCI's collapse. Gokal's company, the Gulf Group, owed almost $1 billion in illegal, unsecured, and under-secured loans when BCCI collapsed in 1991. In 1994, while bedridden and dying in Pakistan, Agha Hassan Abedi was tried and convicted in absentia by a court in Abu Dhabi. He died in Pakistan in August 1995.

The lawsuits also continue. See, for example, *BCCI Holdings (Luxembourg) S.A., et al. v. Clifford, et al.*, 964 F. Supp. 468 (D. DC 1997), a suit by the court-appointed fiduciaries of the demised BCCI Group against the Group's former attorneys, including Clark Clifford and Robert Altman, for damages arising from the attorneys' alleged breach of fiduciary duty and conflicts of interest in representing all parties in the First American Bank deal.

In various RICO forfeiture proceedings brought by the U.S. government against the BCCI Group, a number of other banks have petitioned for relief from forfeiture of money or deposits held by BCCI for their credit. See, for example, the claims of American Express Bank to $23 million held by BCCI as a result of uncompleted currency transactions, described in *United States v. BCCI Holdings (Luxembourg), S.A. (petition of American Express Bank*, 961 F. Supp. 287 (D. DC 1997) (the claims were rejected because American Express continued to do business with BCCI despite the known improprieties and ongoing criminal and regulatory investigations regarding BCCI's activities). See also *United States v. BCCI Holdings (Luxembourg), S.A. (petition of Banque Indosuez*, 961 F. Supp. 282 (D. DC 1997); and other (unreported) petitions of two individuals Zaman and Bhandari (over uncompleted wire transfers); of the Central Bank of Uruguay (over BCCI's Uruguayan subsidiary); and of the State Trading Organization of the Republic of the Maldives (over a letter of credit in connection with the sale of frozen fish and over some foreign exchange accounts).

Money Laundering in Non-Bank Financial Institutions (NBFIs)

5

I. Introduction

The Bank Secrecy Act reporting requirements apply only to "financial institutions" as that term is defined in the Act. As originally enacted in 1970, section 5312 of the BSA defined the term "financial institution" as meaning any one of 19 enumerated entities. Five of these were "banks" (FDIC insured banks, commercial banks or trust companies, private banks, thrifts, and an agency or branch of a foreign bank in the U.S.) and the other 15 have become known as "non-bank financial institutions," or NBFIs. These included all SEC-registered and other securities or commodities brokers or dealers, investment banks or companies, currency exchanges, traveler's check and money order issuers, redeemers, and cashiers, operators of credit card systems, insurance companies, precious metals or jewel dealers, pawnbrokers, loan or finance companies, travel agencies, and telegraph companies. In 1986, four more entities were added to the NBFI list: any business engaged in vehicle sales (cars, planes, and boats); real estate brokers, dealers, and financiers; the U.S. Postal Service; and casinos.

Looking at this exhaustive list of NBFIs, it is clear that this term includes the entire spectrum of financial institutions operating outside the highly regulated world of banks and thrifts that engage in exchanging money, wire transfers of money, cashing checks, and selling money orders and traveler's checks. Although subject to the reporting requirements of the BSA, non-bank financial institutions generally escape notice, and are often subject to only minor state licensing requirements. The NBFIs most synonymous with money laundering are the peso–dollar exchange businesses, known as *casas de cambio;* small wire-transfer businesses known as "Giro houses"; major wire transfer, traveler check, and money order businesses such as American Express and Western Union; and insurance companies.

NBFIs are primarily regulated by the Money Laundering Suppression Act of 1994. They can be classified into two major types: money services businesses, or MSBs, whose primary business is to offer money-related services (examples of MSBs include money exchangers and check cashing services); and all other businesses that, by their nature, deal in or generate large amounts of cash.

II.   Money Services Businesses (MSBs)

A.   Proposed Regulations Relating to MSBs

Money services businesses, or MSBs, include money transmitters, traveler's check and money order issuers and sellers, retail currency exchangers, check cashers, and issuers of stored value services and cards (see Section III.C of chapter 3, *"Cybercrime and Cyberbanking,"* for a description of "Smart Cards" or stored value cards). FinCEN coined the term "money services businesses" as part of its first comprehensive study of the NBFI's potential vulnerability to money laundering. Conducted by Coopers & Lybrand, this study provides an in-depth examination of the entire MSB industry, estimated to include over 160,000 entities in the U.S., handling about $200 billion per year. They were essentially unregulated, except for state licensing requirements. However, on May 21, 1997 (relying on FinCEN's MSB study), the Treasury Department announced three proposed new regulations aimed at preventing and detecting money laundering in MSBs. These regulations also came about as a result of Operation El Dorado and a Geographic Targeting Order (GTO) operation conducted by Customs, FinCEN, the IRS, and the NYPD targeting money transmitters in the New York area (see Chapter 10, *"Law Enforcement Operations"*).

The proposed regulations were published in the Federal Register on May 21, 1997, as Notices of Proposed Rulemaking. The first regulation would first define money services businesses, and then require these entities to register with the Department of the Treasury. The second regulation would require these MSBs to report suspicious activity (in essence, extend the suspicious reporting requirements of financial institutions to the MSBs: unlike financial institutions, MSBs cannot "know their customer" because their customers do not maintain accounts). The third proposed regulation would require MSBs to maintain a current list of their authorized agents, and to report transactions in currency or monetary instruments of at least $750 (studies show the vast majority of legitimate remittances are between $200 and $500) in connection with the transmission or other transfer of funds to any person outside the U.S.

B.   Money Order Transmitters

Money order firms, or money transmitters, such as Western Union, American Express, and MoneyGram, remit upwards of $11 billion annually, exclusive of fees, through over 43,000 locations in the U.S. The vast majority of these are handled by Western Union and MoneyGram, concentrating in California, New York, Texas, New Jersey, Florida, and Illinois. A number of Geographic Targeting Orders, or GTOs, aimed at New York money transmitters are an example of the effectiveness of law enforcement efforts against money order firms (see Chapter 10, "Law Enforcement Operations").

Postal money orders have long been considered one of the safest and most efficient ways to smuggle cash and negotiable instruments out of the U.S. (due, in part, to the reliability of the U.S. Postal Service and the heightened protection the U.S. Mail is given against warrantless searches). For example, in 1992 alone, Panamanian banks negotiated over $180 million in postal money orders originating in the U.S. In response to this abuse of using postal money orders for international money laundering, the U.S. Postal Service published a final rule in 1995 that restricted the negotiation of domestic postal money orders to the U.S. itself. Consequently, if a domestic money order is mailed overseas and negotiated at a foreign bank, the U.S. Postal Service will not honor the money order when it is presented for payment by the bank.

American Express, Western Union, and Travelers Express are the three largest money transmitters in the U.S., specializing in the domestic and international transfer of funds by wire, check, computer network, and other means. Although they all claim to be free of money laundering, they are most certainly not: American Express, for example, has over 37,000 locations where it sells money orders, 19,000 of which are at NBFIs. American Express does not run criminal background checks on all of its agents, nor does it continually monitor its locations for CTR compliance. In addition, only a few states require licensing of the actual agents that perform the transfers. Senate investigators, in a 1992 probe of money laundering through NBFIs, continuously ran across American Express products being used for money-laundering purposes.

A local (for the author) example of using wire transfers to launder money was a 1992 case involving the Chelsea, Massachusetts, businesses World Travel Service, a money transmitter and franchise of Vigo Remittance Corporation of New York and World Telecom, which offered fax services, post office boxes, beeper rentals, and money exchange. Both of these businesses were owned by Dominican-born German Cadavid, who also had interests in the same businesses, but based out of Rhode Island. U.S. Customs soon noticed that these businesses appeared to be laundering money for Dominican-based drug traffickers. They set up a sting operation in which an undercover agent convinced Cadavid to handle three transfers totaling more than $100,000, which would have meant various reporting and record-keeping obligations. However, Cadavid agreed to get around these rules, and structured the transactions so that they were partitioned into $4,500 parcels in various fictitious names and transmitted over a number of days. He was arrested and convicted.

C.   Casas de Cambio

The non-bank financial institution most synonymous with money laundering are the *casas de cambio*, which are basically peso–dollar exchange businesses prevalent in the southwestern U.S. These sprang up following the devaluation of the peso in 1982. Although subject to CTR reporting requirements, their regulation and supervision is in the hands of state and local authorities, if at all. In many Central and Latin American countries, the *casas* serve as an alternative to the official banking systems.

It is estimated that 80% of the over 1,000 *casas de cambio* along the U.S.–Mexican border are involved in money laundering. Although there are hundreds of unregulated casas on both sides of the Mexican–U.S. border, very few are licensed by state banking regulators (75 in Texas, 35 in California). A joint U.S.–Mexican offensive in 1995 resulted in the seizure of $65 million in illicit funds, the arrest of 40 people, and the indictments of 40 others. The average *casa* launders approximately $5 million per month, with the largest doing over $200 million every six months. They charge between 2% and 5%. In Colombia, *casas de cambio* are known as "*giro* houses" (*giro*, pronounced "hero," means "wire" in Spanish).

III.   Casinos

A.   Regulation of Casinos

Forty-eight states now permit legal gambling. In the 10-year period from 1984 to 1994, it is estimated that gross proceeds (cash taken in) of all U.S. casinos increased from approximately $120 billion to over $400 billion (the IRS reports that in 1995, the net revenue of the U.S. gaming industry was over $44 billion on $550 billion in *legal* or reported wagers — see the Treasury Department's Office of Enforcement website at *www.treas.gov\irs\ci*). The proliferation of casinos and casino gambling has resulted in the proliferation of money laundering in casinos.

In the context of anti-money laundering efforts, casinos fall into one of three types: BSA, Nevada, or IRS (tribal) casinos. Casinos generally have been subject to BSA money-laundering rules since 1985 as non-bank financial institutions if they had gross annual gaming revenues over $1 million. Regulatory changes in 1994 required casinos to establish and maintain written BSA compliance programs. These 1994 regulations also enhanced requirements for customer identification when deposit or credit accounts are opened at casinos. Casinos have their own CTR form, called a CTR-C (IRS Form 8362).

By agreement with the Treasury Department, Nevada casinos are exempt from certain BSA reporting requirements; the Nevada Gaming Commission, with its own sophisticated suspicious activity reporting system, rivaling that of FinCEN, also monitors Nevada casinos. In February 1996, regulations to the BSA and MLCA were passed to codify authority over tribal casinos, which are casinos operated pursuant to the Indian Gaming Regulatory Act (IGRA) of 1988, by Indians who belong to one of the federally recognized tribes (such as the Mashantucket-Pequot Tribe, operators of Foxwoods Resort Casino in Ledyard, CT). Prior to 1996, tribal casinos were not required to report cash payments over $10,000.

Casinos that fall under the BSA requirements (such as those in Atlantic City and the Mississippi riverboat casinos) must identify customers who buy more than $10,000 in chips with cash, by way of a CTR-C form. Nevada and tribal casinos also are required to do this; unlike BSA casinos, however, they did not report on payouts over $10,000 in verified winnings until the 1996 amendments.

Specifically, the Code of Federal Regulations, 31 CFR section 103, requires casinos to report currency transactions over $10,000 (section 103.22(2)), to keep certain records of these and other transactions (section 103.36), and to develop and implement compliance programs (section 103.54).

On July 17, 1997, FinCEN issued a revised currency transaction report for casinos (see Chapter 8, "Regulatory (Anti-Money Laundering) Forms").

B. Laundering Money Through Casinos

Laundering money through casinos is an effective way of placing and layering illicit funds. For example, there was testimony during the 1985 Senate Hearings that in the 1970s an organized crime figure entered an Atlantic City casino with almost $1.2 million in small bills. The Bureau of Engraving estimated that the cash weighed almost 300 pounds and would have filled a large duffel bag. After sustaining some losses, this person cashed in $800,000 worth of chips for $100 bills. This cash, the Bureau estimated, weighed 16 pounds and would have fit in an attaché case. The money was deposited into a Swiss bank a few days later.

Laundering money through casinos is effective, in part, because of the huge volume of business, almost all of it in cash, done by casinos. In 1994, the gross annual gaming revenue of Nevada casinos was almost $7 billion; New Jersey casinos' GAGR was almost $3.5 billion; the 60 odd riverboat casinos was $3.3 billion; and tribal casinos $3 billion. Between 1994 and 1996, the least regulated of the casinos — the tribal — saw their GAGR increase over 50% to almost $4.7 billion on $27 billion in business — a 17% return.

Laundering money through casinos is difficult, but possible on a smaller scale. For employees, chip skimming is common. For bettors, structuring remains the method of choice. However, BSA, Nevada, and IRS regulations require that cash purchases of less than $10,000 be aggregated if they exceed $10,000 and are made in the same gaming area (in Nevada casinos, one gaming area is the blackjack tables, another is the slots, a third is roulette, etc.) within certain periods of time — BSA and Nevada use a 24-hour "gaming day," while the IRS-regulated tribal casinos use a calendar year. Therefore, cash amounts of less than $10,000 can be spread across different gaming areas (Nevada), or different gaming days (BSA and Nevada), or laundered across several different BSA, Nevada, or tribal casinos.

C.   Tribal Casinos

Tribal casinos have been called the "new buffalo" for the riches they have bestowed on the various tribes. There are now about 130 tribal casinos in 16 states. Although state-licensed casinos were brought under the BSA reporting umbrella in 1985, and Indian Tribal casinos operate no differently, they were not subject to BSA reporting requirements until the Money Laundering Suppression Act of 1994 was passed. Due to extensive lobbying by the tribal governments, the National Indian Gaming Commission (NIGC), and the National Indian Gaming Association (NIGA), these 1994 changes were watered down, so that tribal casinos enjoyed a number of advantages that other casinos did not. This changed in 1996, when Treasury used its codified authority over gaming institutions generally to equalize treatment of tribal casinos, requiring them to report and keep records, including those of their customers, as do all other casinos and gaming institutions.

D.   On-Line Casinos

In early 1997, Executone Information Systems, a Milford, Connecticut-based company, introduced the National Indian Lottery, based out of the Coeur d'Alene Reservation in Idaho. This "virtual" or "on-line" casino is available to anyone in the world with a computer and modem. However, in May 1997, the Attorney General in Missouri sued the company for violating Missouri's anti-gambling laws. Other states have taken similar action; the Minnesota Attorney General's office sued Granite Gate Resorts, Inc., for offering an Internet-based sports betting company (operating in Belize!); and Wisconsin's Attorney General sued a company for offering Internet-based gambling from a company operating out of the Cook Islands in the South Pacific.

Notwithstanding these challenges, the on-line casino is here to stay. In July 1997, the Senate Technology, Terrorism and Government Information Subcommittee heard testimony that on-line or virtual casinos now account for millions of dollars of illegal gambling per year. The number of on-line casinos has gone from zero just a few years ago (Internet access has only been practically available since 1993) to 12 in January 1997, to over 30 by July 1997. Most of these are established offshore, particularly in places such as Antigua and Belize, where regulations are, at best, lax.

In an effort to avoid excessive regulation, or even prohibition, Internet casinos have formed the Interactive Gaming Council (IGC). The IGC has professed a goal of self-regulation, and is actively involved in lobbying efforts.

The ramifications for money laundering are staggering; rather than having to wire money or provide a credit card number over the Internet, the newest breed of on-line casinos (located "offshore" and often using cellular or digital telephone technology and laptop computers) rely on encrypted "electronic money" payments (see Chapter 3, "Cybercrime and Cyberbanking), which are practically impossible to detect and control.

Senator Jon Kyl (R., Arizona), chairman of the Technology Subcommittee of the Senate Judiciary Committee, introduced a bill in March 1997 aimed at regulating Internet betting, cell-phone cloning, and telemarketing fraud. The Internet Gambling Prohibition Act of 1997 would amend the Wire Communications Act, which makes it illegal to use a telephone to contact a bookmaker, by extending that law to using modems to contact on-line or Internet gambling sites. The bill proposes sentences of six months and $2,500 fines for bettors and four years and $20,000 for online "bookies."

IV.   Card Clubs

Common in California, card clubs are casino-like operations, except that they offer only the physical facilities for gaming by customers who bet against one another, rather than against the house. In addition to gaming facilities, card clubs offer their members deposit and credit accounts, facilities for transmitting and receiving funds transfers, check cashing, and currency exchange. In 1996, card club members wagered almost $9 billion against each other. In January 1998, FinCEN issued a final rule (supplanting its December 1996 "notice of proposed rule making") that would amend the Bank Secrecy Act definition of "financial institution" to include card clubs. The result is to extend non-financial institution casino reporting and record-keeping requirements to card clubs. The final rule goes into effect on August 1, 1998.

V.   Race Tracks

Although not technically a casino, racetracks provide money launderers with the same atmosphere and opportunities to launder money as do casinos. Very simply, if you win a certain amount of money (e.g., $600 on a $2.00 bet), you must present identification to collect — the IRS is interested in such winnings. The basis for laundering money through a race track, then, is the reluctance of winners to declare their winnings to the IRS (and perhaps their spouse!). A winning ticket is negotiable, like a bearer bond, and can be sold by the winner for something less than the winning amount to "flies" or "ten percenters" (for their willingness to but the ticket at a 10% discount). These flies then present the ticket to a cooperative mutual clerk (a teller) who then dutifully fills out the proper forms — but with fictitious or manufactured identifications. The actual bettor is satisfied as he has 90% of his winnings for which he does not have to account (to the government or to his spouse!), and the launderer has been able to "clean" his money at a reasonable cost — 90% to purchase the winning bet, and a further 10% to 20% to pay off the cooperating mutual clerk.

VI.   Insurance Companies

Insurance companies, a class of non-bank financial institutions, are being used more frequently to launder money. For example, a launderer will purchase a single premium annuity under a false name or through a corporate entity. The annuity can later be canceled, with a small penalty, and the insurance company will remit a check for the balance, or wire the proceeds to a specified account. Once that is accomplished, the funds appear legitimate and can be negotiated or sent out of the U.S. at will. Any queries as to the source of the money are met by documentation of a settlement of an insurance contract. Simple schemes such as this depend on this existence of funds already having been placed into the financial system, as insurance companies (and brokers) generally do not accept cash from customers or clients.

OCDETF concluded two investigations in 1992, Operations Teal and Bramson, in which insurance brokers were indicted for money laundering when it was established that they diverted insurance premiums for their personal use, leaving the insureds completely unprotected. In other words, these brokers did not rely on their own illicit funds to launch their schemes, but instead relied on policyholders' legitimate funds. In both cases, insurance agents or brokers accepted premium payments from the victims in the form of checks, which were then deposited in financial institutions. Using a sophisticated system of holding companies, offshore bank accounts and foreign trusts, the subjects transferred premiums, commissions, and fees to various offshore bank accounts. They then "repatriated" the money by obtaining loans from these offshore banks, using the deposits as collateral. Each of these investigations involved losses of over $100 million. At no time was cash ever introduced into the system.

Offshore insurance companies are used by sophisticated launderers to place, layer, and integrate funds. For example, the launderer will purchase or create a corporation in a country with little or no insurance regulations. That corporation will then purchase or create an insurance or reinsurance company, and create some sort of legitimate sales force in the U.S., being licensed to do so on the state level by the various state Commissioners of Insurance. Cash generated from criminal activities, such as drug distribution, is then funneled through various "placement" schemes and placed with the company as insurance premiums. The company creates a realistic audit trail to give the appearance of legitimacy. Then, false claims are filed and paid to the "insured" entities or individuals, who then can "integrate" these seemingly legitimate funds into the mainstream financial world. Adding reinsurance companies (reinsurance is, at its most basic form, the insurance of insurance contracts) to the mix greatly complicates the operation.

VII. Securities Dealers and Brokers

Securities dealers and brokers — from small brokerage firms across the country to the large Wall Street securities firms — have long been the targets of money launderers. As late as March 1996, securities dealers were not required to maintain BSA compliance programs, nor did they have a standard SAR form as banks do. As a result of the Miranda case, and others, described below, brokers and securities dealers are now required to obtain taxpayer identification numbers or the passport number of each person maintaining an account. In addition, as a "financial institution," they are subject to the Bank Secrecy Act and Money Laundering Control Act reporting and record-keeping requirements set out at 31 U.S.C. section 5313 and 31 CFR sections 103.23 (reporting) and 103.35 (record-keeping). Notwithstanding these regulations, it appears that Wall Street's vigilance is lacking; an investigation conducted in 1995 revealed that of the 20,000 suspicious transactions reported to the IRS annually by the financial services industry, only about 300 originate from Wall Street investment firms. Some examples of laundering money through securities dealers and brokers include the following.

In 1986, Drexel, Burnham, Lambert investment banker Dennis Levine was arrested for laundering over $13 million in illegal (insider trading) profits through two Panamanian companies — Diamond Holdings SA and International Gold, Inc. — and the Luxembourg-registered Banque Leu in the Bahamas.

In 1988, E.F. Hutton was fined $1 million for its role in a money-laundering scheme in which the firm accepted, but did not report, large investments in cash. As a result, the firm — and all firms under the auspices of the SEC — now do not accept cash payments or deposits.

In 1994, David Witter, the grandson of Dean Witter, pled guilty to money laundering by knowingly accepting and attempting to launder over $1 million in drug profits.

In 1996, a New York-based stockbroker, Mark Simon, was convicted of various structuring offenses after he deposited more than $130,000 in cash into one account through 14 deposits at eight Citibank locations over the course of 1 week (to avoid filing a CTR for cash transactions of $10,000 or more, Simon made deposits of between $8,800 and $9,920). The case is reported as *United States v. Simon*, 85 F.3d 906 (2d Cir. 1996).

On June 2, 1997, a Miami-based Prudential Bache Securities stockbroker, Edilberto J. Miranda, was convicted on various money laundering charges. Miranda invested money, facilitated wire transfers, and bought and sold real estate for at least nine known Colombian drug traffickers, two of whom testified against him. Most of the estimated $2 million originated in the U.S., was smuggled out (placed and layered), and then brought back in for investment (integrated).

On November 25, 1997, a federal grand jury in New York indicted 19 people on racketeering charges arising from a classic "pump and dump" stock manipulation scheme. Eleven members of the Genovese and Bonanno organized crime families, six stockbrokers at Meyers Pollock Robbins, Inc., and two executives at Arizona-based HealthTech International Inc. made over $1.3 million by manipulating the stock price (Nasdaq) of HealthTech.

Part III
The Good Guys

United States Federal Government Agencies and Task Forces

6

I.   Introduction

The federal agencies or departments primarily involved in the fight against money laundering include the Justice Department (including the DEA, FBI, and OCDETF), the Department of State, the Department of the Treasury (including the OCC, Customs, the IRS, the OTS, and FinCEN), the Federal Deposit Insurance Corporation (FDIC), and the Federal Reserve Board. Other agencies include the Bureau of Alcohol, Tobacco & Firearms (ATF), the Immigration and Naturalization Service (INS), the Department of the Navy's Naval Criminal Investigative Services, the U.S. Border Patrol, the U.S. Coast Guard, and the U.S. Postal Service.

In 1986, and in order to coordinate enforcement of the (then new) MLCA, the Attorney General and the Secretary of the Treasury signed a Memorandum of Understanding (MOU), granting joint investigative authority for money laundering to four federal agencies: IRS, Customs, DEA, and the FBI. All of these agencies are described in greater detail below.

II.   Justice Department

The Justice Department is one of the five major federal governmental agencies involved in combatting money laundering. Since taking over the OCDETF's functions in September 1994, its Asset Forfeiture and Narcotics sections have been the primary units responsible for anti-money-laundering investigations.

A.   Drug Enforcement Administration (DEA)

The DEA is the principal agency involved in narcotics-related money-laundering investigations. The DEA Administrator reports to the Attorney General through the Director of the FBI. There are 21 regional offices in the U.S., each responsible for its own geographic area. In addition to these domestic offices, the DEA maintains approximately 70 offices in 55 foreign countries. Its total budget is just over $1 billion (compared to the Cali Cartel's annual "profits" of over $8 billion!). The DEA maintains an extensive facility, called the El Paso Intelligence Center (EPIC), that maintains a database on drug cartels, transportation systems, money laundering, etc., which it shares with other federal agencies.

B.   Federal Bureau of Investigation (FBI)

The FBI is the Justice Department's principal investigative arm. Its roots go back to 1908, when Attorney General Charles Bonaparte created a a force of "Special Agents" to act as the DOJ's investigators. This force was renamed the Bureau of Investigation in 1909. Following a number of minor name changes, the Federal Bureau of Investigation was officially created in 1935.

The FBI's self-described mission is "to uphold the law through the investigation of violations of federal criminal statutes; to protect the United States from hostile intelligence efforts; [and] to provide assistance to foreign and other U.S. federal, state, and local law enforcement agencies".*

Along with DEA, the FBI is one of the principal federal agencies engaged in anti-money-laundering efforts. The FBI has primary investigative jurisdiction over violations of federal criminal law not specifically assigned to another investigative agency by statute. The FBI has concurrent jurisdiction with the DEA in drug-related crimes.

The FBI has identified five areas of major concern: counter-terrorism, drugs and organized crime, foreign counterintelligence, violent crime, and white-collar crime. In 1995, the FBI opened an international police training academy in Budapest, Hungary, to promote anti-drug smuggling and money-laundering expertise. It has also established offices in Moscow (1994) and Denmark (1995) to monitor money laundering emanating from or through the Eastern Bloc. The FBI also maintains what might be the largest database on crime, criminals, and related matters — the National Crime Information Center (NCIC).

C.   Organized Crime Drug Enforcement Task Force (OCDETF)

In 1982, the Department of Justice initiated this program and task force to mount coordinated investigations involving all federal investigative agencies, state and local law enforcement, and the various U.S. Attorneys' offices (and,

---

* Quoted from the FBI's "official" website at *http://www.odci/gov/ic/usic/fbi.html.*

to some extent, foreign law enforcement). Until 1994, there was a special Money Laundering Section; it was abolished and its functions (generally to provide advice and assistance in the prosecution of money-laundering offenses) and personnel divided between the Asset Forfeiture and Narcotics sections of the Justice Department.

OCDETF (pronounced Oh-Sah-Deaf) has conducted over 5,000 major investigations since its inception. In 1992, it had 875 ongoing investigations, 75% of which involved money-laundering. Virtually every major money laundering investigation in the U.S. has been handled through OCDETF.

III. Department of State

A. Introduction

The U.S. Department of State is actively involved in anti-money-laundering efforts; its annual International Narcotics Control Strategy Report, last released in February 1998, is an excellent source of information. Among other things, the Report includes country-by-country profiles of approximately 200 nations, and a comparative ranking according to their efforts to control and prevent money laundering.

The Department of State's Bureau for International Narcotics and Law Enforcement Affairs, Office of International Criminal Justice (INL/ICJ), has developed a program of multi-agency training to address international organized crime, financial crime, and narcotics trafficking. During 1997, the INL budgeted and spent over $36 million on developing and sponsoring a number of anti-money-laundering training sessions and technical assistance missions throughout the world.

B. Certification of Drug-Producing/Transit Countries

Each year, the State Department's Bureau for International Narcotics and Law Enforcement Affairs (the INL) releases its "International Narcotics Control Strategy Report," which serves as the basis for a determination of which countries are identified as being narcotics-producing or narcotics-transit countries, and whether and what steps they are taking to combat narcotics production, distribution, and money laundering. Working with other federal agencies, the INL submits this report to the President who identifies which of these countries are subject to a "certification" process by the President. Essentially, the President must certify that the "major" drug-producing or transit countries on this list — in 1997, there were 32; in 1998, there were 30 — have cooperated fully with the U.S. and taken the necessary steps to meet the goals and objectives of the 1988 U.N. Convention Against Illicit

Narcotics Drugs and Psychotropic Substances (known as the Vienna Convention, described in detail in Section II.B of Chapter 12, *International Organizations and Treaties*).

The INL considers 16 elements in determining whether a country is cooperating in the fight against international drug trafficking and money laundering. These elements are:

1. Criminalized drug money laundering: whether the government has enacted laws criminalizing money laundering related to drug trafficking
2. Record large transactions: whether banks and financial institutions are required, by law or regulation, to maintain records of large transactions in currency or other monetary instruments (a "know your customer" policy is a prerequisite for satisfaction of this element)
3. Maintain records over time: whether banks and financial institutions are required, by law or regulation, to keep records of large or unusual transactions for a specified period of time, with 5 years considered the benchmark (again, a "know your customer" policy is a prerequisite for satisfaction of this element)
4. Report suspicious transactions: whether banks and financial institutions are required *or permitted,* by law or regulation, to record and report suspicious or unusual transactions to designated authorities
5. System of identifying and forfeiting assets: whether the government has enacted laws authorizing the tracing, seizure, freezing, and forfeiture of assets identified as relating to or being generated by certain criminal offenses, including drug trafficking and money laundering
6. Asset sharing: whether the government permits the sharing of seized assets with third-party governments that assisted in the underlying investigation (this element requires both domestic laws and regulations and bilateral treaties or agreements)
7. Cooperates with domestic law enforcement: whether banks are required, by law or regulation, to cooperate with domestic law enforcement agencies in criminal investigations, including the production of banking records
8. Cooperates with international law enforcement: whether banks are required, by law, regulation, or bilateral agreement, to cooperate with third-party governments' law enforcement agencies in criminal investigations, including the sharing of banking records
9. International transportation of currency: whether the government controls or (at least) monitors the flow of currency and monetary instruments crossing its borders or entering its domestic financial markets, particularly through the use of wire-transfer regulations,

customer identification reports, and control of money exchange and remittance businesses

10. Mutual legal assistance: whether the government has agreed, through formal MLATs or otherwise, to provide and receive mutual legal assistance, including the sharing of data and records

11. Non-drug money laundering: whether the government has extended anti-money-laundering statutes and regulations to include non-drug-related money laundering

12. Non-bank financial institutions: whether the government, by law or regulation, requires non-bank financial institutions (NBFIs) to meet the same customer identification standards and to adhere to the same reporting and record-keeping requirements that it imposes on its banks

13. Disclosure protection: whether the domestic laws provide "safe harbor" protections to banks or other financial institutions that provide otherwise confidential banking data to authorities

14. Offshore banking: whether the government authorizes the licensing of offshore banking facilities

15. 1988 Vienna Convention: whether the government has formally ratified the 1988 United Nations Convention Against Illicit Trafficking in Narcotic Drugs and Psychotropic Substances

16. Compliance: whether the government actually is meeting the goals and objectives of the Vienna Convention

The certification process is required by section 490 of the Foreign Assistance Act of 1961. The Act requires the President to create a list of "majors," or countries, that are subject to the certification process (as stated above, there are 30 such countries on the 1998 list). Once so designated, a country is subject to one of three determinations by the President: full certification, a denial of certification, or a "national interests" certification. The decision of the President can be overturned by a joint resolution of Congress within 30 days.

If the President denies certification, there is a complete cut-off of all foreign aid except for humanitarian and counter-narcotics assistance. In addition, the U.S. will then vote against any loans or other assistance from the World Bank and other like development banks. The Act also gives the President the ability to deny certification but nevertheless continue foreign aid if it is in the "vital national interests" of the U.S. to do so.

On February 26, 1998, the President signed Presidential Determination No. 98-15, a memo to the Secretary of State, entitled "Certification for Major Illicit Drug Producing and Drug Transit Countries." Twenty-two of the thirty major countries were granted full certification; four, including Colombia, were given "vital national interest" certification; and four were denied certification:

> *Full Certification:* Aruba, Bahamas, Belize, Bolivia, Brazil, China, Dominican Republic, Ecuador, Guatemala, Haiti, Hong Kong, India, Jamaica, Laos, Malaysia, Mexico, Panama, Peru, Taiwan, Thailand, Venezuela, Vietnam
>
> *Vital National Interest Certification:* Cambodia, Colombia, Pakistan, Paraguay
>
> *Denied Certification:* Afghanistan, Burma (Myanmar), Iran, Nigeria

The certification process is seen by the U.S. Government as an integral and highly effective part of its anti-drug efforts. Its stated purpose is not to punish those countries that are denied certification, but to use the threat of economic sanctions to hold all countries to "an acceptable standard of cooperation" in the worldwide fight against drug production, distribution, and consumption.

IV. Department of the Treasury

One of the five major "players" among the various federal agencies involved in the fight against money laundering, the Treasury Department is organized into 12 bureaus and 11 offices. The 12 bureaus are Alcohol, Tobacco & Firearms (ATF); Bureau of Engraving and Printing (BEP); Bureau of Public Debt; Office of the Comptroller of the Currency (OCC); Federal Law Enforcement Training Council (FLETC); Financial Crimes Enforcement Network (FinCEN); Financial Management Service; Internal Revenue Service (IRS); Office of Thrift Supervision (OTS); the United States Customs Service (USCS); the United States Mint; and the United States Secret Service (USSS). The 11 offices are: Archives; the Office of Budget Execution; the Office of the Chief Financial Officer and Council; the Office of Chief Information Officer; the Office of Domestic Finance; the Office of Equal Opportunity Programs; the Office of Enforcement; the Office of Foreign Assets Control (OFAC); the Office of Public Correspondence; the Office of Small and Disadvantaged Business Utilization; and the Office of Tax Policy.

The Treasury Department's money-laundering efforts are shared by seven bureaus (OCC, FLETC, FinCEN, IRS, OTS, Customs, and the Secret Service) and two offices (Enforcement and OFAC). Distinct organizations, each one is described herein. Five of these nine agencies — FinCEN, Enforcement, Customs, the IRS's Criminal Investigation Division (CID), and OFAC —

operate under the oversight authority of the Treasury Department's Under Secretary (Enforcement), James Johnson. The other four bureaus come within the purview of the Under Secretary of Domestic Finance. (Within the organizational structure of the Treasury Department, three Under Secretaries — International Affairs, Domestic Finance, and Enforcement — report to the Deputy Secretary, who reports to the Secretary).

A.   Office of the Comptroller of the Currency (OCC)

The Office of the Comptroller of the Currency (OCC) charters, regulates, and supervises over 3,600 national banks. It is also responsible for BSA compliance examinations of these banks. The examinations of banks with more than $1 billion in assets are performed biannually; all others are examined randomly (with about 1/6 of these others covered each year). The Comptroller's Office publishes Examiner's Manuals for large banks to ensure that their personnel are trained in all aspects of the BSA regulatory and reporting requirements.* The OCC notifies the banking community of particularly relevant matters through "Alerts" published by year and volume number. For example, Alert 98-4, published February 6, 1998, notified the banking community of a "Suspicious Transaction — Industrial Bank, Inc." The OCC also publishes Advisory Letters (e.g., "AL-98-02"), which are published in response to particular inquiries by member banks. Finally, the OCC promulgates formal and binding rules on member banks by way of Bulletins (e.g., "OCC 98-4"). These Bulletins first notify the banking community of the OCC's Introductory Rulings. After a period of time for comment and review, an IR is published as a Notice of Proposed Rulemaking. Once the proposed Rule is adopted, it is published as a Final Rule.

B.   United States Customs Service (USCS)

The U.S. Customs Service, headed by Commissioner George J. Weise, is primarily involved in policing U.S. ports of entry. Customs is the Treasury Department's front-line defense against narcotics and contraband interdiction and cash smuggling.

In 1997, Customs processed over 457 million people, 126 million vehicles, and $800 billion in trade, and collected over $22 billion in duties, taxes, and fees. These figures are impressive when compared to the resources available; there are only 6,200 Customs agents assigned to patrol 11,000 miles of coastline, 7,000 miles of land borders, and to police more than 300 air, land, and sea ports of entry. (For a detailed look at the U.S. Customs Service's law

---

* The OCC maintains an excellent website at *http://www.occ.treas.gov*.

enforcement role, see "Smuggling" in Chapter 2, "Money-Laundering Techniques and Tools.")

1.   Customs Service Currency Interdiction Efforts

The BSA requires any person transporting monetary instruments worth more than $10,000 into or out of the U.S. to declare those instruments (including cash) by way of a CMIR form. Failure to file the form — whether inbound or outbound — amounts to "smuggling" and subjects the smuggled instruments to seizure and forfeiture, and the smuggler to arrest and prosecution. In the 4 years prior to September 1992, Customs seized $171 million in outbound, smuggled currency and monetary instruments, almost $50 million of which was seized at New York's JFK Airport. In 1992 alone, Customs made 862 seizures of currency and monetary instruments valued at $42.4 million. These inspectors, organized through Operation Buckstop, have become increasingly effective in targeting certain types of outbound carriers, certain geographic locations, and particular modes of transportation (air and ocean carriers remain the most common smuggling vehicles) but still lack the resources to become truly effective.

2.   Customs Service Narcotics Interdiction Efforts

In 1996, Customs seized more narcotics than all other federal agencies combined: 774,711 pounds of marijuana, 180,947 pounds of cocaine, and 2,895 pounds of heroin. The majority of the marijuana seizures (70%) occur on the Mexico–U.S. border (the southwest border — see "Operation Hard Line" in Chapter 10); and Southern Florida remains the major point of entry for cocaine (42% of the total domestic cocaine seizures).

Beginning in February 1998, Customs embarked on a 6-month concentrated operation to increase drug seizures at "high-risk" ports of entry. This operation, dubbed "Operation Brass Ring," is described in detail in Chapter 10, "Law Enforcement Operations."

3.   Seizures and Forfeitures by Customs

U.S. Customs seizes prohibited property (narcotics, hazardous materials), restricted property (subject to trade embargoes), or undeclared or under-declared property that a person or company attempts to import in violation of U.S. law.

Once the property is seized, the importer and anyone else deemed to have an interest in the property receives a Notice of Seizure, listing the items seized, the law or laws violated, and the importer's options to contest the seizure (petition rights, whether and how to elect judicial or administrative proceedings).

After initial seizure, the property is turned over to the port's Fines, Penalties & Forfeiture Officer (FPFO), who assigns the case to a specialist. If the importer seeks to have his case determined by filing a petition for administrative relief, the specialist reviews the importer's petition (setting out his or its version of the facts and circumstances), together with the Customs report, and makes a recommendation. The options are limited. The specialist can recommend to: forfeit some or all of the property and issue a penalty; release the property; or return some or all of the property upon payment of a sum of money based on the value of the property in lieu of forfeiture.

If the importer does not petition for administrative relief, or fails to comply with the specialist's decision, forfeiture proceedings are initiated. First, public notice of the proceedings are published in various local or national trade and other publications, depending on the type and value of the property sought for forfeiture. If there are no claimants to the property, or any claimants cannot prove their legitimate and innocent ownership of the property, it is forfeited to the government. Depending on the type of property, it may be destroyed, shared with other government agencies, retained for Customs use (radios, computers, etc.), or sold at auction (jewelry, boats, cars, etc.). For a detailed look at seizures and forfeitures, see Chapter 9, "Asset Forfeiture."

C. Internal Revenue Service (IRS)

One of the few absolutes in the United States today (and since 1917) is that all income is taxable. The term "all income" includes illegally earned, unreported, and under-reported income (a fact that Al Capone learned the hard way when he was charged with and convicted of income tax evasion in 1932). Therefore, it follows that the agency responsible for collecting all income and other non-tariff taxes, the IRS, must or should have a great role in investigating and detecting money laundering.

In fact, the IRS plays a dual role in money laundering. Its Examination Division has the regulatory responsibility for ensuring BSA compliance of all non-banking institutions and of all businesses. Among other tools, IRS regulations require the submission (to Detroit) of all Form 8300s. In 1992, the IRS conducted 3,350 compliance examinations of non-bank financial institutions and 8,178 compliance examinations of businesses subject to the Form 8300 requirements. The IRS also maintains a database, separate from FinCEN's, on all Form 8300 reports. This information is only available to the IRS itself, FinCEN (but not through Project Gateway), and the U.S. Customs Service.

The second role of the IRS is carried out by its Criminal Investigation Division (CID), which conducts investigations of all general financial crimes.

The CID was created in 1917 (as the "Intelligence Unit") in response to widespread tax fraud after the enactment of the Revenue Act of 1917. Because the IRS is concerned with collecting income taxes and enforcing the various tax laws, the IRS-CID investigations into fraud, money laundering, or narcotics offenses (and any other activity that generates legal or illegal income) are from the perspective of income; under-reported income, over-reported expenses, or non-reported income. These elements, taken alone or together, create what is known as the "tax gap," which is the total true tax liability less taxes paid voluntarily; in other words, what Americans really owe versus what they pay, either by under or not reporting income, or by over-reporting deductible expenses. The estimated tax gap is over $125 billion per year, and over half of the IRS-CID enforcement activity focuses on tax investigations of *legal* income to reduce this tax gap.

As a result of these elements of financial crimes, the CID has divided its investigative efforts into two areas: fraud and narcotics. Both of these areas generate unreported or under-reported income that, if desired to be spent, must be "laundered." Therefore, money laundering is an element of most CID fraud investigations, such as excise tax fraud (see Section II.B of Chapter 1, "Transnational Criminal Organizations" for a review of the Russian Mafiya's gas tax scams); gaming fraud (see Section III of Chapter 5, "Money Laundering in Non-Bank Financial Institutions" for a review of casinos); general white-collar income tax fraud; healthcare fraud (estimated by the IRS to cost each American family almost $450 per year), including fraudulent home healthcare schemes, false claims, kickbacks or bribes, and staged accidents; insurance fraud (see Section VI of Chapter 5, "Money Laundering in Non-Bank Financial Institutions" for a review of insurance companies), including fraudulent property and casualty claims, staged car accidents, reinsurance fraud, and premium diversion; pension plan fraud (with $3.5 trillion invested in private pension plans, the potential for fraud and theft is staggering); public corruption; and telemarketing fraud.

Notwithstanding this long shopping list of pure fraud areas, approximately 65% of CID's money-laundering investigations either focus on or relate back to illegal income generated from narcotics sales. Therefore, whether the CID initiates a tax investigation and discovers narcotics-related income, or is called in to work the "income" side of a narcotics case, it is the one agency that is involved in almost every major money laundering case at the local, state, or federal level. Often, the ability of the CID to analyze and reconstruct a drug organization's financial activity as it relates to unreported income leads back to the source of the illegal funds; the source often being the narcotics production and distribution kingpins and organizations.

The CID has a long and stellar history in combating narcotics-related money laundering. As set out above, the CID was created in 1917. The first

IRS narcotics-related investigation appears to have occurred in 1919, when a Hawaiian opium dealer was prosecuted for income tax evasion. It wasn't until 1976, however, that the IRS formally began working with the DEA (by way of a Memorandum of Understanding, or MOU) to focus on narcotics-related cases.

In 1980, CID teamed up with Customs and the Narcotics and Dangerous Drug Section of the Department of Justice in a task force dubbed "Operation Greenback," an operation in south Florida that coined the term "smurfing" to describe the "little people" that were used by the launderers to deposit narcotics cash into banks. The work of this task force led to, among other things, the criminalizing of "structuring" transactions to avoid reporting requirements. In 1983, the CID teamed up with the DEA, among other agencies, in the Organized Crime Drug Enforcement Task Force, or OCDETF program. By 1992, the CID made or was responsible for 1,669 seizures totaling $165.5 million in money laundering-related matters.

In 1994, the CID established a "National Strategy for the Enforcement of Money Laundering and Currency Reporting Laws." The thrust of this report was a more focused strategy, targeting the larger and more sophisticated launderers. In the three years following the Report, the CID initiated over 7,500 investigations, recommending prosecution on over 5,600. The CID effected over 3,800 seizures of assets totaling over $236 million.

In 1996, the CID became a "founding member" of the Interagency Coordinating Group (ICG), established to share narcotics money laundering intelligence for multi-agency investigations. The other member agencies include DEA, Customs, Postal Service, FBI, Justice, and FinCEN.

D. Office of Thrift Supervision (OTS)

The Office of Thrift Supervision is the primary regulator of all federal- and many state-chartered thrift institutions. It was established as a Treasury Department bureau in 1989. The OTS has five regional offices: Jersey City, Atlanta, Chicago, Dallas, and San Francisco.

The OTS is responsible for conducting BSA compliance inspections of the nation's thrifts. Inspections are conducted biannually for those with a satisfactory compliance rating, and every six months for those without.

The importance of the OTS in the fight against money laundering comes from its supervision over thrift holding companies. Thrift holding companies have historically been less structured or regulated than Federal Reserve System bank holding companies. The thrift holding companies also have had broader powers to own and operate thrift (savings and loan) institutions than those given to Federal Reserve holding companies to own and operate banks. At the risk of oversimplifying a horribly complex topic, holding companies that own a single thrift are generally allowed to engage in almost any activities that "do not threaten the safety and soundness" of their subsidiary thrift institution (for a mind-numbing but editorial-free look at the range of permissible activities, see the governing Savings and Loan Holding Company Act of 1967 and its regulatory sisters, the 1956 and 1970 Bank Holding Company Acts, and the Glass-Steagall Act of 1933).

With the savings and loan debacle of the 1980s still fresh in our minds, it appears reasonable to assume that money launderers are actively using OTS-regulated thrifts to launder money; there are over 1,300 such thrifts, with assets of almost $800 billion. Over half of these thrifts are in turn controlled by holding companies, which can conduct any other type of business so long as they "do not threaten the safety and soundness" of their subsidiary thrift institution.

E.   Financial Crimes Enforcement Network (FinCEN)*

In many ways, FinCEN is the most important of the six Treasury Department organizations involved in anti-money-laundering operations. FinCEN was created on April 25, 1990, by Treasury Order 105-08 to provide strategic analysis and intelligence to foreign, federal, and state law enforcement and regulatory organizations concerning financial crimes in general and money laundering in particular. In 1994, it was given BSA regulatory responsibilities, and in 1996 was given sole responsibility for SARs.

Located in Vienna, Virginia, FinCEN employs approximately 200 people in 12 offices, as well as analysts and agents ("detailees") from 14 other federal law enforcement and regulatory agencies. FinCEN is the United States' Financial Intelligence Unit, as established pursuant to an FATF initiative. The director of FinCEN is Stanley E. Morris.

FinCEN maintains a financial database that contains the data from all of the reports generated nationwide under the BSA. In 1994 alone, FinCEN assisted 150 agencies in over 6,000 investigations.

In October 1994, Treasury's Office of Financial Enforcement was merged with FinCEN to create a single agency for prescribing BSA reporting requirements. Since 1996, FinCEN has been the sole location for financial institutions to submit Suspicious Activity Reports (SARs). Prior to 1996, financial institutions filed CTRs to the IRS in Detroit. If the bank elected to note that the subject of the CTR was suspicious, the CTR form itself had to be checked. Criminal Referral Reports were also filed with different federal agencies, including FinCEN, the IRS, and the FBI (each of which had their own form). Through lobbying efforts of the American Bankers Association, regulations were passed in 1996 so that banks could file one Suspicious Activity Report

* See FinCEN's website at *http://www.ustreas.gov/treasury/bureaus/fincen.*

(SAR) with one agency, FinCEN. Note that FinCEN does "not" have access to the IRS Form 8300.

Since March 1996, FinCEN has published "Advisories," organized by volume and issue, which sets out current issues of concern. FinCEN is also working with a system to promote "proactive" investigations of money laundering through its FAIS (artificial intelligence) computer system.

In 1997, FinCEN and the Caribbean Financial Action Task Force (CFATF, described in Chapter 12, "International Organizations and Treaties") co-sponsored a Casino Regulatory Conference aimed at identifying money laundering methods, trends, and patterns unique to the gambling industry, and to develop effective anti-money-laundering measures. In July 1997, FinCEN issued the first comprehensive study of money services businesses (MSBs) and their vulnerability to money laundering (see the detailed discussion of MSBs in Chapter 5, "Money Laundering in Non-Bank Financial Institutions").

1. Office of Financial Enforcement (OFE)

The Office of Financial Enforcement, or OFE, was responsible for collection and maintenance of the BSA report databases at Detroit (IRS) and Virginia (FinCEN) until it was merged into FinCEN in 1994. The OFE still works in the areas of promulgating regulations regarding the BSA for Treasury, and is currently working with the Federal Reserve Board to promulgate regulations regarding wire transfers. The OFE was also responsible for imposing civil sanctions against violators of the BSA when such violations were brought through to their attention by the IRS, Customs, DEA, FBI, Justice, or federal or state regulators.

2. FinCEN Artificial Intelligence System (FAIS)

FinCEN's extensive computing capabilities were enhanced in March 1993 with an "artificial intelligence" computer system designed to promote "proactive" investigations of money laundering. Called by its acronym FAIS, this system has the job of examining all of the BSA reports submitted with a goal of generating "proactive" targeting data.

3. Project Gateway

A major initiative of FinCEN has been Project Gateway, which allows state and local law enforcement direct, on-line access to FinCEN's databases, including the 100 million BSA reports in the Treasury database, a database that shows who has made queries on the same suspects (called the "Alert" system, which coordinates queries between states on the same target or subject, allowing for interstate cooperation), and the sophisticated manipulations capabilities of the FinCEN system. In addition, queries through Project Gateway can include access to all major commercial and state databases (Dun

& Bradstreet, Social Security indexes, airplane and boat registries, land ownership, corporation and partnership records, RMV records, etc.).

Project Gateway was fully implemented in 1995. To date, use is concentrated among a few states; five states account for about one-half of all monthly queries. Project Gateway users have been trained in all 50 states, Washington, D.C., and, in the near future, Puerto Rico. This Project is now active in 48 states; from October 1996 to March 1997, there were 27,560 queries made by various state and local law enforcement agencies.

F.   Office of Foreign Assets Control (OFAC)

Acting under Presidential Directives through the International Emergency Economic Powers Act (see Chapter 7, "Domestic Money Laundering Statutes and Laws"), OFAC administers and enforces economic and trade sanctions against targeted countries, terrorists, and drug traffickers. Sanctions are currently in place against Iran, Iraq, Libya, the Yugoslavian states of Serbia, Montenegro, and Serb-controlled Bosnia, Cuba, North Korea, Myanmar, and Sudan; more than 400 Colombian drug traffickers, called Specially Designated Narcotics Traffickers (SDNTs), have also been sanctioned through the efforts of OFAC. A complete list of these SDNTs is set out in Section II.E of Chapter 1, "Transnational Criminal Organizations."

G.   United States Secret Service (USSS)

The United States Secret Service was established in 1865 to combat currency counterfeiting. In 1901, its charter was increased to include protective responsibility for the President. Later, changes to the charter added the protection of the Vice-President and visiting world leaders to the Secret Service's duties.

The Secret Service's investigative authority currently extends to include a variety of financial crimes. Its Financial Crimes Division investigates bank and financial institution fraud. Since the enactment of the Crime Control Act of 1984 (see Chapter 7, "Domestic Money Laundering Statutes and Laws"), the FCD's Electronic Crimes Branch has been responsible for investigating credit card and access device fraud (violations of 18 U.S.C. section 1029) and computer fraud (violations of 18 U.S.C. s. 1030). The American Banking Association has identified access device fraud and the production of counterfeit negotiable instruments using desktop publishing technology as the two biggest areas of bank fraud.

H.   Federal Law Enforcement Training Council (FLETC)

FLETC, pronounced *Flet-C* is Treasury's central training agency. Opened in 1970, FLETC is used by over 70 state and federal agencies for over 200 different training programs, including money laundering and asset forfeiture programs offered by FLETC's Financial Fraud Institute (FFI). In addition, over 5,000 foreign law enforcement officials from 102 countries have received training at FLETC.

FLETC has two principal offices: its main training center in Glynco, Georgia, and a second location in Artesia, New Mexico. FLETC's Director, Charles F. Rinkevich, resigned March 8, 1998. He was replaced by a career Secret Service agent, W. Ralph Basham.

V.   Federal Deposit Insurance Corporation (FDIC)

The FDIC conducts biannual BSA compliance inspections of the 7,100 insured, state-chartered banks that are not members of the Federal Reserve system, as well as the (approximately) 50 insured, state-licensed branches of foreign banks.

VI.   Federal Reserve Board

The Federal Reserve Board is one of the five major "players" among the various federal agencies involved in the fight against money laundering. It is responsible for the annual BSA compliance examinations of state banks that are members of the Federal Reserve, and also American branches of foreign banks (the examinations of the approximately 7,100 state-chartered banks that are not part of the Federal Reserve are carried out by the FDIC). The Board shares responsibility with Treasury in developing regulations regarding wire transfers of funds. For a detailed discussion of the Federal Reserve Board and the banking industry in general, see Chapter 4, "Money Laundering in the Banking Industry."

VII.   Office of National Drug Control Policy (ONDCP)

Established by President Clinton, the Executive (White House)-level Office of National Drug Control Policy is a executive level "clearing house" for drug policies and initiatives. The ONDCP administers the highly effective HIDTA Program, or High Intensity Drug Trafficking Area Program, which identifies drug problem areas and then creates and coordinates local, state, and federal task forces to combat them (see Chapter 12, "Investigative Techniques").

The ONDCP is headed by the "Drug Czar," former Marine Corps General Barry McCaffrey. On September 16, 1997, General McCaffrey reported to

Congress that Mexico had made significant progress in implementing its new anti-money laundering laws, reforming its judiciary, and establishing a corruption-free anti-narcotics unit.

The ONDCP has the legal authority to certify the amount the Defense Department budgets each year on "drug control programs." For example, the Pentagon's proposed 1999 drug control budget (released in November 1997) was originally set at $809 million, almost the same amount as budgeted for 1998 and only 1.3% more than 1990. General McCaffrey advised Defense Secretary William Cohen that the ONDCP would not certify that budget unless a further $141 million was added — $75 million for cocaine interdiction efforts in the Andes region of South America, $24 million for U.S. interdiction and monitoring efforts along the Mexican border, $30 million increase in spending for the National Guard's counterdrug operations, and $12 million for drug interdiction efforts in the Caribbean.

VIII. Central Intelligence Agency

The CIA, established by the National Security Act of 1947, is an independent agency, responsible to the President through the Director of Central Intelligence (DCI) and accountable to the U.S. Congress through various intelligence oversight committees.

The mission of the CIA is to support the President, the National Security Council, and federal officials who make and execute U.S. national security policy by providing foreign intelligence and conducting counterintelligence activities and other functions related to foreign intelligence and national security, as directed by the President, through a variety of clandestine and overt means.*

The CIA is organized into various multidisciplinary "centers," such as nonproliferation, counter-terrorism, counterintelligence, international organized crime and narcotics trafficking, and arms control intelligence.

* See the CIA's website at *http://www.odci.gov/ic/usic/cia.html.*

Part IV
Anti-Money-Laundering Tools

Domestic Money-Laundering Statutes and Laws

7

I.   Milestones in American Anti-Money-Laundering Efforts

1970: Three important statutes were passed. First, the **Bank Secrecy Act,** or BSA, codified at 31 U.S.C. ss. 5311–5322, required certain banks and other financial and non-bank financial institutions to retain records and report certain financial transactions over $10,000. Structuring transactions to avoid the reporting requirements, and money laundering itself, were not criminal offenses. Second, Congress passed the Organized Crime Control Act, Title IX of which was the **RICO Statute,** which included both civil and criminal forfeiture provisions. Third, Congress directed its attention specifically at major drug trafficking organizations by passing the **Continuing Criminal Enterprise Statute,** codified at 21 U.S.C. ss. 848 *et seq.,* as part of the Controlled Substances Act of 1970. The CSA also contained forfeiture provisions. However, neither RICO nor CCE forfeitures were commonly used (due to procedural defects) until the enactment of the Comprehensive Crime Control Act of 1984.

    1974: The constitutionality of the BSA was upheld by the United States Supreme Court in *California Bankers Assn. v. Shultz.*

    1984: The BSA, RICO, and CCE statutes were amended by the Comprehensive Crime Control Act of 1984. This new statute cleaned up some procedural problems with forfeitures, and also added section 5323 to the BSA to provide for rewards for informants in cases where the government recovered more than $50,000 (the reward was the lesser of 25% of the amount recovered or $150,000).

    1985: Casinos became subject to BSA requirements.

    1986: The Anti-Drug Abuse Act of 1986 (Pub. l. 99-570) was passed. Subtitle H was the Money Laundering Control Act (MLCA) of 1986, incorporated as part of chapter 53 of Title 31. Money-laundering and structuring transactions so as to avoid reporting requirements became crimes; the MLCA made the laundering of monetary instruments a crime (31 U.S.C. s. 5316), and criminalized structuring financial transactions so as to avoid the BSA reporting requirements (31 U.S.C. s. 5324).

In addition, the Federal Sentencing Guidelines were passed. Part S of chapter 2 sets out the guidelines for money-laundering and monetary transaction reporting violations.

1988: The MLCA was amended by the addition of section 5325, which compelled financial institutions to obtain identification from customers purchasing certain monetary instruments.

1990: A number of events took place that bear on money laundering. First, FinCEN was formed. Second, the World Wide Web was "created" by a non-profit group led by American Tim Berners-Lee. It was this group that was credited by many with developing the three technical keystones of the Web: the language for encoding documents (HTML, hypertext markup language), the system for linking documents (HTTP, hypertext transfer protocol), and the "www.whatever" system for addressing documents (URL, universal resource locator).

1991: The collapse of the Soviet Union on Christmas Day, coupled with the Balkanization of Eastern Europe, are perhaps the single biggest factors in the globalization of organized crime.

1992: The Annunzio-Wylie Anti-Money Laundering Act was passed, amending the BSA to require financial institutions' officers to report any suspicious transactions by way of a Suspicious Activity Report (SAR). The Act also allowed for the forfeiture of "substitute assets" (see Chapter 10, "Asset Forfeiture").

1994: The Money Laundering Suppression Act (MLSA) was passed, easing some of the reporting requirements of the BSA, expanding the Exempt Businesses list, and loosening the criteria to get on the list. Also, casinos became subject to stricter requirements for customer identification.

1995: For the first time, BSA reporting rules became applicable to wire transfers by the addition of section 5330 to Title 31, in force as of May 1996. The CTR form was revised, reducing the information needed by 30%.

1996: SAR forms were simplified, and could be filed with only one agency, FinCEN, replacing six overlapping methods of reporting. Tribal casinos became subject to BSA requirements. Regulations relating to exempt businesses were further revised.

II.   Evolution of American Money-Laundering Laws

A.   Bank Secrecy Act of 1970 (BSA) 31 U.S.C. ss. 5311-5324

The Bank Secrecy Act of 1970, formally known as Title II of the Currency And Foreign Transaction Reporting Act of 1970, is the cornerstone of bank reporting requirements. The express purpose of the BSA, codified at 31 U.S.C. ss. 5311-5314, 5316-5324, was to create a paper trail of suspicious activity for law enforcement, and to provide sanctions for laundering money. Section 5311 ("Declaration of Purpose") provides that "[i]t is the purpose of this subchapter ... to require certain reports or records where they have a high degree of usefulness in criminal, tax, or regulatory investigations or proceedings."

The BSA requires banks and other financial institutions to produce certain reports or records for use to combat customs, tax, and criminal violations. The Office of the Comptroller of the Currency (the OCC) is responsible for BSA compliance examinations of the 3,600 national banks. Examinations of banks with more than $1 billion in assets are done biannually; examinations of all others are done randomly (with about 1/6 of these others covered each year). The Office of Thrift Supervision (OTS), also a branch of the Treasury Department, is responsible for conducting BSA compliance inspections of the nation's thrifts.

The centerpiece of the BSA is a requirement that financial institutions file an IRS Form 4789, Currency Transaction Report (CTR), whenever an individual or a person acting on the individual's behalf conducts one or more transaction(s) in a single day that involves, in the aggregate, over $10,000. Other reports include CMIRs and FBARs (Foreign Bank Account Reports). Note that this reporting requirement (set out in Title II of the Act) is coupled with a requirement that banks and financial institutions retain these records for up to 5 years. This requirement is set out in Title I of the BSA, codified at 12 U.S.C. s. 1829b, 1951–1959.

Another major provision of the BSA requires any person transporting monetary instruments (as defined by 31 U.S.C. s. 5312(a)(3) and 31 C.F.R. s. 103.11 to include coins, currency, travelers' checks, and bearer bonds, securities, and negotiable instruments) worth more than $10,000 into or out of the U.S. to declare the action on a Currency and Monetary Instrument Report (CMIR). Note that the CMIR applies only to the physical transportation across the border and not to wire transfers, but it does apply to currency of a foreign country! In addition, failure to file CMIRs or to otherwise declare monetary instruments subjects them to forfeiture under 31 U.S.C. 5317(c).

The BSA was recodified in 1982 to include other nontraditional financial institutions in its reporting requirements, such as travel and insurance agencies, money exchanges, wire services, and vehicle dealerships. In 1984, the BSA was again amended, imposing much greater penalties for noncompliance (most offenses were escalated from misdemeanors to felonies).

Notwithstanding these changes, the BSA had little, if any, effect until the introduction of the Money Laundering Control Act of 1986. Launderers

avoided the reporting requirements in a number of ways: by avoiding traditional financial institutions and going to, for example, casinos, by using front
companies, and by simple smuggling. The most common method to avoid
the CTR requirement was by structuring (or "smurfing") the transactions by
dividing large deposits into many smaller transactions of less than $10,000
each. In addition, an effective way to avoid detection was to file a CTR on
the laundered money, which satisfied the BSA and only rarely led to an
investigation. This obvious loophole (the only criminal offense under the
BSA was "failure" to file) was closed with the passing of the MLCA of 1986.

Along with criminal sanctions, the BSA provides for civil money penalties
for noncompliance. The first such penalty ($500,000) was imposed on the
Bank of Boston in February 1985. Prior to that case, the CTR requirement
was generally overlooked by the banking community. A routine regulatory
review of the Bank of Boston in the early 1970s revealed that it had failed to
file CTRs on 1,163 currency transactions valued at $1.2 billion. As a result,
it paid a $500,000 fine. During the course of the case, which ended up in the
U.S. Supreme Court, the constitutionality of the BSA was upheld (it was
alleged by the Bank that the reporting requirements violated the Fourth
Amendment's prohibition against unreasonable search and seizure). Other
banks came forward, or were audited and fined: Crocker National Bank paid
a fine of $2.25 million for failing to report 7,877 transactions totaling $3.98
million; Republic National Bank of Miami was fined $1.95 million for failure
to "promptly" file CTRs; and the Bank of New England was found guilty of
31 offenses and fined $1.2 million.

As of early 1996, the Treasury Department had imposed a total of 101
such civil penalties, averaging just under $300,000 each, with more than 100
pending penalty referrals (the maximum penalty is $100,000 "per day").
Interestingly, no institution or person has ever suffered more than one BSA
penalty, making a case for their deterrent effect. Of the 101 civil penalties,
72 were imposed on banks, 23 on non-bank financial institutions, 4 on
individuals, and only 2 on import/export companies. None have been
imposed on any of the 5,300 securities firms in the U.S. In addition, as of
early June 1997, there were 127 penalty cases pending, with an average age
of 2.8 years (some are as old as 6 or more years, which is the limitation period
under the BSA).

The Treasury Department created the "BSA Advisory Group" as a think-
tank to monitor compliance with BSA, and to recommend ways to implement
anti-money-laundering efforts. Comprised of 30 private (bank and non-
bank) and government members, its recommendations have led to legislation
eliminating unnecessary reporting requirements, simplifying reporting
forms, and refining wire transfer record-keeping rules.

The constitutionality of the BSA was upheld by the United States Supreme Court in *California Bankers Ass'n v. Shultz,* 416 U.S. 21 (1974). Here, the Supreme Court rejected claims that various parts of the BSA violated constitutional due process, the Fourth Amendment protection against unreasonable search and seizure, and the Fifth Amendment privilege against self-incrimination. A later Supreme Court decision, *United States v. Miller* (425 U.S. 435, 1976), settled a question reserved in *Shultz* by ruling that bank customers possess no privacy interests protected by the Fourth Amendment in records of their affairs maintained at banks with which they deal.

One effective tool arising from the BSA is the "know your customer" policy, (described in detail in Chapter 4, "Money Laundering in the Banking Industry"), which requires all financial institutions to verify the identity of all customers who open accounts and purchase negotiable instruments, cashiers checks, and travelers' checks in excess of $3,000. As discussed in greater detail in Chapter 4, the regulations include "safe harbor" provisions and all banks to exempt certain businesses or types of businesses from the CTR reporting requirement.

B. Racketeer Influenced and Corrupt Organizations (RICO) Statute 18 U.S.C. s. 1961-1968

Congress passed the Racketeer Influenced and Corrupt Organizations (RICO) statute in 1970 as part of the Organized Crime Control Act (Title IX of the OCCA). The legislative history of the RICO statute is replete with references to "known mobsters" and the "pervasive influence of organized crime" threatening "the integrity of the American economy."* These concerns go back to the Kefauver Committee hearings in the early 1950s and the McClelland Committee hearings in the early 1960s (the latter including the testimony of Joseph Valachi, of *The Valachi Papers* fame, which was the first public mention of the phrase "La Cosa Nostra"). The RICO statute makes it unlawful for any person to engage in a pattern of racketeering activity or use the proceeds thereof to invest in, acquire control over, or conduct the affairs of, any formal or informal interstate enterprise. The stated purpose of the statute was "the elimination of the infiltration of organized crime and racketeering into legitimate organizations operating in interstate commerce."

The RICO statute is codified at 18 U.S.C. ss. 1961–1968. Section 1961 defines the critical terms, including "racketeering activity," "pattern of racketeering activity," and "enterprise." Section 1962 sets out the four prohibitions on conduct involving a RICO enterprise. Sections 1963 and 1964 describe

---

* See Senate debate at S.Rep. No. 617, 91st Cong., 1st Sess., 79-79 (1969).

the criminal penalties and civil remedies, respectively, for section 1962 violations. Sections 1965 to 1968 contain various procedural matters.

A number of the RICO violations are predicate offenses for money-laundering prosecutions. RICO prosecutions were commonly used for organized crime money-laundering groups prior to the enactment of the MLCA.

C.   Money Laundering Control Act of 1986 (MLCA) 18 U.S.C. ss. 1956 *et seq.*

The MLCA was enacted as part of the Anti-Drug Abuse Act of 1986, passed as P.L. No. 99-570 and signed by President Reagan on October 27, 1986. This act contained three significant (for money-laundering purposes) sections: (1) Subtitle H of Title I, known as the Money Laundering Control Act of 1986; (2) provisions relating to the forfeiture of property involved in money laundering; and (3) allowing Customs agents to freely stop and search outbound traffic to ensure that all monetary instruments over $10,000 were declared. The prelude to Pub. L. 99-570 provides that the Act's intent is "to strengthen Federal efforts to encourage foreign cooperation in eradicating illicit drug crops and in halting international drug traffic, to improve enforcement of Federal drug laws and enhance interdiction of illicit drug shipments, to provide strong Federal leadership in establishing effective drug abuse treatment and rehabilitation efforts, and for other purposes."

The MLCA was passed by Congress as a result of the failure of the BSA to either compel financial institutions to report money laundering or to provide the necessary prosecutorial "teeth" to prevent laundering. The MLCA criminalized money laundering and provided for both civil and criminal forfeitures of funds or property implicated in the laundering. The MLCA also criminalized structuring, attempted structuring, and aiding and abetting in structuring transactions for the purpose of avoiding the CTR filing requirements.

The Senate Committee on the Judiciary held extensive hearings on the proposed MLCA. The final published hearing report, with copies of testimony, is over 900 pages long and is a wealth of information on early anti-money-laundering efforts. It can be found in most major libraries as *1985 Senate Hearings on Money Laundering, 99th Cong., 1st Sess. (1985), S. Rep. No. 433, 99th. Cong., 2d Sess. (1986).**

The MLCA consists of two parts: 18 U.S.C. s. 1956 ("Laundering of Monetary Instruments"), and 18 U.S.C. s. 1957 ("Engaging in Monetary Transactions in Property Derived from Specified Unlawful Activity"). Section 1956 is directed at the criminals and conspirators who seek "either" to hide

---

* The Senate Report and accompanying exhibits, and other public records produced with or in conjunction with the Report form the basis for this section.

the origins of tainted money "or" to use the money to further their criminal operations. Section 1957 casts a much broader net by criminalizing the "knowing acceptance" of tainted funds. Both sections apply extraterritorially to reach both Americans and non-American citizens who are outside the U.S. but are conducting some or all of their laundering activities within the U.S.

Section 1956 of the MLCA contains ten separate money-laundering crimes based on the defendant's knowledge and intent and is divided into three broad categories: (1) four transaction offenses; (2) three transportation offenses, or crimes involving the movement of monetary instruments across U.S. borders; and (3) three crimes involving law enforcement sting operations.

Each of the three categories of prohibited money laundering contains several common elements that the government must show to establish a violation. They are: (1) the funds involved were derived from a particular group — approximately 200 — of specified unlawful activities or, in the case of a sting operation, were represented to be from unlawful activities by law enforcement officers ("origin"); (2) the defendant knew or ought to have known or was willfully blind to the fact of the funds' illicit origins ("knowledge"); (3) the defendant either executed or attempted to execute the prohibited conduct ("prohibited conduct"); and that the defendant executed the prohibited conduct with an unlawful intention ("intent").

In *Ratzlaf v. United States*, 114 S.Ct. 655 (1994), the Supreme Court overturned the convictions of the defendants who had "deliberately" structured a cash transaction of $100,000 used to pay a gambling debt to a casino to avoid triggering the BSA's reporting requirement. The Court held that the "willfulness" component of the BSA reporting statute required the government to prove that the defendants had actual knowledge that their actions were illegal (as a result of this case, Congress amended the BSA and MLCA to dispense with willfulness: see, the "Money Laundering Suppression Act of 1994," below).

The effect of the MLCA has been profound. In 1987, only 17 people were charged with money laundering and only one of those were convicted. In 1993, 1,546 people were charged with money laundering. Of those, 857 were convicted and 22 were acquitted.

1. Money Laundering Involving Financial Transactions MLCA s. 1956(a)(1)

A transaction offense is any attempt to make a financial transaction using the proceeds of any illegal activity. In this subsection, the prohibited action is conducting a "financial transaction." To establish a violation of the first of the three categories of money laundering, the government must first show that the funds involved in the laundering were derived from a "specified unlawful activity," defined as one of over 200 criminal offenses. Most common offenses are drug trafficking, fraud, espionage, environmental crimes, tax evasion, etc.

The second element (knowledge) can be inferred from circumstantial evidence that the accused actually knew or was willfully blind to that fact that he involved himself in a financial transaction that was designed to launder, in some fashion, the proceeds from some criminal activity.

The third element (prohibited conduct) is that the defendant conducted or attempted to conduct a "financial transaction" with funds he knew were derived from an unlawful activity and were in fact derived from an unlawful activity. The term "financial transaction" was drafted broadly and has been interpreted liberally to include almost any disposition of illicit funds. An attempt requires something more than simple preparation.

The fourth element (intent) is satisfied by proving that the offender acted with one of four specific intents (thus creating four separate crimes). First: that he conducted a financial transaction with the intent to promote the carrying on of one of the specified unlawful activities (this crime has been labeled the "Promotion Statute"). Second: that he engaged in a transaction with the intent of evading taxation or fraudulently concealing assets from taxation by filing false tax documents. Third: that he acted with the intent to conceal or disguise the nature, location, source, ownership, or control of the proceeds of the specified unlawful activity. Last: that he attempted to conduct a transaction intending to avoid a transaction reporting requirement under state or federal law.

Each transaction conducted in violation of this subsection carries a 20-year term of imprisonment and a fine of $500,000 or twice the value of the laundered property, whichever is greater, or both.

2.   Crossing the Border Without Declaring Monetary Instruments MLCA s. 1956(a)(2)

A *transportation* offense is any attempt to transfer money across the border when the money was obtained illegally or will be used for illegal purposes. The first two elements of this category of money laundering — origin and knowledge — are the same as those for the transaction offenses; the government must first show that the funds involved in the laundering were derived from a "specified unlawful activity," and the accused actually knew or was willfully blind to the fact that he involved himself in a financial transaction that was designed to launder, in some fashion, the proceeds from some criminal activity.

The third element (prohibited conduct) requires a showing that the defendant attempted or did transport, transmit, or transfer a monetary instrument across U.S. borders. As the term "financial transaction" is defined broadly and interpreted loosely *vis à vis* a category one violation (money laundering involving financial transactions), so is the term "monetary instruments" defined and interpreted, covering everything from simple smuggling to wire transfers.

The fourth element (intent) is satisfied by proving that the offender acted with one of "three" (as compared to four for laundering involving financial transactions — the difference is the exception here of the intent to commit tax fraud) specific intents (thus creating three crimes). First: that he conducted a financial transaction with the intent to promote the carrying on of one of the specified unlawful activities. Second: that he acted with the intent to conceal or disguise the nature, location, source, ownership, or control of the proceeds of the specified unlawful activity. Last: that he attempted to conduct a transaction intending to avoid a transaction reporting requirement under state or federal law.

Each transaction conducted in violation of this subsection carries a 20-year term of imprisonment and a fine of $500,000 or twice the value of the laundered property, whichever is greater, or both. In addition, sanctions for violating this provision include the seizure of any unreported currency. However, a number of federal courts of appeal have ruled that the forfeiture of large amounts of cash amounts to "punishment" and, if the amount is disproportionate to the culpability of the defendant, in violation of the excessive fines clause of the Eighth Amendment.

The most common defense to a charge of failing to file a CMIR is that the currency was seized prior to the "time of departure." For example, money seized from a person boarding a connecting flight from Connecticut to New York is not forfeitable, and no offense has occurred, because the reporting requirement arose only when the person failed to file a report at the time of departure in New York (the international leg of the journey). See *United States v. $500,000 in United States Currency*, 62 F.3d 59 (2nd Cir. 1995). The critical "time of departure" "turns on a reasonable proximity both in space and time to the physical point of departure coupled with a manifest intention to leave the country," quoting *United States v. $122,043 in United States Currency*, 792 F.2d 1470 (9th Cir. 1986) (here, an offense occurred where the claimant had checked her baggage, passed through security, and presented her boarding pass at the jetway).

3. Money-Laundering Sting Operations MLCA s. 1956(a)(3)

Sting operations are the third of three categories of money-laundering offenses in the MLCA. The elements of a sting operation duplicate those of the first category (financial transaction offenses) with two exceptions. First, the proceeds need not "actually" be derived from an unlawful activity, so long as the law enforcement officer represents, and the offender reasonably believes, that the object of the transaction is derived from those activities.

Second, this section does not criminalize transactions conducted with funds represented by law enforcement as derived from a criminal activity in cases where the intent of the launderer is to evade or conceal assets from taxation. Like transportation of monetary instruments across U.S. borders, the sting operations subsection creates three crimes.

4.   Underlying Offenses MLCA s. 1956(c)(7)

This subsection lists approximately 200 criminal offenses for which the handling of the proceeds derived from the offenses will be punishable as money laundering. The list of prohibited offenses changes constantly as new crimes are created in other federal statutes. The most recent additions to the list include terrorism, healthcare fraud, and immigration offenses.

5.   Engaging in Transactions with Property Derived from Unlawful Activity MLCA s. 1957

Where subsection 1956 specifies ten potential crimes, subsection 1957 specifies only one. This subsection goes beyond subsection 1956 by covering situations in which the defendant's only "bad act" is having accepted funds, valued in excess of $10,000, which he knows are tainted. The government does not have to prove any of the impermissible intentions found in section 1956: it need only prove that the defendant knowingly engaged or attempted to engage in a monetary transaction in criminally derived property that was of a value greater than $10,000 and that was derived from specified unlawful activity. Edilberto Miranda, a Prudential Bache Securities broker, was convicted in June, 1997 under this (and other) subsections for investing, wiring, and brokering the drug profits of nine known Colombian drug traffickers.

Each transaction conducted in violation of this subsection carries a 10-year term of imprisonment and a fine of $250,000 or twice the value of the laundered property whichever is greater, or both.

a.   Attorneys' Fees*.   The Congressional record relating to the debates over this section is dominated by references of whether an attorney's fees could, or should, be subject to this subsection. In short, could an attorney violate this subsection if the fee or retainer he accepted was "tainted"?

The National Association of Criminal Defense Attorneys (NACDL) lobbied unsuccessfully for an express exemption for bona fide attorney fees. They succeeded in the House, but eventually lost out in the final negotiation

---

* For a fairly comprehensive review of the impact of anti-money-laundering laws on the attorney-client privilege, see the law review article of the same title at 19 Suffolk Transnational L.R., 507-522 (Summer 1996). For a Canadian perspective, see T.M. Brucker, *Money Laundering and the Client: How Can I Be Retained Without Becoming a Party to the Offense?* 39 Crim. L.Q. 312-333 (Fall 1997).

between the House and Senate. The compromise language excluded from section 1957 "any transaction necessary to preserve a person's right to representation as guaranteed by the Sixth Amendment to the Constitution."

Note that DOJ guidelines require approval from Washington for any federal prosecutor to prosecute an attorney for money laundering under section 1957, or to seek forfeiture of these fees under 18 U.S.C. s. 981-982. Although the anti-money-laundering provisions of the MLCA may not apply to attorneys in certain circumstances, the currency transaction reporting requirements of the BSA compel an attorney to file a Form 8300 (discussed in Chapter 9, herein) whenever a client pays more than $10,000 in cash, regardless of the nature or purpose of the attorney–client relationship. Typical money-laundering/reporting cases involving attorneys and their clients' accounts arise from the attorney's refusal to turn over information on the client's identity and fee arrangements. In most cases, courts compel disclosure of such information, with some exceptions. One court even went so far as to hold that there is "no reason to grant law firms a monopoly on money laundering simply because their services are personal and confidential" [*United States v. Ritchie*, 15 F.3d 592, 601 (6th Cir. 1994)].

b. Forfeiture of Property Involved in Money Laundering. A detailed look at asset forfeiture generally is contained in Chapter 10, "Asset Forfeiture." With regard to property involved in money laundering specifically, such property was not subject to forfeiture until Congress included certain forfeiture provisions in the BSA (codified at 18 U.S.C. ss. 981 and 982) as part of the Anti-Drug Abuse Act of 1986.

Subsection 981(a)(1)(A) allows for the civil forfeiture of any property used or intended to be used to facilitate the money laundering, or any property traceable to such property. Note that the original (1986) text only authorized the forfeiture of the "gross receipts" a person obtained as a result of a violation of the MLCA. The phrase "gross receipts" was limited to mean only the profits, or commissions earned, not the laundered amount itself. Amendments made by the Anti-Drug Abuse Act of 1988 expanded the scope of the forfeitable property to include "any property involved" in money-laundering activity.

c. Border Searches for Monetary Instruments. The third key aspect of the Anti-Drug Abuse Act of 1986 was aimed at stemming the flood of currency being smuggled out of the U.S. From 1970 to 1984, Customs agents needed a search warrant to stop and search traffic for unreported monetary instruments. Search warrants require a judge's finding that there is probable cause to believe an offense has occurred. The Comprehensive Crime Control Act of 1984 amended the statute, 31 U.S.C. s. 5317, to allow searches without a warrant where the officer had "reasonable cause to believe there is a monetary instrument being transported."

However, even this reasonable cause standard was thought to be too onerous; among other arguments, it was noted that this standard to search specifically for monetary instruments was more restrictive than Customs' authority to search for any other purposes. Accordingly, in 1986, the statute was again amended, this time by the Anti-Drug Abuse Act of 1986, to abolish the "reasonable cause" requirement.

D. Anti-Drug Abuse Act of 1988

Among other things, this statute amended the MLCA 1986 by authorizing the use of governmental sting operations to expose money laundering. Sting operations thus became the third category of offense under 18 U.S.C. s. 1956. In addition, the Act significantly increased civil, criminal, and forfeiture sanctions for money-laundering crimes and BSA violations, and permitted Treasury to require financial institutions to file geographically targeted reports.

Note that 1988 also saw the passing of what is known as the Kerry Amendment, codified at 31 U.S.C. ss. 5311 (1988), which authorized the Treasury Department to negotiate with other countries to "export" the BSA reporting requirements and to allow the U.S. access to that information. The Amendment included a ban on conducting banking in the U.S. as the "hammer" for noncompliance. There are treaties with Venezuela, Peru, Colombia, Panama, among others. However, drafting compromises have rendered these agreements almost useless.

E. Annunzio-Wylie Anti-Money-Laundering Act of 1992

In 1992 Congress enacted the Annunzio-Wylie Anti-Money-Laundering Act in order to clean up what were perceived to be deficiencies in various anti-money-laundering statutes. In particular, the BSA was amended in several respects, most noticeably (1) to compel any financial institution and its officers to report any suspicious transactions relevant to a possible violation of law, protected from civil liability for doing so by certain "safe harbor provisions"; and (2) to provide for termination of a bank's charter, insurance, or license to conduct business in the U.S. if convicted of money laundering. If a *domestic* bank is convicted of money laundering, the statutes provide for hearings to determine whether the bank's deposit insurance should be revoked or whether a conservator should be appointed. In the case of a *foreign* bank branch, the statutes provide for the Federal Reserve Board to begin immediate termination proceedings for the bank, and the branch is then shut down. A bank official convicted of money laundering can be banned from the industry.

Another important provision of the Annunzio-Wylie Act was to amend the BSA to allow the Secretary of the Treasury to require all financial institutions to institute money-laundering training and to report suspicious transactions. The Annunzio-Wylie Act also authorized the formation of a Bank Secrecy Act Advisory Group, consisting of personnel from Treasury, Justice, and representatives of private banking.* These amendments are set out in the Code of Federal Regulations, 31 CFR 103.

Finally, the Annunzio-Wylie Act also amended the civil forfeiture statute (discussed in detail in Chapter 9) to allow for the forfeiture of money in a bank account even when that money is not directly traceable to money laundering so long as the account previously contained funds involved in or traceable to illegal activity. See, for example, *United States v. $814,254.76 in United States Currency*, 51 F.3d 207 (9th Cir. 1995) (a case involving a Customs-run sting operation targeting the Banco de Nationale de Mexico, or Banamex).

F. Money-Laundering Suppression Act of 1994 (MLSA)

The MLSA is the primary legislative tool to regulate non-bank financial institutions, or NBFIs. This statute was passed by Congress in response to *Ratzlaf v. United States*, 114 S.Ct. 655 (1994), where the Supreme Court overturned the convictions of the defendants who had "deliberately" structured a cash transaction of $100,000 used to pay a gambling debt to a casino to avoid triggering the BSA's reporting requirement.

In addition, anti-money laundering efforts were becoming so successful between 1986 and 1990 that the MLSA 94 actually loosened those reporting requirements that did not adversely impact money laundering. The Act contains a provision for the creation of a set of Uniform Laws for states to regulate "businesses that provide check cashing, currency exchange, or money transmitting or remittance services, or issue or redeem money orders, travelers' checks, and other similar instruments." Such regulations would include provisions for background checks and to ensure compliance with the BSA reporting requirements. In addition, there was a requirement that all money transmitting businesses and casinos register with the Secretary of the Treasury.**

---

* The Congressional record on the Annunzio-Wylie Anti-Money Laundering Act, and Senate Committee on Governmental Affairs hearings on money exchange houses and money laundering generally, can be found in most major libraries as the *1992 Senate Hearings on Casas de Cambio, 102d Cong., 2nd Sess. (1992)*.

** The history and background of, and rationale for, the MLSA 1994 can be found in the report of the House Committee on Banking, Finance, & Urban Affairs, June, 1993, available in most major libraries as *1993 H.R. Hearings on Money Laundering, 103d Cong., 1st Sess. (1993)*.

Unfortunately, as of early June, 1998, regulations required to implement and enforce most of the provisions of the MLSA 1994 had yet to be enacted, including regulations relating to federal registration for non-bank financial institutions (NBFIs), implementing a system of mandatory cash reporting exemptions to reduce bank compliance burdens, and regulations requiring the reporting of foreign bank drafts. In addition, NBFIs and securities dealers have been without a standard form to report suspicious activities.

G. International Emergency Economic Powers Act (IEEPA) and PDD 42

The International Emergency Economic Powers Act ("IEEPA"), codified at 50 U.S.C. s. 1701, gives the President the ability to impose economic and other sanctions where he declares (by Executive Order) that there is an "unusual and extraordinary threat" to the United States. The IEEPA has been used to sanction (and invade) Iraq, and sanction Iran, Syria, Algeria, Libya, Panama, Colombia, and other nations.

On October 21, 1995, President Clinton used the authority given him by the IEEPA to sign Presidential Directive Decision 42, an Executive Order invoking economic sanctions against certain Colombian individuals and companies involved in drug trafficking and money laundering. This, and other Executive Orders, can be found in the Federal Register, both in hard copy and on-line.

The preamble to PDD 42/Executive Order No. 12978 reads as follows:

> By the authority vested in me as President by the Constitution and the laws of the United States of America, including the International Emergency Economic Powers Act, ... the National Emergencies Act (50 U.S.C. s.1601 "et seq.") ...

> I, WILLIAM J. CLINTON, President of the United States of America, find that the actions of significant foreign narcotics traffickers centered in Colombia, and the unparalleled violence, corruption, and harm that they cause in the United States and abroad, constitute an unusual and extraordinary threat to the national security, foreign policy, and economy of the United States, and hereby declare a national emergency to deal with that threat ...

PDD 42 makes it illegal for any U.S. company or individual to trade directly or indirectly with the sanctioned entities. The original list of "Specially Designated Narcotics Traffickers," or SDNTs, included the four principal Cali Cartel kingpins — Pacho Herrera Buitrago, Gilberto Rodriguez Orejuela, Miguel Angel Rodriguez Orejuela, and Jose Santacruz Londono —

33 related or controlled businesses, and 43 other individuals involved with the four principals.

On November 29, 1995, the list was amended to include three more individuals and one more business. On March 8, 1996, 138 more individuals and 60 businesses were added, bringing the total to 188 individuals and 94 businesses. On January 15, 1997, the Treasury Department identified an additional 21 businesses and 57 individuals determined to be involved with Pacho Herrera's organization, bringing the total number of businesses and individuals sanctioned under PDD 42 to 359. All of these SDNTs were determined to be directly involved with one of the four original "kingpins" and their so-called legitimate business empires, which include poultry farms and processing plants, investment, consulting, and import/export firms, real estate development companies, a lumber distributor, and a construction company. A list of the major SDNTs is set out in Appendix 1.1.

H. International Crime Control Act of 1996 (ICCA)

The ICCA was a response to a speech given by President Clinton to the United Nations General Assembly on October 22, 1995. According to the White House Fact Sheet issued when the ICCA was enacted, it was designed to accomplish five main objectives: deny safe haven to international fugitives, strike at the financial underpinnings of international crime, punish acts of violence committed against U.S. citizens abroad, respond to emerging international organized crime problems, and foster multilateral cooperation against international criminal activity.

In addition to specific provisions relating to each of these five objectives, the ICCA streamlined certain federal court rules regarding the introduction of evidence collected overseas.

Objective 1: Denying a safe haven to international fugitives. The ICCA allows the Attorney General to deny entry into the U.S. of persons who attempt to enter in order to avoid prosecution in another country for certain designated crimes. The Act also allows the U.S. to "transfer" foreign nationals convicted of crimes and imprisoned in the U.S. to their home country without their consent; and it gives the Attorney General certain discretion in extraditing "international criminals" to countries with which the U.S. has no extradition treaty.

Objective 2: Striking at the financial underpinnings of international crime. The ICCA expanded the list of money laundering predicate crimes listed in 18 U.S.C. s. 1957(c)(7) to include certain crimes committed abroad against Americans or American interests, including terrorism and public corruption against foreign governments. In addition, the Act expanded the definition of "financial institution" to include foreign banks, closing a loophole by covering offenses involving criminally derived funds that involve foreign banks but occur in any way in the U.S.

Objective 3: Punishing acts of violence committed against Americans abroad. Included in these provisions is the elimination of the statute of limitations for all federal crimes committed outside the U.S. against U.S. citizens to ensure that international criminals are not shielded from prosecution due to delays (often caused by or exacerbated by corrupt local officials) in gathering evidence from abroad.

Objective 4: Responding to emerging international organized crime problems. The ICCA added extraterritorial provisions regarding alien smuggling, the smuggling of precursor chemicals used to manufacture methamphetamine, and fraud involving "access devices" (ATM cards, etc). In addition, these crimes were added to the money-laundering and asset forfeiture list of predicate crimes.

Objective 5: Improving multilateral cooperation against international crime. The ICCA authorized U.S. law enforcement agencies to better share seized assets with other nations' law enforcement agencies, and to train these foreign law enforcement agencies.

III. Proposed Money Laundering and Financial Crimes Strategy Bill of 1997

Keep your eyes on Senate Bill S.1003, introduced on July 10, 1997 (House Bill 1997CRH3280D), as it wends its way through Congress. This Bill was intended to amend the Bank Secrecy Act (chapter 53 of Title 31) by allowing the President (acting through the Secretary of the Treasury) to develop and submit annually to Congress a national strategy for combating money laundering and related crimes. The Bill's underlying premise is based on the recognition that money launderers are often one step ahead of law enforcement. Therefore, the Bill proposes a system allowing local, state, and federal law enforcement and prosecutors to request that a specific geographic area, industry, sector, or institution be designated a substantial risk for money laundering; once designated, federal grants and formal collaboration would be forthcoming.

As described earlier in this chapter, the BSA is codified in two subchapters of chapter 53 of Title 31 of the U.S. Code. This new Bill proposes adding a third subchapter comprising five sections: definitions (section 5341); development and submission to Congress for a national money laundering and related financial crimes strategy (section 5342); factors for designating high-risk money laundering and related financial crimes areas (section 5343); grant programs for assistance in fighting money-laundering and related financial crimes (section 5344); and authorization for appropriations to funds these programs (section 5345).

IV. Federal Sentencing Guidelines

A. Introduction and Basic Concepts

The Federal Sentencing Guidelines are used by judges, prosecutors, and defense attorneys to determine the possible sentence, or the range of a possible sentence, for any federal crime. They are based on the concept that each type of offense should result in a sentence within a determined range, adjusted to the high or low end of the range, depending on certain known factors, including the defendant's criminal history.

The U.S. Sentencing Commission, an independent agency of the judicial branch consisting of seven voting and two non-voting members, was created by the Sentencing Reform Act of 1984 (Title II of the Comprehensive Crime Control Act of 1984). The Commission's original mandate was to enhance the ability of the criminal justice system to combat crime through an effective, fair sentencing system. To achieve this end, the Sentencing Reform Act abolished the parole system and altered the "good behavior credits" system (essentially reducing the maximum allowable reduction for good behavior to 15% of the total original sentence). Armed with this "honesty in sentencing" mandate, the Commission then sought to create a sentencing system that balanced *uniformity* in sentencing for similar offenses with *proportionality* in sentencing between different offenses. Over a three-year period from 1984 to April 1987, the Commission created various offense categories, a uniform range of sentences within a category, and proportionality between categories. The sentence for any category of offense had to fall within a designated range (the maximum could not exceed the minimum by more than the greater of 25% or six months) unless the case presented atypical features. In other words, a court can depart from the guidelines when it finds "an aggravating or mitigating circumstance of a kind, or to a degree, not adequately taken into consideration by the Sentencing Commission in formulating the guidelines that should result in a sentence different from that described." (18 U.S.C. section 3553(b).) Note that these circumstances do *not* include race, sex, socioeconomic background, lack of guidance as a youth, drug or alcohol dependence, coercion, or duress.

The guidelines were promulgated in 1986 as part of the Anti-Drug Abuse Act, and enacted or put in effect in April 1987 (they apply to all federal offenses committed on or after November 1, 1987). They are organized into seven chapters: (1) Introduction and General Principles, (2) Offense Conduct, (3) Adjustments, (4) Criminal History and Criminal Livelihood, (5) Determining the Sentence, (6) Sentencing Procedures and Plea Agreements, and (7) Violations of Probation and Supervised Release. The guidelines were changed in 1994 by the Violent Crime Control & Law Enforcement Act by adding the "three strikes and you're out" provision for violent career criminals, as well as a "safety valve" provision to allow a court to go below the guidelines for certain drug offenses committed by low-level, nonviolent offenders.

B.   How the Guidelines Work

As described above, the Guidelines provide for an offense "base level," and then add or subtract from that base level to come up with a sentence or sentence range. The backbone of the guidelines is the Sentencing Table, set out in chapter 5 of the guidelines. The table is essentially a grid containing 43 levels organized into four zones on the vertical axis, and 6 criminal history categories based on criminal history points (0 to 13 or more) on the horizontal axis. For example:

- Offense Level 1 with criminal history category I results in a sentence of 0 to 6 months.
- Offense Level 22 with criminal history category I results in a sentence of 41 to 51 months.
- Offense Level 22 with criminal history category VI results in a sentence of 84 to 105 months.
- Offense Level 37 with criminal history category I results in a sentence of 210 to 262 months.
- Offense Level 37 with criminal history category VI results in a sentence of 360 months to life.
- Offense Level 43 with criminal history category I results in a sentence of life.
- Offense Level 43 with criminal history category VI results in a sentence of life.

Note that a change or increase of six levels roughly doubles a sentence range. Note also that the original base level for most money-laundering offenses was 23, which translates to 46 to 57 months (this offense conduct is described in greater detail below).

Chapter 2 of the guidelines contains the offense conduct, organized by type or category of offense, each with a corresponding base offense level and one or more specific offense characteristics that adjust the offense level upward or downward. This chapter is broken down into Parts A through X. For example, Part A lists "offenses against the person," which include all homicides, ranging in seriousness from involuntary manslaughter (level 10) to first degree murder (level 43), to assault (ranging from level 6 to 28), criminal sexual abuse (10 to 27), and even air piracy (level 12).

Part D of Chapter 2 lists the "offenses involving drugs," which include all trafficking, importing, exporting, and possessory offenses. The range for these drug offenses (base offense level 6 to 43) is based on the drug quantity table and/or the precursor chemical quantity table, and/or whether death resulted. For example, the guidelines provide for a base offense level of 38 for trafficking or importing 30 kilos or more of heroin, 150 kilos or more of cocaine or methamphetamine, 300 grams or more of LSD, or 30,000 kilos of marijuana.

Part E of Chapter 2 lists "racketeering" offenses (range of between 9 and 19). Part F lists the "offenses involving fraud or deceit," and includes counterfeiting (range of between 6 and 24, depending on the amount counterfeited). Part L lists offenses involving immigration, naturalization, and passports (range of between 6 and 20).

Part M of Chapter 2 lists a wide range of offenses, including "prohibited financial transactions and exports" (offense level 22).

Chapter 3 of the guidelines sets out the adjustments: victim-related adjustments, the defendant's role in the offense, obstruction of justice, multiple counts, and acceptance of responsibility.

Chapter 4 of the guidelines provides for further adjustments based on the defendant's criminal history and livelihood, and whether the defendant can be considered a "career offender."

Chapter 5 of the guidelines contains the factors used to determine the sentence range and type of sentence, from probation to imprisonment, restitution, fines, forfeitures, and departures.

C. Sentencing Guidelines for Money Laundering Offenses

Part S of Chapter 2 sets out an offense category entitled "money laundering and monetary transaction reporting." There are three subparts (2S1.1 to 2S1.3) based on the different types of money-laundering offenses: Parts 2S1.1 and 2S1.2 for Money Laundering Control Act (MLCA) offenses under 18 U.S.C. sections 1956 and 1957, respectively; and Part 2S1.3 for Bank Secrecy Act (BSA) offenses under 31 U.S.C. sections 5313 - 5324.

1. Part 2S1.1: Laundering of Monetary Instruments (18 U.S.C. s. 1956)

Part 2S1.1 lists the offense of laundering of monetary instruments. The base offense level is 23 if the offense is set out in the MLCA, 18 U.S.C. subsections

1956(a)(1)(A), (a)(2)(A), or (a)(3)(A). The base offense level is 20 for all other money-laundering offenses. There are two specific offense character-istics: (1) "if the defendant knew or believed that the funds were the proceeds of unlawful activity involving the manufacture, importation, or distribution of narcotics or other controlled substances, increase by 3 levels"; and (2) the offense level could be increased by as much as 13 levels if the value of the funds laundered exceeded $100,000 (for $100,000 to $200,000, the increase was 1; for $10,000,000 to $20,000,000, the increase was 9; for $60,000,000 to $100,000,000, the increase was 12; over $100,000,000, the increase was 13). The maximum term of imprisonment is 20 years, which is higher than that specified in 2S1.2 or 2S1.3 because of the higher maximum for the underlying offenses and the added elements as to source of funds, knowledge, and intent.

2. Part 2S1.2: Engaging in Monetary Transactions (18 U.S.C. s. 1957)

Part 2S1.2 lists the offense of engaging in monetary transactions in property derived from specified unlawful activity. This offense carries a base level of 17. The specific offense characteristics increase the offense level by as much as 5 ("if the defendant knew that the funds were the proceeds of an unlawful activity involving the manufacture, importation, or distribution of narcotics or other controlled substances") or as little as 2 for all other specified unlawful activity set out in 18 U.S.C. s. 1956 (c)(7). In addition, the same dollar amounts apply to this subpart. The maximum term of imprisonment is 10 years. This subpart focuses on 18 U.S.C. s. 1957 offenses, which are similar to those in section 1956 but do not require that the recipient exchange or launder funds, nor that he have any intent to further or conceal specified unlawful activity, but do require that the person have knowledge that the funds were criminally derived property (thus the 2-level increase for all other specified unlawful activity in 1956(c)(7), which carries an intent element missing from section 1957 offenses).

3. Part 2S1.3: Bank Secrecy Act Violations (31 U.S.C. ss. 5313–5324)

Where Parts 2S1.1 and 1.2 list MLCA offenses, Part 2S1.3 lists the BSA offenses (31 U.S.C. sections 5313, 5314, 5316, and 5324) of structuring trans-actions to evade reporting requirements, failure to report cash or monetary transactions, failure to file CTRs or CMIRs, and knowingly filing false reports. The base offense level for these offenses is 6 *plus* the number of offense levels from the "fraud and deceit" table (section 2F1.1), including increases for the value of the funds from section 2F1.1. There are two specific offense char-acteristics: (1) if the defendant "knew or believed that the funds were proceeds of unlawful activity, or were intended to promote unlawful activity," there is an increase of 2 levels; and (2) there would be a *decrease* of 6 levels if the defendant did not know or believe the funds were proceeds of unlawful activity, and he did not act with reckless disregard as to the source of the funds.

D. Future of the Sentencing Guidelines

In the later 1980s, it came to the attention of the Commission that the guidelines appeared to sanction money-laundering offenses disproportionately to the underlying criminal conduct. In 1992, the Commission convened a Money Laundering Working Group to assess these concerns. The Working Group has published two reports, one in 1992 and one in 1995. They can both be found online at *www.ussc.gov/moneylau.html.*

As a result of the Working Group's efforts generally, and reaction from a U.S. Supreme Court's decision in *United States v. LaBonte* (117 S.Ct. 1673, 1997), the Sentencing Commission amended the guidelines in early October 1997, to clarify the career offender (three strikes and you're out) provisions. New Proposed Guidelines were released on January 21, 1998, for public comment. Offense levels and increases for fraud, theft, and tax-related offenses have been changed: money-laundering offenses were not touched.

V. States' Money-Laundering and Reporting Legislation

As of October 1997, 31 of the 50 American states had anti-money-laundering legislation in place. Of those, only seven had anti-money-laundering *and* reporting requirements for both financial institutions accepting cash (a CTR-type requirement) and businesses accepting cash (a Form 8300-type requirement). Of the 18 states that had the CTR-type reporting requirements, three had no anti-money-laundering legislation (Alabama, Nebraska, and North Carolina). Nine states have no anti-money-laundering legislation and no cash transaction reporting requirements. Those are Alaska, Delaware, Kentucky, West Virginia, Wyoming, and four New England states: Maine, Massachusetts, New Hampshire, and Vermont. Finally, 29 states had a casino reporting requirement (a CTR-C type requirement).*

VI. Current State of American Money-Laundering Laws

The two key statutes remain the Money Laundering Control Act, 31 U.S.C. sections 1956 through 1957, as amended from 1986 through 1996, and the

---

* Information provided by FinCEN.

Bank Secrecy Act, 31 U.S.C. sections 5311 through 5324, as amended from 1970 through 1996. The MLCA is sufficiently described in Section II.E of this chapter. The BSA is set out in Appendix 7.1, with the actual text of each section followed by a common-sense "translation" or explanation of the more relevant sections.

APPENDIX 7.1

BANK SECRECY ACT, 31 U.S.C. 5311–5324 and Regulations

Section 5311 Declaration of Purpose

It is the purpose of this subchapter (except section 5315) to require certain reports or records where they have a high degree of usefulness in criminal, tax, or regulatory investigations or proceedings.

Chapter 53 of Title 31 generally deals with domestic or international transactions involving U.S. currency or monetary instruments. The exception is section 5315, which deals with foreign currency transactions. The language of section 5311 has not changed since the enactment of the Bank Secrecy Act in 1970. Note the reference to "reports or records": the statute's regulations, set out at 31 CFR section 103, reflect these types of documents. Reports, such as CTRs, CMIRs, and SARs, are described in subpart B of 31 CFR 103 (sections 103.20 to 103.29). Records are described in subpart C. Essentially, a regulatory or law enforcement agency will either receive *reports* on certain designated transactions from a financial institution, which may be used to trigger an investigation, or the agency can request or subpoena a financial institution's historical *records* of these transactions.

Bottom line: send reports, keep records.

Section 5312 Definitions and Application

(a) In this subchapter —

(1) **"financial agency"** means a person acting for a person (except for a country, a monetary or financial authority acting as a monetary or financial authority, or an international financial institution of which the United States Government is a member) as a financial institution, bailee, depository trustee, or agent, or acting in a similar way related to money, credit, securities, gold, or a transaction in money, credit, securities, or gold.

The definition of "financial agency" closes a loophole of using a person(s) or entity(ies) as a buffer between the money launderer and his financial institution. This definition seeks to include transactions with or between intermediaries.

(2) **"financial institution"** means —

(A) an insured bank (as defined in section 3(h) of the Federal Deposit Insurance Act (12 U.S.C. 1813(h)));

(B) a commercial bank or trust company;

(C) a private banker;

(D) an agency or branch of a foreign bank in the United States;

(E) an insured institution (as defined in section 401(a) of the National Housing Act (12 U.S.C. 1724(a)));

(F) a thrift institution;

(G) a broker or dealer registered with the Securities and Exchange Commission under the Securities Exchange Act of 1934 (15 U.S.C. 78a et seq.);

(H) a broker or dealer in securities or commodities;

(I) an investment banker or investment company;

(J) a currency exchange;

(K) an issuer, redeemer, or cashier of travelers' checks, checks, money orders, or similar instruments;

(L) an operator of a credit card system;

(M) an insurance company;

(N) a dealer in precious metals, stones, or jewels;

(O) a pawnbroker;

(P) a loan or finance company;

(Q) a travel agency;

(R) a licensed sender of money;

(S) a telephone company;

(T) a business engaged in vehicle sales, including automobile, airplane, and boat sales;

(U) persons involved in real estate closings and settlements;

(V) the United States Postal Service;

(W) an agency of the United States Government or of a State or local government carrying out a duty or power of a business described in this paragraph

(X) a casino, gambling casino, or gaming establishment with an annual gaming revenue of more than $1,000,000 which:

(i) is licensed as a casino, gambling casino, or gaming establishment under the laws of any State or any political subdivision of any State; or

(ii) is an Indian gaming operation conducted under or pursuant to the Indian Gaming Regulatory Act other than an operation which is limited to class I gaming (as defined in section 4(6) of such Act);

(Y) any business or agency which engages in any activity which the Secretary of the Treasury determines, by regulation, to be an activity which is similar to, related to, or a substitute for any activity in which any business described in this paragraph is authorized to engage; or

(Z) any other business designated by the Secretary whose cash transactions have a high degree of usefulness in criminal, tax, or regulatory
matters.

Whether Congress was reluctant to begin again at subparagraph (aa),
this cumbersome definition of "financial institution" conveniently includes
or stops at twenty-six different entities defined as being a "financial institution" for the purpose of the statute's reporting and record keeping requirements. Those entities listed (A) through (S) appeared in the original 1970
version of the BSA; (T) through (Z) were added between 1986 and 1992.

A better definition, or at least a more comprehensible one, of financial
institution appears in the regulations at 31 CFR 103.11(n). Although this
latter definition actually encompasses all 26 types of entities contained in
section 5312(a)(2), it lists them in a more orderly fashion:

1. banks (defined elsewhere in the regulations)
2. securities dealers and brokers (defined elsewhere in the regulations)
3. money exchangers and check cashers
4. issuer, seller, or redeemer of travelers checks or money orders
5. transmitter of funds
6. telegraph companies
7. casinos (defined elsewhere in the regulations)
8. any person subject to state or federal banking supervision
9. the U.S. Postal Service regarding the sale of money orders

(3) **"monetary instruments"** means —

(A) United States coins and currency;
(B) as the Secretary may prescribe by regulation, coins and currency
of a foreign country, travelers' checks, bearer negotiable instruments, bearer
investment securities, bearer securities, stock on which title is passed on
delivery, and similar material; and
(C) as the Secretary of the Treasury shall provide by regulation for
purposes of section 5316, checks, drafts, notes, money orders, and other
similar instruments which are drawn on or by a foreign financial institution
and are not in bearer form.

Parts B and C of this definition invite the Secretary of the Treasury to
expand on the definition of "monetary instrument." The Secretary has, in
fact, taken us up on the invitation. In addition to coins and currency, 31 CFR
section 103.11(u) adds the following: currency (defined as "coin or paper
money of the United States *or of any other country* ...")); traveler's checks in
any form; all stock or bond certificates in bearer form (recall the movie

Die Hard where Bruce Willis battled German criminals intent on stealing $650 million in "bearer bonds"); all negotiable instruments (any kind of check or money order with the payee's name included); and all "incomplete instruments" (sort of a non-negotiable negotiable instrument, or a check or money order without the payee's name filled in). These "incomplete instruments" were included in the regulations because of the common practice of "smurfs" mailing blank checks — signed and with the amount properly filled in, but not dated and without a payee — to an unknown handler or intermediary, who would fill in the date and payee name once proper instructions were received. Typically, a mid- to high-level launderer will set up a number of smurfs with identification, a place to live, an identity (often as a student), and a bank account. The smurf will establish a normal, routine "banking identity," complete with normal deposits (often in the form of wire transfer deposits in amounts and frequencies that do not trigger regulatory or internal reports) and withdrawals (checks, credit card payments, ATM transactions, etc.). Over the course of a few months, the smurf will establish him or herself as a good customer, well known to the local branch personnel. At some point, the smurf might write out a series of checks for designated amounts, payable to a designated payee or simply left blank. These checks are then mailed to a central location, where they are held by the launderer until needed. At some point, the smurf will receive a huge infusion of money into his or her account — money that has been placed into the financial system at another point and routed to or through the smurf's account. The smurf will then direct that some, or perhaps even all, of it be routed on to the next smurf (seeking to layer the funds). The balance, if any, will be drawn down over a few days with the checks that were sent out earlier. Detection is not critical at this point, as the smurf usually has moved on to a new city or location, with a new ID, to perform his or her task all over again. Typically, smurfs such as these receive $2,500 to $5,000 per month as "spending money" to establish their "bona fides." In exchange, they facilitate the movement of hundreds of thousands, and in some cases, millions of dollars.

(4) **"person,"** in addition to its meaning under section 1 of title 1, includes a trustee, a representative of an estate and, when the Secretary prescribes, a governmental entity.

(5) **"United States"** means the States of the United States, the District of Columbia, and, when the Secretary prescribes by regulation, the Commonwealth of Puerto Rico, the Virgin Islands, Guam, the Northern Mariana Islands, American Samoa, the Trust Territory of the Pacific Islands, a territory or possession of the United States, or a military or diplomatic establishment.

The words "Virgin Islands, Guam, the Northern Mariana Islands, American Samoa, the Trust Territory of the Pacific Islands, a territory or possession of the United States, or a military or diplomatic establishment" were added in 1986 after some creative challenges to a number of money-laundering cases arising in or involving the the U.S. Virgin Islands.

(b) In this subchapter —

(1) **"domestic financial agency"** and **"domestic financial institution"** apply to an action in the United States of a financial agency or institution.

(2) **"foreign financial agency"** and **"foreign financial institution"** apply to an action outside the United States of a financial agency or institution.

Section 5313 Reports on domestic coins and currency transactions
(a) When a domestic financial institution is involved in a transaction for the payment, receipt, or transfer of United States coins or currency (or other monetary instruments the Secretary of the Treasury prescribes), in an amount, denomination, or amount and denomination, or under circumstances the Secretary prescribes by regulation, the institution and any other participant in the transaction the Secretary may prescribe shall file a report on the transaction at the time and in the way the Secretary prescribes. A participant acting for another person shall make the report as the agent or bailee of the person and identify the person for whom the transaction is being made.

This is the CTR section. It simply tells the reader to turn to the regulations, in this case, 31 CFR section 103.22 "Reports of Currency Transactions."

The magic number for *reports* of currency transactions is $10,000. Remember, do not confuse *reports* with *records*. For example, a financial institution need not *report*, but must maintain a *record* of any cash purchase of bank checks, money orders, or travelers' checks over $3,000.

The regulations separate the reporting requirements of casinos and Postal Service money orders from other financial institutions. Every financial institution is required to file a CTR of each deposit, withdrawal, exchange or currency, or transfer by, through, or to it which involves a transaction in currency of **more than $10,000.** Remember, "currency" includes U.S. paper or coin or the paper or coin of any other country.

The section deals with the threat of structuring: "multiple currency transactions shall be treated as a single transaction if the financial institution has knowledge that they are by or on behalf of any person and result in either cash in or cash out totaling more than $10,000 during any one business day."

Casinos are also required to file a report (a CTRC) of "each transaction in currency, involving either cash in or cash out of more than $10,000." Such transactions include purchases or redemption of chips or tokens or markers, deposits or withdrawals of front money, payments on any form of credit or marker, currency received by or given out by a casino by wire transfer for or to a customer, or even reimbursement of a customer's travel and entertainment expenses. For a detailed look at casinos, see Chapter 5, "Money Laundering in Non-Bank Financial Institutions."

The **Postal Service** is also required to report each cash purchase of postal money orders in excess of $10,000.

(b) The Secretary may designate a domestic financial institution as an agent of the United States Government to receive a report under this section. However, the Secretary may designate a domestic financial institution that is not insured, chartered, examined, or registered as a domestic financial institution only if the institution consents. The Secretary may suspend or revoke a designation for a violation of this subchapter or a regulation under this subchapter (except a violation of section 5315 of this title or a regulation prescribed under section 5315), section 411 of the National Housing Act (12 U.S.C. 1730d), or section 21 of the Federal Deposit Insurance Act (12 U.S.C. 1829b).

(c)(1) A person (except a domestic financial institution designated under subsection (b) of this section) required to file a report under this section shall file the report —

(A) with the institution involved in the transaction if the institution was designated;

(B) in the way the Secretary prescribes when the institution was not designated; or

(C) with the Secretary.

(2) The Secretary shall prescribe —

(A) the filing procedure for a domestic financial institution designated under subsection (b) of this section; and

(B) the way the institution shall submit reports filed with it.

(d) Mandatory exemptions from reporting requirements —

(1) In general. — The Secretary shall exempt, pursuant to section 5318(a)(6), a depository institution from the reporting requirements of subsection (a) with respect to transactions between the depository institution and the following categories of entities:

(A) Another depository institution.

(B) A department or agency of the United States, any State, or any political subdivision of any State.

(C) Any entity established under the laws of the United States, any State, or any political subdivision of any State, or under an interstate compact between 2 or more States, which exercises governmental authority on behalf of the United States or any such State or political subdivision.

(D) Any business or category of business the reports on which have little or no value for law enforcement purposes.

(2) Notice of exemption. — The Secretary of the Treasury shall publish in the Federal Register at such times as the Secretary determines to be appropriate (but not less frequently than once each year) a list of all the entities whose transactions with a depository institution are exempt under this subsection from the reporting requirements of subsection (a).

(e) Discretionary exemptions from reporting requirements —

(1) In general. — The Secretary shall exempt, pursuant to section 5318(a)(6), a depository institution from the reporting requirements of subsection (a) with respect to transactions between the depository institution and a qualified business customer of the institution on the basis of information submitted to the Secretary by the institution in accordance with procedures which the Secretary shall establish.

(2) Qualified business customer defined. — For purposes of this subsection, the term "qualified business customer" means a business which —

(A) maintains a transaction account (as defined in section 19(b)(1)(C) of the Federal Reserve Act) at the depository institution;
(B) frequently engages in transactions with the depository institution which are subject to the reporting requirements of subsection (a); and
(C) meets criteria which the Secretary determines are sufficient to ensure that the purposes of this subchapter are carried out without requiring a report with respect to such transactions.

(3) Criteria for exemption. — The Secretary of the Treasury shall establish, by regulation, the criteria for granting an exemption under paragraph (1).

(4) Guidelines. —

(A) In general. — The Secretary of the Treasury shall establish guidelines for depository institutions to follow in selecting customers for an exemption under this subsection.
(B) Contents. — The guidelines may include a description of the types of businesses or an itemization of specific businesses for which no exemption will be granted under this subsection to any depository institution.

This entire section was added by the Money Laundering Suppression Act of 1994 to ease the burden on banks reporting on the routine transactions of their regular, legitimate business customers. The guidelines and criteria for exempting certain persons are described in the section's complimentary regulation, 31 CFR section 103.22(b) through (h). These exempt businesses include the following:

Retail businesses, defined as "a business primarily engaged in providing goods to ultimate consumers and for which the business is paid in substantial portions by currency." The exception to this exempt class are vehicle, boat, and airplane dealerships (cash deposits by these entities are subject to the reporting requirements); sports arenas, race tracks, amusement parks, bars, restaurants, hotels, licensed check cashing services, vending machine operators, theaters, passenger carriers, and public utilities; and any business that regularly pays its employees in cash.

In any case, these exemptions cannot exceed amounts which the bank "may reasonably conclude do not exceed amounts commensurate with the customary conduct of the lawful, domestic business of that customer." 31 CFR section 103.22(c).

In addition, in order to gain exempt status, customers must sign a written statement attesting to their reason for seeking an exemption. These statements must be retained by the bank so long as the customer is exempt, and for five years thereafter.

(5) Annual Review. — The Secretary of the Treasury shall prescribe regulations requiring each depository institution to —

(A) review, at least once each year, the qualified business customers of such institution with respect to whom an exemption has been granted under this subsection; and

(B) upon the completion of such review, resubmit information about such customers, with such modifications as the institution determines to be appropriate, to the Secretary for the Secretary's approval.

(6) 2-Year phase-in provision. — During the 2-year period beginning on the date of the enactment of the Money Laundering Suppression Act of 1994, this subsection shall be applied by the Secretary on the basis of such criteria as the Secretary determines to be appropriate to achieve an orderly implementation of the requirements of this subsection.

This two-year phase in period expired on April 30, 1996, and the regulations specifically required all banks to "redesignate" their exempt customers within 30 days of that customer's first transaction after April 30, 1996, or by August 30, 1996, whichever was sooner.

The regulations clearly put the onus on the banks to ensure their customers are truly exempt: a bank "must take such steps to assure itself that a person is an exempt person ... that a reasonable and prudent bank would take to protect itself from loan or other fraud or loss based on misidentification of a person's status." 31 CFR section 103.22(h)(4).

(f) Provisions applicable to mandatory and discretionary exemptions. —

(1) Limitation on liability of depository institutions. — No depository institution shall be subject to any penalty which may be imposed under this subchapter for the failure of the institution to file a report with respect to a transaction with a customer for whom an exemption has been granted under subsection (d) or (e) unless the institution —

(A) knowingly files false or incomplete information to the Secretary with respect to the transaction or the customer engaging in the transaction; or

(B) has reason to believe at the time the exemption is granted or the transaction is entered into that the customer or the transaction does not meet the criteria established for granting such exemption.

(2) Coordination with other provisions. — Any exemption granted by the Secretary of the Treasury under section 5318(a) in accordance with this section, and any transaction which is subject to such exemption, shall be subject to any other provision of law applicable to such exemption, including —

(A) the authority of the Secretary, under section 5318(a)(6), to revoke such exemption at any time; and

(B) any requirement to report, or any authority to require a report on, any possible violation of any law or regulation or any suspected criminal activity.

FinCEN has been given the authority under (f)(2)(A) to revoke exemptions by regulation, 31 CFR section 103.22(h)(8), by publishing notice in the Federal Register.

The language of subsection (f)(2)(B) means simply that even where a transaction is conducted by a Qualified Business Customer or exempt person, a financial institution is not relieved of its obligation to report if that transaction is otherwise "suspicious."

(g) Depository institution defined. — For the purposes of this section, the term "depository institution" —

(1) has the meaning given to such term in section 19(b)(1)(A) of the Federal Reserve Act; and

(2) includes —

(A) any branch, agency, or commercial lending company (as such terms are defined in section 1(b) of the International Banking Act of 1978);

(B) any corporation chartered under section 25A of the Federal Reserve Act; and

(C) any corporation having an agreement or undertaking with the Board of Governors of the Federal Reserve System under section 25 of the Federal Reserve Act.

Section 5314 Records and reports on foreign financial agency transactions

(a) Considering the need to avoid impeding or controlling the export or import of monetary instruments and the need to avoid burdening unreasonably a person making a transaction with a foreign financial agency, the Secretary of the Treasury shall require a resident or citizen of the United States or a person in, and doing business in, the United States, to keep records, file reports, or keep records and file reports, when the resident, citizen, or person makes a transaction or maintains a relation for any person with a foreign financial agency. The records and reports shall contain the following information in the way and to the extent the Secretary prescribes:

(1) the identity and address of participants in a transaction or relationship.

(2) the legal capacity in which a participant is acting.

(3) the identity of real parties in interest.

(4) a description of the transaction.

(b) The Secretary may describe —

(1) a reasonable classification of persons subject to or exempt from a requirement under this section or a regulation under this section;

(2) a foreign country to which a requirement or a regulation under this section applies if the Secretary decides applying the requirement or regulation to all foreign countries is unnecessary or undesirable;

(3) the magnitude of transactions subject to a requirement or a regulation under this section;

(4) the kind of transaction subject to or exempt from a requirement or a regulation under this section; and

(5) other matters the Secretary considers necessary to carry out this section or a regulation under this section.

(c) A person shall be required to disclose a record required to be kept under this section or under a regulation under this section only as required by law.

Section 5315 Reports on foreign currency transactions

(a) Congress finds that —

(1) moving mobile capital can have a significant impact on the proper functioning of the international monetary system;

(2) it is important to have the most feasible, current, and complete information on the kind and source of capital inflows, including transactions by large United States businesses and their foreign affiliates; and

(3) additional authority should be provided to collect information on capital flows under section 5(b) of the Trading With the Enemy Act (50 App. U.S.C. 5(b)) and section 8 of the Bretton Woods Agreement Act (22 U.S.C. 286f).

(b) In this section, "United States person" and "foreign person controlled by a United States person" have the same meanings given those terms in section 7(f)(2)(A) and (C), respectively, of the Securities and Exchange Act of 1934 (15 U.S.C. 78g(f)(2)(A), (C)).

(c) The Secretary of the Treasury shall prescribe regulations consistent with subsection (a) of this section requiring reports on foreign currency transactions conducted by a United States person or a foreign person controlled by a United States person. The regulations shall require that a report contain information and be submitted at the time and in the way, with reasonable exceptions and classifications, necessary to carry out this section.

Section 5316 Reports on exporting and importing monetary instruments

(a) Except as provided in subsection (c) of this section, a person or an agent or bailee of the person shall file a report under subsection (b) of this section when the person, agent, or bailee knowingly —

(1) transports, is about to transport, or has transported, monetary instruments of more than $10,000 at one time —

(A) from a place in the United States to or through a place outside the United States; or

(B) to a place in the United States from or through a place outside the United States; or

(2) receives monetary instruments of more than $10,000 at one time transported into the United States from or though a place outside the United States.

This section imposes a duty on a person transporting, mailing, or shipping currency or a "monetary instrument" (remember the definition) into or out of the U.S. in an amount more than $10,000 to report that act by way of a CMIR — an International Currency and Monetary Instrument Report. The original (1970) threshold amount was $5,000. It was raised to $10,000 by the Money Laundering Control Act of 1986.

The MLCA also added the "about to transport, mail, or ship" language to close a loophole where the person had not actually transported the monetary instrument but was attempting to do so. There is an entire series of cases on whether a person committed an offense under this section where they were stopped by Customs before they passed through airport security, where they had dropped off a package for shipment to Mexico, etc.

(b) A report under this section shall be filed at the time and place the Secretary of the Treasury prescribes. The report shall contain the following information to the extent the Secretary prescribes:

(1) the legal capacity in which the person filing the report is acting.

(2) the origin, destination, and route of the monetary instruments.

(3) when the monetary instruments are not legally and beneficially owned by the person transporting the instruments, or if the person transporting the instruments personally is not going to use them, the identity of the person that gave the instruments to the person transporting them, the identity of the person who is to receive them, or both.

(4) the amount and kind of monetary instruments transported.

(5) additional information.

(c) This section or a regulation under this section does not apply to a common carrier of passengers when a passenger possesses a monetary instrument, or to a common carrier of goods if the shipper does not declare the instrument.

(d) Cumulation of closely related events. — The Secretary of the Treasury may prescribe regulations under this section defining the term "at one time" for purposes of subsection (a). Such regulations may permit the cumulation of closely related events in order that such events may collectively be considered to occur at one time for the purposes of subsection (a).

The regulations referred to in subsection (d) are set out at 31 CFR section 103.23, entitled "Reports of transportation of currency or monetary instruments." Note that it is not illegal to transport over $10,000 in currency or other monetary instruments across the border; it is the failure to report that leads to criminal liability and possible forfeiture of the instruments and fines.

The subsection and complimentary regulations also apply equally to legally derived money that is not reported. In the early 1990s, singer James Brown failed to report over $300,000 in cash that he had earned on an Eastern European concert tour. The money was forfeited and he faced criminal charges.

Among other things, this subsection and regulation expands the term "transports" to include mailing or shipping, but limits it to a *physical* transportation by excluding transfers of funds through normal banking channels.

Section 5317 Search and forfeiture of monetary instruments

(a) The Secretary of the Treasury may apply to a court of competent jurisdiction for a search warrant when the Secretary reasonably believes a monetary instrument is being transported and a report on the instrument under section 5316 of this title has not been filed or contains a material omission or misstatement. The Secretary shall include a statement of information in support of the warrant. On a showing of probable cause, the court may issue a search warrant for a designated person or a designated place or physical object. This subsection does not affect the authority of the Secretary under another law.

(b) Searches at border. — For purposes of ensuring compliance with the requirements of section 5316, a customs officer may stop and search, at the border and without a search warrant, any vehicle, vessel, aircraft, or other conveyance, any envelope or other container, and any person entering or departing from the United States.

A more detailed look at seizure and forfeiture is contained in Chapter 9, "Asset Forfeiture."

(c) If a report required under section 5316 with respect to any monetary instrument is not filed (or if filed, contains a material omission or misstatement of fact), the instrument and any interest in property, including a deposit in a financial institution, traceable to such instrument may be seized and forfeited to the United States Government. Any property, real or personal, involved in a transaction or attempted transaction in violation of section 5324(b), or any property traceable to such property, may be seized and forfeited to the United States Government. A monetary instrument transported by mail or a common carrier, messenger or bailee is being transported under this subsection from the time the instrument is delivered to the United States Postal Service, common carrier, messenger, or bailee through the time it is delivered to the addressee, intended recipient, or agent of the addressee or intended recipient without being transported further in, or taken out of, the United States.

Section 5318 Compliance, exemptions, and summons authority

(a) General powers of the Secretary. — The Secretary of the Treasury may (except under section 5315 of this title and regulations prescribed under section 5315) —

(1) except as provided in subsection (b)(2), delegate duties and powers under this subchapter to an appropriate supervising agency and the United States Postal Service;

(2) require a class of domestic financial institutions to maintain appropriate procedures to ensure compliance with this subchapter and regulations prescribed under this subchapter or to guard against money laundering;

(3) examine any books, papers, records, or other data of domestic financial institutions relevant to the record keeping or reporting requirements of this subchapter;

(4) summon a financial institution, an officer or employee of a financial institution (including a former officer or employee), or any person having possession, custody, or care of the reports and records required under this subchapter, to appear before the Secretary of the Treasury or his delegate at a time and place named in the summons and to produce such books, papers, records, or other data, and to give testimony, under oath, as may be relevant or material to an investigation described in subsection (b);

(5) exempt from the requirements of this subchapter any class of transactions within any State if the Secretary determines that —

(A) under the laws of such State, that class of transactions is subject to requirements substantially similar to those imposed under this subchapter; and

(B) there is adequate provision for the enforcement of such requirements; and

(6) prescribe an appropriate exemption from a requirement under this subchapter and regulations prescribed under this subchapter. The Secretary may revoke an exemption by actually or constructively notifying the parties affected. A revocation is effective during judicial review.

(b) Limitations on summons power. —

(1) Scope of power. — The Secretary of the Treasury may take any action described in paragraph (3) or (4) of subsection (a) only in connection with investigations for the purpose of civil enforcement of violations of this subchapter, section 21 of the Federal Deposit Insurance Act, section 411 of the National Housing Act, or chapter 2 of Public Law 91-508 (12 U.S.C. 1951 et seq.) or any regulation under any such provision.

(2) Authority to issue. — A summons may be issued under subsection (a)(4) only by, or with the approval of, the Secretary of the Treasury or a supervisory level delegate of the Secretary of the Treasury.

(c) Administrative aspects of summons. —

(1) Production at designated site. — A summons issued pursuant to this section may require that books, papers, records, or other data stored or maintained at any place be produced at any designated location in any State or in any territory or other place subject to the jurisdiction of the United States not more than 500 miles distant from any place where the financial institution operates or conducts business in the United States.

(2) Fees and travel expenses. — Persons summoned under this section shall be paid the same fees and mileage for travel in the United States that are paid witnesses in the courts of the United States.

(3) No liability for expenses. — The United States shall not be liable for any expense, other than an expense described in paragraph (2), incurred in

connection with the production of books, papers, records, or other data under this section.

(d) Service of summons. — Service of a summons issued under this section may be by registered mail or in such other manner calculated to give actual notice as the Secretary may prescribe by regulation.

(e) Contumacy or refusal. —

(1) Referral to Attorney General. — In case of contumacy by a person issued a summons under paragraph (3) or (4) of subsection (a) or a refusal by such person to obey such summons, the Secretary of the Treasury shall refer the matter to the Attorney General.

(2) Jurisdiction of court. — The Attorney General may invoke the aid of any court of the United States within the jurisdiction of which —

(A) the investigation which gave rise to the summons is being or has been carried on;
(B) the person summoned is an inhabitant; or
(C) the person summoned carries on business or may be found, to compel compliance with the summons.

(3) Court order. — The court may issue an order requiring the person summoned to appear before the Secretary or his delegate to produce books, papers, records, and other data, to give testimony as may be necessary to explain how such material was compiled and maintained, and to pay the costs of the proceeding.

(4) Failure to comply with order. — Any failure to obey the order of the court may be punished by the court as a contempt thereof.

(5) Service of process. — All process in any case under this subsection may be served in any judicial district in which such person may be found.

(f) Written and signed statement required. — No person shall qualify for an exemption under subsection (a)(5) unless the relevant financial institution prepares and maintains a statement which —

(1) describes in detail the reasons why such person is qualified for such exemption; and

(2) contains the signature of such person.

(g) Reporting of suspicious transactions. —

(1) In general. — the Secretary may require any financial institution, and any director, officer, employee, or agent of any financial institution, to report any suspicious transaction relevant to a possible violation of law or regulation.

The requirement to report suspicious activity was first created in 1992. The history and fundamentals of this requirement, and the nature of the

Suspicious Activity Report (SAR) form itself, is set out in detail in Chapter 7, "Domestic Money Laundering Statutes and Laws," and Section II.F of Chapter 8, "Regulatory (Anti-Money-Laundering) Forms."

(2) Notification prohibited. — A financial institution, and a director, officer, employee, or agent of any financial institution, who voluntarily reports a suspicious transaction, or that reports a suspicious transaction pursuant to this section or any other authority, may not notify any person involved in the transaction that the transaction has been reported.

This is the "whistleblower" section — a bank or one of its officers is prohibited from tipping off its customer that he, she, or it is either under suspicion or that a particular transaction is suspicious. The corollary to this provision is the "safe harbor" provision found in the next section.

(3) Liability for disclosures. — Any financial institution that makes a disclosure or any possible violation of law or regulation or a disclosure pursuant to this subsection or any other authority, and any director, officer, employee, or agent of such institution, shall not be liable to any person under any law or regulation of the United States or any constitution, law, or regulation of any State or political subdivision thereof, for such disclosure or for any failure to notify the person involved in the transaction or any other person of such disclosure.

This is the "safe harbor" provision. So long as a financial institution acts in good faith and pursuant to legal process or authority, it cannot be held liable for any damage that it causes by disclosing a "possible violation."

(4) Single designee for reporting suspicious transactions. —

(A) In general. — In requiring reports under subparagraph (1) of suspicious transactions, the Secretary of the Treasury shall designate, to the extent practicable and appropriate, a single officer or agency of the United States to whom such reports shall be made.

FinCEN has been designated as the sole recipient of all SARs.

(B) Duty of designee. — The officer or agency of the United States designated by the Secretary of the Treasury pursuant to subparagraph (A) shall refer any report of a suspicious transaction to any appropriate law enforcement agency or supervisory agency.

(C) Coordination with other reporting requirements. — Subparagraph (A) shall not be construed as precluding any supervisory agency for any financial institution from requiring the financial institution to submit any information or report to the agency or another agency pursuant to any other applicable provision of law.

(h) Anti-money laundering programs. —

(1) In general. — In order to guard against money laundering through financial institutions, the Secretary may require financial institutions to carry out anti-money laundering programs, including at a minimum

(A) the development of internal policies, procedures, and controls,
(B) the designation of a compliance officer,
(C) an ongoing employee training program, and
(D) an independent audit function to test programs.

(2) Regulations. — The Secretary may prescribe minimum standards for programs established under paragraph (1).

Section 5319 Availability of reports

The Secretary of the Treasury shall make information in a report filed under section 5313, 5314, or 5316 of this title available to an agency, including any State financial institution's supervisory agency, on request of the head of the agency. The report shall be available for a purpose consistent with those sections or a regulation prescribed under those sections. The Secretary may only require reports on the use of such information by any State financial institution's supervisory agency for other than supervisory purposes. However, a report and records of reports are exempt from disclosure under section 552 of title 5.

Section 5320 Injunctions

When the Secretary of the Treasury believes a person has violated, is violating, or will violate this subchapter or a regulation prescribed or order issued under this subchapter, the Secretary may bring a civil action in the appropriate district court of the United States or appropriate United States court of a territory or possession of the United States to enjoin the violation or to enforce compliance with the subchapter, regulation, or order. An injunction or temporary restraining order shall be issued without bond.

Section 5321 Civil penalties

(a)(1) A domestic financial institution, and a partner, director, officer, or employee of a domestic financial institution, willfully violating this subchapter or a regulation prescribed under this subchapter (except sections 5314 and 5315 of this title or a regulation prescribed under sections 5314 and 5315) is liable to the United States Government for a civil penalty of not more than the greater of the amount (not to exceed $100,000) involved in the transaction (if any) or $25,000. For a violation of section 5318(a)(2) of this title or a regulation prescribed under section 5318(2), a separate violation occurs for each day the violation continues and at each office, branch, or place of business at which a violation occurs or continues.

(2) The Secretary of the Treasury may impose an additional civil penalty on a person not filing a report, or filing a report containing a material omission or misstatement, under section 5316 of this title or a regulation prescribed under section 5316. A civil penalty under this paragraph may not be more than the amount of the monetary instrument for which the report was required. A civil penalty under this paragraph is reduced by an amount forfeited under section 5317(b) of this title.

(3) A person not filing a report under a regulation prescribed under section 5315 of this title or not complying with an injunction under section 5320 of this title enjoining a violation of, or enforcing compliance with, section 5315 or a regulation prescribed under section 5315, is liable to the Government for a civil penalty of not more than $10,000.

(4) Structured transaction violation. —

(A) Penalty authorized. — The Secretary of the Treasury may impose a civil money penalty on any person who violates any provision of section 5324.

(B) Maximum amount limitation. — The amount of any civil money penalty imposed under subparagraph (A) shall not exceed the amount of the coins and currency (or such other monetary instruments as the Secretary may prescribe) involved in the transaction with respect to which such penalty is imposed.

(C) Coordination with forfeiture provision. — The amount of any civil money penalty imposed by the Secretary under subparagraph (A) shall be reduced by the amount of any forfeiture to the United States in connection with the transaction with respect to which such penalty is imposed.

(5) Foreign financial agency transaction violation. —

(A) Penalty authorized. — The Secretary of the Treasury may impose a civil money penalty on any person who willfully violates or any person willfully causing any violation of any provision of section 5314.

(B) Maximum amount limitation. — The amount of any civil money penalty imposed under subparagraph (A) shall not exceed —

(i) in the case of violation of such section involving a transaction, the greater of —

(I) the amount (not to exceed $100,000) of the transaction; or
(II) $25,000; and

(ii) in the case of violation of such section involving a failure to report the existence of an account or any identifying information required to be provided with respect to such account, the greater of —

(I) an amount (not to exceed $100,000) equal to the balance in the account at the time of the violation; or

(II) $25,000.

(6) Negligence. —

(A) In general. — The Secretary of the Treasury may impose a civil money penalty of not more than $500 on any financial institution which negligently violates any provision of this subchapter or any regulation prescribed under this subchapter.

(B) Pattern of negligent activity. — If any financial institution engages in a pattern of negligent violations of any provision of this subchapter or any regulation prescribed under this subchapter, the Secretary of the Treasury may, in addition to any penalty imposed under subparagraph (A) with respect to any such violation, impose a civil money penalty of not more than $50,000 on the financial institution.

(b) Time limitations for assessments and commencement of civil actions. —

(1) Assessments. — The Secretary of the Treasury may assess a civil penalty under subsection (a) at any time before the end of the 6-year period beginning on the date of the transaction with respect to which the penalty is assessed.

(2) Civil actions. — The Secretary may commence a civil action to recover a civil penalty assessed under subsection (a) at any time before the end of the 2-year period beginning on the later of —

(A) the date the penalty was assessed; or

(B) the date any judgment becomes final in any criminal action under section 5322 in connection with the same transaction with respect to which the penalty is assessed.

(c) The Secretary may remit any part of a forfeiture under subsection (c) or (d) of section 5317 of this title or civil penalty under subsection (a)(2) of this section.

(d) Criminal penalty not exclusive of civil penalty. — A civil money penalty may be imposed under subsection (a) with respect to any violation of this subchapter notwithstanding the fact that a criminal penalty is imposed with respect to the same violation.

(e) Delegation of assessment authority to banking agencies. —

(1) In general. — The Secretary of the Treasury shall delegate, in accordance with section 5318(a)(1) and subject to such terms and conditions as the Secretary may impose in accordance with paragraph (3), any authority of the Secretary to assess a civil money penalty under this section on depository institutions (as defined in section 3 of the Federal Deposit Insurance Act) to the appropriate Federal banking agencies (as defined in such section 3).

(2) Authority of agencies. — Subject to any term or condition imposed by the Secretary of the Treasury under paragraph (3), the provisions of this section shall apply to an appropriate Federal banking agency to which is delegated any authority of the Secretary under this section in the same manner such provisions apply to the Secretary.

(3) Terms and conditions. —

(A) In general. — The Secretary of the Treasury shall prescribe by regulation the terms and conditions which shall apply to any delegation under paragraph (1).

(B) Maximum dollar amount. — The terms and conditions authorized under subparagraph (A) may include, in the Secretary's sole discretion, a limitation on the amount of any civil penalty which may be assessed by an appropriate Federal banking agency pursuant to a delegation under paragraph (1).

Section 5322 Criminal penalties

(a) A person willfully violating this subchapter or a regulation prescribed under this subchapter (except section 5315 of this title or a regulation prescribed under section 5315 or 5324) shall be fined not more than $250,000, imprisoned for not more than five years, or both.

(b) A person willfully violating this subchapter or a regulation prescribed under this subchapter (except section 5315 or 5324 of this title or a regulation prescribed under section 5315 or 5324), while violating another law of the United States or as part of a pattern of illegal activity involving transactions of more than $100,000 in a 12-month period, shall be fined not more than $500,000, imprisoned for not more than 10 years, or both.

(c) For a violation of section 5318(a)(2) of this title or a regulation prescribed under section 5318(a)(2), a separate violation occurs for each day the violation continues and at each office, branch, or place of business at which a violation occurs or continues.

Section 5323 Rewards for informants

(a) The Secretary may pay a reward to an individual who provides original information which leads to a recovery of a criminal fine, civil penalty, or forfeiture, which exceeds $50,000, for a violation of this chapter.

(b) The Secretary shall determine the amount of a reward under this section. The Secretary may not award more than 25 per centum of the net amount of the fine, penalty, or forfeiture collected or $150,000, whichever is less.

(c) An officer or employee of the United States, a State, or a local government who provides information described in subsection (a) in the performance of official duties is not eligible for a reward under this section.

(d) There are authorized to be appropriated such sums as may be necessary to carry out the provisions of this section.

Section 5324 Structuring transactions to evade reporting requirement prohibited

(a) Domestic coin and currency transactions. — No person shall for the purpose of evading the reporting requirements of section 5313(a) or 5325 or any regulations prescribed under any such section —

(1) cause or attempt to cause a domestic financial institution to fail to file a report required under section 5315(a) or 5325 or any regulation prescribed under any such section;

(2) cause or attempt to cause a domestic financial institution to fail to file a report required under section 5315(a) or 5325 or any regulation prescribed under any such section that contains a material omission or misstatement of fact; or

(3) structure or assist in structuring, or attempt to structure or assist in structuring, any transaction with one or more domestic financial institutions.

(b) International monetary instrument transactions. — No person shall, for the purpose of evading the reporting requirements of section 5316 —

(1) fail to file a report required by section 5316, or cause or attempt to cause a person to fail to file such a report;

(2) file or cause or attempt to cause a person to file a report required under section 5316 that contains a material omission or misstatement of fact; or

(3) structure or assist in structuring, or attempt to structure or assist in structuring, any importation or exportation of monetary instruments.

(c) Criminal penalty. —

(1) In general. — Whoever violates this section shall be fined in accordance with title18, United States Code, imprisoned for not more than 5 years, or both.

(2) Enhanced penalty for aggravated cases. — Whoever violates this section while violating another law of the United States or as part of a pattern of any illegal activity involving more than $100,000 in a 12-month period shall be fined twice the amount provided in subsection (b)(3) or (c)(3) (as the case may be) of section 3571 of title 18, United States Code, imprisoned for not more than 10 years, or both.

Section 5325 Identification required to purchase certain monetary instruments

(a) In general. — No financial institution may issue or sell a bank check, cashier's check, traveler's check, or money order to any individual in connection with a transaction or group of such contemporaneous transactions which involves United States coins or currency (or such other monetary instruments as the Secretary may prescribe) in amounts or denominations of $3,000 or more unless —

(1) the individual has a transaction account with such financial institution and the financial institution —

(A) verifies that fact through a signature card or other information maintained by such institution in connection with the account of such individual; and

(B) records the method of verification in accordance with regulations which the Secretary of the Treasury shall prescribe; or

(2) Report to Secretary upon request. — Any information required to be recorded by any financial institution under paragraph (1) or (2) of subsection (a) shall be reported by such institution to the Secretary of the Treasury at the request of such Secretary.

(c) Transaction account defined. — For purposes of this section, the term "transaction account" has the meaning given to such term in section 19(b)(1)(C) of the Federal Reserve Act.

Section 5326 Records of certain domestic coin and currency transactions

(a) In general. — If the Secretary of the Treasury finds, upon the Secretary's own initiative or at the request of an appropriate Federal or State law enforcement official, that reasonable grounds exist for concluding that additional record keeping and reporting requirements are necessary to carry out the purposes of this subtitle and prevent evasions thereof, the Secretary may issue an order requiring any domestic financial institution or group of domestic institutions in a geographic area —

(1) to obtain such information as the Secretary may describe in such order concerning —

(A) any transaction in which such financial institution is involved for the payment, receipt, or transfer of United States coins or currency (or such other monetary instruments as the Secretary may describe in such order) the total amounts or denominations of which are equal to or greater than an amount which the Secretary may prescribe; and

(B) any other person participating in such transaction;

(2) to maintain a record of such information for such period of time as the Secretary may require; and

(3) to file a report with respect to any transaction described in paragraph (1)(A) in the manner and to the extent specified in the order.

(b) Authority to order depository institutions to obtain reports from customers. —

(1) In general. — The Secretary of the Treasury may, by regulation or order, require any depository institution (as defined in section 3(c) of the Federal Deposit Insurance Act) —

(A) to request any financial institution (other than a depository institution) which engages in any reportable transaction with the depository institution to provide the depository institution with a copy of any report filed by the financial institution under this subtitle with respect to any prior transaction (between such financial institution and any other person) which involved any portion of the coins or currency (or monetary instruments) which are involved in the reportable transaction with the depository institution; and

(B) if no copy of any report in subparagraph (A) is received by the depository institution in connection with any reportable transaction to which such subparagraph applies, to submit (in addition to any report required under this subtitle with respect to the reportable transaction) a written notice to the Secretary that the financial institution failed to provide any copy of such report.

(2) Reportable transaction defined. — For purposes of this subsection, the term "reportable transaction" means any transaction involving coins or currency (or such other monetary instruments as the Secretary may prescribe in the regulation or order) the total amounts or denominations or which are equal to or greater than an amount which the Secretary may prescribe.

(c) Nondisclosure of orders. — No financial institution or officer, director, employee, or agent of a financial institution subject to an order under this section may disclose the existence of, or terms of, the order to any person except as prescribed by the Secretary.

(d) Maximum effective period for order. — No order issued under subsection (a) shall be effective for more than 60 days unless renewed pursuant to the requirements of subsection (a).

Section 5327 Repealed, September 30, 1996.

Section 5328 Whistleblower protections

(a) Prohibition against discrimination. — No financial institution may discharge or otherwise discriminate against any employee with respect to compensation, terms, conditions, or privileges of employment because the employee (or any person acting pursuant to the request of the employee) provided information to the Secretary of the Treasury, the Attorney General, or any Federal supervisory agency regarding a possible violation of any provision of this subchapter or section 1956, 1957, or 1960 of title 18, or any regulation under any such provision, by the financial institution or any director, officer, or employee of the financial institution.

(b) Enforcement. — Any employee or former employee who believes that such employee has been discharged or discriminated against in violation of subsection (a) may file a civil action in the appropriate United States district court before the end of the 2-year period beginning on the date of such discharge or discrimination.

(c) Remedies. — If the district court determines that a violation has occurred, the court may order the financial institution which committed the violation to —

(1) reinstate the employee to the employee's former position;

(2) pay compensatory damages; or

(3) take other appropriate actions to remedy any past discrimination.

(d) Limitation. — The protections of this section shall not apply to any employee who —

(1) deliberately causes or participates in the alleged violation of law or regulation; or

(2) knowingly or recklessly provides substantially false information to the Secretary, the Attorney General, or any Federal supervisory agency.

(e) Coordination with other provisions of law. — This section shall not apply with respect to any financial institution which is subject to section 33 of the Federal Deposit Insurance Act, section 213 of the Federal Credit Union Act, or section 21A(q) of the Home Owners' Loan Act (as added by section 251(c) of the Federal Deposit Insurance Corporation Improvement Act of 1991).

Section 5329 Staff commentaries

The Secretary shall —

(1) publish all written rulings interpreting this subchapter; and

(2) annually issue a staff commentary on the regulations issued under this subchapter.

Section 5330 Registration of money transmitting businesses

(a) Registration with Secretary of the Treasury required. —

(1) In general. — Any person who owns or controls a money transmitting business shall register the business (whether or not the business is licensed as a money transmitting business in any State) with the Secretary of the Treasury not later than the end of the 180-day period beginning on the later of —

(A) the date of the enactment of the Money Laundering Suppression Act of 1994; or

(B) the date on which the business is established.

(2) Form and manner of registration. — Subject to the requirements of subsection (b), the Secretary of the Treasury shall prescribe, by regulation, the form and manner for registering a money transmitting business pursuant to paragraph (1).

(3) Businesses remain subject to State law. — This section shall not be construed as superseding any requirement of State law relating to money transmitting businesses operating in such State.

(4) False and incomplete information. — The filing of false or materially incomplete information in connection with the registration of a money transmitting business shall be considered as a failure to comply with the requirements of this subchapter.

(b) Contents of registration. — The registration of a money transmitting business under subsection (a) shall include the following information:

(1) The name and location of the business.

(2) The name and address of each person who —

   (A) owns or controls the business;
   (B) is a director or officer of the business; or
   (C) otherwise participates in the conduct of the affairs of the business.

(3) The name and address of any depository institution at which the business maintains a transaction account (as defined in section 19(b)(1)(C) of the Federal Reserve Act).

(4) An estimate of the volume of business in the coming year (which shall be reported annually to the Secretary).

(5) Such other information as the Secretary of the Treasury may require.

(c) Agents of money transmitting businesses

(1) Maintenance of lists of agents of money transmitting businesses. — Pursuant to regulations which the Secretary of the Treasury shall prescribe, each money transmitting business shall —

   (A) maintain a list containing the names and addresses of all persons authorized to act as an agent for such business in connection with activities described in subsection (d)(1)(A) and such other information about such agents as the Secretary may require; and
   (B) make the list and other information available on request to any appropriate private law enforcement agency.

(2) Treatment of agent as money transmitting business. — The Secretary of the Treasury shall prescribe regulations establishing, on the basis of such criteria as the Secretary determines to be appropriate, a threshold point for

treating an agent of a money transmitting business as a money transmitting business for purposes of this section.

(d) Definitions. — For purposes of this section, the following definitions shall apply:

(1) Money transmitting business. — The term "money transmitting business" means any business other than the United States Postal Service which —

   (A) provides check cashing, currency exchange, or money transmitting or remittance services, or issues or redeems money orders, travelers' checks, and other similar instruments;
   (B) is required to file reports under section 5313; and
   (C) is not a depository institution (as defined in section 5313(g)).

(2) Money transmitting service. — The term "money transmitting service" includes accepting currency or funds denominated in the currency of any country and transmitting the currency or funds, or the value of the currency or funds, by any means through a financial agency or institution, a Federal reserve bank or other facility of the Board of Governors of the Federal Reserve System, or an electronic funds transfer network.

(e) Civil penalty for failure to comply with registration requirements. —

(1) In general. — Any person who fails to comply with any requirement of this section or any regulation prescribed under this section shall be liable to the United States for a civil penalty of $5,000 for each such violation.

(2) Continuing violation. — Each day a violation described in paragraph (1) continues shall constitute a separate violation for purposes of such paragraph.

(3) Assessments. — Any penalty imposed under this subsection shall be assessed and collected by the Secretary of the Treasury in the manner provided in section 5321 and any such assessment shall be subject to the provisions of such section.

Regulatory (Anti-Money-Laundering) Forms

8

I. Introduction

The Bank Secrecy Act, 31 U.S.C. sections 5311–5324, and its complementary regulations, Part 103 of Title 31 of the Code of Federal Regulations (31 CFR 103) set out in excruciating detail the who's, when's, where's, and why's of filing the various reports designed to report and record activity that is or could be related to criminal activity. The five major reports required by Title 31, and IRS Form 8300, are each described below.

Note that, in addition to these reports, financial institutions are required to maintain certain records; this chapter is limited to the *reports*. A more detailed discussion of the statutes and theory behind the reports and the records is contained in Chapter 7, "Domestic Money Laundering Statutes and Laws."

II. The Six Major Regulatory Reporting Forms

A. Currency Transaction Report (CTR)

From 1970 until 1992, the centerpiece of the Bank Secrecy Act was the Currency Transaction Report (CTR) (Appendix 8.1), a report that all "financial institutions" are required to file whenever an individual or a person acting on the individual's behalf conducts one or more transactions in a single day that involve, in the aggregate, over $10,000. Since their 1992 introduction, Suspicious Activity Reports, or SARs, have become the primary report for law enforcement authorities.

Why are CTRs not as effective as SARs? There certainly are a great number being filed; in 1992, there were almost 9 million CTR reports filed; FinCEN estimated it would receive more than 14 million in 1996. One problem is that CTRs are filed whether or not the transaction is facially legitimate; the IRS estimates that 30 to 40% of CTR filings relate to routine deposits by legitimate businesses. A second problem is the cost; the banking industry estimates the cost at approximately $130 million per year, or between $3 and $15 per CTR report. In addition, it costs the federal agencies approximately $2 per report to process and store the data.

Although the CTR filing requirement was first imposed in 1970, it was generally overlooked by the banking community until the mid-1980s when a regulatory review of the Bank of Boston revealed that it had failed to file CTRs on currency transactions valued at $1.2 billion. As a result, it paid a $500,000 fine. Other banks came forward, or were audited and fined: Crocker National Bank paid a fine of $2.25 million for failing to report 7,877 transactions totaling $3.98 million; Republic National Bank of Miami was fined $1.95 million for failure to "promptly" file CTRs.

In May 1995, as a result of a joint effort by the BSA Advisory Group and FinCEN, new regulations were issued, cutting the information required on the CTR by 30% to include basic information of who conducted the transaction, on whose behalf, the amount, the description of the transaction, and where it originated and was destined.

The corollary to the CTR is IRS Form 8300, which must be submitted by any person engaged in trade or business who engages in either a single or series of related transactions involving cash or cash equivalents involving an aggregate in excess of $10,000. This form, in theory, catches the "other end" of the cash transaction — the CTR requires the bank to report the deposit, while the Form 8300 requires the depositor to report the source of the funds for deposit.

B.   Currency Transaction Report by Casinos (CTRC)

Since 1985, state-licensed casinos with annual gaming revenues of at least $1 million have been subject to BSA and IRS record-keeping and reporting requirements. The Money Laundering Suppression Act of 1994 extended these requirements to tribal casinos. The primary reporting form has been IRS Form 8362 (and its counterpart for Nevada-based casinos, IRS Form 8852), the Currency Transaction Report by Casinos, or CTRC (Appendix 8.1). During 1996, casinos filed approximately 150,000 CTRCs, reporting cash transactions exceeding $3.2 billion. The CTRC is the twin to the CTR. The regulations relating to CTRCs are found at 31 CFR 103.22(a)(2).

On July 17, 1997, the Treasury Department, through FinCEN, issued a revised CTRC designed to help casinos report large currency transactions. These new forms simplified the reporting of the required information and clarified the instructions to make it clear that a form must be filed for each deposit, withdrawal, exchange of currency or gambling tokens or chips, or other payment or transfer by, through or to such casino that involves a transaction in currency of more than $10,000.

For a detailed look at casinos, see Section III of Chapter 5, "Money Laundering in Non-Bank Financial Institutions."

C.   Currency and Monetary Instrument Report (CMIR)

The CMIR, formally known as U.S. Customs Form 4790, "Report of International Transportation of Currency or Monetary Instruments," was created by the Bank Secrecy Act of 1970. The BSA (specifically 31 U.S.C. s. 5316) and its complimentary regulation, 31 CFR section 103.23, require any person who transports, mails, or ships, or causes to be physically transported, mailed, or shipped, or even attempts to transport, mail, or ship monetary instruments worth more than $10,000 into or out of the U.S. to declare the action on a CMIR. Note that the CMIR applies only to the physical transportation across the border and not to wire transfers. The domestic twin of a CMIR is the CTR; but note that the obligation to prepare and file a CMIR (Appendix 8.1) is on the person exporting or importing the monetary instrument, whereas the obligation to prepare and file a CTR is on the financial institution.

The most infamous CMIR case may well be *United States v. $173,081.04 in United States Currency,* 835 F.2d 1141 (5th Cir. 1988). Here, Raoul Arvizo-Morales, an employee of Casa de Cambio Juarez, a money exchange located in Juarez, Mexico, was asked by the owner (his brother Francisco) to transport $172,081.04 in cash and checks to the Texas Commerce Bank in El Paso, Texas, to settle accounts owed to some Texan *casas.* Raoul prepared a CMIR for that amount. Just before leaving the *casa,* Raoul was asked by Francisco to take another $19,865.04 to a second bank in El Paso. Raoul put the first bundle of money in a nylon bag, and the second bundle — miscounted as $20,865.04 — into a paper bag.

Raoul presented the CMIR to the Customs agent at the border crossing, who asked Raoul to produce the actual monetary instruments for verification. Raoul returned to his vehicle and returned with both bags. When asked if all the money was going to the Texas Commerce Bank, Raoul responded that it was, except for the "contents of the brown paper sack." When asked why he did not declare those funds, Raoul could only shrug; he then asked if he could add them to his CMIR form. The Customs agent refused and seized all of the money.

The Court of Appeals for the Fifth Circuit allowed the forfeiture of the entire sum (the $172,081.04 and the miscounted $1,000.00 in the paper bag — the brothers did not contest the undeclared $19,081.04), but they expressed their displeasure at the defense lawyer for failing to seek remission or mitigation. They also expressed displeasure with the apparent harshness of the statute.

D.   Foreign Bank Account Report (FBAR)

The FBAR is formally known as Treasury Form 90-22.1, "Report of Foreign Bank and Financial Accounts" (Appendix 8.1). Every person ("person" is a defined term including companies, trusts, etc.) having a financial interest in or signing authority over a bank, securities, or other financial account in a foreign country with aggregate deposits above $10,000 must report that relationship each year by filing an FBAR with Treasury on or before June 30th of the following year. The statutory authority over FBARs is set out at 31 U.S.C. s. 5314.

E.   Form 8300

The mirror image to a CTR is IRS Form 8300 (Appendix 8.1), which must be submitted by any person engaged in trade or business who engages in either a single or series of related transactions involving cash or cash equivalents involving an aggregate in excess of $10,000. Whereas a financial institution must file a CTR, any defined "trade or business" must file a Form 8300. The applicable statute for Form 8300 is 26 U.S.C. s. 6050I.

A "trade or business" is defined as any activity constituting the sale of goods or the performance of services that produce income. Examples include wholesale and retail sellers of: aircraft, antiques, art, vehicles, boats, coins, entertainment, equipment, furniture, furs, jewelry, and perishables. Accountants, airlines, attorneys, auction houses, consumer finance companies, hotels, insurance companies, leasing companies, pawn brokers, real estate agents, and travel agents are also covered by the statute.

Until February, 1992, trades and businesses were only required to report the receipt of "cash" over $10,000 received in any revolving 12-month period. Since that date, however, the regulations have been amended to include other types of monetary instruments used in payment for consumer durables, collectibles, and travel and entertainment.

These trades and businesses must aggregate "related transactions," which are defined as any transaction conducted between a payer or its agent and a recipient of cash in a 24-hour period or during a period of more than 24 hours if the recipient knows or has reason to know that each transaction is one of a series of connected transactions. In addition, multiple cash transactions that are conducted during the course of a rolling 12-month period by or on behalf of the same person also must be aggregated if the trade or business knows or has reason to know the transactions are related. Cash payments for the purchase of a single item in different days clearly triggers the filing requirements.

In addition to filing Form 8300, the trade or business must retain a copy for a period of five years. It is a five-year and/or $10,000 fine felony to willfully fail to file Form 8300 or to file a false or fraudulent form. In addition, the statute provides for civil fines of up to $100,000 per transaction where the form was not filed.

Reporting by businesses was spotty, at best, from 1986 (enactment) until the early 1990s, when the IRS began to clamp down. For example, in 1990, there were 30,800 Form 8300 filings. A 1991 IRS sweep of car dealerships and marine dealerships resulted in the assessment of $6 million in civil penalties and 44 criminal investigations. Thereafter, filings rose to 71,400 in 1991 and 142,400 in 1992. By 1994, Form 8300 filings had fallen to 121,100, while the corresponding CTR filings rose by 14%. This resulted in a second sweep in 1995, this time focusing on specific, targeted auto dealerships and jewelry stores (using a cross-referencing system of identifying those businesses with large cash deposits, per the CTR filings by banks, but which had made relatively few Form 8300 filings). Again, hefty civil fines and numerous criminal convictions ensued.

The first and one of the largest cases against a business for failing to file IRS Form 8300 was a 1991 case against five New York area car dealerships: Mercedes-Benz Manhattan, Gidron Ford, Manhattan Nissan, Bronx Acura, and Manhattan Mazda. Cars and dealership bank accounts were seized, and 15 persons pled guilty to various money laundering, structuring, and cash reporting offenses.

F. Suspicious Activity Report (SAR)

Since its creation in 1992, the Suspicious Activity Report (SAR) has been the cornerstone of anti-money-laundering reporting requirements. Whenever a financial institution's employee "knows, suspects, or has reason to suspect" he has processed a suspicious transaction, he is required to file "TDF 90-22.47," or "Treasury Department Form 90-22.47," a Suspicious Activity Report. The statutory authority for SARs is set out at 31 U.S.C. section 5318(g).

Financial institutions covered by the SAR reporting requirements are those 23,000 institutions regulated by the Federal Reserve Board, the Office of the Comptroller of the Currency, the Office of Thrift Supervision, the National Credit Union Administration, and the FDIC. Essentially, all financial institutions operating in the U.S. have an obligation to report suspicious activity.

The term "suspicious activity" mirrors the operative language of money laundering contained in section 1956 of Title 18. The term, defined in 31 CFR 103.21, also includes any activity that "has no business or apparent lawful purpose or is not the sort in which the particular customer would normally be expected to engage, and [the institution] knows of no reasonable explanation for the transaction after examining the available facts, including the background and possible purpose of the transaction." The dollar limits vary depending on the suspect and his activity. For violations where a suspect can be identified or where the transaction or transactions involve potential money laundering or Bank Secrecy Act violations, the amount is an aggregate of $5,000 or more. For violations where the suspect cannot be identified or where the transaction or transactions do not involve potential money laundering or Bank Secrecy Act violations, the amount is an aggregate of $25,000 or more.

A financial institution is required to submit an SAR within 30 days of the initial detection of the suspicious activity (a further 30 days, to a total of 60, are allowed to enable the financial institution to identify the suspect). If there is an ongoing violation, the financial institution is required to immediately notify its regulator and "law enforcement authorities."

Failure to file an SAR, or failure to file an SAR in a timely manner, exposes the financial institution and its responsible officers to "supervisory action," which includes civil monetary penalties. In addition, a finding that the financial institution was willfully blind to the suspicious activity could lead to a section 1956 criminal money-laundering charge. SARs must be retained for 5 years.

Since April 1, 1996, FinCEN has been the sole location for financial institutions to submit SARs. Prior to this date, financial institutions filed CTRs to the IRS in Detroit. If the bank elected to note that the subject of the CTR was "suspicious," the CTR form itself had to be checked, and Criminal Referral Reports were filed with seven different federal agencies, including FinCEN, the IRS, and the FBI, each of which had their own form. Through lobbying efforts of, among others, the American Bankers Association, regulations were passed so that, in addition to the usual CTR filings, a bank could file one SAR with FinCEN. As of early 1997, new interim SAR regulations were being unveiled to encompass securities brokers, mutual funds, etc.

The law enforcement value of SARs is limitless; since April 1996, there have been 82,000 SARs filed, 40% of which involve possible money laundering, structuring, etc. The difference between the utility of the CTR database and the SAR database is striking; one FinCEN employee describes the utility of the CTR database as the equivalent of looking for a needle in a haystack; he describes the SAR database as a "haystack full of needles."

The only flaw with SARs is that a degree of discretion is left in the hands of clerks, tellers, compliance officers, and other financial institution personnel as to whether any transaction or transactions are suspicious; what is suspicious to one may not be suspicious to another, and a crooked teller or clerk can easily avoid noticing anything "suspicious." In fact, the FATF has acknowledged that those countries that do not have any mandatory reporting requirements, but only "suspicious" reporting requirements, often miss many transactions that would otherwise be caught (in other words, structuring is more possible).

APPENDIX 8.1

The Reporting Forms

A. Currency Transaction Report (CTR)

Form **4789**	**Currency Transaction Report**	
(Rev. October 1995) Department of the Treasury Internal Revenue Service	▶ Use this 1995 revision effective October 1, 1995. ▶ For Paperwork Reduction Act Notice, see page 3. ▶ Please type or print. (Complete all parts that apply—See instructions).	OMB No. 1545-0183

1 Check all box(es) that apply:

a ☐ Amends prior report   b ☐ Multiple persons   c ☐ Multiple transactions

Part I   Person(s) Involved in Transaction(s)

Section A—Person(s) on Whose Behalf Transaction(s) Is Conducted

2 Individual's last name or Organization's name		3 First name	4 M.I.
5 Doing business as (DBA)		6 SSN or EIN	
7 Address (number, street, and apt. or suite no.)		8 Date of birth M M D D Y Y	
9 City	10. State 11 ZIP code 12 Country (if not U.S.)	13 Occupation, profession, or business	

14 If an individual, describe method used to verify identity:

a ☐ Driver's license/State I.D.   b ☐ Passport   c ☐ Alien registration   d ☐ Other ....

e Issued by: f Number:

Section B—Individual(s) Conducting Transaction(s) (if other than above).

If Section B is left blank or incomplete, check the box(es) below to indicate the reason(s):

a ☐ Armored Car Service   b ☐ Mail Deposit or Shipment   c ☐ Night Deposit or Automated Teller Machine (ATM)

d ☐ Multiple Transactions   e ☐ Conducted On Own Behalf

15 Individual's last name		16 First name	17 M.I.
18 Address (number, street, and apt. or suite no.)		19 SSN	
20 City	21 State 22 ZIP code 23 Country (if not U.S.)	24 Date of birth M M D D Y Y	

25 If an individual, describe method used to verify identity:

a ☐ Driver's license/State I.D.   b ☐ Passport   c ☐ Alien registration   d ☐ Other ....

e Issued by: f Number:

Part II   Amount and Type of Transaction(s). Check all boxes that apply.

		26 Date of Transaction M M D D Y Y
26 Cash In $ _____ .00	27 Cash Out $ _____ .00	

29 ☐ Foreign Currency _____ (Country)   30 ☐ Wire Transfer(s)   31 ☐ Negotiable Instrument(s) Purchased

32 ☐ Negotiable Instrument(s) Cashed   33 ☐ Currency Exchange(s)   34 ☐ Deposit(s)/Withdrawal(s)

35 ☐ Account Number(s) Affected (if any):   36 ☐ Other (specify)

_____   _____

_____   _____

_____   _____

Part III   Financial Institution Where Transaction(s) Takes Place

37 Name of financial institution	Enter Federal Regulator or BSA Examiner code number from the instructions here. ▶ [ ]
38 Address (number, street, and apt. or suite no.)	39 SSN or EIN
40 City	41 State 42 ZIP code 43 MICR No.

Sign Here ▶	44 Title of approving official	45 Signature of approving official	46 Date of signature M M D D Y Y
	47 Type or print preparer's name	48 Type or print name of person to contact	49 Telephone number ( )

Cat. No. 42004W   Form **4789** (Rev. 10-95)

B. Currency Transaction Report by Casinos (CTRC)

| Form **8362**
(Rev. September 1993)
Department of the Treasury
Internal Revenue Service | **Currency Transaction Report by Casinos**
▶ Please type or print.
(Complete all applicable parts—see instructions) | OMB No. 1545-0906
Expires 5-31-95 |

1 Check appropriate boxes if: a ☐ amends prior report   b ☐ suspicious transaction

Part I   Identity of individual who conducted this transaction with the casino

2 If more than one individual is involved, see instructions and check here . . . . ▶ ☐
3 If the casino was not required by law or regulation to obtain identifying information on this individual, see instructions and check here . ▶ ☐

4 Last name	5 First name	6 Middle initial	7 Social security number
8 Address (number, street, and apt. or suite no.)	9 Occupation, profession, or business		10 Date of birth (see instructions)
11 City	12 State	13 ZIP code	14 Country (if not U.S.)	15 Customer's account number

16 Method used to verify identity: a (check applicable box) ☐ Driver's license ☐ Passport ☐ Alien registration ☐ Other ▶ .... (Specify)
    b Issued by ▶   c Number ▶

Part II   Person for whom this transaction was conducted (See Definitions)

17 If this transaction was conducted on behalf of more than one person, see instructions and check here . . . . ▶ ☐

18 Individual's last name or Organization's name	19 First name	20 Middle initial	21 Social security number

22 Alien identification: a Describe identification ▶ ....   Employer identification number
    b Issued by ▶   c Number ▶

23 Address (number, street, and apt. or suite no.)	24 Occupation, profession, or business	25 Date of birth (see instructions)
26 City	27 State	28 ZIP code	29 Country (if not U.S.)	30 Account number

Part III   Description of transaction. If more space is needed, attach a separate schedule and check this box . . ☐

31 CASH IN: (in U.S. dollar equivalent)		32 CASH OUT: (in U.S. dollar equivalent)	
Purchase of chips, tokens, and plaques	$ _____ .00	Redemption of chips, tokens, and plaques	$ _____ .00
Deposit (front money or safekeeping)	_____ .00	Withdrawal of deposit (front money or safekeeping)	_____ .00
Payment on credit (including markers)	_____ .00	Advance on credit	_____ .00
Bets of currency	_____ .00	Payments on bets (including slot jackpots)	_____ .00
For wire transfer	_____ .00	From wire transfer	_____ .00
Purchase of casino check	_____ .00	Negotiable instrument cashed (including checks)	_____ .00
Currency exchange	_____ .00	Currency exchange	_____ .00
Other (specify) ▶	_____ .00	Payment for customer's expenses	_____ .00
		Other (specify) ▶	_____ .00

33 Total amount of currency transaction (round up)
    Cash in (from item 31) $ .... .00
    Cash out (from item 32) $ ____ .00

34 Amount of item 33 in U.S. $100 bills or higher
    Cash in $ .... .00
    Cash out $ ____ .00 ☐ Unknown

35 Date of transaction (see instructions)

36 If other than U.S. currency is involved, please furnish the following information: a Exchange made ☐ for, or ☐ from U.S. currency
    b Country   c Amount of currency (in U.S. dollar equivalent) $ .... .00

37 If a negotiable instrument was involved in this transaction, furnish the following:
    If more than one instrument was involved, see instructions and check here . . ▶ ☐
    a Identify instrument (Check applicable box): ☐ Check ☐ Money order ☐ Traveler's check ☐ Other (specify)

b Date	c Amount (in U.S. dollars)	d Payee of instrument
	.00	

    e Maker of instrument   f Drawee or issuer and location

Part IV   Casino reporting this transaction

38 Name	39 Employer identification number (EIN)

40 Address (number, street, and apt. or suite no.) where transaction occurred

41 City	42 State	43 ZIP code	44 Telephone number of contact person ( )

Sign Here ▶	45 Signature (preparer)	46 Title	47 Date
	48 Type or print preparer's name	49 Approving official (signature)	50 Date

For Paperwork Reduction Act Notice, see page 3.   Cat. No. 62291Z   Form **8362** (Rev. 9-93)

C.   Currency and Monetary Instrument Report (CMIR)

Form Approved
OMB No. 1515-0079

(U.S. Customs Use Only)

Control No.
31 U.S.C. 5316; 31 CFR 103.23 and 103.25
▶ Please type or print.

DEPARTMENT OF THE TREASURY
UNITED STATES CUSTOMS SERVICE

**REPORT OF INTERNATIONAL
TRANSPORTATION OF CURRENCY
OR MONETARY INSTRUMENTS**

▶ This form is to be filed with the United States Customs Service

▶ For Paperwork Reduction Act Notice and Privacy Act Notice, see back of form.

Part I   FOR INDIVIDUAL DEPARTING FROM OR ENTERING THE UNITED STATES

1. NAME (Last or family, first, and middle)
2. IDENTIFYING NO. (See instructions)
3. DATE OF BIRTH (Mo./Day/Yr.)

4. PERMANENT ADDRESS IN UNITED STATES OR ABROAD
5. OF WHAT COUNTRY ARE YOU A CITIZEN/SUBJECT?

6. ADDRESS WHILE IN THE UNITED STATES
7. PASSPORT NO. & COUNTRY

8. U.S. VISA DATE
9. PLACE UNITED STATES VISA WAS ISSUED
10. IMMIGRATION ALIEN NO. (If any)

11. CURRENCY OR MONETARY INSTRUMENT WAS: (Complete 11A or 11B)

A. EXPORTED		B. IMPORTED	
Departed From: (City in U.S.)	Arrived At: (Foreign City/Country)	From: (Foreign City/Country)	At: (City in U.S.)

Part II   FOR PERSON SHIPPING, MAILING, OR RECEIVING CURRENCY OR MONETARY INSTRUMENTS

12. NAME (Last or family, first, and middle)
13. IDENTIFYING NO. (See instructions)
14. DATE OF BIRTH (Mo./Day/Yr.)

15. PERMANENT ADDRESS IN UNITED STATES OR ABROAD
16. OF WHAT COUNTRY ARE YOU A CITIZEN/SUBJECT?

17. ADDRESS WHILE IN THE UNITED STATES
18. PASSPORT NO. & COUNTRY

19. U.S. VISA DATE
20. PLACE UNITED STATES VISA WAS ISSUED
21. IMMIGRATION ALIEN NO. (If any)

22. CURRENCY OR MONETARY INSTRUMENTS
DATE SHIPPED
DATE RECEIVED

23. CURRENCY OR MONETARY INSTRUMENTS
☐ Shipped To ▶
☐ Received From ▶

NAME AND ADDRESS

24. IF THE CURRENCY OR MONETARY INSTRUMENT WAS MAILED, SHIPPED, OR TRANSPORTED COMPLETE BLOCKS A AND B.
A. Method of Shipment (Auto, U.S. Mail, Public Carrier, etc.)
B. Name of Transporter/Carrier

Part III   CURRENCY AND MONETARY INSTRUMENT INFORMATION (SEE INSTRUCTIONS ON REVERSE)(To be completed by everyone)

25. TYPE AND AMOUNT OF CURRENCY/MONETARY INSTRUMENTS   Value in U.S. Dollars

Coins.................................... ☐ A. ▶ $

Currency................................ ☐ B. ▶

Other Instruments (Specify Type) ⟋ .... ☐ C. ▶

(Add lines A, B and C)........................ TOTAL AMOUNT ▶ $

26. IF OTHER THAN U.S. CURRENCY IS INVOLVED, PLEASE COMPLETE BLOCKS A AND B. (SEE SPECIAL INSTRUCTIONS)
A. Currency Name
B. Country

Part IV   GENERAL - TO BE COMPLETED BY ALL TRAVELERS, SHIPPERS, AND RECIPIENTS

27. WERE YOU ACTING AS AN AGENT, ATTORNEY OR IN CAPACITY FOR ANYONE IN THIS CURRENCY OR MONETARY INSTRUMENT ACTIVITY? (If "Yes" complete A, B and C)   ☐ Yes   ☐ No

PERSON IN WHOSE BE-HALF YOU ARE ACTING ▶

A. Name
B. Address
C. Business activity, occupation, or profession

Under penalties of perjury, I declare that I have examined this report, and to the best of my knowledge and belief it is true, correct and complete.

28. NAME AND TITLE
29. SIGNATURE
30. DATE

(Replaces IRS Form 4790 which is obsolete.)

Customs Form 4790 (031695)

D. Foreign Bank Account Report (FBAR)

Department of the Treasury TD F 90-22.1 10/92 SUPERSEDES ALL PREVIOUS EDITIONS	REPORT OF FOREIGN BANK AND FINANCIAL ACCOUNTS For the calendar year 19 Do not file this form with your Federal Tax Return	Form Approved: OMB No. 1505-0063 Expiration Date: 9/95

This form should be used to report financial interest in or signature authority or other authority over one or more bank accounts, securities accounts, or other financial accounts in foreign countries as required by Department of the Treasury Regulations (31 CFR 103). You are not required to file a report if the aggregate value of the accounts did not exceed $10,000. Check all appropriate boxes. SEE INSTRUCTIONS ON BACK FOR DEFINITIONS. File this form with Dept. of the Treasury, P.O. Box 32521, Detroit, MI 48232.

1. Name (Last, First, Middle)	2. Social security number or employer identification number if other than individual	3. Name in item 1 refers to ☐ Individual
4. Address (Street, City, State, Country, ZIP)		☐ Partnership ☐ Corporation ☐ Fiduciary

5. ☐ I had signature authority over one or more foreign accounts, but had no "financial interest" in such accounts (see instruction J.)
Indicate for these accounts:

(a) Name and social security number or taxpayer identification number of each owner _____

(b) Address of each owner _____

_____

(Do not complete item 9 for these accounts)

6. ☐ I had a "financial interest" in one or more foreign accounts owned by a domestic corporation, partnership or trust which is required to file TD F 90-22.1 (See instruction L). Indicate for these accounts.

(a) Name and taxpayer identification number of each such corporation, partnership or trust _____

(b) Address of each such corporation, partnership or trust _____

(Do not complete item 9 for these accounts)

7. ☐ I had a "financial interest" in one or more foreign accounts, but the total maximum value of these accounts (see instruction I) did not exceed $10,000 at any time during the year. (If you checked this box, do not complete item 9).

8. ☐ I had a "financial interest" in 25 or more foreign accounts. (If you checked this box, do not complete item 9.)

9. If you had a "financial interest" in one or more but fewer than 25 foreign accounts which are required to be reported, and the total maximum value of the accounts exceeded $10,000 during the year (see instruction I), write the total number of those accounts in the box below:
Complete items (a) through (f) below for one of the accounts and attach a separate TD F 90-22.1 for each of the others.
Items 1, 2, 3, 9, and 10 must be completed for each account.
Check here if this is an attachment. ☐

(a) Name in which account is maintained	(b) Name of bank or other person with whom account is maintained
(c) Number and other account designation, if any	(d) Address of office or branch where account is maintained

(e) Type of account. (If not certain of English name for the type of account, give the foreign language name and describe the nature of the account. Attach additional sheets if necessary.)

☐ Bank Account   ☐ Securities Account   ☐ Other (specify)

(f) Maximum value of account (see instruction I)
☐ Under $10,000   ☐ $10,000 to $50,000   ☐ $50,000 to $100,000   ☐ Over $100,000

10. Signature	11. Title (Not necessary if reporting a personal account)	12. Date

PRIVACY ACT NOTIFICATION

Pursuant to the requirements of Public Law 93-579, (Privacy Act of 1974), notice is hereby given that the authority to collect information on TD F 90-22.1 in accordance with 5 U.S.C. 552(e)(3) is Public Law 91-508; 31 U.S.C. 1121; 5 U.S.C. 301, 31 CFR Part 103.

The principal purpose for collecting the information is to assure maintenance of reports or records where such reports or records have a high degree of usefulness in criminal, tax, or regulatory investigations or proceedings. The information collected may be provided to those officers and employees of any constituent unit of the Department of the Treasury who have a need for the records in the performance of their duties. The records may be referred to any other department or agency of the Federal Government upon the request of the head of such department or agency for use in a criminal, tax, or regulatory investigation or proceeding.

Disclosure of this information is mandatory. Civil and criminal penalties, including under certain circumstances a fine of not more than $500,000 and imprisonment of not more than five years, are provided for failure to file a report, supply information, and for filing a false or fraudulent report.

Disclosure of the social security number is mandatory. The authority to collect this number is 31 CFR 103. The social security number will be used as a means to identify the individual who files the report.

Cat. No. 12996O

E.   Form 8300

Form **8300**	**Report of Cash Payments Over $10,000**	
(Rev. August 1994)	**Received in a Trade or Business**	OMB No. 1545-0892
Department of the Treasury Internal Revenue Service	▶ See instructions for definition of cash.	
	Please type or print.	

1 Check appropriate boxes if: **a** ☐ amends prior report;   **b** ☐ suspicious transaction.

Part I   Identity of Individual From Whom the Cash Was Received

2 If more than one individual is involved, see instructions and check here . . . . ▶ ☐

3 Last name	**4** First name	**5** M.I.	**6** Social security number
7 Address (number, street, and apt. or suite no.)			**8** Date of birth (see instructions)
9 City	**10** State **11** ZIP code **12** Country (if not U.S.)		**13** Occupation, profession, or business

14 Method used to verify identity: **a** Describe identification ▶ ....
b Issued by ....   **c** Number

Part II   Person (See Definitions) on Whose Behalf This Transaction Was Conducted

15 If this transaction was conducted on behalf of more than one person, see instructions and check here . . . . . . ▶ ☐

16 Individual's last name or Organization's name	**17** First name	**18** M.I.	**19** Social security number
20 Doing business as (DBA) name (see instructions)			Employer identification number
21 Alien identification: **a** Describe identification ▶			
b Issued by **c** Number			
22 Address (number, street, and apt. or suite no.)			**23** Occupation, profession, or business
24 City	**25** State **26** ZIP code **27** Country (if not U.S.)		

Part III   Description of Transaction and Method of Payment

28 Date cash received	**29** Total cash received	**30** If cash was received in more than one payment, check here . . . ▶ ☐	**31** Total price if different from item 29
	$ .00		$ .00

32 Amount of cash received (in U.S. dollar equivalent) (see instructions):

a U.S. currency $ _____.00   (Amount in $100 bills or higher $ _____.00)
b Foreign currency   _____.00   (Country ▶ _____)
c Cashier's check(s)   _____.00   } Issuer's name(s) and serial number(s) of the monetary instrument(s) ▶ ....
d Money order(s)   _____.00   ....
e Bank draft(s)   _____.00   ....
f Traveler's check(s)   _____.00

33 Type of transaction

a ☐ personal property purchased   **f** ☐ debt obligations paid
b ☐ real property purchased   **g** ☐ exchange of cash
c ☐ personal services provided   **h** ☐ escrow or trust funds
d ☐ business services provided   **i** ☐ other (specify) ▶
e ☐ intangible property purchased

34 Specific description of property or service shown in 33. (Give serial or registration number, address, etc.)
▶ ....
....

Part IV   Business That Received Cash

35 Name of business that received cash	**36** Employer identification number
37 Address (number, street, and apt. or suite no.)	Social security number
38 City	**39** State **40** ZIP code **41** Nature of your business

42 Under penalties of perjury, I declare that to the best of my knowledge the information I have furnished above is true, correct, and complete.

Sign Here

_____	_____	_____	( ) _____
(Authorized signature of business that received cash)	(Title)	(Date signed)	(Telephone number of business)

Cat. No. 62133S   Form **8300** (Rev. 8-94)

Asset Forfeiture

9

I. Introduction

Asset forfeiture is the taking of property without compensation when the property is used in a manner contrary to law. The concept has been used in American law since Colonial times, enabling the government to seize ships (and their cargoes) that violated customs or other laws, even where the owners of the ships were innocent of any wrongdoing. Essentially, the legal theory was that the government was proceeding against the offending ship, rather than against the crew, captain, or owner. Over time, this historical underpinning for forfeiture evolved into various customs laws, including the Tariff Act of 1930 (19 U.S.C. ss 1602–1621), which provides the practical framework for modern forfeitures, including seizure, custody, remission, and mitigation. In addition to these customs laws, the Supplementary Rules for Certain Admiralty and Maritime Claims (now called the Admiralty Rules or Supplementary Rules) provide the procedural framework for contesting civil forfeitures.

In 1969, Congress decided to use these old forfeiture laws to attack organized crime and the major drug traffickers. Their attack was aimed at the profits derived from, and the property used in, the criminals' illegal schemes. Three statutes were passed during the 1970 session that effectively introduced the notion of criminal and civil forfeiture (described below) of property used to facilitate illegal activity or forming the proceeds or profits of such activity. First, Congress directed its attention to organized crime generally, and passed the Organized Crime Control Act of 1970, which contained what is commonly called the RICO statute (see Chapter 7, "Domestic Money Laundering Statutes and Laws"). Second, Congress directed its attention specifically to drug traffickers, and passed the Continuing Criminal Enterprises (CCE) statute (21 U.S.C. s. 848, *et seq.*). Third, Congress included certain forfeiture provisions in the BSA (codified at 18 U.S.C. ss. 981 and 982). After amendments in 1984 (which designated forfeited assets for law enforcement purposes only, rather than for the benefit of the general treasury) and 1986 (including forfeiture provisions for property involved in money laundering schemes as part of the Anti-Drug Abuse Act of 1986), asset forfeitures began to take off, both in terms of numbers and property. In 1988, Congress passed the Anti-Drug Abuse Act, which included a provision (called the Justice Department Organized Crime and Drug Enforcement Enhancement Act) for additional Assistant United States Attorneys to work exclusively in asset forfeiture. In 1992, the Annunzio-Wylie Anti-Money Laundering Act gave U.S. courts *in rem* jurisdiction over property located abroad.*

II. Basic Concepts of Forfeiture

A. Statutory Authority

First and foremost, any forfeiture requires statutory authority. The three most common federal statutes authorizing forfeiture are (1) the RICO statute for organized crime-related forfeitures (18 U.S.C. ss. 1961–1968); (2) the CCE statute for drug-related forfeitures (21 U.S.C. s. 881 for civil forfeitures and s. 853 for criminal forfeitures); and (3) the BSA for money laundering-related forfeitures (18 U.S.C. s. 981 for civil forfeitures and s. 982 for criminal forfeitures). As set out above, these statutes were first passed in 1970.

B. Property Subject to Forfeiture

1. Property Related to Drug Crimes

Sections 881 and 853 of Title 21 of the United States Code provide for civil and criminal forfeiture, respectively, of property related to a list of certain drug offenses. Subsection 881(a) contains the shopping list of property subject to forfeiture: (1) the drugs themselves ("controlled substances") manufactured or distributed in violation of the drug laws; (2) the raw materials, products, and equipment of any kind used or intended to be used for manufacturing, distributing, importing, or exporting controlled substances; (3) any property used as a container for the property described in (1), (2), or (9); (4) conveyances, including aircraft, vehicles, or vessels, used or intended to be used to transport, or in any manner facilitate the transportation, sale, receipt, concealment of the property described in (1), (2) or (9) but subject to the statutory innocent owner protections; (5) all books and records used or intended to be used to violate the drug laws; (6) all money, negotiable instruments, securities, or other things of value used or intended to be used to violate the drug laws or furnished or intended to be furnished by any person in exchange for a controlled substance in violation of the drug laws,

---

* For a look at the future of asset forfeiture, including the proposed Civil Asset Forfeiture Reform Act, see Section V of this chapter.

and all proceeds traceable to such an exchange; (7) real property, or any part thereof, which is used or intended to be used to commit or facilitate the commission of a *felony* violation of the drug laws but subject to the statutory innocent owner protections; (8) any drugs possessed in violation of the drug laws; (9) all chemicals and equipment that have been or are intended to be imported or exported in violation of certain felony provisions of the drug laws; (10) drug paraphernalia, as that term is defined; and (11) firearms used or intended to be used to facilitate the transportation, sale, receipt, possession, or concealment of property described in (1) or (2), and any proceeds traceable to such property. Note that the real property section was not added until 1984.

2.   Property Related to Money-Laundering Crimes

Sections 981 and 982 of Title 18 of the United States Code provide for civil and criminal forfeiture, respectively, of property related to a list of certain money-laundering offenses. Generally, the federal law authorizes the forfeiture of any real or personal property involved in or traceable to property involved in violations of Title 18, subsections 1956(a)(1) (money laundering involving financial transactions), 1956(a)(2) (crossing the border without declaring monetary instruments), and 1956(a)(3) (money laundering sting operations); any one of approximately 200 criminal offenses listed in section 1956(c)(7); section 1957 (engaging in transactions with property derived from specified unlawful activity, or SUA); and the anti-structuring laws contained in 31 U.S.C. sections 5313(a) and 5324.

3.   Other Types of Property Subject to Forfeiture

The list is endless. Perhaps the most unique property ever forfeited was an Afghan Urial Ovis Orientalis Blandfordi fully mounted sheep, confiscated and forfeited from a Pakistani as he tried to bring it into the U.S. It appears that U.S. Customs agents seized the offending sheep pursuant to the federal Lacey Act, which effectively honors the export restriction laws of other countries. Here, the villainous sheep was imported contrary to Pakistan's Imports and Exports Act, which prohibits the export of sheep. Although the sheep's owner possessed an export permit issued from his home province of Baluchistan, the federal Imports and Exports Act trumped the provincial permit. What happened to the sheep remains unknown. See *United States v. One Afghan Urial Ovis Orientalis Blanfordi Fully Mounted Sheep,* 964 F.2d 474 (5th Cir. 1992).

C.   Proceeds of Crime or Property Used to Facilitate Crime

What is the nature of the authority in any forfeiture statute? The property sought to be forfeited must have been "involved in" or "related to" a specifically enumerated federal crime. For example, in order to forfeit a drug trafficker's boat, house, bank account, car, or cash, the government must show that the particular property was used to facilitate the underlying crime, *intended to be used* to facilitate that crime, was acquired by or because of that crime (in other words, constitutes proceeds of the crime), or is somehow traceable to that crime (for example, the government can seek forfeiture of a boat purchased with bank drafts that, in turn, were purchased with cash from the sale of drugs ... the boat is traceable to proceeds from a crime).

D.   Civil or Criminal Forfeiture

As set out above, the major forfeiture statutes all contain provisions allowing for *either* civil forfeiture or criminal forfeiture of the proceeds of criminal activity or property used or intended to be used to facilitate criminal activity. The differences are substantive and procedural.

1.   Civil Forfeiture Proceedings Generally

Civil forfeiture of property is a legal proceeding against the property itself.* The government will bring a separate civil action against the property (even if there is no criminal action against the drug dealer or money launderer, or the criminal charges were dismissed, or the criminal defendant dies or is a fugitive from law). Theses actions appear, or are styled, as *United States v. $435,678.88 in United States Currency* or *United States v. One 1997 Ferrari Testarossa Automobile Bearing VIN No. 4TYH435F5T3578465*, or something similar. The legal theory (some say it is a legal fiction) is that the property itself violated the law by facilitating a criminal offense or being the proceeds of a criminal offense.

In any case, a civil forfeiture action requires the government to show by a standard of *probable cause* that the property violated federal law.** Often, the affidavit of one of the involved law enforcement agents is attached to the civil complaint; in that affidavit, the officer sets out the factual basis for the seizure and forfeiture of the offending property. Note that otherwise impermissible hearsay evidence is allowed to establish probable cause.

Once the government meets its initial burden of showing probable cause, the burden then shifts to any claimant (the government is required to give formal notice to all those with an interest in the property) to establish that the property is not forfeitable or that he or she has a valid preexisting interest

---

* A civil action against a thing is called an *in rem* proceeding; a criminal action against a person is called an *in personem* proceeding.
** A discussion of the "probable cause" standard is best left to a legal text. Suffice it to say, however, that this standard of proof needed to proceed with civil forfeiture actions is the same as that needed to obtain a search warrant or indictment. It is often described in legal circles as "less than *prima facie* proof, but more than mere suspicion."

in the property that is not forfeitable (e.g., a preexisting mortgage on a house or car). The procedures followed in a civil forfeiture proceeding depend on whether the proceeding is an administrative or judicial action. Contested *judicial* civil forfeiture actions can take years to complete. The steps are generally as follows:

1. *Pre-seizure investigation,* including determination of probable cause, appraisal and title investigation, and evaluation of possible innocent owner claims.
2. *Seizure/Arrest* occurs either by way of a seizure warrant obtained from a United States District Court Magistrate by the seizing agency or by a warrant of arrest obtained from a U.S. District Court Magistrate by the U.S. Marshals Service pursuant to a civil complaint filed by the local U.S. Attorney.
3. *Custody and Appraisal* of the seized property by the U.S. Marshals Service.
4. *Notice* of seizure to all potential claimants and for three successive weeks in a local newspaper of general circulation. The notice is intended to advise of the government's intent to forfeit, of the procedures to contest the seizure and forfeiture, and of the right to expedited release.
5. *Expedited release,* commonly where there is insufficient equity in the property, by giving notice to the potential claimants, who petition for expedited release. The U.S. Attorney must respond to the petition within 20 days of receipt.
6. *Judgment of Forfeiture* without trial by one of two ways. First, *default judgment* against the property and all real and potential claimants if no claimants file a claim within 10 days of receiving notice or, if they file a claim, fail to file an answer to the complaint within 20 days thereafter. Second, *summary judgment* against the property and all real and potential claimants if the claimants cannot establish that a genuine issue of material fact exists regarding their claims.
7. *Discovery and Trial* where a claimant or claimants has/have filed an answer to the complaint and have met their threshold burden (there is a genuine issue of material fact regarding their claim or claims), the case proceeds through the judicial process, including reciprocal discovery, depositions, pretrial motions, and trial. If the government prevails, there is a *judicial judgment* against the property and all real and potential claimants.
8. *Remission or Mitigation:* if a petition for remission or mitigation is filed, the U.S. Attorney can then grant relief to the innocent petitioner by complete remission of the forfeiture or by mitigation (granting partial relief).

9. *Disposition* of the forfeiture by transferring the cash from the agency's holding account to its forfeiture fund, or by putting the non-cash property into official use, or by selling non-cash property.
10. *Equitable Sharing* with participating state or local agencies, if any.

2.   Civil Forfeiture: Administrative Proceedings

The federal agency that seizes certain property used in violation of federal law can proceed against that property by way of an administrative forfeiture, rather than referring the case to the Justice Department for a formal civil judicial action. Not all property can be forfeited by administrative proceedings; the federal agency can administratively forfeit personal property appraised at $500,000 or less, any conveyances used to transport contraband (regardless of the value), and any monetary instruments (cash or negotiable instruments) of any value.

After seizing the property incident to the arrest of a person or pursuant to a search or seizure warrant (again, based on a finding that there is probable cause to believe the property was used or intended to be used to violate federal law, or is proceeds of a violation), the agency must serve and file a notice of intent to forfeit on all persons or entities (potential claimants) it believes has an interest in the property. To contest the seizure, a prospective claimant must then post a claim or cost bond (or petition the court to proceed without a bond, called an *in forma pauperis* petition). If the administrative seizure is challenged, the agency is required to refer the matter to a U.S. Attorney to bring a judicial forfeiture proceeding.

Civil administrative proceedings generally take from three to five months to complete, from adoption to uncontested disposition. The steps are as follows:

1. *Pre-seizure investigation*, determination of probable cause, and appraisal and title investigation.
2. *Seizure* with or without a warrant or adoption of a state and/or local seizure.
3. *Custody and appraisal* of seized property.
4. *Notice* of seizure to all potential claimants and for three successive weeks in a local newspaper of general circulation. The notice is intended to advise of the government's intent to forfeit, of the procedures to contest the seizure and forfeiture, and of the right to expedited release.
5. *Expedited release*, commonly where there is insufficient equity in the property, by giving notice to the potential claimants, who petition for expedited release. The head of the agency must respond to the petition within 20 days of receipt.

6. *Decree of Forfeiture,* where no claim or cost bond (cash, check or surety equal to the lower of $5,000 or 10% of the value of the property to a minimum of $250) or *in forma pauperis* claim is made to the seized property within 20 days of the last publication of notice. The decree is issued by the head of the seizing agency.

7. *Remission or Mitigation:* if a petition for remission or mitigation is filed, the head of the agency can then grant relief to the innocent petitioner by complete remission of the forfeiture or by mitigation (granting partial relief).

8. *Disposition* of the forfeiture by transferring the cash from the agency's holding account to its forfeiture fund, or by putting the non-cash property into official use, or by selling non-cash property.

9. *Equitable Sharing,* if any.

3. Criminal Forfeiture Proceedings

Whereas civil forfeiture is an *in rem* proceeding against the property, criminal forfeiture is an *in personem* proceeding against the person alleged to have committed the crime; one or more of the counts in the criminal complaint is or are against the property alleged to have been used or intended to be used to facilitate the crimes or that constitutes proceeds of the crimes.

The major differences between civil and criminal forfeiture proceedings are as follows. First, a civil forfeiture is not dependent on the initiation or successful completion of a criminal action against the defendant, whereas criminal forfeiture is dependent on the conviction of the defendant. If the defendant dies or remains a fugitive from justice, the criminal forfeiture counts cannot proceed. Second, criminal forfeiture requires the government to prove beyond a reasonable doubt that the defendant committed the offenses charged and by a preponderance of the evidence (a standard higher than probable cause, but lower than beyond a reasonable doubt) that the property was involved in the crime. Third, hearsay evidence cannot be used to establish the government's burden or to rebut the claimant's allegations. Fourth, criminal forfeiture statutes generally allow for the substitution of a defendant's legitimate property where the defendant has placed his illegitimate assets beyond the reach of the government or has commingled illegitimate with legitimate assets.

Criminal forfeiture proceedings are governed by the Speedy Trial Act, which requires the trial to commence within 70 days of the defendant's first appearance. This time frame is subject to waiver and other vagaries, including the concept of "excluded time." Generally, the steps are as follows:

1. *Pre-indictment investigation,* including determination of probable cause, and appraisal and title investigation.

2. *Pre-indictment restraining and seizure orders* against the property can be obtained to preserve the property (including substitute property).

3. *Indictment* returned by the federal grand jury, charging the defendant with any number of federal offenses and naming the property sought to be forfeited.

4. *Post-indictment restraining and seizure orders* against the property can be obtained to preserve the property (including substitute property).

5. *Motion(s) to set aside the pre- and/or post-indictment restraining orders* can be filed by the defendant (not by any other innocent parties, who are not parties to the criminal proceeding).

6. *Trial and Special Verdict of Forfeiture:* if the fact finder (jury or judge) convicts the defendant of the criminal offense(s) charged, they then return a special verdict that finds the property to be forfeited, subject to an ancillary hearing and/or a petition for remission or mitigation.

7. *Preliminary Order of Forfeiture* is issued by the court, directing the U.S. Marshals Service to seize the property.

8. *Seizure, Custody, and Appraisal* of the property by the U.S. Marshals Service.

9. *Notice* of the preliminary order of forfeiture is given by the Marshall to all potential claimants and to the public generally (by publication) that forfeiture will be ordered within 30 days of notice unless a petition asserting an interest in the property is filed.

10. *Petition by Potential Claimants,* if any, are heard by a judge or magistrate sitting without a jury.

11. *Final Order of Forfeiture* is issued if the potential claimants' claims are rejected. The final order will acknowledge any valid interests, and directs the sale or other disposition of the forfeited assets (if substitute assets were sought, the final order will also direct the acquisition of those assets, as well as their sale or other disposition).

12. *Remission or Mitigation:* if a petition for remission or mitigation is filed, the U.S. Attorney General's office can then grant relief to the innocent petitioner by complete remission of the forfeiture or by mitigation (granting partial relief).

13. *Disposition* of the forfeiture by transferring the cash from the agency's holding account to its forfeiture fund, or by putting the non-cash property into official use, or by selling non-cash property.

14. *Equitable Sharing,* if any.

E.   Relation Back Doctrine

Criminals often try to transfer, encumber, or otherwise hide their illegitimate property in order to shield it from potential or pending forfeiture. However, because of the "relation back doctrine," such efforts are useless, as this doctrine holds that the forfeiture "relates back" in time to when it was used in violation of law, or to the time of the act giving rise to the forfeiture occurred. The doctrine holds that title to forfeited property passes to the government as of the time of the act giving rise to the forfeiture, thus thwarting criminals' efforts to hide or encumber their ill-gotten assets. The only protections from the relation back doctrine are afforded to those whose claim or title to the property is obtained without knowledge of the illegal activities — the so-called "innocent owners."

F.   Innocent Owners

All forfeiture statutes contain legal protections for persons innocent of any wrongdoing or innocent of any involvement of the property in the illegal activity. As a general rule, a person is entitled to the "innocent owner" protections where he or she had no knowledge of the illegal activity, did not consent to the illegal activity, could not have known of the illegal activity, or took all reasonable and possible steps to prevent the illegal activity. Depending on the nature of the innocent owner's interest, the forfeiture itself will be defeated or the value of the innocent owner interest will be paid to the owner after forfeiture and sale of the property (e.g., the owner of a stolen car used in violation of law might get his or her car back, whereas the holder of a note on that same car might simply get the value of the note after the car is forfeited and sold).

A person claiming innocent ownership must establish this claim by a preponderance of the evidence. Even where property is forfeited, an innocent party can file a petition for remission or mitigation. Here, the interested party is admitting the forfeitability of the property, but is seeking equitable relief from the court (judicial forfeiture) or head of the agency (administrative forfeiture).

G.   Constitutional and Other Protections

Forfeitures, both civil and criminal, are constrained by due process considerations (right to notice and an opportunity to be heard), and the Eighth Amendment's prohibition against excessive fines. Any issues regarding double jeopardy (the Double Jeopardy Clause of the Fifth Amendment prohibits a person from being punished twice for the same offense in the same proceeding) were resolved by the Supreme Court in the June 1996 decision of *United States v. Ursery*.

In addition to these constitutional protections, the Department of Justice has promulgated guidelines to protect innocent interests in real property, for expedited release procedures for conveyances and expedited settlement procedures for innocent lien holders for conveyances or real property, and to ensure that prospective attorney fee forfeitures are handled properly. These guidelines or policies are contained in the Attorney General's Guidelines on Seized and Forfeited Property, first issued in 1990, and in the Department of Justice's Asset Forfeiture Manual.*

III. Equitable Sharing and Adoption of State Forfeitures

Federal statutes and regulations allows state agencies to share in federal agencies' forfeitures, and the federal seizing agencies can "adopt" a state or local agency's seizures.

The Department of Justice publishes (annually) a Guide to Equitable Sharing of Federally Forfeited Property for State and Local Law Enforcement Agencies, which allows local agencies to share in federally forfeited property where (1) there is a joint investigation (equitable sharing) or (2) where the local agency commences a forfeiture investigation, and turns it over to the federal government for jurisdictional, practical, or financial reasons, within 30 days of the local seizure (an "adoptive forfeiture"). For joint investigation seizures, each agency involved in the case shares according to their participation in the law enforcement efforts leading to the seizure, up to 80% of the value of the property (the federal agency or agencies get a minimum of 20%). For adoptive seizures, the federal agency retains 20% of the net proceeds. In addition, there are minimum equity requirements in order for the federal agency to accept any adoptive seizure: $5,000 for vehicles; $10,000 for aircraft and vessels; the greater of $20,000 or 20% of the appraised value of real property; $5,000 for all other property, and any firearm, without regard to value.** The uses to which the local agencies can put these proceeds is strictly regulated.

IV. Disposition of Seized and Forfeited Property

Once property is seized, it becomes the responsibility of the Marshals Service to manage.*** Seized cash must be deposited into a seized asset deposit fund within 60 days of seizure or 10 days of indictment. Seized property cannot be used until confirmation of the forfeiture. If the property is something other than cash, there must also be approval of official use.

---

* The Asset Forfeiture Manual was first published in 1993. Volumes I and II contain the law and practice basics of federal forfeiture; Volume III contains the Justice Department's policies on asset forfeitures.
** Practically, these dollar figures are much higher.
*** The exception being property seized by a Treasury Department agency, which is then managed by Treasury.

All property is forfeited either by confirmation in a non-contested proceeding, or by order of a court. Once forfeited, there are a number of uses or destinations, depending on the type of property or intended use for that property. Forfeited cash is deposited into the seizing agency's or Justice Department's asset forfeiture fund. Any other forfeited property that is intended for official use (planes, boats, houses, cars, etc.) is then put into such use, after meeting certain requirements. Finally, any other non-cash property that is not intended for official use is sold, and the proceeds are used to pay any preexisting liens, claims or innocent owners, and expenses of seizure, storage, and sale. The proceeds, if any, are then deposited into the appropriate asset forfeiture fund.

V.   The Future of Asset Forfeiture

As set out in Section I of this chapter, federal forfeiture law has been the subject of reform since its introduction in the Bank Secrecy Act and RICO and CCE (Continuing Criminal Enterprise) statutes in 1970. In 1993, Representative Henry Hyde (R.-Ill.), now the Chairman of the House Judiciary Committee, introduced a sweeping forfeiture reform bill, the Civil Asset Forfeiture Reform Act (CAFRA) of 1993. Among other changes, the bill sought to raise the government's burden of proof to a "clear and convincing" standard. The Democrats filed their own reform bill; and in early 1994, these bills were met by the Department of Justice's own proposed Forfeiture Act of 1994. None of these efforts met with any legislative success.

In 1995, and now as the Chairman of the House Judiciary Committee, Representative Hyde reintroduced his (revised) CAFRA. This bill had six main provisions:

1. to remove the government's immunity from lawsuits seeking damages for the negligent destruction, loss or damage of seized property
2. to enlarge the time frame a claimant had to file a claim against seized property from 10 to 30 days in civil forfeiture proceedings, and from 20 to 30 days for administrative seizures
3. to place the burden of proof on the government by a standard of clear and convincing evidence (rather than the lesser standard of balance of probabilities)
4. to authorize the appointment of counsel for indigent claimants
5. to allow for the release of the seized property pending final adjudication if the claimant showed substantial hardship and he/she could post security for the value of the property

6. to provide that the lack of consent to unlawful use by the owner as a defense provided the owner took reasonable steps to prevent the property from being used for the alleged illegal use (a statutory "innocent owner" provision)

The House conducted numerous hearings on the 1995 CAFRA throughout 1996, without a consensus being reached. In June 1996, the U.S. Supreme Court released two forfeiture-related decisions: (1) in *Michigan v. Bennis,* the Court rejected a spouse's "innocent owner" defense in the face of a prostitution-related seizure and forfeiture of the family car; and (2) in *United States v. Ursery, et al.,* which held that civil forfeiture did not constitute punishment for the purposes of the Fifth Amendment's prohibition against double jeopardy. As a result, further additions were made to the draft bill, which was reintroduced in the 105th Congress.

Law Enforcement
Operations

10

I. Introduction

The two principal U.S. federal agencies charged with waging the "war on drugs" are the Customs Service and the DEA. However, they do not, and cannot, work alone. Bank and financial institution regulators, such as the OCC, OTS, and Federal Reserve; the IRS's Criminal Investigations Division (CID); and, of course, state and local law enforcement all contribute to fighting crime. In addition, U.S. law enforcement agencies would be powerless to stop the global, transnational criminal organizations without the assistance and cooperation of foreign police agencies, such as Britain's MI-5 and MI-6 (domestic and foreign intelligence agencies, respectively), Colombia's National Police, and Canada's Royal Canadian Mounted Police.

II. Law Enforcement Tools

A. Geographic Targeting Orders (GTOs)

Targeting money transmitters, these orders are issued under the authority of the Treasury Department's anti-money-laundering initiatives. Specifically, 31 CFR 103.26 provides as follows:

> "(a) If the Secretary of the Treasury finds, upon the Secretary's own initiative or at the request of an appropriate Federal or State law enforcement official, that reasonable grounds exist for concluding that additional record keeping and/or reporting requirements are necessary to carry out the purposes of this part and to prevent persons from evading the reporting/record keeping requirements of this part, the Secretary may issue an order requiring any domestic financial institution or group of financial institutions in a geographic area and any other person participating in the type of transaction to file a report in the manner and to the extent specified in such order."

GTOs allow federal, state, and local law enforcement authorities to impose stricter reporting and record-keeping requirements on specified financial service providers in a certain geographical area for a limited time (for a detailed look at a GTO operation, see Section II.E "Operation El Dorado," in this chapter).

Operation El Dorado, or the El Dorado Task Force, included the first GTO, directed at New York money transmitters wiring money to Colombia. On September 4, 1997, the Treasury Department issued two more GTOs against 15 money remitters in New York and their 3,400 agents, and against five remitters in Puerto Rico, requiring all of them to report all cash remittances of $750 or more sent to the Dominican Republic after September 2nd. These latter two GTOs came about as a result of information received by Treasury that more than $500 million was being wired through these money remitters from New York to the Dominican Republic each year, most of which was believed to be drug money.

One of the results of GTOs has been a shift from wiring money to smuggling money, further resulting in an increase in the number and amount of cash seizures. The original New York (Colombian) GTO resulted in a 400% increase in cash seizures at New York area airports.

B. Mobile Enforcement Teams (METs)

Initially deployed in 1995, these DEA teams are sent out to work with state and local law enforcement authorities to target specific problem areas to help combat drug-related violence. Where programs such as the Southwest Border Initiative target the cause of the drug violence — the drug kingpins and their communications and financial networks — the METs go to the streets to curb the street-level violence itself.

C. High Intensity Drug Trafficking Areas (HIDTA)

The Office of National Drug Control Policy (ONDCP) (see Chapter 6, "United States Federal Government Agencies," for a full description of this executive-level agency) administers the HIDTA Program, which is designed to target those areas of the U.S. that are seen as having the most critical drug trafficking problem. In 1997, the ONDCP coordinated over 150 joint ventures between local, state, and federal law enforcement task forces, many of which focused on particular HIDTAs.

The HIDTA Program was established by the Anti-Drug Abuse Act of 1988. Since 1990, the following areas or cities have been designated as a HIDTA:

1990   Houston, Los Angeles, New York/New Jersey, South Florida, and the Southwest border area (known as the SWBI, see below)

1994   Puerto Rico, U.S. Virgin Islands, Washington/Baltimore
1995   Atlanta, Chicago, Philadelphia/Camden
1996   The Rocky Mountain states of Colorado, Utah, and Wyoming;
        the Gulf Coast states of Alabama, Louisiana, and Mississippi; Indiana;
        Washington, the San Francisco Bay area; and Southeastern Michigan
        (Detroit)

One of the most successful HIDTA task forces has been established as part of the Southwest Border Initiative (SWBI). The Mexican–U.S. border is the primary smuggling and money-laundering region in the U.S. For example, Brownsville–Laredo, Texas, is considered by many agencies to be the major money-laundering and drug-smuggling town. A FinCEN study of money declared along the U.S.–Mexico border between 1988 and 1990 showed that this border town and area had the most funds declared on entry to the U.S. — almost $8 billion. Second on the list was the small town area of Nogales, Arizona, with $5 billion. The largest population centers along the Mexican border — El Paso and San Diego — placed third and fourth. The SWBI was launched by a myriad of federal, state, and local law enforcement agencies, working with prosecutors, to target this area. The goal of the SWBI was to identify and arrest the leadership, and to seize and forfeit the proceeds and property of those drug traffickers operating along the southwest border — the Mexican Federation and their "partners," the Cali Cartel. The primary tactic used was to target the communications systems of the command and control infrastructure of the Mexican Federation and Cali Cartel. In 1996, the strategy was found effective in Operation Zorro I. As a result, it has been employed in other regions, notably Puerto Rico (see "Operation Hard Line" and "Operation Gateway," below).

II.   Multi-Agency Drug-Money-Laundering Operations

Since the mid-1980s, federal law enforcement and regulatory agencies have worked together, either formally through memoranda of understanding (MOUs) or as members of task forces, or by sharing intelligence and information. Although the operations listed below all involve multi-agency task forces, there are still a large number of operations involving single agencies. For example, Customs often works alone, simply because of their unique jurisdiction along the borders and at ports of entry; Customs Operations Casacam in Miami and Omega in Los Angeles resulted in the two largest seizures of cash by any federal law enforcement agencies: $22 million in Casacam and $19 million in Omega (Customs also is credited with the largest border seizure of cash — $15 million — which occurred at the Port of Miami in 1996).

A. Operation Big Ticket

This operation was conducted by the Criminal Investigations Division (CID) of the IRS. Initiated in 1991, the operation began as a series of nationwide undercover investigations that focused on automobile dealers who sold cars to narcotics dealers for cash without filing the requisite Form 8300. Over the course of the operation, dozens of arrests were made and millions of dollars seized.

B. Operation Cat's Eye

The Italian organized-crime group 'Ndrangheta, operating through cells in Toronto, Canada, and Tampa, Florida, was the target of a multi-agency undercover operation that ended in mid-1997 with indictments in U.S. Federal Court for various heroin trafficking and money-laundering violations. Of great concern to law enforcement authorities was evidence of alliances between the 'Ndrangheta cells and Mafia groups in New York City and Providence, Rhode Island; Colombian traffickers in Miami; and various Asian gangs in New York City. The RCMP was instrumental in this operation.

C. Operation C-Chase

Operation C-Chase ("C" for currency) was a joint Customs, IRS, DEA, FBI, and Justice sting operation, played out over five years and based out of Tampa; this operation investigated links between Manuel Noriega, the Medellín Cartel, and the Bank of Credit and Commerce International (BCCI). It led to the indictments of Luxembourg-based BCCI, two of its subsidiaries, nine bank officials, and 75 other individuals who were laundering approximately $20 million per month in drug proceeds.

The money-laundering scheme involved the placement of drug proceeds into various U.S. bank "undercover accounts." At its most basic, the launderers (actually their agents or employees) would sign blank checks drawn on these undercover accounts, then mail these checks to the head of the laundering operation. After a cash pick-up/placement occurred, the head of the laundering operation would enter a corresponding amount onto one of the blank checks and either forward it to the owner of the funds or sell it on the black market at a discount. As the launderers became more sophisticated, they began to use more wire transfers to layer the funds from the undercover accounts, by wire transferring funds to similar accounts in Panama or through a U.S. bank to a U.S.-based foreign bank. These funds were then used to purchase 90-day certificates of deposit; these CDs were then used as collateral on loans made by the Panamanian bank to its launderers. The loan proceeds were then layered again, eventually ending up in the owner's accounts in Uruguay.

D. Operation Dinero

Operation Dinero involved two undercover DEA agents, working with the advice of the IRS and banking consultants out of Atlanta and England (and the blessing of the Attorney General), who established and ran a "bank" based out of Anguilla in order to root out the kingpins of a drug trafficking ring. It took a year to find a bank to purchase and another year to get it set up and running so as to appear to be a legitimate Caribbean bank (the details were crucial, including using the standard-sized British paper, which is $11^{1/4}$ inches long, versus standard American-sized paper, 11 inches long). The bank finally opened in July 1994, backed up by dozens of front companies and more than 50 corporate accounts set up in other banks. They were in business. The agents had done such a good job of setting up their bank, that it took them only six months of operation to collect enough evidence to complete the sting operation.

After "advertising" in Colombia — overtly catering to the money-laundering "needs" of a small elite group of clients who all happened to be money launderers. Over the course of the sting, agents laundered money for the Cali Cartel, the Italian Mafia, Spanish and Croatian mobsters, and Russian criminals operating out of New York with ties to the former KGB. Their bank cashed checks drawn on Mexican banks, prepared loans to purchase ships, and wired money throughout the world.

The Operation eventually resulted in the seizure of $54 million, nine tons of cocaine, and the arrest of 58 suspected drug traffickers and money launderers in the U.S., and 30 more in France, Italy, Spain, and Canada. During the course of the sting operation, the agents actually laundered over $50 million for their various customers, tracing the proceeds as they went. The Operation actually ran at a profit as the "bank" was charging its customers a hefty fee for their services.

E. Operation El Dorado

Beginning on August 7, 1996, certain licensed money transmitters in the New York area were made subject to an BSA Order issued by then Under Secretary of the Treasury (Enforcement) Raymond Kelly. This order, the New York Geographic Targeting Order (GTO) required these money transmitters to report information about the senders and recipients of all cash-purchased money transfers to Colombia of $750 or more. The GTO was the result of a joint federal/state/local law enforcement operation, called the El Dorado Task Force, that had developed evidence that certain New York area money remitters were moving drug money to Colombia by structuring transfers so as to avoid BSA reporting requirements. For example, the Task Force determined that, in 1995 alone, New York City area money remitters wired over

$1.5 billion to Colombia. Under Secretary Kelly noted that "to account for the money legitimately, each Colombian household in the area would have had to wire $30,000 to Colombia each year — an amount that exceeds the $27,000 average annual income for this community." (From testimony before the House Judiciary Subcommittee on Crime, July 24, 1997.)

As a result, Treasury issued the GTO requiring 12 New York City money transmitters and their 1,600 agents (expanded in October, 1996 to a further 10 licensed transmitters and 1,900 agents, and again in April 1997 to include another licensed transmitter) to report all wire transfers exceeding $750 destined for Colombia. The result was an immediate and dramatic reduction in the flow of narcotics proceeds to Colombia through New York money transmitters and the seizure of over $29 million in illegal funds being sent to Colombia. Customs has also seen a fourfold increase in the amount of money seized at borders, and a ninefold increase in cash seizures at JFK Airport, both believed to be a direct result of the GTO. One of the transmitters stopped sending money to Colombia entirely, one went out of business, and another — Vigo Remittance Corp. — has pled guilty to structuring violations.

The New York GTO has been so successful that Treasury is looking to issue additional GTOs in other cities. In addition, the GTO has spawned new regulations aimed at all money transmitters (see Chapter 7, "Money Services Businesses, or MSBs").

F.   Operation Gateway

See Section II.J, "Operation Hard Line," in this chapter.

G.   Operation Green Ice

Operation Green Ice was one of the most successful undercover operations ever run by American law enforcement. Organized under the auspices of OCDETF, and headed by DEA Supervisory Special Agent Tom Clifford, its targets were several Colombian cartel "kingpins." The main objectives of Operation Green Ice were to (1) identify, disrupt, and dismantle cartel cells in the U.S. and the United Kingdom; (2) identify and arrest the launderers and drug traffickers in those cells; (3) identify and seize cartel assets; and (4) disrupt the cartels' money flow back to Colombia.

Beginning in January 1990, this operation was first established in San Diego and Los Angeles. The money brokers in Colombia instructed the undercover agents to pick up and launder money in Miami, Ft. Lauderdale, New York, and Chicago. The DEA then established a national network of import/export companies, located in those cities, as well as in Houston and San Diego. Soon, the Colombian money launderers instructed the agents to establish leather stores in the various cities to act as their retail "fronts." The launderers' scheme was to import leather goods to the U.S., grossly inflating the invoices to show more merchandise than was actually shipped, and allowing them to legitimize the import/export businesses and to justify the U.S. currency deposits then made in their bank accounts in Colombia.

After establishing a credible national corporate structure, known as Trans Americas Ventures Associates, the DEA agents were invited by the Colombian money brokers to move into the international markets in Canada, Spain, Italy, and the United Kingdom. On September 25, 1992, with the cooperation of law enforcement authorities in Canada, Italy, England, Costa Rica, Holland, and Colombia, agents took down the operation and made 200 arrests, including those of seven ranking figures of the drug cartels' money-laundering operations, the former inspector general of Colombia's national bank, Jose "Tony the Pope" Duran, described by the Italian government as the world's largest cocaine distributor (he had 20 aliases), and various leaders of the Sicilian Mafia and Italian Camorra. In addition, law enforcement agencies throughout the world seized 15 money-laundering front companies, over $50 million from over 100 bank accounts, and three-quarters of a ton of cocaine.

While Operation Green Ice was underway, an FBI undercover money-laundering investigation, called Operation Cabbage Farm, was found to have overlapping targets. As a result, a "working group" based out of Washington, D.C. coordinated their activities. Operation Cabbage Farm identified over 90 bank accounts all over the world used by the Yunez money-laundering group, money brokers based out of Colombia.

H. Operation Green Ice II

This operation was recently completed by the DEA. Here, Jack Hook of the DEA's San Diego office led a team that made 50 arrests and seized over $15 million in cash and thousands of pounds of cocaine. Agents operated fake storefronts and jewelry wholesale companies in southern California and Florida, where Mexican couriers would arrive with suitcases of cash (all captured on videotape!). Once these funds were placed, agents offered to "layer" the money for a 3% fee.

I. Operation Greenback

One of the first multi-agency operations, this IRS-CID and Customs Service operation began in 1980 to investigate the unusual currency deposits in southern Florida and whether there was a link between these deposits and the growing drug trade in the Miami area. Agents of this task force coined the term "smurfing." The ultimate results of Operation Greenback and its progeny were the enactment of the currency-reporting requirements of the

Comprehensive Crime Control Act of 1984 and the criminalization of structuring by the Money Laundering Control Act of 1986.

J.   Operation Hard Line

Operation Hard Line was launched by the U.S. Customs Service in 1995 to permanently "harden" the southwestern border ports of entry to prevent "port runners," or drug smugglers, from smuggling drugs into the U.S. The southwestern border accounts for the majority of cross-border traffic: 3.5 million trucks (70% of the U.S. total), 75 million cars (60% of the U.S. total), and 250 million people (55% of the U.S. total). The Operation has resulted in a 60% decrease in port running, with drug seizures up 29% (to 6,956) and the amount of seized drugs up 24% (to 545,922 pounds). The Operation has proven so successful that Customs has started Operation Gateway, an identical operation aimed at Puerto Rico.

K.   Operation La Mina

Operation La Mina involved two jewelry companies, Adonian Brothers and Ropex Corp., which had successfully laundered almost $1 billion in Medellín Cartel cocaine profits through business locations in New York, Los Angeles, Houston, Canada, and Switzerland.

Very simply, the scheme involved the deposit of fictitious jewelry sales (really drug proceeds) into accounts held by various jewelry stores owned or controlled by Adonian and Ropex. Money was then wired to Latin America and supported by documentation showing gold purchases from Uruguay (in some cases, the documents themselves were supported by the importation of lead bars coated with gold paint).

The scheme came to the attention of federal authorities as a result of two incidents. First, figures from the Department of Commerce showed that, in the span of three years, Uruguay went from having no gold trade with the U.S. to being the second largest exporter of gold to the U.S., even though it had no usable gold reserves. Second, Wells Fargo Bank in Los Angeles reported to the FBI that the Adonian Brothers' jewelry stores were making cash deposits in sums greater than Tiffany & Co. In addition, there are some reports that indicate that a Ropex shipment of "scrap metal" accidentally "broke open" in transit, revealing bundles of cash.

L.   Operation Polar Cap

Operation Polar Cap was a series of five OCDETF multi-agency investigations started in 1988 for the purpose of targeting Colombian drug-money launderers. It began very simply by two separate banks reporting suspicious activities related to changes in customer's banking habits. Those two separate reports, analyzed by Customs, helped uncover an operation that had laundered approximately $1.2 billion over two years and led to the arrests of more than 125 people, the indictment of a Colombian bank, and the seizure of one ton of cocaine.

Operation Polar Cap V targeted five specific money-laundering groups. One group, led by Cranston, Rhode Island, "mobster" Stephen Saccoccia, laundered between $200 million and $750 million for the Colombian Cartels (it is rumored that Saccoccia was one of the few launderers ever to work for both the Medellín and Cali Cartels simultaneously without incurring their wrath). Saccoccia's methods were simple: drug cash was shipped from New York and Los Angeles by Colombian native and New York resident Duvan Arboleda to Saccoccia's offices in Rhode Island, New York, and California. This bulk cash was packaged and labeled as "gold bullion."

Relying on instructions received by facsimile from Arboleda, Saccoccia converted the cash to cashier's checks, which he then sent on to various business accounts. These transactions were then followed by a complex array of deposits, wire transfers, falsified invoices, and sales receipts, with the ultimate beneficiary transfers being made to accounts in Colombia and Miami. In a 15-month period, Saccoccia laundered at least $130 million, charging a flat 10% fee for his services. He was convicted of various money-laundering and conspiracy charges, and was fined $15.8 million, ordered to forfeit over $130 million, and was sentenced to 660 years in federal prison. For a full description of the various schemes, see *United States v. Saccoccia*, 58 F.3d 1129 (1st Cir. 1995), and its sister case, *United States v. Hurley, DeMarco, Saccoccia, Cirella, et al.*, 63 F.3d 1 (1st Cir. 1995).

M. Operation Q-Tip

Another OCDETF investigation, Operation Q-Tip, was started in 1991 and was based on repeated findings of transshipment and undervaluation of Chinese textiles and wearing apparel into and through the U.S. Since its inception, it has resulted in the seizure of several million dollars of laundered assets.

N. Operation Zorro II

Part of the DEA's Southwest Border Initiative, this eight-month operation involved over 40 state and local law enforcement agencies, the DEA, FBI, DOJ's Criminal Division, 10 U.S. Attorney's Offices, and seven other federal agencies. It targeted a Mexican-run cocaine smuggling and distribution network within the U.S. and with ties to the Colombian Mafia that smuggled drugs into southern California, stored them in Los Angeles for shipment to Miami, Chicago, Philadelphia, New York, Newark, and Richmond. After more than 90 wiretaps, the operation culminated in May 1996, with the arrests of 156 traffickers, the seizure of 5,600 kilos of cocaine, one-half ton of marijuana, and the seizure of over $17 million. In addition, the Operation resulted in the dismantling of the U.S. infrastructure of the Rodriguez–Orejuela brothers' Cali organization as well as the U.S. infrastructure of two of the four groups of the Mexican Federation — the Arellano-Felix Organization and the Caro-Quintero Organization.

O.   Pizza Connection Case

In 1987, E.F. Hutton, among other Wall Street investment firms, had accepted millions of dollars in investment cash from a Mafia heroin-smuggling operation. This came to light in what is known as the "Pizza Connection Case" because of the involvement of the Sicilian Mafia. Investigators concluded that these drug traffickers had made approximately $6 million per year for over 10 years. The investment firms and the drug smugglers escaped any liability because they had filed the required CTRs on their transactions. The money-laundering scheme was fairly basic: they deposited cash into various accounts; withdrew the funds in the form of bank drafts; used the brokerage firms to transfer the drafts to Swiss bank accounts; then used various financial service companies to wire transfer the funds from the Swiss accounts to their Sicilian bank accounts. Cases like this one led to the criminalization of money laundering itself under the MLCA of 1986.

Investigative Techniques

11

I.   Four Basic Steps of Money-Laundering Investigations

A.   Step 1: Identify the Unlawful Activity

Most local money laundering investigations begin as a result of an investigation into a target's unlawful activity, whether it be drug dealing, gambling, smuggling, etc. It is imperative that investigators ensure that this unlawful activity is one of the types of specially designated or "specified unlawful activity" giving rise to a money-laundering and/or forfeiture case; all known money laundering, forfeiture, and bank reporting statutes require that, in order to prove a money-laundering offense, the target must have engaged in a financial transaction using the proceeds of an "unlawful activity." In the case of the federal money-laundering statutes (sections 1956 and 1957 of Title 18), the government must prove that the funds were derived from at least one of approximately 200 "specified unlawful activities." The most common offenses are drug trafficking, fraud, environmental crimes, banking violations, and racketeering.

B.   Step 2: Identify and Track the Financial Transactions

This is the "show me the money" part of the investigation. As set out above, most local money-laundering investigations begin as a result of a narcotics-related arrest or investigation. Typically, a street-level dealer's arrest leads to an investigation into his supplier's drug activities. As part of this latter investigation, investigators should identify and track the target's financial trail using:

1.   Documents seized during the execution of search warrants: look for money exchange receipts, brokerage statements (often the target will retain only envelopes with the broker's return address, which is enough information to start an investigation into any accounts the target

might hold), wire transfer receipts, postal money order receipts, safety deposit box records, automobile records, credit card statements (overpaying a credit card gives the target instant access to cash later on), casino membership cards, and documents relating to travel agents (who are notorious for laundering money; the target purchases open return tickets, then sells those tickets later).

2. Law-enforcement databases: FinCEN's database, accessed by state and local agencies through FinCEN's Gateway system, should be the starting point for all financial investigations.

3. Commercial databases: including credit bureau reports and legal, or court dockets (the latter may lead to witnesses who have been sued or sued the target; they could be a wealth of information about the target).

4. Public records: corporate records, social security, bankruptcy courts, divorce (probate court) records, land registry.

5. Licensing bureaus: motor vehicle records, marriage licenses, liquor licenses, notary public records.

Often, the target will be laundering money through a storefront business, such as a pizza parlor, sub shop, towing business, wire-transfer business (caution: those wire-transfer businesses that also sell pagers, beepers, fax machines, and cellular phones are often simply a "one-stop" shop for drug dealers!), or any other cash-intensive business. If the target has some connection to a small business, the investigator should consider a review of the business's books to determine if the target is commingling legal revenues with illicit money, comparing sales and profit ratios with other similar businesses, determining the volume of business by observing traffic patterns, checking with suppliers and wholesalers to see if the product purchased is consistent with the reported sales, analyzing bank records and deposit patterns, and comparing deposits with sales.

In 1995, prosecutors in Houston, Texas, uncovered a number of *giro* houses that reported wire transfers of $30,000 to $50,000 per day from 20 to 30 customers. Receipts showed transfers of less than $10,000 (below the reporting threshold). However, physical surveillance showed that only a handful of clients went into the business each day. Further analysis of the names of the clients on the receipts showed that the names had actually been taken from a Cali, Colombia, telephone directory; the business was actually limited to two or three major drug dealers bringing in hundreds of thousands of dollars in cash each day, to be wire-transferred to Colombia. The *giro* house's banks filed CTRs when the *giro* house deposited the bulk cash into its accounts for settlement with the beneficiaries in Colombia, but the CTRs simply noted the name of the *giro* house, not the name(s) of the clients. After closing this *giro* house and others like it (and even more simply closed their doors so as to avoid possible prosecution), law enforcement officers noticed a huge increase in the amount of cash seized during the execution of search warrants at local crack houses. The thinking was that the dealers were stockpiling their cash until they were able to make alternative arrangements to move it out of Houston.

It is important to assume that the target might not be the source of the funds being laundered; rather, the target is acting as an intermediary in the laundering process. It might seem obvious that the dealer or supplier being investigated is taking his proceeds and laundering them. What might not be obvious, however, is that this dealer or supplier is only one of a number of others like him, all working for a greater organization. He could be laundering money received from others like him, and then moving that money along the laundering path.

C.   Step 3: Perform a Financial Analysis of the Target

There are two main financial investigation tools used to determine if the target's spending habits reflect an "honest living." The first is known as a "net worth analysis," generally used where the target has conspicuous assets, and a "source and application of funds analysis," generally used where the target has conspicuous spending habits.

1.   Net Worth Analysis

Net worth analysis is an investigative tool used to determine if a target has acquired assets at a rate in excess of his income from "legitimate" sources in order to conclude whether he had income from "illegitimate" sources. This technique is useful when the target's spending patterns reflect acquisition and disposal of tangible assets; where the target's spending habits are of a more transient nature, such as maintaining a lavish lifestyle, a "source and application of funds analysis" is more appropriate. In *United States v. Sorrentino*, the court described the net worth analysis method as follows:

> The government makes out a prima facie case ... if it establishes the defendant's opening net worth ... with reasonable certainty and then shows increases in his net worth for each year in question which, added to his non-deductible expenditures and excluding his known non-taxable receipts for the year, exceed his reported taxable income by a substantial amount ... . The jury may infer that the defendant's excess net worth increases represent unreported taxable income if the government either shows a likely source, ... or negates all possible non-taxable sources.

2.   *Source and Application of Funds Analysis*

Source and application of funds analysis is an investigative tool used to determine if a target has acquired assets at a rate in excess of his income from "legitimate" sources in order to conclude whether he had income from "illegitimate" sources. This technique is useful when the target's spending patterns are of a transient nature (e.g., maintaining a lavish lifestyle); where the target's spending habits reflect acquisition and disposal of tangible assets, a "net worth analysis" is more appropriate.

The formula for this analysis is very simple: unidentified cash equals total cash expenditures less total cash income (UC = TCE − TCI). Like the net worth analysis, this analysis is based on the basic fact that, for any given period of time, a person's income is applied to items that are either known and reported, or unknown and unreported.

D.   Step 4: Freeze and Confiscate Assets

The seizure and forfeiture of money-laundering proceeds is beyond the scope of this chapter. However, the key to any successful seizure is timing, as most launderers — particularly those acting as an intermediary in the laundering cycle — will accumulate funds over a period of time, then disperse them in blocks at the end of that period. It would be futile to seize a target's business and bank accounts immediately after large withdrawals have been made.

II.   Compelling the Production of Documents

A.   Letters Rogatory

Letters rogatory are an internationally recognized procedural device that allows a judicial body in one country to petition the courts of a foreign country for assistance in a criminal investigation. Because this device is slow and costly, U.S. law enforcement agencies turned to simple subpoenas to pressure banks with American branches to produce records from accounts held in branches in other countries.

B.   Subpoenas

The most common tool to compel production of documents is the use of a grand jury subpoena (to compel a person to appear) or a subpoena *duces tecum* (to compel specified documents to appear). The most common use of a subpoena in money-laundering investigations is for bank records. Any such subpoena should seek all documents (including those stored electronically) relating to the following: account records (signature cards, monthly statements, deposit slips, canceled checks), bank checks, certificates of deposit, travelers checks, correspondence on file, credit cards (including applications, credit reports, and monthly statements), CTRs, loan records (applications and records of payments), safe deposit box records (particularly entry records), security or investment account records, and wire-transfer logs.

Subpoenas issued by U.S. courts or grand juries are territorially limited to the court's or grand jury's specific territorial jurisdiction. Any power to compel the production of documents located outside the U.S. lies in "letters rogatory." However, U.S. law enforcement agencies have turned to subpoenas to pressure foreign banks with American branches to produce records from accounts held in branches in other countries. Because many of these countries have strict bank secrecy laws that often make the production of a bank client's records a criminal offense, the "act of state doctrine" (protecting the bank from prosecution if their actions were compelled by an act of state) comes into play. Some courts will enforce a subpoena against a foreign bank with American branches; others will not. In two cases involving the Bank of Nova Scotia, the Eleventh Circuit held that subpoenas "could" be enforced, while the D.C. Circuit held that they could not be enforced. In the Eleventh Circuit case, *In re Grand Jury Proceedings the Bank of Nova Scotia*, 740 F.2d 817 (11th Cir. 1984), cert. denied, 469 U.S. 1106 (1985), the U.S. government delivered a subpoena to an American branch of the Bank of Nova Scotia, headquartered in Canada with branches in the U.S., Bahamas, and the Cayman Islands, compelling it to produce records of a customer account held at its Bahamian and Cayman Islands branches. The Eleventh Circuit compelled the production, notwithstanding that both the Bahamas and the Cayman Islands made it a criminal offense to do so. After imposing fines of $25,000 per day, the Bank finally caved in and produced the records. In the D.C. Circuit case, *In re Sealed Case*, 825 F.2d 494 (D.C. Cir. 1987), the court held that, although it would not compel the bank to produce records in violation of the laws of its country, it did uphold a subpoena that required a bank official who had formerly worked at the foreign branch to testify as to his knowledge of the accounts.

III. The ABA Numerical System Identification Code

All bank checks printed for use by U.S. banks contain a series of numbers strung out on the bottom left of the check, called the MICR (Magnetic Image Character Recognition) Code. These same numbers also appear in the upper right-hand corner of each check, right below the check number. Known as the "ABA Transit Number," or "routing" number, these numbers are an identification code developed by the American Bankers' Association in order to identify the city, state, bank, Federal Reserve District, and whether it is a head office or branch office of the FRD, and the terms of credit for the check (immediate credit, deferred credit, or any special collection arrangements). All of this information can be critical in tracing originators of checks, which Federal Reserve districts the checks are processed through, etc.

The ABA Transit Number, as it appears in the upper right-hand corner of a check (below the check number), looks like this:

$$\frac{68-1}{1210}$$

The first number, in this case "68," identifies the city (numbers 1 through 49) or state (numbers 50 through 99). The second number ("1") identifies the particular bank (in the New York Federal Reserve District, this number can have as many as three digits). The first number in the denominator, or first two numbers if there are four numbers in the denominator (in this case, the number "12"), identifies the Federal Reserve District (between 1 and 12). The next number ("1"), which will be between 1 and 5, distinguishes between a Federal Reserve head office ("1") or one of the branch offices (2 through 5, as no Federal Reserve District has more than four branches). The last number on the denominator (in this case "0") identifies the type of credit ("0" for immediate credit, 1 through 5 for deferred credit) or whether there are any special collection arrangements (6 through 9).

Note that there are 12 district banks in the Federal Reserve System, with 25 regional offices. Each Federal Reserve Banks and branches is represented by a number:

Federal Reserve Bank	Regional Offices
Boston (1)	None
New York (2)	Buffalo (2)
Philadelphia (3)	None
Cleveland (4)	Cincinnati (2), Pittsburgh (3)
Richmond, VA (5)	Baltimore (2), Charlotte (3)
Atlanta (6)	Birmingham (2), Jacksonville (3), Nashville (4), New Orleans (5)
Chicago (7)	Detroit (2)
St. Louis (8)	Little Rock (2), Louisville (3), Memphis (4)
Minneapolis (9)	Helena (2)
Kansas City (10)	Denver (2), Oklahoma City (3), Omaha (4)
Dallas (11)	El Paso (2), Houston (3), San Antonio (4)
San Francisco (12)	Los Angeles (2), Portland (3), Salt Lake City (4), Seattle (5)

As described above, the first two numbers on the top line of the ABA Transit Number designate the city or state in which the check is drawn: 1 through 49 for major cities and 50 through 99 for states. Numbers 50 to 58 are eastern states; 59 is Alaska, Samoa, Guam, Hawaii, Puerto Rico, and the U.S. Virgin Islands; 60 to 69 are southeastern states; 70 to 79 are central states; 80 to 88 are southwestern states; and 90 to 99 are western states.

Numbers of Cities in Numerical Order

1. New York	18. Kansas City, MO	35. Houston, TX
2. Chicago	19. Seattle	36. St. Joseph, MO
3. Philadelphia	20. Indianapolis	37. Fort Worth, TX
4. St. Louis	21. Louisville, KY	38. Savannah, GA
5. Boston	22. St. Paul, MN	39. Oklahoma City
6. Cleveland	23. Denver	40. Wichita, KA
7. Baltimore	24. Portland, OR	41. Sioux City, IA
8. Pittsburgh	25. Columbus, OH	42. Pueblo, CO
9. Detroit	26. Memphis, TN	43. Lincoln, NE
10. Buffalo	27. Omaha, NE	44. Topeka, KA
11. San Francisco	28. Spokane, WA	45. Dubuque, IA
12. Milwaukee	29. Albany, NY	46. Galveston, TX
13. Cincinnati	30. San Antonio	47. Cedar Rapids, IA
14. New Orleans	31. Salt Lake City	48. Waco, TX
15. Washington, D.C.	32. Dallas, TX	49. Muskogee, OK
16. Los Angeles	33. Des Moines, IA	
17. Minneapolis	34. Tacoma, WA	

Numbers of States in Numerical Order

50. New York	64. Georgia	82. Colorado
51. Connecticut	65. Maryland	83. Kansas
52. Maine	66. North Carolina	84. Louisiana
53. Massachusetts	67. South Carolina	85. Mississippi
54. New Hampshire	68. Virginia	86. Oklahoma
55. New Jersey	69. West Virginia	87. Tennessee
56. Ohio	70. Illinois	88. Texas
57. Rhode Island	71. Indiana	89.
58. Vermont	72. Iowa	90. California
59. Alaska, Samoa,	73. Kentucky	91. Arizona
Guam, Hawaii, Puerto	74. Michigan	92. Idaho
Rico, U.S. Virgin Islands	75. Minnesota	93. Montana
60. Pennsylvania	76. Nebraska	94. Nevada
61. Alabama	77. North Dakota	95. New Mexico
62. Delaware	78. South Dakota	96. Oregon
63. Florida	79. Wisconsin	97. Utah
	80. Missouri	98. Washington
	81. Arkansas	99. Wyoming

The second series of numbers across the bottom of each check identifies the bank branch number and the actual bank account number. The final series of numbers are entered by the processing bank, and consist of the check number and the amount of the check, all written in MICR Code.

Part V
The World Stage

International Organizations and Treaties

12

I. Introduction

U.S. federal and state agencies, working alone or in task forces, have begun to recognize the transnational or international nature of the criminal organizations they are trying to fight. These domestic agencies, and their foreign counterparts, are turning more and more to each other and to the various international organizations and treaties to bolster their efforts. Therefore, any discussion of international criminal organizations and money laundering requires a basic understanding of the major international organizations and treaties available in opposition.

II. The United Nations

A. Structure and Organization

The United Nations (UN) is an organization of 185 nations providing an organization and forum to address and resolve any conceivable issue of concern to the international community. The UN is headquartered in New York, with five of its six main organs based at the UN Headquarters:

1. the General Assembly (all 185 members are represented, each having one vote)
2. the Security Council (15 member nations, five of which have permanent status — China, France, Great Britain, the Russian Federation, and the United States)
3. the Economic and Social Council (54 member nations coordinating the 14 specialized agencies of the UN)

4. the Trusteeship Council (established to ensure that trust territories began full-fledged nations, the work of this Council was finished in 1994 with the admission of the Pacific Island nation of Palau, the last of the 11 original UN trusteeships)
5. the International Court of Justice, or World Court (15 judges elected by the General Assembly decide cases between nations)
6. the Secretariat (the "executive branch" of the UN, headed by the Secretary General)

B.   The 1988 Vienna Convention

The United Nations' 1988 Convention Against Illicit Traffic in Narcotic Drugs and Psychotropic Substances, known as the Vienna Convention, is considered a watershed event in the development of a coordinated international response to global money laundering. Compliance with the Convention is a prerequisite to certification of drug-producing and -transit countries by the State Department.

The origins of the 1988 Vienna Convention can be traced back to two earlier anti-drug conventions: the 1961 Single Convention on Narcotic Drugs, and the 1971 Convention on Psychotropic Substances. Using these two conventions as models, the 1988 Convention (in effect since November 11, 1990) urged its (roughly) 75 signatory nations to exchange information and enforce their domestic money-laundering statutes. A by-product of the Convention was a law enforcement treaty, signed by 44 nations, which established money laundering as domestic criminal offenses. The Convention also allows for asset forfeiture, extradition, and general mutual assistance between law enforcement agencies.

The Convention is enforced by the International Narcotics Control Board that, in turn, reports to the Commission on Narcotic Drugs of the Economic and Social Council of the United Nations. The Convention itself consists of 34 articles:

Article 1: Definitions
Article 2: Scope of the Commission
Article 3: Offenses and Sanctions
Article 4: Jurisdiction
Article 5: Confiscation
Article 6: Extradition
Article 7: Mutual Legal Assistance
Article 8: Transfer of Proceedings
Article 9: Other forms of cooperation and training
Article 10: International cooperation and assistance for transit states
Article 11: Controlled delivery

Article 3 — Offenses and Sanctions — is the critical article *vis à vis* drug trafficking and money laundering. Section 1 of Article 3 requires each nation, or "Party" to the Convention, to criminalize drug trafficking (subparagraph (a)) and money laundering (subparagraph (b)(i) and (ii)). The proposed money-laundering offenses are described as follows:

(b)(i) the conversion or transfer of property, knowing that such property is derived from any offense or offenses established in accordance with subparagraph (a) of this paragraph, or from an act of participation in such offense or offenses, for the purpose of concealing or disguising the illicit origin of the property or of assisting any person who is involved in the commission of such an offense or offenses to evade the legal consequences of his actions;

(b)(ii) the concealment or the disguise of the true nature, source, location, disposition, movement, rights with respect to, or ownership of property, knowing that such property is derived from an offense or offenses established in accordance with subparagraph (a) of this paragraph or from an act of participation in such an offense or offenses.

III. The Financial Action Task Force (FATF)

A. Creation and Mandate

Formed in 1989 with a 10-year mandate, the FATF is an international organization whose sole purpose is to combat global financial crime. Twenty-six countries and two international organizations are members: Australia, Austria, Belgium, Canada, Denmark, Finland, France, Germany, Greece, Hong Kong, Iceland, Ireland, Italy, Japan, Luxembourg, the Netherlands, New Zealand, Norway, Portugal, Singapore, Spain, Sweden, Switzerland, Turkey, the United Kingdom, the United States, and the European Commission and the Gulf Co-operation Council.

The FATF was created by the Group of Seven (G-7) nations at their July 1989 Heads of State and Finance Ministers Economic Summit. Its goal is to fight money laundering by having its members enact and enforce certain domestic, bilateral, and multilateral anti-money-laundering laws and initiatives, based on its "40 Recommendations." These recommendations, revised in 1996, set out a basic framework for anti-money-laundering efforts and are designed to be of universal application. They cover the criminal justice system and law enforcement (numbers 1–7), the financial system and its regulation (numbers 8–29), and international cooperation (numbers 30–40). They are designed as guidelines only, recognizing that each of the member's political and legal systems are different. Each of the member countries engages in an annual self-assessment of their implementation and application of the principles, as well as being subject to multilateral surveillance and peer review. For example, the FATF issued a formal statement in September 1996, condemning Turkey for failing to implement anti-money-laundering legislation. By December 1996, Turkey had implemented such laws. As of early 1998, all FATF member nations have anti-money-laundering legislation that comports with the 40 Recommendations.

B. The Forty Recommendations

Like the 34 Articles of the Vienna Convention, the 40 Recommendations of the FATF form the background by which all nations' anti-money-laundering efforts are gauged. They are as follows:

1. Each country should take immediate steps to ratify, and to implement fully, the 1988 United Nations Convention against Illicit Traffic in Narcotic Drugs and Psychotropic Substances (the Vienna Convention).

2. Financial institution secrecy laws should be conceived so as not to inhibit implementation of these recommendations.

3. An effective money-laundering enforcement program should include increased multilateral cooperation and mutual legal assistance in money-laundering investigations and prosecutions and extradition in money-laundering cases, where possible.

4. Each country should take such measures as might be necessary, including legislative ones, to enable it to criminalize money laundering as set forth in the Vienna Convention. Each country should extend the offense of drug money laundering to one based on serious offenses. Each country would determine which serious crimes would be designated as money-laundering predicate offenses.

5. As provided in the Vienna Convention, the offense of money laundering should apply at least to knowing money-laundering activity, including the concept that knowledge can be inferred from objective financial circumstances.

6. Where possible, corporations themselves — not only their employees — should be subject to criminal liability.

7. Countries should adopt measures similar to those set forth in the Vienna Convention, as necessary, including legislative ones, to enable their competent authorities to confiscate property laundered, proceeds from, instrumentalities used in or intended for use in the commission of any money-laundering offense, or property of corresponding value, without prejudicing the rights of *bona fide* third parties. Such measures should include the authority to: (1) identify, trace, and evaluate property that is subject to confiscation; (2) carry out provisional measures, such as freezing and seizing, to prevent any dealing, transfer, or disposal of such property; and (3) take any appropriate investigative measures. In addition to confiscation and criminal sanctions, countries should also consider monetary and civil penalties, and/or proceedings including civil proceedings, to void contracts entered into by parties, where parties knew or should have known that as a result of the contract, the State would be prejudiced in its ability to recover financial crime, e.g., through confiscation or collection of fines and penalties.

8. Recommendations 10 to 29 should apply not only to banks, but also to non-bank financial institutions, or NBFIs. Even for those NBFIs that are not subject to a formal prudential supervisory regime in all countries (e.g., *bureaux de change*), governments should ensure that these institutions are subject to the same anti-money-laundering laws or regulations as all other financial institutions and that these laws or regulations are implemented effectively.

9. The appropriate national authorities should consider applying Recommendations 10 to 21 and 23 to the conduct of financial activities as a commercial undertaking by businesses or professions that are not financial institutions, where such conduct is allowed or not prohibited. Financial activities include, but are not limited to, those listed in the attached annex. It is left to each country to decide whether special situations should be defined where the application of anti-money-laundering measures is not necessary; for example, when a financial activity is carried out on an occasional or limited basis.

10. Financial institutions should not keep anonymous accounts or accounts in obviously fictitious names; they should be required (by law, by regulations, by agreements between supervisory authorities and financial institutions, or by self-regulatory agreements among financial institutions) to identify, on the basis of an official or other reliable identifying document, and record the identity of their clients, either occasional or usual, when establishing business relations or conducting transactions (in particular opening of accounts or passbooks, entering into fiduciary transactions, renting of safe deposit boxes, performing large cash transactions). To fulfill identification requirements concerning legal entities, financial institutions should, when necessary, take measures to (1) verify the legal existence and structure of the customer by obtaining either from a public register or from the customer or both, proof of incorporation, including information including the customer's name, legal form, address, directors, and provisions regulating the power to bind the entity; and (2) verify that any person purporting to act on behalf of the customer is so authorized and identify that person.

11. Financial institutions should take reasonable measures to obtain information about the true identity of the persons on whose behalf an account is opened or a transaction conducted if there are any doubts as to whether these clients or customers are acting on their own behalf e.g., in the case of domiciliary companies (institutions, corporations, foundations, trusts, etc. that do not conduct any commercial or manufacturing business or any other form of commercial operation in the country where their registered office is located).

12. Financial institutions should maintain, for at least five years, all necessary records on transactions, both domestic or international, to enable them to comply swiftly with information requests from the competent authorities. Such records must be sufficient to permit reconstruction of individual transactions (including the amounts and types of currency involved if any) so as to provide, if necessary, evidence for prosecution of criminal behavior. Financial institutions

should keep records on customer identification (e.g., copies of records of official identification documents like passports, identity cards, driving licenses or similar documents), account files, and business correspondence for at least five years after the account is closed. These documents should be available to domestic competent authorities in the context of relevant criminal prosecutions and investigations.

13. Countries should pay special attention to money-laundering threats inherent in new or developing technologies that might favor anonymity, and take measures, if needed, to prevent their use in money-laundering schemes.

14. Financial institutions should pay special attention to all complex, unusual, large transactions, and all unusual patterns of transactions, that have no apparent economic or lawful purpose. The background and purpose of such transactions should, as far as possible, be examined, the findings established in writing, and be available to help supervisors, auditors and law enforcement agencies.

15. If financial institutions suspect that funds stem from a criminal activity, they should be required to report promptly their suspicions to the competent authorities.*

16. Financial institutions, their directors, officers, and employees should be protected by legal provisions from criminal or civil liability for breach of any restriction on disclosure of information imposed by contract or by any legislative, regulatory, or administrative provision, if they report their suspicions in good faith to the competent authorities, even if they did not know precisely what the underlying criminal activity was, and regardless of whether illegal activity actually occurred.**

17. Financial institutions, their directors, officers, and employees, should not, or, where appropriate, should not be allowed to, warn their customers when information relating to them is being reported to the competent authorities.***

18. Financial institutions reporting their suspicions should comply with instructions from the competent authorities.

19. Financial institutions should develop programs against money laundering. These programs should include, as a minimum: (1) the development of internal policies, procedures and controls, including the designation of compliance officers at management level, and adequate

* This is the "Suspicious Activity" concept adopted by most nations. See Section V in Chapter 4, "Money Laundering in the Banking Industry," for a discussion of this concept.
** This is the "Safe Harbor Provisions" concept adopted by some nations. See Section V in Chapter 4, "Money Laundering in the Banking Industry," for a discussion of this concept.
*** This is the "Tip Off Provisions" concept adopted by some nations. See Section V in "Money Laundering in the Banking Industry," for a discussion of this concept.

screening procedures to ensure high standards when hiring employees; (2) an ongoing employee training program; and (3) an audit function to test the system.

20. Financial institutions should ensure that the principles mentioned above are also applied to branches and majority-owned subsidiaries located abroad, especially in countries that do not or insufficiently apply these Recommendations, to the extent that local applicable laws and regulations permit. When local applicable laws and regulations prohibit this implementation, competent authorities in the country of the mother institution should be informed by the financial institutions that they cannot apply these Recommendations.

21. Financial institutions should give special attention to business relations and transactions with persons, including companies and financial institutions, from countries that do not or insufficiently apply these Recommendations. Whenever these transactions have no apparent economic or visible lawful purpose, their background and purpose should, as far as possible, be examined, the findings established in writing, and be available to help supervisors, auditors, and law enforcement agencies.

22. Countries should consider implementing feasible measures to detect or monitor the physical cross-border transportation of cash and bearer negotiable instruments, subject to strict safeguards to ensure proper use of information and without impeding in any way the freedom of capital movements.

23. Countries should consider the feasibility and utility of a system where banks and other financial institutions and intermediaries would report all domestic and international currency transactions above a fixed amount, to a national central agency with a computerized database, available to competent authorities for use in money-laundering cases, subject to strict safeguards to ensure proper use of the information.

24. Countries should further encourage, in general, the development of modern and secure techniques of money management, including increased use of checks, payment cards, direct deposit of salary checks, and book entry recording of securities, as a means to encourage the replacement of cash transfers.

25. Countries should take notice of the potential for abuse of shell corporations by money launderers and should consider whether additional measures are required to prevent unlawful use of such entities.

26. The competent authorities supervising banks or other financial institutions or intermediaries, or other competent authorities, should ensure that the supervised institutions have adequate programs to guard against money laundering. These authorities should cooperate

with and lend expertise spontaneously or on request to other domestic judicial or law enforcement authorities in money-laundering investigations and prosecutions.

27. Competent authorities should be designated to ensure an effective implementation of all these Recommendations, through administrative supervision and regulation, in other professions dealing with cash as defined by each country.

28. The competent authorities should establish guidelines that will assist financial institutions in detecting suspicious patterns of behavior by their customers. It is understood that such guidelines must develop over time, and will never be exhaustive. It is further understood that such guidelines will primarily serve as an educational tool for financial institutions' personnel.

29. The competent authorities regulating or supervising financial institutions should take the necessary legal or regulatory measures to guard against control or acquisition of a significant participation in financial institutions.

30. National administrations should consider recording, at least in the aggregate, international flows of cash in whatever currency, so that estimates can be made of cash flows and reflows from various sources abroad, when this is combined with central bank information. Such information should be made available to the International Monetary Fund and the Bank for International Settlements to facilitate international studies.

31. International competent authorities, perhaps Interpol and the World Customs Organization, should be given responsibility for gathering and disseminating information to competent authorities about the latest developments in money laundering and money-laundering techniques. Central banks and bank regulators could do the same on their network. National authorities in various spheres, in consultation with trade associations, could then disseminate this to financial institutions in individual countries.

32. Each country should make efforts to improve a spontaneous or "upon request" international information exchange relating to suspicious transactions, persons and corporations involved in those transactions between competent authorities. Strict safeguards should be established to ensure that this exchange of information is consistent with national and international provisions on privacy and data protection.

33. Countries should try to ensure, on a bilateral or multilateral basis, that different knowledge standards in national definitions — i.e., different standards concerning the intentional element of the infraction

— do not affect the ability or willingness of countries to provide each other with mutual legal assistance.

34. International cooperation should be supported by a network of bilateral and multilateral agreements and arrangements based on generally shared legal concepts with the aim of providing practical measures to affect the widest possible range of mutual legal assistance.

35. Countries should be encouraged to ratify and implement relevant international conventions on money laundering, such as the 1990 Council of Europe Convention on Laundering, Search, Seizure, and Confiscation of the Proceeds from Crime.

36. Cooperative investigations among countries' appropriate competent authorities should be encouraged. One valid and effective investigative technique in this respect is controlled delivery related to assets known or suspected to be the proceeds of crime. Countries are encouraged to support this technique, where possible.

37. There should be procedures for mutual assistance in criminal matters regarding the use of compulsory measures, including the production of records by financial institutions and other persons, the search of persons and premises, seizure and obtaining of evidence for use in money-laundering investigations and prosecutions and in related actions in foreign jurisdictions.

38. There should be authority to take expeditious action in response to requests by foreign countries to identify, freeze, seize and confiscate proceeds or other property of corresponding value to such proceeds, based on money laundering or the crimes underlying the laundering activity. There should be arrangements for coordinating seizure and confiscation proceedings that could include the sharing of confiscated assets.

39. To avoid conflicts of jurisdiction, consideration should be given to devising and applying mechanisms for determining the best venue for prosecution of defendants in the interests of justice in cases that are subject to prosecution in more than one country. Similarly, there should be arrangements for coordinating seizure and confiscation proceedings that could include the sharing of confiscated assets.

40. Countries should have procedures in place to extradite, where possible, individuals charged with a money-laundering offense or related offenses. With respect to its national legal system, each country should recognize money laundering as an extraditable offense. Subject to their legal frameworks, countries could consider simplifying extradition by allowing direct transmission of extradition requests between appropriate ministries, extraditing persons based only on warrants of arrests or judgments, extraditing their nationals, and/or introducing a sim-

plified extradition of consenting persons who waive formal extradition proceedings.

C. Future of the FATF

In 1996, the 40 Recommendations were revised to (1) add more predicate offenses; (2) make reporting of suspicious activities mandatory; (3) include nonfinancial institutions in the mandatory reporting requirements; (4) focus on cyberpayment money laundering; and (5) provide for more support for placement-level enforcement.

On February 6, 1997, the FATF released its Annual Report for 1996–1997, which reviewed current money-laundering methods and countermeasures, reviewed the efforts of the FATF countries in promoting and implementing the 40 Recommendations, and looked to the global problems, in general. Stanley Morris, chairman of FinCEN, chaired the group that authored the Report.

The FATF's 1998 report, released on February 12, 1998, focused on money-laundering typologies. The report was a result of a November 1997 summit between 22 member countries, the European Commission, and other international organizations such as Interpol, the World Customs Organization (WCO), the International Organization of Securities Commissions (IOSCO), and the UNDCP, and their discussions on recent trends in money laundering, emerging threats, and effective countermeasures. The 1998 Report focused on the new payment technologies and the shift from the banking sector to non-bank financial institutions and nonfinancial entities (such as lawyers, accountants, and insurance companies).

IV. Caribbean Financial Action Task Force (CFATF)

A. Introduction

Modeled after its parent, Paris-based FATF, the 26 member countries from the Caribbean Basin (and the United States) of the CFATF have banded together to promulgate and implement various anti-money-laundering efforts. Its goal is to fight money laundering through mutual cooperation and evaluation. The CFATF grew from a conference initiated in 1991 by the Prime Minister of Aruba because of his concern about the influx of drug money into Aruba. However, the organization was not formed until October 1996, when it issued a Memorandum of Understanding (MOU) that outlined its purpose and goals. Non-member, but "cooperating" nations include the United States, Canada, Mexico, France, Great Britain, Argentina, and Holland. Colombia was invited as an observer nation to the 1996 conference.

The CFATF is taking an active role in anti-money-laundering intiatives in the Caribbean and Latin American region. For example, in July 1997, the CFATF and FinCEN co-sponsored a Casino Regulatory Conference that addressed money-laundering methods, practices, trends, and effective countermeasures in the casino and gaming industry.

B.   The Nineteen Aruba Recommendations

The centerpiece of the CFATF is its "19 Recommendations" modeled after the FATF's 40 Recommendations. Proponents argue that these recommendations have been instrumental in the CFATF's efforts; detractors argue that the member nations have been slow to adopt or implement the recommendations because of their fear of eliminating all financial activity, not just illegal activity. Regardless, the 19 Aruba Recommendations are as follows.

Anti-Money-Laundering Authority

1. Adequate resources need to be dedicated to fighting money laundering and other drug-related financial crimes. In countries where experience in combatting money laundering and other drug-related financial crimes is limited, there need to be competent authorities that specialize in money-laundering investigations and prosecutions and related forfeiture actions, advise financial institutions and regulatory authorities on anti-money-laundering measures, and receive and evaluate suspicious transaction information from financial institutions and regulators and currency reports, if required, to be filed by individuals or institutions.

Crime of Money Laundering

2. Consistent with Recommendation 5 of the Financial Action Task Force and recognizing that the objectives of combating money laundering are shared by members of this Conference, each country in determining for itself what crimes ought to constitute predicate offenses, should be fully aware of the practical evidentiary complications that might arise if money laundering is made an offense only with respect to certain very specific predicate offenses.

3. In accordance with the Vienna Convention, each country should, subject to its constitutional principles and the basic concepts of its legal system, criminalize conspiracy or assocation to engage in, and aiding and abetting drug trafficking, money laundering and other serious drug-related offenses and subject such activities to stringent criminal sanctions.

4. When criminalizing money laundering, the national legislature should consider:

(a) whether money laundering should only qualify as an offense in cases where the offender actually knew that he was dealing in funds derived from crime or whether it should also qualify as an offense in cases where the offender ought to have known that this was the case;

(b) whether it should be relevant that the predicate offense might have been committed outside the territorial jurisdiction of the country where the laundering occurred;

(c) whether it is sufficient to criminalize the laundering of illegally obtained funds, or whether other property that might serve as a means of payment should also be covered.

5. Where it is not otherwise a crime, countries should consider enacting statutes that criminalize the knowing payment, receipt or transfer, or attempted payment, receipt or transfer of property known to represent the proceeds of drug trafficking or money laundering, where the recipient of the property is a public official, political candidate, or political party. In countries where it is already a crime, countries should consider the imposition of enhanced punishment or other sanctions, such as forfeiture of office.

Attorney-Client Privilege

6. The fact that a person acting as a financial advisor or nominee is an attorney should not in and of itself be sufficient reason for such person to invoke an attorney–client privilege.

Confiscation

7. Confiscation measures should provide for the authority to seize, freeze, and confiscate, at the request of a foreign state, property in the jurisdiction in which such property is located, regardless of whether the owner of the property or any persons who committed the offense making the property subject to confiscation are present or have ever been present within the jurisdiction.

8. Countries should provide for the possibility of confiscating any property that represents assets which have been directly or indirectly derived from drug offenses or related money-laundering offenses (property confiscation), and can also provide for a system of pecuniary sanctions based on an assessment of the value of assets that have been directly or indirectly derived from such offences. In the latter case, the pecuniary sanctions concerned might be recoverable from any asset of the convicted person that might be available (value confiscation).

9. Confiscation measures can provide that all or part of any property confiscated be transferred directly for use by competent authorities, or be sold and the proceeds of such sales deposited into a fund dedicated to the use by competent authorities in anti-narcotics and anti-money-laundering efforts.

10. Confiscation measures should also apply to narcotic drugs and psychotropic substances, precursor and essential chemicals, equipment and materials used or destined for the illicit manufacture, preparation, distribution, and use of narcotic drugs and psychotropic substances.

Administrative Authority

11. In order to implement effectively the recommendations of the Financial Action Task Force, each country should have a system that provides for bank and other financial institutions supervision, including:

- Licensing of all banks, including offices, branches, and agencies of foreign banks, whether or not they take deposits or otherwise do business in the country (so-called offshore shell banks), and
- Periodic examination of institutions by authorities to ensure that the institutions have adequate anti-money-laundering programs in place and are following the implementation of other recommendations of the Financial Action Task Force.

Similarly, in order to implement the recommendations of the Financial Action Task Force, there needs to be effective regulation, including licensing and examination, of institutions and businesses such as securities brokers and dealers, *bureaux de change,* and casinos, that offer services that make them vulnerable to money laundering.

12. Countries need to ensure that there are adequate border procedures for inspecting merchandise and carriers, including private aircraft, to detect illegal drug and currency shipments.

Recordkeeping

13. In order to ensure implementation of the recommendations of the Financial Action Task Force, countries should apply appropriate administrative, civil, or criminal sanctions to financial institutions that fail to maintain records for the required retention period. Financial institution supervisory authorities must take special care to ensure that adequate records are being maintained.

Currency Reporting

14. Countries should consider the feasibility and utility of a system that requires the reporting of large amounts of currency over a certain specified amount received by businesses other than financial institutions, either in one transaction or in a series of related financial transactions. These reports would be analyzed routinely by competent authorities in the same manner as any currency report filed by financial institutions. Large cash purchases of

property and services such as real estate and aircraft are frequently made by drug traffickers and money launderers and, consequently, are of similar interest to law enforcement. Civil and criminal sanctions would apply to businesses and persons who fail to file or falsely file reports or structure transactions with the intent to evade the reporting requirements.

Administrative Cooperation

15. In furtherance of Recommendation 30 of the Financial Action Task Force, information acquired about international currency flows should be shared internationally and disseminated, if possible, through the services of appropriate international or regional organizations, or on existing international networks. Special agreements can also be concluded for this purpose.

16. Member states of the OAS should consider signing the OAS Convention on Extradition, concluded at Caracas on February 25, 1981.

17. Each country should endeavor to ensure that its laws and other measures regarding drug trafficking and money laundering, and bank regulation as it pertains to money laundering, are to the greatest extent possible as effective as the laws and other measures of all other countries in the region.

Training and Assistance

18. As a follow-up, there should be regular meetings among competent judicial, law enforcement, and supervisory authorities of the countries of the Caribbean and Central American region in order to discuss experiences in the fight against drug money laundering and emerging trends and techniques.

19. In order to enable countries with small economies and limited resources to develop appropriate drug money laundering prevention programs, other countries should consider widening the scope of their international technical assistance programs, and to pay particular attention to the need of training and otherwise strengthening the quality and preserving the integrity of the judicial, legal, and law enforcement systems.

V.   Organization of American States (OAS)*

What is now the OAS was first established in 1890 as the International Union of American Republics. Originally created to promote commercial relations between its 18 member nations, the IUAR added a system of collective security in 1947 (the Rio Treaty). In 1948, the OAS Charter was adopted (Pact of Bogotá). In 1959, the 20 member nations established the Inter-American Development Bank; and the following year, the members produced the Act

* This section is from the OAS website at *http://www.oas.org,* and a State Department website at *http://www.state.gov/www/background_notes/oas.*

of Bogotá, a hemispheric commitment to economic and social development. The 1948 Charter has been amended three times: by the 1967 Protocol of Buenos Aires, the 1985 Protocol of Cartegena, and the 1993 Protocol of Managua. In the end, the basic objectives of the OAS are to strengthen peace and security; promote democracy; ensure peaceful settlement of disputes; seek solutions to political, juridical, and economic problems; promote economic, social, educational, scientific, and cultural development; and limit conventional weapons. Currently, there are 35 member nations (Cuba is a member, but its present government has been excluded from participation since 1962 for incompatibility with the principles of the OAS) and 41 nations with "permanent observer" status:

Member Nations		Permanent Observer Nations	
Antigua and Barbuda	Argentina	Algeria	Angola
The Bahamas	Barbados	Austria	Belgium
Belize	Bolivia	Bosnia & Herzegovina	
Brazil	Canada	Croatia	Cyprus
Chile	Colombia	Czech Republic	Egypt
Costa Rica	Cuba*	Equatorial Guinea	European Union
Dominica	Dominican Rep	Finland	France
Ecuador	El Salvador	Germany	Ghana
Grenada	Guatemala	Greece	The Holy See
Guyana	Haiti	Hungary	India
Honduras	Jamaica	Israel	Italy
Mexico	Nicaragua	Japan	Kazakstan
Panama	Paraguay	Korea	Latvia
Peru	Saint Lucia	Lebanon	Morocco
St. Kitts and Nevis	Saint Vincent & Grenadines	Netherlands	Pakistan
Suriname	Trinidad & Tobago	Poland	Portugal
United States	Uruguay	Rumania	Russian Federation
Venezuela		Saudi Arabia	Spain
		Sri Lanka	Sweden
		Switzerland	Tunisia
		Ukraine	United Kingdom

The OAS is headquartered in Washington, D.C., and operates as a regional "United Nations." The Secretary General of the OAS is Colombian Cesar Gaviria Trujillo (elected to a 5-year term in 1994). Almost 60% of its operating budget of $84 million is contributed by the U.S. The OAS is comprised of various committees, councils, commissions, and foundations. For the purposes of international crime and money laundering, the principal entities and treaties are the Inter-American Drug Abuse Control Commission (CICAD), created in 1986, which meets biannually as the Inter-American Specialized Conference on Traffic in Narcotic Drugs; the 1996 Inter-American

Convention Against Corruption; and the Inter-American Juridical Committee. CICAD has been particularly effective. For example, in 1992, the OAS General Assembly approved model regulations on money laundering and asset forfeiture; currently, OAS nations, through CICAD, are working on improving banking and other financial institution controls to fight money laundering. In 1997, CICAD developed a program to assist countries in implementing and enforcing chemical control laws. This program, called the Monitoring System for the Control of Precursors and Other Chemical Substances Used in the Production of Illicit Drugs, uses mathematical models to estimate the quantities of these chemicals (ether, hydrochloric acid, ephedrines, etc.) required for domestic industrial use and what portion of any excess is liable for diversion to the producers or manufacturers of illicit drugs.

VI. Other International Organizations or Entities

A. Phare Project on Money Laundering

The Phare Project on Money Laundering is a project or task force established by various Central and Eastern European countries designed to promote legislative and other actions to enhance measures against money laundering in that region.

B. Association of Southeast Asian Nations (ASEAN)

The nine-member ASEAN is emerging as a powerful economic and political bloc. Its members include Burma (Myanmar), Malaysia, Indonesia, the Philippines, Thailand, Vietnam, Singapore, Brunei, and Laos.

C. Asia/Pacific Group on Money Laundering (APG)

The APG was formally established in February 1997, at the Fourth Asia/Pacific Money Laundering Symposium. The APG is made up of most of the ASEAN countries, as well as Australia. It has yet to adopt a formal statement of principles, but has recognized, in principle, the FATF 40 Recommendations.

D. Financial Intelligence Units (FIUs)

Through a Financial Action Task Force (FATF) initiative, member countries created Financial Intelligence Units (FIUs) as cross-agency/private and public sector "super" agencies designed as clearing-houses of information and data to combat money laundering. The FATF has defined or described FIUs as serving as a central point for the receipt, and as permitted by domestic law, analysis and dissemination to competent authorities of suspicious activity report information and data.

FinCEN is the U.S. version of an FIU. Similar organizations have been created in 30 countries, including Great Britain (Financial Intelligence Unit of the National Criminal Intelligence Service, or NCIS); France ("TRACFIN" — "traitement du renseignement et action contre les circuits financiers clandestins," or treatment of information and action against illicit financial circuits); Belgium ("CTIF" — French for "cellule de traitement des informations financieres," or bureau of treatment of financial information, or the Flemish "CFI" — "cel voor financiele informatie-verwerking"); Mexico (created with the assistance, and funded through, FinCEN, and opened in April 1997); Panama ("FAU" — Financial Analysis Unit — was created with the assistance, and funded through, FinCEN); and Australia ("AUSTRAC" — Australian Transactional Analysis Center).

Those organizations with FIUs have formed an organization, called the Egmont Group, which first met in 1995 and most recently met in San Francisco in 1996. The Egmont Group has grown from 14 members in 1995 to 28 members in 1997. A recent meeting of its members resulted in the development and implementation of a system to allow FIUs to communicate and exchange financial information securely through a "virtual private network" or website on the Internet.

E.   Interpol

Interpol is an international organization of over 170 member nations established to facilitate information sharing and coordination among nations in worldwide criminal investigations. In 1995, for the first time in its 64-year history, Interpol unanimously passed a resolution establishing the first major anti-money-laundering declaration. The former President of Interpol is a Canadian, Norman Inkster. Prior to his term as President of Interpol, Mr. Inkster was head of the RCMP.

VII. International Banking Organizations

A.   The International Monetary Fund (IMF)

The International Monetary Fund is a group of nations that have formed what is now known as the "World Bank" (its formal name is the International Bank for Reconstruction and Development, or IBRD). As the lender of last resort to the world's financial systems, the IMF and its World Bank is one of the world's most influential and dominant financial organizations. In fact, though, the World Bank is not a bank at all, but an organizer or broker of money pooled then lent by developed nations to undeveloped nations in order to encourage economic growth and stability in order to encourage global trade.

The World Bank was originally created to facilitate short-term loans to underdeveloped countries whose cash reserves were too low to pay for their imports at fixed exchange rates. In 1971, the U.S. moved away from a gold standard so that, instead of trading at a fixed exchange rate, currencies traded at a floating rate, depending on supply and demand.

In the early to mid-1970s, there were huge currency surpluses caused by the glut of OPEC "petrodollars." The IMF had no major role to play. In the late 1970s and early 1980s, the U.S. Federal Reserve pushed up interest rates and the value of the dollars that many countries could not repay their debts. Rather than risk a widespread economic collapse (of the countries and private banks that had lent money), loans were restructured with the aid of the IMF and World Bank. The IMF facilitated short-term loans and, more importantly, imposed economic and political restrictions on the borrowing countries to ensure repayment; the lending nations (including the U.S.) used these restrictions to fashion political, as well as economic changes, to the borrowing nations.

The two most infamous "bailouts" by the IMF are the 1985 Mexico bailout and the more recent bailouts of Indonesia and South Korea.

B. Basle Committee on Banking Supervision

The Basle Committee on Banking Supervision is composed of banking supervisory authorities and central banks of the Group of Ten countries. (Note that the Group of Ten actually has "12" members: the United States, Great Britain, Belgium, Canada, France, Germany, Italy, Japan, Luxembourg, Netherlands, Sweden, and Switzerland.)

Established in 1975, the Committee works on international banking and money transfer issues, and its reports are considered authoritative. Its 1988 report on "Prevention of Criminal Use of the Banking System for the Purposes of Money Laundering" is a landmark study on international money laundering.

C. Offshore Group of Banking Supervisors (OGBS)

The OGBS was established in 1980 as a forum for cooperation among banking supervisory authorities in the offshore financial centers of the Bahamas, Cayman Islands, Hong Kong, and Singapore.

D. International Bank Security Association

Most of the world's largest international banks are members of the IBSA, either as a full voting member (52 banks) or as an associate member (six banks). All 12 of the world's major financial centers (defined as the 12 member nations of the Group of Ten) are represented, except Japan.

VIII. International Agreements and Treaties

A. Financial Information Exchange Agreements (FIEAs)

FIEAs are bilateral Executive Agreements designed to facilitate the exchange of currency transaction information between governments. They provide a mechanism for the exchange of such information between the Treasury Department, through FinCEN, and the other government's finance ministry. Currently, the U.S. has FIEAs in effect with Colombia, Ecuador, Panama, Peru, Venezuela, Paraguay, and Mexico.

B. Mutual Legal Assistance Treaties (MLATs)

Currently, the U.S. maintains 22 Mutual Legal Assistance Treaties with various nations, including the Bahamas, Canada, Italy, Mexico, Panama, Switzerland, the United Kingdom, and (the U.K. Dependent Territories of) the Cayman Islands, Anguilla, and the British Virgin Islands.

Negotiated by the Department of State, MLATs are intended to increase the level of cooperation between U.S. officials and foreign governments in international criminal matters, including money laundering and asset forfeiture. In this area, the mutual assistance is often in the form of expediting the flow of information from foreign-based banks.

One of the most effective MLATs is with Switzerland. In late 1994, Switzerland cooperated in one of the largest cash seizures of drug profits: over $170 million in a Swiss account belonging to Colombian Cartel members was held for forfeiture under a U.S. court order.

The Pan American Countries: Canada, Mexico, Panama, and Colombia

13

I. Canada

"Canada still remains an easy target for drug-related and other types of money laundering."

— **U.S. State Department's 1998 International Narcotics Control Strategy Report**

A. Background

Canada is the second largest country in the world in area, yet has only 29 million people (1996 census). One-third of Canada's population resides in the four largest urban areas: the Toronto–Hamilton–Oshawa urban area (called "HOT") with a population of 5.5 million; Montreal with 3.3 million; Vancouver with 2.0 million (and growing at a rate of approximately 14% per year); and Ottawa–Hull with 1.0 million people. Two other major cities in the western province of Alberta are Edmonton (900,000 people) and Calgary (800,000 people). Almost two-thirds of Canadians live in the provinces of Ontario and Quebec.

According to the U.S. Department of State's "Background Notes: Canada, April 1997," Canada's ethnic groups include British (28%), French (23%), other European (15%), Asian/Arab/African (6%), Indian and Eskimo (2%), and other (26%). Canada's gross domestic product (1996) was $580 billion, and it enjoys a per capita GDP of almost $19,500.

By all economic indicators, Canada is considered one of the world's leading economies and a major player in most of the world's major financial and international organizations, including the Group of Ten, the Group of Seven (now "eight," with Russia), the FATF, the United Nations, etc. However, this stature does not immunize Canada from being considered a major drug-money laundering country; Canada is currently ranked as a "high priority" country in the U.S. Department of State's "1998 International Narcotics Control Strategy Report."

B.   Canada's Relationship with the United States

The relationship between Canada and the U.S. is arguably the closest and most extensive in the world. Trade between the two countries is nearly $1 billion "per day," and nearly 100 million people cross the border each year. Canada's primary trading partner is the United States — 81% of all of Canada's foreign exports of $185 billion is with the U.S. (6% with Europe and 4% with Japan). The U.S. imports nearly one-third of all of Canada's food exports, two-thirds of its forest products, and three-quarters of its newsprint. Canada currently (1996) has a $91 billion trade surplus with the U.S.

Canada and the U.S. share many common interests and values. Canada was a charter signatory to the United Nations and NATO, is a member of the Organization of American States, and was the host of the 1997 Asia-Pacific Economic Cooperation forum (the U.S. is a member). In 1989, Canada and the U.S. entered into the bilateral Free Trade Agreement (trade between the two countries increased 50% since the FTA went into effect), and they were signatories, with Mexico, to the 1994 North American Free Trade Agreement (NAFTA), which superseded the FTA.

Notwithstanding these close ties, Canada and the U.S. have differences in foreign policy (Canada allows trade with and travel to Cuba), bilateral trade (the "salmon wars"), and disputes over softwood lumber harvesting.

C.   Organized Crime Activity in Canada

Canada's Criminal Intelligence Service (CISC) has identified six major organized crime groups operating in Canada:

1. *Asian gangs:* Asian gangs are involved in heroin smuggling, credit card fraud, and money laundering throughout the country, primarily in Vancouver and Toronto. Asian gangs in Canada are dominated by the Big Circle Boys.
2. *Eastern European groups:* Called "FSU" groups, or Former Soviet Union groups, these gangs are dominated by wealthy "import/export" individuals, primarily based in Toronto.*
3. *Italian criminal groups:* Like their counterparts in the U.S., the "IOC" or Italian Organized Crime groups, dominated by the Mafia and

---

* See the detailed description of the Russian Mafiya in Chapter 1, "Transnational Criminal Organizations," and in Chapter 14, "Russia and the Former Soviet Union (FSU) Nations."

Camorra, have been severely compromised in recent years. Notable law enforcement successes have included 1994 arrests and seizures of heroin traffickers and money launderers in Montreal (one defendant confessed to having laundered almost $50 million in a scheme where over 550 kilos of heroin were smuggled into Canada); a 1995 raid and seizure on a Quebec-based counterfeiting ring (police seized $132 million in counterfeit $100 bills); and a 1996 international narcotics ring investigation leading to over 30 arrests of IOC figures, airport baggage handlers, and a brokerage firm executive. In addition, the RCMP was instrumental in the investigation and prosecution of an 'Ndrangheta international heroin trafficking ring (see the description of Operations Cat's Eye in Chapter 10, "Law Enforcement Operations"). A detailed history of the Mafia is also set out in Chapter 1, "Transnational Criminal Organizations."

4. *Aboriginal groups:* The Canadian aboriginal criminal groups dominate the cigarette and alcohol smuggling along the Canada–U.S. border. It is estimated that smuggled tobacco supplied as much as one-third of the Canadian market during the smuggling heyday of the early 1990s.*

5. *Outlaw biker gangs:* You name it, they do it. A 1995 seizure of 305 kilos of cocaine in Vancouver proved the existence of ties between the Hell's Angels and Colombian drug traffickers.

6. *Colombian drug cartels:* These cartels are involved in cocaine and heroin smuggling and distribution; other organized crime groups are now turning to the Colombians' "professional money launderers" for expertise in money laundering. One Colombian kingpin actually wrote several checks (drawn on his Canadian bank account) to various individuals as payment for the purchase of a cocaine base from a Bolivian trafficker. The checks were ultimately deposited into European banks.

D.   Canada's Anti-Money-Laundering Efforts

1.   *Background*

Why is Canada used by major money-laundering rings? Canada's positive economic attributes attract money launderers: its proximity to the U.S., its stable economy, currency, and governments, and its sophisticated financial sector are attractive to all investors, including money launderers. However, Canada's negative attributes — its lack of mandatory reporting requirements (the RCMP and the Canadian Bankers Association have a memorandum of understanding so that banks report suspicious activities), and lack of controls

* Porteous, Samuel, *Commentary 70, The Threat from Transnational Crime — An Intelligence Perspective,* Canadian Security Intelligence Service, 1996.

on currency crossing the world's longest undefended border — make it attractive. In addition, there could be a belief — certainly mistaken — among some criminal elements that Canadian law enforcement agencies are not as sophisticated as those in the U.S. In fact, the Royal Canadian Mounted Police have a worldwide reputation within the law enforcement community as being a highly sophisticated and effective agency.

At least $10 billion (U.S.) is laundered in or through Canada and Canadian financial institutions each year. How does this compare with the U.S.? Using a ratio of the estimated amount laundered in or through each country ($300 billion in the U.S., $10 billion in Canada) over the gross domestic product of each country ($6,928 billion, or $6.9 trillion, in the U.S. and $694 billion in Canada, both figures as reported by *The Wall Street Journal Almanac 1998*, Random House, 1997), the "money laundering problem" in the U.S. is three times as serious as it is in Canada (this "analysis" is for illustrative purposes only, and is not meant to imply that there is a correlation between a country's economic output and money laundering).

Most of the estimated $10 billion in laundered money flows through Canada's banks — Canadian banks traditionally have branch offices in most Caribbean tax haven countries — and currency exchange houses located along the U.S. border. Currently, these exchange houses are not required to report large transactions, although they are required to maintain these records.

Canada and the U.S. have a long history of cooperating in money-laundering investigations.* In addition, the first Canada/U.S. money laundering conference was held in Windsor, Ontario, in May 1997. Among other matters discussed, Canadian officials indicated that they were taking steps to strengthen Canada's money-laundering laws, including provisions to require financial institutions to report all transactions over $10,000 (Cdn), customer identification verification (note that Ontario has implemented one of the first Smart Card identification systems — a card that contains the holder's personal driving, medical, criminal, and other information), and an expansion of those institutions subject to reporting requirements (including casinos).**

---

* See, for example, "Operation Dinero" and "Operation Green Ice II," described in detail in Chapter 10, "Law Enforcement Operations."
** An excellent summary of organized crime and money laundering in Canada is the *Annual Report on Organized Crime in Canada 1996*, published by the Criminal Intelligence Service Canada (CISC), a branch of the Royal Canadian Mounted Police, available on its website at *http://www.cisc.gc.ca*. Another good source is the United Nations, April 1996 Report of the Secretary General entitled *Implementation of the Naples Political Declaration and Global Action Plan Against Organized Transnational Crime*, specifically paragraphs 11, 14, 16, 53, and 73 as they relate to Canada.

2.   Anti-Money-Laundering Legislation

Canada's money-laundering criminal statutes have only recently been used to prosecute large-scale money laundering. These laws — a 1988 law criminalizing money laundering and the 1991 Proceeds of Crime (Money Laundering) Act, requiring banks and non-bank financial institutions to maintain records on certain financial transactions — have been effective, but do not go far enough. For example, the regulations to the 1991 law (amending the Criminal Code) require every person who in the course of a business transaction receives cash in excess of $10,000 to "keep and maintain" records; however, the regulations do not require those people to "report" these transactions.

Specifically, the object of the Proceeds of Crime (Money Laundering) Act of 1991 "is to establish record-keeping requirements in the financial field in order to facilitate the investigation and prosecution of" certain narcotics offenses (section 1). The Act applies to federally regulated banks, provincially regulated credit unions and caisse populaire, insurance companies, trust and loan companies, securities dealers and brokers, and foreign exchange businesses (section 2).

The substance of the Act (section 4) is a requirement that the financial institutions keep and retain certain records, as set out in the accompanying regulations. The Regulations to the Act define the various substantive terms, set out the minimum reporting amount ($10,000), detail the contents of the various reports, and describe the period for which such records must be retained (at least 5 years; section 10). Failure to comply with the Act and Regulations exposes the offender (which includes officers of corporate offenders; section 7) to criminal sanctions, including fines up to $500,000 and imprisonment for up to 5 years (section 6). Of interest is an express provision that appears to exclude lawyers from keeping such records for retainers (section 3 of the Regulations).

II.   Mexico

There is not one single law enforcement institution [in Mexico] with whom the DEA has a really trusting relationship.

— Thomas Constantine, head of the DEA, testifying before the House Government Reform and Oversight Subcommittee on National Security, International Affairs and Criminal Justice on February 25, 1997; 3 days before the U.S. certified Mexico as a cooperating nation in the fight against drug trafficking

A.   Background

The United Mexican States, or Mexico, has a population of 95 million, composed of peoples of Indian–Spanish descent (60%), Indian (30%), and

Caucasian (9%). There are more than one-half million American citizens living in Mexico. Mexico is a federal republic, with 31 states and one federal district. The gross domestic product of Mexico (projected for 1997) is $370 billion, with a per capita GDP of $3,900. The annual inflation rate is running at approximately 18% (down from 28% in 1996).

Total exports and imports are approximately $200 billion. Mexico is almost totally dependent on trade with the U.S.: 84% of its exports go to and 76% of its imports come from the U.S. The United States is also very dependent on trade with Mexico, which is its third largest trading partner, behind only Canada and Japan. There is approximately $120 billion in "legal" trade between the two nations (the "illegal" drug trade is estimated to be between $30 billion and $50 billion, and might account for anywhere between 8 and 15% of Mexico's GDP).

Politically, Mexico's 1917 constitution provides for a federal republic organized much like the United States. The head of the executive branch of the government is the President, elected to a single six-year term (compared to the American president, allowed to hold office for no more than two consecutive four-year terms). The legislative branch — the Congress — is composed of a Senate and a Chamber of Deputies. Members of both bodies are prohibited from holding office for consecutive terms. There are 128 seats in the Senate, with senators elected for a six-year term. Beginning with the elections of July 6, 1997, 32 of these seats are now based on nationwide elections. These 32 senators will serve three-year terms so that all 128 seats will be contested in the year 2000. The 500 Deputies serve three-year terms: 300 are directly elected to represent single-member districts, and 200 are selected by a form of proportional representation from five electoral regions.

In elections in early July 1997, the Institutional Revolutionary Party (PRI), which had held power in Mexico for the last 70 years, was defeated in a number of elections, losing three of six governor's races, the mayorship of Mexico City (critical, as Mexico City accounts for about one-quarter of Mexico's GNP), and control of the Mexican National Congress. President Ernesto Zedillo will face the first opposition legislature since 1913, which will be a major obstacle in his bid to halt the 27% inflation rate.

The third branch of government, the judiciary, is also similar to that in the U.S. The Mexican judiciary is divided into federal and state court systems. The federal courts have jurisdiction over most major felonies; trial is generally by judge alone, sitting without a jury.*

---

* All statistics are courtesy of the U.S. Department of State's "Background Notes: Mexico, April 1997."

B.   Organized Crime and Money Laundering in Mexico

1.   Background

As set out above, Mexico and the U.S. share $120 billion in "legal" trade. The amount of "illegal" trade in drugs and drug profits is not known, but it is clear that most of the drugs on the streets of the U.S. come from Mexico. One report suggests that 70% of the cocaine, 50% of the marijuana, 5% of the heroin, and almost all of the methamphetamine comes via Mexico, while a second report suggests slightly different numbers: 70% of the cocaine, 25% of the heroin, 80% of the marijuana, and 90% of the ephedrine used to make methamphetamine come via Mexico.* Either way, as a result of this drug trade, money laundering is an increasing problem between Mexico and the U.S. In addition, money laundering is rampant in Mexico because of its historically lax (or nonexistent) regulations, corruption at all levels, and the newly opened economy (including the North American Free Trade Agreement, or NAFTA).

The single biggest problem facing international efforts to combat the Mexican drug problem is rampant corruption in Mexico. For example, in 1996, Mexico sought the extradition of two Arellano-Felix contract killers. Mexico submitted extradition papers that stated that the State Attorney General and almost 90% of the law enforcement officers, prosecutors, and judges in Tijuana and the State of Baja California are on the Tijuana Cartel's payroll. In March 1997, a little-known lawyer, Mariano Herran Salvatti, was appointed to head Mexico's war on drugs, with a mandate to root out corruption. He replaced former General Jesus Gutierrez Rebello, jailed in February 1997, after only 3 months in office, for accepting bribes from Amado Carrillo Fuentes, head of the Juarez Cartel. In early 1997, the Swiss national police chief acknowledged that most of the $120 million in Swiss accounts held by Raul Salinas de Gertari, the jailed brother of the former president of Mexico (Carlos Salinas, living in voluntary exile in Ireland), is probably drug related. Mexican authorities agree; as of June 1997, they had discovered 53 properties, and 13 domestic and 23 foreign bank accounts, held by Raul Salinas or in one of the four aliases he uses. On May 12, 1997, over 1000 pounds of seized cocaine was stolen from a Sonora police station. Two of the region's military commanders, army generals Antonio Ramon Mimendi and Antonio Morales, were implicated in the theft. As of August 5, 1997, they were being held at a military prison.

In addition, it is thought that many Mexican banks are owned or controlled by Colombian or Mexican drug dealers and money launderers, and

---

* See, Statement of Senator Dianne Feinstein, State Department Explanation of Mexico's Certification, March 10, 1997, at *http://.senate.gov/~feinstein/mexstmt2.html.*

that these banks often maintain two sets of books, only one of which bears the scrutiny of regulators. Further, the Bilateral Task Forces (BTFs) established in Juarez, Tijuana, and Monterey by the Mexican government and the DEA have met with little success, primarily due to the corruption of the leaders of the Mexican police agencies, as well as a 1996 decision by the Mexican government to refuse to allow American federal agents working in Mexico under the BTFs to arm themselves (resulting in the rescission of their travel authority). To put it diplomatically, the DEA is constantly working to improve its working relationships with its Mexican counterpart, the National Institute to Combat Drugs.

2.   Anti-Money-Laundering Efforts

Mexico's legislative efforts at combating organized crime, drug trafficking, and money laundering have, until very recently, been abysmal. They are, in effect, at the same stage the American laws were 25 years ago. In November 1996, Mexico finally passed an Organized Crime Law that authorizes the use of wiretap/electronic surveillance, undercover operations, and informants; provides for a witness protection program; allows for plea bargaining; and contains conspiracy laws. Asset forfeiture provisions are still awaiting approval from the Mexican states. One reason for the delays is the control that the Mexican Federation has over legislators and the banking lobby.

To enforce these new laws, Organized Crime Units (ostensibly free of corruption) have also been established. In May 1996, Mexico criminalized money laundering under its Penal Code, providing for 5- to 12-year prison sentences with 50% enhancements if the violator is a government official in charge of prevention, prosecution, or investigation of money laundering. Prior to these changes, money laundering was simply a tax violation with the penalty based on the amount laundered.

Mexico's former deputy attorney general Mario Ruíz Massieu and chief drug prosecutor have been indicted for accepting bribes (from the Gulf Cartel) and laundering millions of dollars through U.S. banks. Ironically, Massieu was in charge of investigating the assassination of his brother, Jose Francisco Ruiz Massieu, the secretary-general of the ruling PRI, who was killed by cartel-related hit men controlled by the brother of the former president of Mexico, Carlos Salinas. Massieu was first detained by U.S. Customs agents in March 1997, for failing to declare about $40,000 before trying to board a flight from New Jersey to Spain. Authorities later found and forfeited about $8 million in suspected drug profits or bribes in his Texas Commerce Bank accounts (note that although the bank reported all of the massive cash deposits, it could face civil penalties under the BSA). Mexico is seeking his extradition to face charges that he blocked a probe into his brother's assassination in 1994.

In March 1997, the Mexican Treasury, or *Hacienda*, issued new regulations designed to insulate financial institutions from money laundering, including customer identification rules, mandatory reporting of transactions over $10,000, mandatory reporting of suspicious transactions, Safe Harbor Rules, and Tip Off Provisions, all modeled after American laws and regulations. In addition, Mexico created an FIU to monitor and track money laundering in the financial sector. Using FinCEN expertise, computer systems, and personnel, this new FIU should prove to be effective. A bilateral agreement with Mexico allows both countries access to each other's FIU databases.

C.   Certification/Decertification of Mexico

On February 6, 1997, Mexico's top anti-drug official, General Jesus Gutierrez Rebello, was arrested on charges he accepted bribes from the Juarez drug cartel (he was convicted in February 1988, and sentenced to 14 years in prison). On February 16, 1997, the Mexican magazine *Proceso* reported that documents from the Mario Ruiz Masseau trial in Houston, Texas, revealed that the family of former President Carlos Salinas de Gortari was linked to drug traffickers. On February 23, 1997, the *New York Times* reported that two Mexican governors — Manlio Bafio Beltrones Rivera of Sonora and Jorge Carrillo Olea of Morelos — had ties to drug traffickers. On February 25, 1997, the head of the DEA, Thomas Constantine, testified before a House subcommittee that there was not a single Mexican law enforcement agency trusted by the DEA.

Notwithstanding the obvious corruption, on February 28, 1997, the Clinton administration certified Mexico as a cooperating nation in the fight against drug trafficking (Colombia, Myanmar (formerly Burma), and Nigeria were decertified).

This certification was part of a report presented annually to the U.S. Congress on the anti-drug efforts of 32 countries identified as major drug production or transportation centers receiving U.S. aid. According to various presidential directives, such aid is dependent on the recipient country being "certified" as taking all reasonable and necessary steps to combat drug abuse and trafficking. Decertification could result in the cutting off of military and economic aid, as well as opposing international loans to a decertified country, unless the President exercised a "national interest" waiver (decertification without economic sanctions). For a full discussion of certification, see Section IV of Chapter 6, "United States Federal Government Agencies."

The 1997 certification of Mexico followed intense negotiations between the two countries, and promises by Mexico that it would extradite more suspected drug traffickers, prosecute more money-laundering cases, wipe out corruption, and, perhaps most importantly, allow DEA agents to carry weapons while participating in joint operations along the U.S.–Mexico border. The certification was also seen as an endorsement of President Ernesto Zedillo Ponce de Leon's efforts to root out the deeply entrenched corruption, and a clear acknowledgment of Mexico's status as a U.S. trading partner (and a clear need to support Mexico's economy, for fear of repeating the December, 1994 collapse of the *peso*). However, legislators on both sides of the border were clearly offended; even more so in the U.S. when it was revealed that Mexico delayed reporting — until after the certification — the earlier (approximately three hours earlier) "release" of Humberto Garcia Abrego, brother of the Gulf Group's leader, Juan Garcia Abrego, jailed on money-laundering charges to great fanfare on February 27th.

On March 6, 1997, the House International Relations Committee voted to immediately decertify Mexico. Amid howls of protest from Republicans from states along the Mexican border, the House of Representatives tempered that finding, instead voting to decertify Mexico unless the President demonstrated within 90 days that Mexico had made significant progress (or unless the President exercised his "national interest" veto). On March 20, 1997, the Senate approved a watered-down resolution that gave the President until September 1, 1997, to report to Congress that Mexico had made sufficient progress in 10 designated areas; but the Senate did not threaten decertification.

Throughout 1997, Mexico took many steps to improve its perilous certification status. On April 30, 1997, the National Institute to Combat Drugs, Mexico's version of the DEA, was abolished and replaced with a smaller, ostensibly corruption-free agency (the Institute's former chief was Gen. Jesus Gutierrez Rebello).

In May 1997, Presidents Clinton and Zedillo issued a "Declaration of the U.S.–Mexico Alliance Against Drugs" and released the "Binational Drug Threat Assessment." These agreements led to the creation of the U.S.–Mexico High-Level Contact Group on Narcotics (HLCG), a senior-level group that prepared the February 1998 United States–Mexico Binational Drug Strategy. This Strategy targeted the five drug cartels of the Mexican Federation. It was designed to strengthen cooperation between U.S. and Mexican state and federal law enforcement agencies; improve the exchange of intelligence on producers, traffickers, and money launderers; facilitate extradition; and provide U.S. assistance in screening and training members of Mexico's new anti-drug force. The Strategy has drawn heavy criticism: U.S. politicians allege that corruption is so rampant in Mexico that any U.S. efforts are not only wasted, but any cooperative efforts could endanger U.S. law enforcement personnel and compromise existing operations.

Due to the obvious efforts and apparent progress of the Mexican government to comply with international standards of combating drug trafficking and money laundering, President Clinton certified Mexico as a cooperating nation on February 26, 1998. As it did following the 1997 certification, criticism has followed the 1998 decision.

III.   Panama and the Colon Free Zone

A.   Introduction

Notwithstanding the fact that Panama is a major transit point for Colombian cocaine and heroin en route to the U.S., and a major transit point for cash and drug proceeds flowing back to Colombia, Panama was certified as a "cooperating nation" by the President in February 1998.

Panama has two parallel economies: the normal economic activity of any country, and the Panama Free Zone, or Colon Free Zone, a 740-acre site in the city of Colon on the northern, or Atlantic, end of the Panama Canal. The Zone is served by the ports of Cristobal, Coco Solo, and Manzanillo on the Atlantic, and Balboa on the Pacific. There are four "transshipment terminals" in the Zone, each with a 20-year concession obtained from the Panamanian government. The largest of these terminals is Manzanillo International Terminal, operated jointly by Motores Internacionales S.A. (MOINSA), a Panamanian distributor of automobiles, and SSA Panama, an affiliate of Stevedoring Services of America, based out of Seattle, Washington.

Established in the 1950s, and now the second largest duty-free trading center in the world, behind only Hong Kong, the Colon Free Zone (CFZ) accounts for the vast majority of the commerce and banking in Panama. Nearly $11 billion worth of customs, excise, and duty-free goods are traded annually through the CFZ throughout Latin America, South America, and the Caribbean (a market of over 500 million people). PanamaInfo, a Panamanian state-run "chamber of commerce" (see their website at *http://www.panamainfo.com/tables/cfz.html*) reports that, for 1995:

1. Imports to the CFZ totaled $5.2 billion and exports totaled $5.7 billion.
2. The CFZ's largest importing nations were Hong Kong (27%), Japan (13%), United States (11%), South Korea (10%), Taiwan (8%), Italy (5%), and all others (26%).
3. The most important imports to the CFZ were electronics (22% of the value), apparel (17%), textiles (7%), footwear (5%), jewelry (5%), watches (4%), and all other products (40%).
4. The CFZ's largest markets, or the destinations of the exports, were Colombia (27%), Ecuador (9%), Panama (6%), Venezuela (5%), United States (5%), Chile (4%), and all others (44%).

The CFZ is home to over 2,300 legitimate, shady, illegitimate, and outright illegal companies engaged in various types of trade and commerce, including drug trafficking (recent seizures include 19 tons of cocaine found in containers of Brazilian tiles bound for the eastern U.S. and over 5 tons of cocaine found inside coffee bound for Miami).

Although there are legitimate businesses operating in the Free Zone — most businesses have some sort of presence there in order to effectively do business in Latin, Central, and South America — most of these 2,300 entities exist in order to launder Colombian drug money. One estimate has almost 90% of the purchasers of goods from these companies being Colombian companies or individuals or their nominees. The most common method of using Free Zone companies to launder drug proceeds is by the process of dollar discounting.

B.   Panama's Anti-Money-Laundering and Drug-Control Efforts

The 1998 certification of Panama was based on the belief that, notwithstanding the country's status as a drug and money transit point between the U.S. and Colombia, and its low-level corruption, the Panamanian government has continued to press its counter-narcotics efforts, including:

1. implementing a counter-narcotics "master plan" dealing with prevention, treatment, and rehabilitation; control of supply; illicit trafficking; and tightening its border with Costa Rica
2. hosting the first "Hemispheric Congress on the Prevention of Money Laundering"
3. becoming the first Latin American country to be admitted to the Egmont Group of FIUs
4. actively participating in CICAD, the CFATF, and the Basel Committee's Offshore Group of Bank Supervisors
5. negotiating a bilateral agreement with the U.S. government on the creation of a Multinational Counter-Narcotics Center at Howard Air Force Base

IV.   Colombia

"We've had enough."

— Colombian President Belisario Betencur Cuartas, declaring a "war without quarter" against the Medellín Cartel, November 1984

A.   Introduction

To state the obvious, Colombia has a severe drug and money-laundering problem. Colombia has now passed Peru and Bolivia as the world's largest producer of coca paste (Peru's coca cultivation has dropped 40% over the last 2 years, whereas Colombia's has increased by almost 60%).

Colombia has always been a "major" or "high-priority" country in the U.S. Department of State's International Narcotics Control Strategy Reports. It was only marginally certified in 1998 because of the "vital national interest" exception given by the President (for a full discussion of certification, see Section IV of Chapter 6, "United States Federal Government Agencies"). This qualified certification followed two successive years of decertification in 1996 and 1997. The President of Colombia, Ernesto Samper, himself linked to drug money (it is alleged that his 1994 election campaign received $6 million from Cali Cartel traffickers), called the 1997 decertification "a unilateral sanction of Colombia that is totally unjust."

President Samper's cries over unjust treatment ring hollow, however. A Berlin-based anti-corruption organization, Transparency International, ranked Colombia as the world's third most corrupt nation (behind only Nigeria and Bolivia, with Russia fourth) in its 1997 survey of 52 nations. Indeed, some would argue that Colombia has been taken over — economically, politically, legally, and militarily — by the Colombian drug cartels.

Available statistics appear to support the theory that narcotics have taken over the country. For example, Colombia's largest legal export, oil, accounts for about $1.5 billion in annual revenue, and the country's total exports are valued at approximately $11 billion. Compare these figures with the annual "profits" from narcotics — estimated to be between $4 billion and $8 billion. In addition, between 1985 and 1990, over 1000 policemen, 70 journalists, 60 judges, and 4 presidential candidates were killed by drug traffickers. Others attribute some of these killings to the Revolutionary Armed Forces of Colombia, or FARC, the largest and oldest (30 years old) left-wing guerrilla faction in Colombia, the National Liberation Army (ELN), or the People's Liberation Army (EPL). In a recent article entitled "A New Cottage Industry: Kidnapping in Colombia," author Thomas B. Hunter writes that kidnapping-for-ransom is a $530 million per year "industry" in Colombia. Mr. Hunter's article includes the full text of the U.S. Department of State Fact Sheet on International Terrorism and American Hostages.*

B.   Colombian Anti-Money-Laundering Efforts

Notwithstanding its history, the Colombian government has taken some positive steps in the fight against drug trafficking, but their efforts usually seem to fall short of their stated goals. For example:

---

* For a detailed look at the Colombian drug trafficking "community," see Chapter 1, "Transnational Criminal Organizations."

1. In December 1996, the Colombian Congress passed a law making asset forfeiture retroactive to the date on which the original criminal activity generating the ill-gotten assets became a crime. Prior to this law, authorities could seize but not sell drug dealers' property. On August 13, 1997, Colombia's high court denied a series of lawsuits brought by various drug lords, and affirmed that the law can be applied retroactively. As of August 1997, more than 360 properties valued at $500 million have been seized since the law took effect. Most of these properties are located in and around Medellín and Cali, and include choice urban real estate and hotel resorts purchased by drug kingpins such as Pablo Escobar, Gonzalo Rodriguez Gacha, and the Rodriguez Orejuela brothers (as reported by the *Washington Post*, August 14, 1997).

2. On January 17, 1997, Cali kingpins and brothers Miguel and Gilberto Rodriguez Orejuela received nine- and $10^1/_2$-year sentences, respectively, for various drug trafficking offenses (each faced 24 years in jail, but their sentences were reduced because they "confessed" ... they can be released in four years, although U.S. authorities liken their incarceration to house arrest). On February 22nd, a judge extended Miguel's sentence to 23 years.

3. On January 30, 1997, Colombian troops seized the largest cocaine processing plant ever seized, capable of producing over $1^1/_2$ tons of cocaine per day. They also seized eight tons of cocaine. The plant was run by the Cali Cartel under the protection of FARC.

4. On February 20, 1997, the U.S. and Colombia signed a bilateral agreement allowing the U.S. Coast Guard greater rights in intercepting vessels thought to be smuggling drugs.

5. In November 1997, the Colombian Congress approved a constitutional reform to remove a six-year old ban on extraditing its citizens for trial in foreign countries. Colombia's refusal to extradite notorious drug traffickers had been one of the main reasons the U.S. had determined that Colombia had not previously been certified as participating fully in the fight against the narcotics trade. The law has no retroactive application, so that Colombian drug lords remain beyond the reach of U.S. justice for any crimes committed before December 1997. As of early January 1998, Colombia's high court had not yet ruled on the legality of the new law.

6. The U.S. and Colombia have created a joint elite drug unit, charged with tracking down and arresting known drug kingpins. This unit appears to be having some success; on August 10, 1997, Waldo Simeon Vargas, aka "The Minister," and reputed to be one of Colombia's top heroin traffickers, was captured in Bogotá by this joint U.S./Colombian drug unit.

7. On August 14, 1997, Colombian police seized 1,675 kilos of cocaine bound for the U.S. or Canada. The cocaine had a street value of over $30 million.
8. In 1997, responsibility for the maximum-security prisons housing the major drug lords was transferred to the Colombian National Police (CNP), a move that appears to have drastically curtailed the ability of the drug lords to run their cartels from their jail cells.

Not all steps are positive, however. In apparent "retaliation" for the 1997 decertification, Colombia suspended its aerial drug crop eradication program, viewed by the U.S. as the most important element of Colombia's anti-drug effort (Colombia is second to Peru in coca cultivation). In addition, corruption remains rampant, evidenced by the arrests and convictions of several congressmen and the mayor of Cali on corruption charges. It is this continuing corruption, poor government performance on the extradition issue, failure to meet the requirements of the 1988 U.N. Convention, and failure to enforce all counter-narcotics laws, that led to the decision to decertify Colombia but allow foreign and other aid because of the perceived "vital national interests" of the U.S.

The closing paragraph of the State Department's "explanation of President Clinton's 1998 narcotics certification decision for Colombia" is very telling (reproduced from the Internet version of the text from the United States Information Agency's website at *www.usia.gov*):

In making the decision to provide a vital national interests certification to Colombia this year, the USG [United States Government] is mindful of the deteriorating security and human rights environment in Colombia, the threat to that country's democracy, and the threat posed to Colombia's neighbors and to regional stability. The cumulative effects of Colombia's 40-year old insurgency, narco-corruption, the rise of paramilitaries, the growing number of internally displaced Colombians, growing incidents of human rights abuses, and the potential threat that Colombia's violence and instability pose to the region all require a vital national interests certification. Such a certification is necessary so that the USG can provide assistance in order to broaden and deepen its engagement with this and the next Colombian government in an effort to effectively confront and eliminate narco-trafficking. The threats to U.S. vital national interests posed by a bar on assistance outweigh the risks posed by Colombia's inadequate counter-narcotics performance.

Russia and the Former Soviet Union (FSU) Nations

14

I. Introduction

The demise of the old Soviet Union on Christmas Day, 1991, brought 21 new quasi-democratic nations and 280 million people into the world of free-market capitalism. The dominant country to emerge from the FSU was the Russian Federation, or Russia, which formally declared its independence on August 24, 1991. Russia inherited much of the U.S.S.R.'s legacy, including its seat on the U.N. Security Council, and the bulk of its assets and debt. Almost all of the former Soviet republics agreed to join a loose association, called the Commonwealth of Independent States (CIS).

Russia has a population of roughly 150 million. The official language is Russian, but there are an estimated 140 other languages and dialects. The executive branch of the government is composed of the President (presently Boris Yeltsin, elected in June, 1991) and Prime Minister, who is the chairman of the Duma. The legislative branch, the Federal Assembly, is made up of the Federation Council and the State Duma. From 1991 to September 1993, the communist-dominated Assembly blocked almost all of Yeltsin's efforts. On September 21, 1993, Yeltsin dissolved the Assembly and called for December elections. Yeltsin (and Russia!) survived a failed insurrection on October 3, 1993, and elections were safely held on December 12, 1993. The upper Federation Council (170 seats) and the lower State Duma (450 seats) now have functions similar to the U.S. Senate and House of Representatives, respectively.

The new Russian Constitution also took effect on December 12, 1993. The Constitution gives the President a great deal of power, allowing him to appoint (with Duma approval) the Prime Minister, pass decrees without Duma consent, and control the armed forces. The Constitution divides the Russian Federation into 21 autonomous republics and 68 autonomous territories (the latter including the two "cities of federal significance," Moscow and St. Petersburg). Their powers, and relationships with each other and to the Federation, remain unclear and changing as the new nation grapples with its newfound independence.

The judicial branch includes the Constitutional Court, the Supreme Court, the Supreme Court of Arbitration, and the Office of Procurator General. Basically, the judicial system is in a state of chaos, with reforms needed in the criminal justice system and institutions. Legal enforcement of private business disputes is nonexistent, and there are virtually no regulatory systems in place for the banking and securities industries.

The gross domestic product of Russia is estimated to be $250 billion, with a per capita GDP of between $1,700 and $5,300, and an annual growth rate of between 0.4% and *negative* 4% (the low end of both ranges is based on figures provided by the Russian Central Bank; the high end of both ranges is based on figures provided by the U.S. State Department). For the period 1992 to 1996, the average annual inflation rate was close to 400%. On January 12, 1998, the Russian Central Bank announced that the "official" 1997 inflation rate was down to 11%.

Russia was ranked as the world's fourth most corrupt nation — trailing only Nigeria, Bolivia, and Colombia — in a 1997 survey of 52 nations. It is an ideal country for large-scale money laundering; its regulatory agencies are nonexistent or corrupt, and its law enforcement agencies have little or no resources with which to fight organized crime. Stories abound about Moscow law enforcement taking subways and buses to crime scenes. According to Izvestia, Russia's homicide rate of 84 murders per day is more than double that of the next closest country — the U.S. It is also believed that four of five Russian businesses are paying protection money. Russian law enforcement agencies seized a mere six tons of narcotics in 1995 (although up from only 50 kilograms in 1992, it is still a minuscule amount).

II.   Drug Trafficking Activity in Russia

The State Department's 1998 International Narcotics Strategy Report recognized that Russia now plays an increasingly important role in drug trafficking in Eastern and Western Europe and Central Asia. The major players are the ethnically based gangs in the Caucasus regions of southern Russia that first rose to prominence during the Soviet–Afghan war in the 1980s. These gangs have taken the skills they learned under the old Soviet regime — smuggling, distribution networks, and money laundering — and adapted them to the new free-market economy to dominate Russian drug trafficking. They work with their Central Asian counterparts in the Former Soviet Union countries (described below) to smuggle Afghan and Pakistani heroin into Russia and then on to the Baltic countries, Eastern Europe, and Western Europe.

In addition to trafficking in heroin, Russian drug rings, usually Mafiya-connected, work with Sicilian Mafia and Colombian drug traffickers to import and distribute cocaine, which sells for three times as much in Russia as it does in the U.S. (roughly $300 per gram retail versus $100 per gram retail in the U.S.). For a detailed look at organized crime in Russia and the FSU countries, see Chapter 1, "Transnational Criminal Organizations."

III. Drug Trafficking Activity in the Former Soviet Union Countries

The FSU "Stan" countries of Kazakstan, Kyrgyzstan, Tajikstan, Turkmenistan, and Uzbekistan, all bordering Afghanistan and/or Iran, have historically been important poppy-growing regions themselves, as well as serving as the overland conduits for the smugglers of Afghanistan and Pakistani heroin destined for Russia and Europe. Opium cultivation and heroin production and smuggling have provided much of the cash used to finance the seemingly constant civil wars that plague the region.

IV. Russian Anti-Money-Laundering Efforts

Until mid-1997, the Russian Central Bank had few, if any, controls over banks; there were few records regarding ownership, capitalization, customers, loans, money transfers, etc. New Russian banks emerged almost daily, and many of them are believed to be controlled by Russian organized crime. John Deutch, former Director of the Central Intelligence Agency, in testimony before the House International Relations Committee in April 1996, responded to a question suggesting that 50 to 80% of all Russian banks were controlled by organized crime, stated that "the number 50% is tremendously much too large an estimate, but there are some financial institutions over there which do have these connections." Interestingly, however, Director Deutch then offered to provide greater detail to this statement, but only in closed testimony.

New legislative controls and improved enforcement efforts begun in late 1996 and early 1997 appear to be having a positive effect. On January 6, 1998, the Russian Central Bank announced it had withdrawn the licenses of 316 Russian banks in 1997. This number represented almost 15% of the total number of 2,035 banks.

An interesting website for Russian banks is the homepage of the "Golden Club of Russia Association," which bills itself as "a non-profit association established in November 1994 to unite Russian banks, gold-producing and gold-processing Russian industries with the aim of forming a civil precious metals and gems market in the country." Twenty-seven Russian banks have their own sites on the Internet. In 1993, Citibank and Chase Manhattan became the first U.S. banks to receive a general license to open a subsidiary in Russia. Four more foreign banks received similar licenses in 1997: Bank America and J.P. Morgan & Co. from the U.S.; and Germany's Deutsche Bank and Commerzbank.

A comprehensive anti-money-laundering bill tabled in the Russian Parliament in late 1996 has still not been passed (as of March 1998). In the summer of 1997, the Central Bank of the Russian Federation issued guidelines to its (roughly 400) member banks on customer identification and the prevention of money laundering generally. The customer identification guidelines were modeled after the FATF's "know your customer" guidelines, which are in place in most nations, including the U.S.

V.   Cooperation Between Russia and the United States

The primary vehicle for formal cooperative efforts between Russia and the U.S. is the United States–Russian Commission on Economic and Technological Cooperation, known by its signatories as the Gore-Chernomyrdin Commission, or GCC (U.S. Vice President Al Gore and former Russian Prime Minister Viktor Chernomyrdin).

In its five-year history, the GCC has resulted in more than 200 bilateral agreements, ranging from reducing lead contamination in Russia to technology transfer agreements to nuclear arms reduction. Since 1993, trade between the two countries has increased 50%, and the Russian economy has improved dramatically. Two of the leading indicators of economic performance — rise in gross domestic product and inflation — confirm this performance. On January 12, 1998, Russia announced that its GDP rose 0.4% in 1997, the first rise since the collapse of the Soviet Union; and that inflation had dropped to 11%, the lowest level since the 1994 economic and financial reforms.

Profiles of Other Countries

15

Profiles for the Pan American countries of Canada, Mexico, Colombia, and Panama, and a profile of Russia, are set out in the preceding two chapters.

I. Introduction

The U.S. Department of State believes that every country suffers, to some degree, from money-laundering activity. The Department publishes an annual report that ranks all countries according to their culpability. This report, the "International Narcotics Control Strategy Report," looks at a myriad of money-laundering factors to assign priorities to these countries using six different categories — from high priority to no priority. These factors include (1) the nature of the money-laundering situation in the country, e.g., drugs, contraband, arms smuggling; (2) whether the government has taken appropriate legislative actions to address the money laundering situation; (3) whether this legislation is effectively implemented and enforced; and (4) the degree of international cooperation in fighting global money laundering.

The DEA has taken a slightly different approach by focusing on the most egregious offenders: 16 "major conduits and repositories for illicit drug money." These include four cities in the U.S. (Houston, New York, Los Angeles, and Miami) and three cities in Canada (Vancouver, Toronto, and Montreal) as well as nine countries: Andorra, Cayman Islands, Channel Islands, Liechtenstein, Luxembourg, Mexico, Singapore, Switzerland, and the United Arab Emirates.

Taken together, these two lists show that the major money-laundering nations include Aruba, Brazil, Canada, Colombia, Hong Kong, Pakistan, Panama, Russia, Singapore, the United States, Uruguay (described by *The Economist* — March 4, 1989 — as having "bank secrecy laws to put the Swiss to shame"), and Venezuela. A recent addition to the list might be Chile, which is fast becoming a favorite of the Mexican and Colombian drug traffickers. In addition to these countries is the roster of "offshore banking havens," such as the Cayman Islands and the Channel Islands, which are used by legitimate and illegitimate entities to increase their profits.

Twenty-seven of the countries listed in this chapter (as well as Mexico, Panama, and Colombia, described in Chapter 13) are considered "major drug-producing or transit countries" and are subject to an annual certification process pursuant to section 490 of the Foreign Assistance Act of 1961. This Act requires the President to certify annually that each major drug-producing or transit country has cooperated fully or has taken adequate steps on its own to meet the goals and objectives of the 1988 U.N. Convention, including rooting out public corruption. Governments that do not meet these standards lose eligibility for most forms of U.S. foreign aid, including military aid, and also face a mandatory veto from the U.S. on loans from various international development banks, such as the World Bank and International Monetary Fund. The details of the certification process are described in Section IV of Chapter 6, "United States Federal Government Agencies."

II. Country Profiles

1. Afghanistan

Afghanistan was one of only four countries that failed to gain certification in 1998 (the other three were Iran, Nigeria, and Myanmar (formerly Burma)). The decision to not grant certification was based on the country's absolute failure to take any steps to control drug production and trafficking. This failure, in turn, was caused primarily by the continuing civil war and absence of a recognized central government. In fact, the most powerful faction in Afghanistan, the Taliban faction, controls almost all of the regions where opium poppies are grown, and it levies an "agricultural tax" on opium production, which is the only cash crop of any substance in the country. With a per capita gross domestic product of only $600, the influences of heroin production are obvious.

Afghanistan is now the world's largest producer of heroin, supplying as much as 50% of the world's supply. Most of the rest comes from Afghanistan's neighbor, Pakistan (the heroin cultivation area of Afghanistan and Pakistan is known as the "Golden Crescent"); the Middle East countries of Syria, Lebanon, Turkey, and Jordan; and the "Golden Triangle" countries of Myanmar (formerly Burma), Laos, and Thailand.

Afghanistan is landlocked, located between Pakistan to the southeast, Iran to the west, and the Former Soviet Union countries of Tajikistan, Uzbekistan, Turkmenistan to the north and northeast (a small finger of Afghanistan pushes east between Tajikistan and Pakistan to border with China). Most of the heroin produced in Pakistan and Afghanistan is smuggled overland through one of two main routes: either through Iraq or Iran, or through the old Soviet Republics of Tajikistan, Uzbekistan, Turkmenistan, and Kazakhstan into Russia, where it is processed and distributed throughout Europe and the oil-rich Persian Gulf states. The smugglers commonly use camels — the same form of transportation used by their ancestors for thousands of years. In early January 1998, Iranian police seized more than 4,600 pounds of opium and heroin after a battle with Afghani smugglers. Also seized were 21 camels that had been carrying the drugs.

2.   *Antigua*

Located in the eastern Caribbean, Antigua has long been known as a small, but active, offshore banking haven. This former British colony has been accused by both Britain and the U.S. as having lax banking, corporate, and tax laws that have allowed organized crime to launder money. In the last few years, the Russian Mafiya have opened up a number of Antiguan offshore banks. Antigua is home to a number of questionable cyberbanks. In addition, its casino industry is open to potential money-laundering activity.

The Antiguan government has launched a complete overhaul of the nation's banking regulations in an effort to change its image as an easy place to launder money. In 1996, the government passed the Money Laundering (Prevention) Act, suspended the issuance of offshore banking licenses, and raised bank capitalization requirements.

The 1996 ML(P)A is in keeping with CFATF and FATF objectives and goals. Among other things, it criminalizes money laundering beyond drug trafficking and related offenses. It also imposes customer identification, record-keeping and reporting requirements on financial institutions; expands the definition of "financial institutions" beyond traditional banks; provides for safe harbor protections for financial institutions and their employees; makes it a criminal offense for financial institutions to fail to comply with the required disclosure regulations; permits law enforcement and regulatory authorities to enlist the assistance of foreign agencies in money laundering investigations; and requires the reporting of outbound currency and other monetary instruments over $50,000.

The impact of the ML(P)A will depend on the government's willingness and ability to enforce and prosecute. Antigua's track record in doing so has been questioned by American authorities. For example, a U.S. District Court (May 1994, Boston) criminal forfeiture order for $7.5 million against John E. Fitzgerald, a convicted racketeer and drug money launderer, has been left unsatisfied, in part because the Antiguan government has failed or refused to enforce the order against funds in Antiguan-based Swiss American Bank. In fact, the Antiguan government appears to have transferred these funds from Swiss American directly into its national treasury.

In 1997, the government continued its focus on offshore banking. In August, the Director of International Business Corporations, Wrenford Ferrance, delivered a four-page letter to each of the island's 51 licensed offshore banks. This letter requires each of these banks to submit, by September 29, 1997, a complete disclosure of their ownership, branch offices, auditing procedures, corresponding banks, insurance coverage, advertising, use of the World Wide Web, and internal policies to prevent money laundering.

Antigua is actively looking to estabish a financial intelligence unit that will be run by a Special Advisor to the Prime Minister on Money Laundering and Counternarcotics, a position created during the 1996 legislative session.

3.   *Argentina*

Argentina has been identified as one of the world's biggest money-laundering countries. For example, George Melloan, in a *Wall Street Journal* article entitled "Drugs — The Argentine Connection," described a personal secretary to the Argentine president who regularly acted as a camel for drug smugglers by bringing at least $1 million dollars, wrapped in a blanket inside a suitcase, into Argentina after each of her trips to New York (protected by diplomatic immunity).

Despite, or perhaps because of, its status as a money-laundering haven, Argentina also is one of the leading South American nations in its efforts to combat money laundering. Among other efforts, it is a member of the Egmont Group, having a FinCEN-like Financial Intelligence Unit.

Argentina has been known for rampant inflation and corruption. However, President Carlos Saul Menem's administration appears to have stabilized Argentina's run-away inflation and improved its economic outlook.

4.   *Aruba*

Aruba is strategically located in the southern Caribbean, immediately north of Venezuela and east of Colombia. Because of its location and historically *laissez-faire* attitude toward investment and banking, it has been ranked as a "high-priority" or "major" drug-producing and transit country in the U.S. Department of State's 1997 and 1998 International Narcotics Control Strategy Reports, therefore subjecting it to the annual certification/decertification process. The country has been fully certified the last 2 years.

Aruba has been taking some steps to improve its reputation. In December 1993, Aruba criminalized money laundering, albeit for a limited number of underlying offenses (narcotics offenses are included offenses). As of March 1996, Aruba passed further money-laundering legislation designed to require certain financial institutions to better identify customers and to file unusual transaction reports with a reporting center, MOT. In the year since its inception, MOT has received approximately 1,700 unusual transaction reports.

Despite these legislative changes, Aruba continues to be a money-laundering haven because of Aruba's proximity to Colombia and Venezuela, its offshore banking facilities, casinos, resorts, high volume of American tourism, and stable currency and government. In addition, the "Aruba Free Zone" flourishes in much the same way as Panama's Colon Free Zone.

As a result of international pressure, the Royal Dutch Government and the Government of Aruba appointed a number of commissions to investigate money-laundering activities. In July 1996, reports by the Aruba Free Zone Commission and the Commission on the Gaming Industry recommended a number of changes, including a tightening of supervision of the Free Zone and gaming industry, strengthening the licensing requirements on the island, including casinos as regulated "financial institutions" subject to the various reporting requirements, and establishing better cross-border currency reporting requirements.

Further legislative changes in 1997 are expected to include provisions on search and seizure, and extradition of nationals.

5.   *Australia*

Australia is a leading member of the Financial Action Task Force (FATF), and has adopted most, if not all, of the 40 Recommendations. Accordingly, it is considered to have an exemplary anti-money-laundering infrastructure. Australia's Financial Intelligence Unit, AUSTRAC (the Australian Transactional Analysis Center), is second-to-none. The Australian Bureau of Criminal Intelligence, the Australian Customs Service, the Australian Federal Police, and the Australian Taxation Office, all coordinated by the National Crime Authority (NCA), have initiated some significant money-laundering prosecutions using information provided by AUSTRAC.

6.   *Bahamas*

The Bahamas has been a center for smuggling for centuries, and has been known as a drug transit and money-laundering center for over 20 years. In fact, it is believed that in the 1980s, the Medellín Cartel's Carlos Lehder bought his own Bahamian island, Norman's Cay, which he used as staging point for plane loads of cocaine bound for the U.S.

This infamous history, as well as the Bahamas' status as one of the largest offshore financial centers in the world, has resulted in its status as a "high-priority" or "major" drug-producing and transit country in the U.S. Department of State's 1998 International Narcotics Control Strategy Report. To its credit, The Bahamas was certified as a cooperating nation.

The Bahamas shares several characteristics with the other small nations that have cultivated their banking industries into tax and secrecy havens, such as Luxembourg, the Cayman Islands, the Netherlands Antilles, Grenada,

Bermuda, and the British Virgin Islands: strict bank secrecy laws, coupled with criminal offenses for divulging banking information regarding customer accounts; stable governments; governments cultivating the financial sector, regardless of its legitimacy (or even in spite of its obvious illegitimacy); and liberal corporate laws allowing the establishment of shell or nominee corporations.

The Bahamas is a very attractive site for offshore business. Its Central Bank regulates and audits the financial sector, which includes over 400 licensed banks and trust companies. The financial sector is second only to tourism in the amount of revenue generated. The Bahamas has no tax treaties with any other country, and there are no corporate or personal income taxes.

Until a few years ago, the government of the Bahamas was actively encouraging and facilitating foreign investment in a financial sector that was largely unregulated *vis à vis* money laundering. Banking secrecy was strictly enforced, with access to bank records available only to the signatories on an account or to law enforcement on a showing that access to the account would "materially aid in the prosecution of a criminal act" (because tax avoidance and evasion are not crimes in the Bahamas — there being no taxes — a court cannot even consider tax issues). However, rising crime and evidence that the Bahamas was becoming an organized crime haven changed the government's position from one that espoused the position that there was "no evidence whatsoever of money laundering in the Bahamas" to one that has passed (as of December 1996) very strong anti-money-laundering and bank reporting laws and regulations. For example, signatories must appear personally to open an account and they must present (1) a personal letter of reference from their mainland (U.S. or Canadian, for example) bank addressed to the Bahamian bank, and (2) originals or notarized copies of either a passport or birth certificate.

In 1997, the Central Bank of the Bahamas established an anti-money-laundering unit to monitor compliance of the new money-laundering and bank reporting laws. Domestically, Bahamian banks are generally subsidiaries of international banks. Some of the larger Bahamian banks are Barclays PLC, Royal Bank of Canada (the first offshore bank to open in The Bahamas), Scotiabank, Canadian Imperial Bank of Commerce (CIBC), and Credit Suisse.

With the gradual demise of the Medellín Cartel, and the 1996 and 1997 arrests of the Cali Cartel's kingpins, the new Colombian drug lords are moving away from the Mexican smuggling routes and going back to the traditional Caribbean smuggling routes. The Bahamas are playing an integral role in this new smuggling chain. For example, on February 28, 1998, Bahamian police, working with the DEA, searched the Panamanian-registered vessel Sea Star II docked in Freeport, Grand Bahama. Approximately 2,000 kilograms of cocaine were discovered.

The drug syndicates use Bahamian criminals as "transit" specialists, moving cocaine and heroin through the Bahamas to the U.S. These transit groups utilize a variety of methods. One method involves picking up drugs either dropped into the ocean or transferred from larger boats by small, "island-hopping" boats and even canoes. These small boats then move the drugs into the labyrinth of the Bahamian island chains, where the drugs are transferred to pleasure craft, which then blend into the inter-island boat traffic. DEA reports show that these groups are using sophisticated global positioning systems to pinpoint drop locations, and cellular telephones to minimize detection from monitoring ship-to-ship radio traffic.

The DEA also reports that the drug syndicates are now using the containerized shipping facilities in Freeport to smuggle drugs and money. These facilities function as a freight-forwarding point for commercial cargo bound for Europe and the U.S. Although the cargo containers are not to be opened, authorities are concerned that they can be compromised. In addition, plans to make Freeport a "free zone" like the Colon Free Zone in Panama would further exasercbate the potential smuggling problem.

To combat these drug smuggling schemes, the U.S. government has entered into a number of joint interdiction operations with the government of the Bahamas. These include the early 1982 Operation Bahamas and Turks and Caicos (OPBAT), which effectively closed the northern Caribbean to the Colombian syndicates and forced them to move to Mexico smuggling routes; 1997 Operations Summer Storm and Blue Skies; and the proposed (April 1998) Operation Frontier Lance. All of these operations had (or will have) agents and bases of operations in Nassau.

7. *Belgium*

A member of the European Union (EU), Belgium has a significant financial sector, heavily involved in foreign exchange. Brussels is home to the world's largest international wire-transfer system, SWIFT (see Chapter 3, "Cybercrime and Cyberbanking"). Belgium has adopted the various EU money-laundering directives, including the criminalization of money laundering itself in 1990, and various financial institution reporting requirements in 1993. Since 1993, financial institutions have been required to keep records of transactions that are suspicious or involve ECU 10,000 (approximately U.S.$13,000) or more. In May 1993, legislation was passed improving the provisions for domestic and international asset seizures. In 1996, the government adopted a plan against organized crime that covers money laundering by or through notaries, financial advisors, accountants, real estate agents, and casinos.

Belgium has developed a successful Financial Investigations Unit (FIU), called CTIF or CFI. The president of CTIF/CFI is the president of the Financial Action Task Force for the 1997–1998 session. The CTIF works closely, and well, with Belgium's principal financial sector regulatory body, the Banking and Financial Commission. The CTIF is also well known for being one of the two founders, along with FinCEN, of the Egmont Group — an international organization of financial intelligence units. Most of the money-laundering cases in Belgium are related to drug trafficking (69%), other organized crime (11%), and smuggling (8%). Money laundering based on diamond smuggling is prominant as many of the Russian and South African mined diamonds are brokered through Brussels-based diamond merchants.

In its 1997 International Narcotics Control Strategy Report, the State Department described a money-laundering scheme involving Belgium. In this case, two members of a well-known drug organization routed (U.S.)$9 million through a trust company managed by a second corporation located in the British Virgin Islands, eventually depositing it electronically in a Swiss bank located in Antwerp, Belgium. Using this deposit as collateral or security, the group then purchased a $10 million letter of credit at a discounted rate of $8.6 million, which was then resold in England for $9,150,000.

8. Belize

Strategically located on Mexico's southernmost border (on the Yucatan Peninsula, northeast of Guatemala), Belize was ranked as a "high-priority" or "major" drug-producing and transit country in the U.S. Department of State's 1998 International Narcotics Control Strategy Report, therefore subjecting it to the annual certification/decertification process. Although Belize has been fully certified the last two years, its rating has gone from "medium" to "high" priority.

Belize is home to over 1,000 international business corporations, or IBCs, for which there are no public records and no Central Bank oversight. This should change with the passage of the Money Laundering Prevention Act in August 1996. This Act criminalized money laundering, imposed reporting and record-keeping requirements on domestic banks and financial institutions regarding large currency and suspicious transactions, and allowed for asset forfeiture.

Belize formalized its membership in the CFATF in October 1996.

9. Bermuda

Although not technically a Caribbean nation because of its mid-Atlantic location, Bermuda is considered one of the main offshore financial centers. Bermuda shares several characteristics with the other small nations that have cultivated their banking industries into tax and secrecy havens, such as Luxembourg, the Bahamas, the Netherlands Antilles, Grenada, the Cayman Islands, and the British Virgin Islands. These are: (1) strict bank secrecy laws, coupled with criminal offenses for divulging banking information regarding customer accounts; (2) a stable government; (3) a government that encourages the financial sector; and (4) liberal corporate laws allowing the establishment of shell or nominee corporations.

Bermuda also enjoys historical and cultural ties to the United Kingdom that foster the stability of the financial sectors of the economy, particularly its insurance industry (many insurance and reinsurance companies are based in Bermuda).

10. British Virgin Islands

The British Virgin Islands (BVI) are one of five island nations making up the United Kingdom's Caribbean Dependent Territories, or CDT (the others are Anguilla, the Cayman Islands, Montserrat, and Turks and Caicos).

The BVI is located immediately east of Puerto Rico, which makes it strategically important in the narcotics and human smuggling trades. In addition, it is known as an offshore banking haven. For example, in the mid-1980s, there were approximately 5,000 corporations registered in the BVI; by 1994, there were more than 120,000 BVI corporations.

11. Bolivia

Bolivia's status as one of only three countries in the world able to cultivate the coca plant (Colombia and Peru are the other two) has resulted in it being designated a "high-priority" or "major" drug-producing and transit country in the U.S. Department of State's annual International Narcotics Control Strategy Reports, therefore subjecting it to the annual certification/decertification process.

Bolivia was fully certified in 1998 because of its efforts to reduce coca cultivation (down 5% in 1997), its efforts in shutting off the "Air Bridge" to Colombia, its implementation of a 1996 U.S.–Bolivia bilateral extradition treaty, and concern over the adverse economic effects of decertification (President Hugo Banzer's government is battling 10 to 15% inflation). The U.S. government is critical of Bolivia's coca crop eradication programs, which do not allow aerial spraying (the most effective and safest means). Certification was also granted notwithstanding Bolivia's failure to criminalize money laundering and its complete lack of effective bank reporting and record-keeping requirements.

12. Brazil

Although Brazil has been ranked as a "high-priority" or "major" drug-producing and transit country in the U.S. Department of State's International Narcotics Control Strategy Reports, it has annually attained full certification.

13. Burma

Burma is now known as "Myanmar" (described below).

14. Cambodia

Cambodia was ranked as a "high-priority" or "major" drug-producing and transit country in the U.S. Department of State's 1998 International Narcotics Control Strategy Reports, but was fully certified.

15. Cayman Islands

Located southwest of Cuba and centrally to Florida and Panama and Colombia, the Cayman Islands have been ranked as a "high-priority" country in the U.S. Department of State's International Narcotics Control Strategy Reports.

In 1964, this tiny Caribbean nation had less than 25,000 inhabitants, two banks, and no "offshore" businesses. By 1993, it was the sixth largest financial center in the world with over 540 banks controlling over $400 billion in assets; and 23,500 corporations registered on the island. By 1996, there were approximately 15 fewer banks (some were shut down, some consolidated) controlling $420 billion in assets, and almost 30,000 corporations. In addition to the banking and corporate sectors, the Cayman Islands are home to a thriving securities industry; they are home to more than 1,300 regulated mutual funds with assets of more than $100 billion.*

Despite its dependence on offshore banking — the per capita income of the Cayman Islands is now one of the highest in the Western Hemisphere — the Caymans have enacted strong anti-money-laundering legislation, including mandatory reporting of suspicious transactions. The 1996 Proceeds of Criminal Conduct Law is equivalent in most respects to British anti-money-laundering legislation (see the section on the United Kingdom, below).

16. Channel Islands and the Isle of Man

The Channel Islands of Guernsey and Jersey, and the Isle of Man — all located off the coast of France in the English Channel — are major tax havens and offshore banking centers. Banking is the islands' largest industry, and is strictly regulated; money laundering is a criminal offense, and banks are required to report suspicious transactions to various Financial Investigation Units. The Islands' appeal lies in its use as a wire-transfer conduit to and from North and South America and Europe.

Although as much as 20% of the $120 billion in assets under management in Jersey alone could be laundered money, cooperation between the Islands

---

* This represents a large chunk of the $5 trillion worldwide mutual funds industry, $1 trillion of which is through offshore funds such as those on the Caymans.

and the U.S. is excellent. In 1996, the State of Jersey was awarded U.S.$1 million from the U.S. Treasury for its role in a U.S. Customs case based out of San Francisco; a Jersey-based trust company disclosed various suspicious activities of two U.S. clients, which led to their arrest, prosecution, and conviction for drug trafficking offenses.

17. Chile

Chile is fast becoming a favorite money-laundering country for Mexican and Colombian drug cartels. Occupying a sliver of land down the west coast of South America, and sharing borders with the drug-producing nations of Bolivia and Peru, Chile enjoys one of the most stable economies in the region, with a balanced budget, low external debt, stable inflation, and, perhaps most important, strict bank secrecy laws and a government that is actively encouraging foreign investment. Chile has had effective counter-narcotics and money-laundring laws since October 1995. These laws criminalize the laundering of drug proceeds and allow (but do not require) banks to report suspicious transactions.

Recent DEA money-laundering investigations show that foreign and domestic banks in Santiago are becoming favorite destinations for laundered money and/or are being used as intermediaries in the wire-transfer schemes commonly used to move and hide money.

18. China

Despite its human rights abuses, widespread corruption in the financial sectors, and being home to the Chinese Triads (see Section II.D of Chapter 1), China was fully certified as a cooperating nation by President Clinton in February 1998.

19. Cyprus

Cyprus has emerged as a key money-laundering center, principally because it is a geographic and cultural bridge between Asia, the Middle East, and Europe. It is generally perceived as a conduit for illegal funds, principally from Russian organized crime groups. Accordingly, it was ranked as a "high-priority" country in the U.S. Department of State's 1997 and 1998 International Narcotics Control Strategy Reports.

Domestic banks are tightly controlled by the Cyprus Central Bank. Offshore banks are also regulated by the Central Bank (e.g., they cannot accept foreign currency cash deposits without customs forms and must report all cash transactions over a fixed amount), but enforcement is negligible.

As a member of the European Union, Cyprus has adopted all of the provisions of the 1988 UN Convention and the Council of Europe Convention. Its Prevention and Suppression of Money Laundering Activities Law of 1996 expands the list of underlying offenses, specifies bank actions to deter money laundering (including "Know Your Customer" policies, records maintenance, personnel training), and creates a financial investigations unit.

The future of Cyprus as a money-laundering haven is uncertain. The Turkish and Greek areas have always feuded, and the Turkish area proclaimed self-rule from the Republic of Cyprus in 1975. There is great disparity between the two areas. For example, the Greek area enjoys a GDP that is roughly 16 times that of the Turkish area; a GDP per capita that is over three times as large; and an inflation rate of approximately 3% versus 100 to 200% that of the Turkish area.

20. Czech Republic

Like the other Central European countries and the Former Soviet Union (FSU, or Newly Independent States, or NIS) nations, the Czech Republic has some anti-money-laundering and counter-narcotics legislation in place, but the infrastructure and political will to enforce this legislation are sketchy, at best. In February 1996, the government passed legislation criminalizing money laundering, imposing reporting and record-keeping requirements on banks and other financial institutions (for unusual or suspicious transactions as well as those over 500,000 Czech crowns, about U.S.$18,000), and creating an FIU (which works closely with FinCEN and has obtained membership in the Egmont Group of FIUs). In addition, the Republic has entered into an agreement with the European Union that necessitates they meet the standards of the EU directive on money laundering.

Although the U.S. government has taken an active role in the development of the Republic's anti-money-laundering laws (including seminars by the DEA, Customs, the FBI, and the Financial Fraud Unit of FLETC), the magnitude of the money-laundering problem is not known with any certainty. The Czech police do know, however, that a number of international criminal organizations are strengthening their hold on the Republic's legitimate and illegitimate economy. The Russian Mafiya, the Italian Camorra, and the Sicilian Mafia dominate the smuggling networks and money-laundering operations.

The Czech Republic is used mainly as a transit country for contraband and narcotics moving from Asia to Western Europe and Russia. Turks, Albanians, Russians, and former Yugoslavs move large amounts of heroin from the Golden Crescent (Afghanistan and Pakistan) via Iran. Colombians, operating alone or in partnership with Russians or Italian Camorra and Mafia, have begun using the Republic to move heroin into Western Europe.

21. Dominican Republic

The Dominican Republic was ranked as a "high-priority" or "major" drug-producing and transit country in the U.S. Department of State's 1998 International Narcotics Control Strategy Report, but was fully certified.

The "positives" were seen as: the Dominican Republic being a party to the 1988 UN Drug Convention; money laundering and asset forfeiture laws that comply with the OAS/CICAD models; and a bilateral maritime agreement with the U.S. that includes a standing authorization for U.S. authorities to board and search Dominican-registered vessels in international waters if suspected of drug smuggling.

The "negatives" were seen as: the country's status as an active transshipment point for drugs arriving by air and sea from Colombia and Panama, as well as drugs crossing its notoriously porous land border with Haiti; its prohibition of extraditing Dominican citizens (resulting in many Hispanic drug dealers claiming Dominican nationality in order to gain sanctuary in the country); and little or no government supervision of currency exchange and remittance businesses.

These currency exchange and remittance businesses were the target of two 1997 Geographic Targeting Orders issued by the Treasury Department requiring certain Puerto Rican and New York City money transmitters to report all money transfers of $750 or more to the Dominican Republic in an effort to stem the flow of drug money back to that country (for a full discussion of these GTOs, see Section II.A of Chapter 10, "Law Enforcement Operations").

Dominicans have emerged as one of the fastest growing criminal elements in the East Coast drug trade. They are now acting as the low- and mid-level distribution "franshisees" for the new Colombian drug syndicates, using their social bases in the major East Coast cities from Charlotte, North Carolina, through Philadelphia and New York, to New England, particularly those in Connecticut (Hartford and New Haven), Massachussetts (Boston, Lowell, and Lynn), and New Hampshire (Concord).

22. Ecuador

Ecuador is located along the Atlantic coast of South America, south of the world's greatest producer of cocaine, Colombia (and adjacent to the southern jungles of Colombia, the main area for the cocaine processing plants), and north of the world's greatest cultivator of coca paste, Peru. This geography alone accounts for Ecuador's status as a money-laundering and drug-transit nation.

Notwithstanding its geographic and cultural ties with Colombia, Ecuador has taken a number of positive steps to counter money laundering and drug trafficking, including the 1990 criminalization of money laundering and enactment of asset forfeiture provisions; the 1992 arrest and conviction of one of Latin America's most notorious drug traffickers, Jorge Reyes Torres; the 1994 regulation of the domestic and offshore banking industries, and bank reporting and record-keeping requirements on all cash transactions over $10,000; and the 1995 creation of a financial intelligence unit, called CONSEP (information stored by CONSEP is available to U.S. law enforcement agencies through a bilateral agreement).

The efficacy of Ecuador's programs and laws is questionable, as there remains a lack of interagency cooperation between the banking regulators, the national and local police, and CONSEP. Efforts are also stymied because the money-laundering legislation itself is very vague; although it purports to make it illegal for anyone to try to hide proceeds of narcotics trafficking, the legislation actually fails to use the term "money laundering"! In addition, the legislation does not require the banks or financial institutions to use due diligence against money-laundering activity, nor does it criminalize the laundering of one's own money (it is illegal to launder a third party's money, or to help that third party launder his money). Finally, banks are not required to report suspicious activity or transactions, and they are reluctant to do so because of the lack of "safe harbor" provisions.

23. *The European Union or European Community*

The European Union (EU), or European Community (EC), was created to seek to unify Europe through economic unification of the European nations into one large economy; the EU is now the world's largest single economy, with a $7 trillion per year gross domestic product (1995) and 375 million consumers (compared to 350 million in Latin and South America and the Caribbean, and 290 million in the U.S.). The member nations of the EU include Austria, Belgium, Denmark, France, Germany, Greece, Ireland, Italy, Luxembourg, the Netherlands, Portugal, Spain, Sweden, and the United Kingdom. Noticeably absent is Switzerland, which has retained its traditional political autonomy (but has entered into a free trade agreement with the EU). The EU has invited five countries to begin discussions about membership. Poland, Hungary, the Czech Republic, Slovenia, and Estonia joined Cyprus, chosen earlier, as potential entrants.

The EU's member nations have passed a series of comprehensive directives on money laundering that are compatible with, and in some parts exceed, the 40 Recommendations of the Financial Action Task Force (note that all members of the EU are members of the FATF).

Of immediate impact *vis à vis* money laundering, the EU is currently working to develop a single European currency; the European Currency Unit, or *Ecu* (pronounced "eck-you") is the currency of denomination for the

European Monetary System. European eurobonds and bank certificates of deposit are presently in *Ecus*. The *Ecu* is a composite of the EU member countries' currency valuations, calculated at the *Ecu* central rate (the value of its component currencies). Note that the central rate is not necessarily the same as the market *Ecu* value (the amount it trades for in the market).

The *Ecu* was born when the European Monetary System was launched in 1979. It is intended to be replaced in 1999 by the *euro* as part of the transition to monetary union by the European Community. This transition, set out in glorious, mind-numbing detail in the 1991 Maastricht Treaty, is to take place in three stages. The first stage involves the elimination of all restrictions on the movement of capital between the member countries. This stage was to have been completed by January 1, 1994, but is (arguably) not yet complete. The second stage began on January 1, 1994, with the creation of the "European Monetary Institute," or EMI, the precursor to the proposed European Central Bank. The third stage is scheduled to begin on January 1, 1999, at which time the member countries will fix their currencies to the *euro*, equal to 1 *Ecu*. Over a 3-year transition period, national currencies and the *euro* will both circulate as the national currencies are phased out. During this period, ending in 2002, the EMI will be folded into the European Central Bank. In 2002, *euro* notes and coins will be circulated (if the member countries can agree on sizes, shapes, symbols, etc.). In order to ensure that the *Ecu, euro*, EMI, and ECB remain stable, any member country must be able to meet and maintain certain economic "convergence criteria."

The European Union's fight against money laundering is unlike that of any single nation or any other organization of nations because of the scope of the changes proposed by the economic union of the Western European nations and the emergence of the Eastern European nations.

A 1991 directive passed by the Commission — the EU's 20-member executive body — contained eight sections about money laundering, including sections on a bank's duty to identify customers ("know your customer") and transactions ("suspicious activities"). The directive has been accepted by most of the member nations (Ireland has accepted only some of the sections). Other nations — Denmark, Spain, Germany, France, the Netherlands, and Great Britain — have applied the directive to include casinos, jewel trading, and art dealers.

However, like other areas of unification, anti-money-laundering efforts remain hampered by lack of coordination and cooperation between countries, inconsistent application of international treaties and accords (like the United Nations' Vienna Convention on drugs, adopted in whole by only seven nations), the structure of a Europol (a European "FBI"), and other problems.

24. Germany

Although Germany is not considered a tax haven or offshore banking center, it was ranked as a "high-priority" country in the U.S. Department of State's 1998 International Narcotics Control Strategy Report.

The money-laundering problem is generally a product of the unification of East and West Germany on October 3, 1990. Since the unification, Germany's regulation of and control over the movement of people and capital from the east has lagged. In particular, Germany's lack of any reporting requirements for large trans-border cash movement is the source of much of the money-laundering problems. There are large numbers of Russian and East Europeans bringing U.S. currency into Germany, converting them to Deutsche marks, and then depositing the Deutsche marks into German bank accounts. Although German banks are required to maintain records of large cash transactions — more than dm 20,000, or about U.S.$13,500 — and report suspicious activities (money laundering is a criminal offense), structuring remains a huge problem.

Article 261 of the German Criminal Law provides for jail sentences of up to five years for individuals who attempt to conceal the origin of illegally obtained funds. The major domestic anti-money-laundering law enforcement agency is the German Federal Intelligence Service, or BRD.

Germany appears to be taking some other positive steps toward combating money laundering. For example, on January 16, 1998, the Bundestag voted to amend the Constitution to expand the circumstances in which police can tap telephones and otherwise eavesdrop (such surveillance having been found to be highly effective in U.S. law enforcement efforts, particularly against organized crime). These changes are designed to give police greater powers to combat Germany's growing organized crime problem — a problem seen by many as emerging from former East German and Soviet criminal elements.

25. Grenada

Located at the southern-most tip of the West Indies and just north of Venezuela, Grenada is one of the small Caribbean island nations known as an offshore banking haven. For example, the government collects a $5,000 fee to register an "off-the-shelf" corporation. These corporations are then resold by local lawyers and accountants to foreign clientele — no questions asked — for an average of $30,000.

26. Guatemala

Strategically located immediately south of Mexico on the Trans-American overland route, Guatemala was ranked as a "high-priority" or "major" drug-producing and transit country in the U.S. Department of State's 1998 International Narcotics Control Strategy Report. Its apparent compliance with the 1988 UN Drug Convention and apparent lack of corruption resulted in it gaining full certification.

27. Haiti

The poorest country in the Western Hemisphere, Haiti would not survive without extensive foreign aid. Therefore, despite its abysmal human rights record, low-level corruption, and porous overland border with the Dominican Republic, it was certified as a cooperating nation in 1988 (note that the mere fact it was subject to the certification process meant that Haiti was ranked as a "high-priority" or "major" drug-producing and transit country in the U.S. Department of State's 1998 International Narcotics Control Strategy Report).

Haiti is strategically located in the central Caribbean, occupying the western half of the island of Hispaniola, which it shares with the Dominican Republic. With the Caribbean to its south, the Bahamas to its north, and Puerto Rico only 80 miles from the east coast of Hispaniola, Haiti is perfectly situated as an ideal narcotics "transit" country. For example, the approximately 430 sea miles between the southern coast of Haiti and the northern coastal cities of Barranquila and Cartegena in Colombia allow "go fast" smuggling boats to negotiate a round-trip in one day. The vast majority of drugs smuggled into Haiti then go overland to cross the Haitian–Dominican border, which has virtually no effective customs or police presence. From the Dominican Republic, the drugs are smuggled into Puerto Rico or the Bahamas, for eventual transport to the U.S.

In addition to its prime geographic location, Haiti's abject poverty also makes it ripe for drug traffickers and money launderers to corrupt or influence the police and judiciary. In addition, Haiti has been hampered by a continuing political impasse and failure to elect an effective prime minister and parliament (a failure that has stalled draft legislation on money laundering and counter-narcotics provisions). Notwithstanding these problems, Haiti has taken some positive steps. For example, in 1997, Haiti and the U.S. entered into a Maritime Counterdrug Agreement, resulting in four marine interdiction seizures yielding over 2 metric tonnes of cocaine and 5 metric tonnes of marijuana (from Jamaica). Also in 1997, Haiti established a Counternarcotics Unit (CNU) within its Haitian National Police. Staffed, trained, and advised with assistance from American law enforcement agencies (particularly the DEA), the CNU appears to be poised to be an effective force.

The DEA has identified three principle individuals responsible for the majority of the drug and money-laundering activity in Haiti.

Fernando Alfonso Burgos-Martinez, a Colombian national, heads an organization that moves over 1,000 kilos of cocaine in and through Haiti each month. Burgos-Martinez uses dozens of "legitimate" businesses in Haiti and the Dominican Republic as front companies for his illicit activities. His specialty is getting the drugs into Haiti and the Dominican Republic. He was indicted in January 1997 in the Southern District of Florida, but remains at-large.

Beaudouin Ketant, a Haitian national, using cocaine and heroin supplied by Burgos-Martinez, is responsible for getting the narcotics from Haiti to the U.S. His principle method is to use commercial cargo flights as well as couriers on passenger flights, destined for Miami, New York's JFK International Airport, and Chicago's O'Hare Airport. To facilitate these schemes, Ketant's organization has corrupted personnel at the outbound end (Port-au-Prince in Haiti, Santo Domingo in the Dominican Republic, San Juan in Puerto Rico, and Nassau in the Bahamas) as well as at the various destination airports, particularly Miami and JFK. Once the product is sold in the U.S., Ketant's organization also launders the proceeds and repatriates them back to Haiti and the Dominican Republic, for eventual return to his Colombian suppliers. Favorite schemes include pure smuggling of currency as well as use of wire-transfer companies (see the discussion of Geographic Targeting Orders in Section II.A of Chapter 10, "Law Enforcement Operations").

The third major drug trafficker operating in Haiti is Fritz Charles Saint Hubert, also known as Mona St. Hubert. A Haitian national, Mona St. Hubert and his brother Ives smuggle cocaine from Haiti to the U.S., using couriers, "go fast" boats, commercial fishing boats, and container or commercial shipping channels.

28. *Hong Kong*

Although Hong Kong's status as a British Colony ceased on July 1, 1997, as it reverted back to Chinese rule, it is expected that it will retain its role as a primary Eastern Asian and Pacific Rim money-laundering center. Hong Kong was ranked as a "high-priority" country in the U.S. Department of State's 1997 and 1998 International Narcotics Control Strategy Reports. While not a signatory to the 1988 Vienna Convention, Hong Kong's vigorous law enforcement and regulatory efforts usually exceed the goals and objectives of the Convention. An example of these efforts is the extradition agreement with the U.S. on December 20, 1996.

Hong Kong's status as a major money-laundering center stems from its proximity to major Asian drug-producing countries, its sophisticated financial sectors, low taxation rates, simple procedures for incorporating and maintaining companies, and an absence of controls on the amount of money that can enter and leave the territory. Hong Kong also has a very sophisticated system of remittance centers and money changers. In addition, Hong Kong is home to the major Chinese Triads (see Chapter 1, "Transnational Criminal Organizations," for a description of the Triads).

29. India

Home to the world's most extensive underground banking system (the "Hawala" banking system, described in detail in Section III of Chapter 4) and centrally located between the two great heroin cultivation and production regions in the world (i.e., the "Golden Triangle" of Southeast Asia and the "Golden Crescent" of Central Asia), India was ranked as a "high-priority" or "major" drug-producing and transit country in the U.S. Department of State's 1998 International Narcotics Control Strategy Report. Its compliance with the 1988 UN Drug Convention and apparent lack of corruption resulted in it gaining full certification.

30. Indonesia

Indonesia gained international notice in late 1997 and early 1998 as one of two Southeast Asian nations (the other being Malaysia) on the verge of financial collapse and subject to an International Monetary Fund bail-out. Although not ranked as a "major" drug-producing or transit country in the U.S. Department of State's 1998 International Narcotics Control Strategy Report, its status as one of the world's most populous nations makes it a significant country.

31. Iran

Iran was ranked as a "high-priority" or "major" drug-producing and transit country in the U.S. Department of State's 1998 International Narcotics Control Strategy Report. Iran was one of only four countries to suffer complete decertification, principally because of its government's absolute failure to enact any meaningful anti-money-laundering legislation, and its failure to control the extensive smuggling networks (Iran is a historical route for heroin smuggled overland from Afghanistan and Pakistan).

32. Israel

In 1996, the U.S. State Department upped its rating of Israel as a money-laundering center from medium to medium-high. This change was a result, in part, of the increase in the number of Russian Mafiya members who have illegally obtained Israeli citizenship, and thus access to Israeli banks and property, through their manipulation of Israel's "Law of Return," which provides for the acceptance of anyone who is Jewish. Through this law, many Russian Jews (and non-Jews who bought their status to take advantage of the law) have emigrated to Israel or obtained Israeli citizenship.

33. Jamaica

Jamaica was ranked as a "high-priority" or "major" drug-producing and transit country in the U.S. Department of State's 1998 International Narcotics Control Strategy Report. Its compliance with the 1988 UN Drug Convention (to which it became a party in 1995) and apparent lack of corruption resulted in it gaining full certification. Other positive factors include an improved marijuana eradication program and the passage of a national drug abuse prevention and control plan modeled after an OAS/CICAD master plan. In addition, in November 1997, the federal government amended its 1996 anti-money-laundering law to mandate reporting of all cash transactions of $10,000 (U.S.) or more.

Jamaica remains a major producer of marijuana and an increasingly significant cocaine transshipment country. Other problems exist, particularly Jamaica's poor compliance with U.S. extradition requests (only three of 29 active extradition cases were acted on in 1997), and its failure to enact anti-money-laundering laws that comply with the basic recommendations of the CFATF.

34. Japan

Organized crime in Japan is dominated by the Yakuza (for a full description, see Chapter 1, "Transnational Criminal Organizations," for a discussion of the Japanese Yakuza and its effect on Japan and its economy). The economic boom years of the 1980s saw a meteoric rise in Yakuza activity and prominence. Elements of the Yakuza (called "jiageya") were used to forcibly evict tenants in order to pave the way (literally) for new construction; sokaiya were used to keep corporate meetings short and quiet. Two major scandals were the direct result of corporations paying off sokaiya. The first involved accusations of payoffs made by the president of Japan's largest securities firm, Nomura Securities. The second involved the former chairman of the Dai-Ichi Kangyo Bank, or DKB (larger than Citibank and Bankers Trust combined). In traditional Japanese style, the former chairman committed suicide rather than face accusations of corruption (although four former executives did not take the honorable way out, and instead pled guilty in January 1988, to making payments to a sokaiya racketeer).

The Yakuza's influence in Japan could have far-reaching and devastating effects on Japan's economy; in 1997, the Japanese government released a report, based on figures provided by the banks, that their bad debts owed to Japanese banks from the boom-to-bust real estate of the 1980s were approximately 30 trillion yen, or U.S.$210 billion, but that these debts were eventually collectible. This official report was scoffed at by the international financial community, which believed that there was anywhere between U.S.$300 billion and U.S.$600 billion in bad debts owed to Japan's banks;

that most of it was owed to Yakuza-affiliated real estate speculators; and that the banks were essentially afraid to liquidate or collect. Faced with this international skepticism, on January 12, 1998, the Japanese Finance Ministry released an independent assessment that debunked their earlier estimate; the assessment found that Japan's banks had 76.7 trillion *yen*, or U.S.$560 billion in bad loans. Although the report was silent as to the Yakuza's influence or involvement in these bad loans, the Nomura Securities and DKB scandals and a number of recent business failures appear to suggest that there is a connection. In November 1997, three of Japan's largest financial businesses collapsed: its 4th- and 7th-largest securities firms (Yamaichi Securities and Sanyo Securities Co., respectively) and one of its largest banks, Hokkaido Takushoku Bank Ltd. (its book assets had dropped $20 billion from 1995 to 1996 — still, with almost $74 billion in assets, it would have been the 7th largest bank in the U.S., larger than the Bank of New York).

35. Laos
Laos was ranked as a "high-priority" or "major" drug-producing and transit country in the U.S. Department of State's 1998 International Narcotics Control Strategy Report. Notwithstanding the fact that Laos accounts for about 10% of Southeast Asian opium gum cultivation, its efforts to comply with the 1988 UN Drug Convention and apparent lack of corruption resulted in it gaining full certification.

36. Luxembourg
Luxembourg has long been considered one of the main "offshore" financial centers (although there is nothing "offshore" about it, as it is a landlocked nation located between France and Germany, just south of Belgium).

Luxembourg's dubious status is attributable in part because it was the (nominal) home of the infamous Bank of Credit and Commerce International (BCCI). In addition, Luxembourg is the home of the Banque Leu, the only non-U.S. bank prosecuted by the U.S. government for violations of the Bank Secrecy Act.

37. Malaysia
Like its neighbor Indonesia, Malaysia suffered from a financial crisis in late 1997 and early 1998, resulting in a bail-out from the International Monetary Fund.

Although not a "major" drug-producing or transit country, Malaysia is attractive to Southeast Asian money launderers because of its geographic proximity to the Golden Triangle nations and Hong Kong, its wide range of financial services, and sophisticated and secure legal and banking systems for establishing trusts its offshore financial center, Labuan.

38. *Myanmar*

Formerly known as Burma, Myanmar remains one of the world's leading producers of heroin (see, Chapter 1, "Transnational Criminal Organizations," for a description of Khun Sa, the world's most notorious heroin trafficker, responsible for as much as 60% of the heroin on the streets of the U.S., until his 1996 "surrender" to DEA Bangkok and Royal Thai Police in Operation Tiger Trap). Myanmar was ranked as a "high-priority" or "major" drug-producing and transit country in the U.S. Department of State's 1998 International Narcotics Control Strategy Report. It was one of only four countries to suffer complete decertification, principally because of its government's absolute failure to enact any meaningful anti-money-laundering legislation, and its failure to control opium gum and heroin production.

Myanmar is located in southeast Asia, east of India, southwest of China, and bordering the "Golden Triangle" nations of Laos and Thailand. Myanmar has been under a military regime since 1988. Its head of state is former General Than Shwe, who now wears the mantel of "Prime Minister and Chairman of the State Law and Order Restoration Council." U.S. Secretary of State Madeleine Albright described Myanmar as "the only member of ASEAN (Association of Southeast Asian Nations) where the government protects and profits from the drug trade. In fact, [Myanmar's] top traffickers have become leading investors in its economy … Drug money is laundered with such impunity in [Myanmar] that it taints legitimate investment." In fact, it appears that Myanmar's own economic statistics might confirm Secretary Albright's position; Myanmar's debt and revenue combined do not match its reported expenditures.

39. *Netherlands Antilles*

Like many other southern Caribbean banking nations, the Netherlands Antilles was ranked as a "high-priority" country in the U.S. Department of State's 1998 International Narcotics Control Strategy Report.

Like Aruba, in 1996, the Netherlands Antilles established a center (called MOT) for certain financial institutions to report unusual financial transactions. However, the country continues to earn its long-held reputation as an offshore banking haven. For example, it was estimated that by the early 1980s, as much as 20% of all real property in the Miami area was owned by entities incorporated in the Netherlands Antilles; one piece of property was traced through three levels of Netherlands Antilles shell corporations, with the final "true" owner being a corporation with bearer shares.

The Netherlands Antilles was the offshore home used by the Bank of Credit and Commerce International (BCCI) to gain a foothold into the U.S. banking system in the mid-1980s.

40. Nigeria

The 1998 International Narcotics Control Strategy Report described Nigeria as the "hub of African narcotics traffic." It was one of only four countries to suffer complete decertification, principally because of its government's absolute failure to control the drug trafficking gangs. Secretary of State Madeline Albright had this to say about Nigeria's decertification (formal statement on the 1998 Presidential certifications as reproduced online at *www.usia.gov):*

> [Nigeria's] gangs run networks that bring in much of the heroin which ends up in the United States. The Nigerian government has failed to make life difficult for international criminal enterprises headquartered there and has broken direct promises on extraditions and related actions.

Nigeria has long been a haven for arms and ivory smugglers. The smuggling infrastructure is reasonably sophisticated, with arms and drugs smuggled both overland and through ports into South Africa; from there, the guns and drugs are smuggled into New York and various European cities. Nigeria is also a staging area for cocaine from Colombia and heroin from Thailand.

Nigeria is the largest (roughly the size of Germany and France combined) and most populous (roughly the same number of people as Mexico — approximately 100 million) nation in Africa. Until the collapse of oil prices in the 1980s, it was also a reasonably wealthy nation. With the drop in oil prices came a drop in income and government services, which in turn fostered crime and led to the creation of a criminal class. Add to these economic and social conditions Nigeria's arms and ivory smuggling history, the emergence of Nigeria as a transshipment point for guns and drugs is not surprising. In addition, this emergence has coincided with the opening up, or decolonization, of Africa generally and South Africa particularly. The election of Nelson Mandela, in April 1994, brought an incredible amount of foreign investment to South Africa; with that investment came a growth in the financial services industries of the African nations. As a result, Africa has opened up to both legitimate business and illegal business, including money laundering.

Nigeria has been under some sort of military rule, by successive regimes, since 1983 (Nigeria obtained independence from Britain in 1960. Various forms of democratic government survived until 1983). In late 1995, the head of state, General Sani Abacha, declared that there would be general elections in October 1998. The chances for a peaceful shift to a democratically elected civilian government appear slim, however; Nigeria is the only African country to have been decertified by the U.S., and a 1997 study found it to be the most corrupt nation on Earth (see, also, the discussion of Nigerian criminal organizations in Chapter 1).

41. Pakistan

Pakistan was ranked as a "high-priority" or "major" drug-producing and transit country in the U.S. Department of State's 1998 International Narcotics Control Strategy Report. Like Paraguay and Colombia, it received the marginal "vital national interests" certification; its abysmal record of cooperation (it failed to convict or even arrest any major drug traffickers in 1997) warranted decertification, but its strategic location and political instability compelled the President to certify it so that it would not lose the economic benefits of certification.

Although Pakistan has always been an opium and heroin source country, its rise to "prominence" really began in 1979 with the invasion of Afghanistan and Iran's fundamentalist crackdown on drug production and use. According to the State Department's 1998 International Narcotics Control Strategy Report of Pakistan and its neighbor, Afghanistan, are now the world's second-leading producers of opium (collectively, this region is known as the "Golden Crescent"), behind the Golden Triangle countries of Myanmar (Burma), Laos, and Thailand. Given Afghanistan's internal strife — Soviet occupation, civil war, and current Islamic fundamentalist rule — Pakistan-based heroin traffickers have taken over cultivation and smuggling of opium, as well as the production, smuggling, and distribution of heroin bound for Europe, the oil-rich Persian states, and, to a lesser degree, the U.S.

The United Nations estimates that one of every twenty young Pakistani males is a heroin addict, giving Pakistan the most serious heroin abuse problem in the world. In addition, the drug trade accounts for about 5% of Pakistan's gross domestic product.

With increases in both heroin trafficking and use, it follows that Pakistan is becoming one of the world's leading money-laundering centers. In fact, it has actively courted those wishing to launder money; in 1991, it liberalized its banking laws, eliminating the reporting of large cash transactions and the identities of bank customers. And in 1992, the State Bank of Pakistan ran an ad in *The Wall Street Journal*, advertising its new issue of government bearer bonds, announcing "No Questions Asked About Source of Funds! No Identity To Be Disclosed!" Originally to be marketed in the U.S., Pakistan withdrew its bond offer from American markets after 5 days due to severe pressure from the international banking community. Pakistan also has the dubious distinction of being the home nation of many of the key players in the Bank of Credit and Commerce International (BCCI) scandal, including BCCI's founder, Agha Hasan Abedi.

42. Paraguay

Like Colombia and Pakistan, Paraguay received the marginal "vital national interests" certification. Its ineffective counter-narcotics measures warranted decertification, but its strategic location in South America and political instability compelled the President to certify it so that it would not lose the economic benefits of certification.

43. Peru

According to the 1998 International Narcotics Control Strategy Report, Peru was the world's largest grower of coca. This distinction could change, however, as Peru has taken great steps in reducing the total area under cultivation. For example, in 1997, Peru reduced cultivation by 40% to the lowest levels in over 10 years. This reduction deprived the Colombian cartels of over 100 metric tonnes of processed cocaine.

44. Puerto Rico

Puerto Rico's commonwealth status with the U.S. and its location in the Caribbean make it the largest staging area in the Caribbean for smuggling Colombian cocaine and heroin into the continental U.S. Once a shipment reaches Puerto Rico, it is free of U.S. Customs inspection en route to the continental U.S. Puerto Rico has the third-busiest seaport in North America, fourteenth busiest in the world. More than 75 daily commercial flights leave San Juan's Luiz Munoz Marin International Airport.

In the 1980s, most Colombian drugs were smuggled into the U.S. through the Caribbean and Florida. Successful interdiction efforts caused a shift to Mexico. Since the early 1990s, the Mexican Federation has been responsible for smuggling 70% of the Colombian cocaine into the U.S., taking as their fee one-half of the drugs transported. With the arrests of the four top Cali kingpins in 1995, Puerto Rico has become a more popular route — the new generation of Colombian drug lords are trying to circumvent their Mexican partners, with the 50% fee, and are using Puerto Ricans and Dominicans, with a 20% fee, to transport their drugs to the U.S. Almost all of these drugs flow through Puerto Rico.

The two largest Puerto Rican groups are operated by Alberto Orlandez-Gamboa (based in Colombia, distributing in and from the New York and New Jersey areas), and Celeste Santana, using the Luis Munoz Marin International Airport and a cadre of baggage handlers, airline service workers, mechanics, etc., to smuggle product to the continental U.S.

A number of federal law enforcement agencies — including the DEA, Customs, the IRS, and Justice — maintain a task force in San Juan to combat drug smuggling and money laundering; the High Intensity Drug Trafficking Area (HIDTA) Task Force is actively involved in a number of operations, including the recent (September 1997) GTOs aimed at New York money transmitters.

45. *Switzerland*

Long a haven of money launderers due to its strict bank secrecy laws, Switzerland adopted tighter financial reporting laws in 1989 as a result of extreme pressure from other nations. Swiss banks, particularly the Big Three — Union Bank of Switzerland, Credit Suisse, and Swiss Bank Corp.* — have recently come under international public and regulatory scrutiny regarding the "Nazi Loot" issue, and various class-action suits by Holocaust survivors and Filipinos seeking repatriation of Jewish and Ferdinand Marcos billions, respectively. On July 22, 1997, Swiss banks released a list of approximately 2,000 foreign (non-Swiss) names of those who opened Swiss accounts before the end of World War II and who might have died during the Holocaust. These accounts, all dormant for at least 10 years, have combined deposits of over $40 million. The banks have asked heirs or people with information on the account holders to contact Ernst & Young.

In early 1997, the Swiss national police chief acknowledged that most of the $120 million in Swiss accounts held by Raul Salinas de Gertari, the brother of the former president of Mexico, is probably drug related.

Article 305 of the Swiss Penal Code, passed in 1990, criminalized money laundering. Prior to that, money laundering was a crime only if the funds were later used in drug trafficking. In addition, it also prohibits individuals who, in the course of their professional duties, fail to establish the identities of the beneficial owners of otherwise anonymous accounts.

To supplement these new laws, in April 1991, the Swiss Banking Commission issued directives eliminating anonymous bank accounts. Prior to that date, attorneys could open accounts for their clients, who would remain anonymous under the cloak of the attorney–client privilege.

Although a marked changed from their long historical adherence to strict banking secrecy laws, the Swiss laws are fundamentally different from most nations' money-laundering laws. Where most nations focus on transactional reporting, the Swiss laws focus on identifying the beneficial owner of the account itself.

46. *Taiwan*

Taiwan was ranked as a "high-priority" or "major" drug-producing and transit country in the U.S. Department of State's 1998 International Narcotics Control Strategy Report. It was one of the 22 of 30 such countries to gain full certification.

---

* The Big Three may soon be the Big Two. On December 7, 1997, Union Bank and Swiss Bank Corp. announced that they will merge, creating the world's second largest bank with assets of almost $600 billion. Combined, the two banks also will be the world's largest money manager, with almost $1 trillion ($900 billion) in assets under management.

47. Thailand

Thailand was ranked as a "high-priority" or "major" drug-producing and transit country in the U.S. Department of State's 1998 International Narcotics Control Strategy Report. Thailand gained full certification, principally because the government's opium gum crop eradication program has dropped Thailand's share of Southeast Asia's heroin production to less than 1%.

48. United Kingdom

Because of its major role in the world's economy, and historical ties to the Caribbean region, the United Kingdom (U.K.) has taken a leading role in the fight against money laundering. This role is also taken on, in part, for purely selfish reasons, as the U.K. continues to be one of the world's largest consumers of narcotics — the single greatest source of illegal (therefore in need of laundering) funds.

The U.K. is a member of most of the international anti-money-laundering organizations, principally the FATF. Domestically, the primary statutes aimed at money laundering and drug trafficking are the 1986 Drug Trafficking Offenses Act, which makes drug money laundering a felony punishable by up to 14 years imprisonment; the Criminal Justice (Scotland) Act 1987; the Criminal Justice Act 1988; and the Criminal Justice (International Cooperation) Act 1990. Since 1992, the British Parliament has passed new penal legislation creating new "all crimes" money-laundering offenses and strengthening the confiscation legislation. The Money Laundering Regulations of 1993 set out requirements as to customer identification ("know your customer"), record-keeping, and the reporting of suspicious transactions for banks, as well as a wide range of businesses.

The U.K.'s financial intelligence unit, the National Criminal Intelligence Service (NCIS), is considered a model unit. In addition, Britain's system of educating and training the financial sectors in money-laundering issues is also considered to be outstanding.

49. Venezuela

In 1997, Venezuela adopted new currency transaction reporting requirements. This step, and others aimed at preventing (too much) influence of the Latin and South American drug lords in the Venezuelan economy, led to Venezuela's certification as a cooperating nation in the fight against narcotics trafficking and money laundering.

50. Vietnam

Vietnam was ranked as a "high-priority" or "major" drug-producing and transit country in the U.S. Department of State's 1998 International Narcotics

Control Strategy Report. Vietnam is a new "player" in Southeast Asian opium gum production. Although its total production remains low (about 25 metric tonnes, or about 2% of the Southeast Asian total), the areas under cultivation have doubled since 1996.

References

Bortner, R. Mark, "Cyberlaundering: Anonymous Digital Cash and Money Laundering," (Univ. of Miami School of Law, Miami, 1996).

Boston College International and Comparative Law Review, "Bankers, Guns and Money," (Winter 1991).

Canadian Security Intelligence Service, "Annual Report on Organized Crime in Canada 1996-1997," (Canadian Security Intelligence Service, Ottawa, 1996) from the website at *www.cisc.gc.ca*.

Code of Federal Regulations (Annotated), Title 31, section 103, and cases cited therein.

Department of Justice, "Asset Forfeiture Manual, Volumes I–III (Washington, D.C., 1993).

Department of Justice, Drug Enforcement Administration, Strategic Intelligence Section, Latin American Unit, June 1996 Report, "The South American Cocaine Trade: An 'Industry' in Transition," (Washington, D.C., 1996).

Department of Justice, Federal Bureau of Investigation, Infrastructure Protection Task Force (from the FBI's website at *www.fbi.gov/programs/iptf*).

Department of Justice, "Financial Investigations Check List," Internal Manual, (Washington, D.C., 1992).

Department of the Treasury websites are generally accessed using the initials or acronym for the particular office or bureau at one of four common URL's (using the OCC as an example): *www.occ.treas.gov*, *www.occ.ustreas.gov*, *www.treas.gov/occ*, or *www.ustreas.gov/treasury/bureaus/occ*. The nine offices or bureaus and their URL "designation" are the Office of the Comptroller of the Currency (*occ*), the Office of Thrift Supervision (*ots*), Federal Law Enforcement Training Council (*fletc*), Financial Crimes Enforcement Network (*fincen*), the Internal Revenue Service (*irs*), the Customs Service (*uscs*), the Secret Service (*usss*), the Office of Foreign Assets Control (*ofac*), and the Bureau of Alcohol, Tobacco and Firearms (*atf*).

Department of the Treasury, Office of the Comptroller of the Currency, "Money Laundering: A Banker's Guide to Avoiding Problems," (from the website at *http://www.occ.treas.gov/launder*).

Department of the Treasury, Office of the Comptroller of the Currency, Examiners' Manuals, Alerts, Advisory Letters, and Bulletins (Washington, D.C., 1997).

Department of the Treasury, Office of Thrift Supervision, "Statement on Retail Online Personal Banking," January, 1998.

Department of the Treasury, United States Customs Service, "1994 Report to the Senate Committee on Governmental Affairs, Permanent Subcommittee on Investigations," (Washington, D.C., 1995).

Department of the Treasury, United States Customs Service, Numerically Integrated Profiling System (NIPS) database on trade fraud and anomolies.

Facts on File, Facts on File News Services, *World News Digest*, Vol. 56 No. 2875, (January 11, 1996) through Vol. 58 No. 2988 (March 12, 1998).

Financial Action Task Force Annual Reports, 1995–1996, 1996–1997.

Financial Action Task Force, "Annual Report 1996-1997," (available at FinCEN's website at *www.ustreass.gov/treasury/bureaus/fincen*).

Financial Action Task Force, "The Forty Recommendations of the Financial Action Task Force on Money Laundering," (Paris, 1990).

Kerry, Senator John, *The New War: The Web of Crime That Threatens America's Security*, (Simon & Schuster, 1997).

Kochan, Nicholas, *Dirty Money: The Inside Story of the World's Sleaziest Bank*, (National Press Books, Washington, D.C., 1992).

Natural History Magazine, "Telltale Tattoos in Russian Prisons." November 1993.

Newspapers: articles consulted by the author appeared in *The Boston Globe, The New York Times, The Vancouver Sun, The Wall Street Journal,* and *The Washington Post.*

Office of the Attorney General of California, California Department of Justice, "Report on Russian Organized Crime," (Sacramento, 1995).

On-line Federal Government Sources consulted include the Census Bureau at *http://census.gov*; the Federal Register at *www.access.gpo.gov*; the Government Information Exchange, or GIX at *www.info.gov*; the United States House of Representatives at *www.house.gov*; the United States Senate at *www.senate.gov*; the United States Congressional website THOMAS at *http://thomas.loc.gov*; C-Span's on-line service at *www.c-span.org*; and the White House, at *www.white-house.gov.*

PanamaInfo website at *www.panamainfo.com.*

Porteus, Samuel, "Commentary 70, The Threat from Transnational Crime — An Intelligence Perspective," (Canadian Security Intelligence Service, Ottawa, 1996).

President's Commission on Critical Infrastructure Protection (PCCIP), Chairman Robert T. Marsh, text of speech given at the National Information Systems Security Conference on October 7, 1997, Baltimore, Maryland, and the text of a speech given for Harvard University's John F. Kennedy School of government, Washington, D.C. Regional Alumni Council Lecture Series entitled "The Role of Government in the 21st Century," September 20, 1997, at Arlington, Virginia (both from the PCCIP's website at *www.pccip.gov*).

President's Commission on Organized Crime, "1984 Interim Report of the President's Commission on Organized Crime, 'The Cash Connection: Organized Crime, Financial Institutions, and Money Laundering,'" (Washington, D.C., 1984).

President's Commission on Organized Crime, "A Report to the President and the Attorney General of the United States: America's Habit — Drug Abuse, Drug Trafficking and Organized Crime," (Washington, D.C., 1986).

President's Commission on Organized Crime, "The Impact: Organized Crime Today," (Washington, D.C., 1986).

Preston, Staff Sgt. Robert, Royal Canadian Mounted Police (retired), "Investigators Manual for Financial Investigations and Money Laundering," United Nations International Drug Control Program, (Edmonton, 1996).

Robinson, Jeffrey, *The Laundrymen: Inside Money Laundering, The World's Third-Largest Business*, (Arcade Publishing, N.Y., 1996).

Sieber, Dr. Ulrich, *The International Handbook on Computer Crime*, (John Wiley & Sons, New York, 1986).

Smith, David B., *Prosecution and Defense of Forfeiture Cases*, Vol. 1, (Matthew Bender & Co., 1997).

State Department, "1996 Patterns of Global Terrorism Report," (Washington, D.C., 1997).

State Department, "Background Notes" on various countries and international organizations, e.g., "Background Notes: Organization of American States," *www.state.gov/www/background_notes/oas*.

State Department, Bureau for International Narcotics and Law Enforcement Affairs, Office of International Criminal Justice, "Annual International Narcotics Control Strategy Report," 1996, 1997, 1998.

Time Magazine, Canadian Edition, July 14, 1997, p. 37.

Uniform Commercial Code (U.C.C.) Article 4A, and cases cited therein.

United Nations Report on the Impact of Organized Criminal Actvities at Large, (New York, 1993).

United Nations, "1988 Convention Against Illicit Narcotic Drugs and Psychotropic Substances," Paris, 1988.

United Nations, Office of the Secretary General, "Implementation of the Naples Political Declaration and Global Action Plan Against Organized Transnational Crime," (New York, April 1996).

United States Code (Annotated), Title 12, section 3401 (Right to Financial Privacy Act), and cases cited therein.

United States Code (Annotated), Title 12, sections 1811 *et seq.* (Federal Deposit Insurance Act), and cases cited therein.

United States Code (Annotated), Title 12, sections 21 *et seq.* (National Bank Act), and cases cited therein.

United States Code (Annotated), Title 12, sections 221 *et seq.* (Federal Reserve Act), and cases cited therein.

United States Code (Annotated), Title 18, sections 1030, 2314, and 2701, and cases cited therein.

United States Code (Annotated), Title 21, section 848 (Racketeer Influenced Criminal Organizations statute), and cases cited therein.

United States Code (Annotated), Title 22, section 2656f, and cases cited therein.

United States Code (Annotated), Title 31, sections 5311–5322 (Bank Secrecy Act), and cases cited therein.

United States Code (Annotated), Title 31, sections 5311–5328, and cases cited therein.

United States Code (Annotated), Title 50, section 1701, and cases cited therein.

United States Congress, Office of Technology Assessment, "Information Technologies for Control of Money Laundering," OTA-ITC-630, (Washington, D.C., September, 1995).

United States Federal Government Foreign Broadcast Information Service.

United States Government, the Central Intelligence Agency, "World Factbook Online," (*www.odci.gov/cia/publications/96fact*), Washington, D.C., 1996.

United States House of Representatives, Hearings of the House Banking Committee, "Money Laundering," (Washington, D.C.,1993).

United States House of Representatives, Hearings of the House Committee on Banking, Finance and Urban Affairs, "Bank of Credit and Commerce International (BCCI) Investigation," (Washington, D.C., 1991, 1992).

United States House of Representatives, Hearings of the House Committee on Government Relations, Legal and Monetary Affairs Subcommittee, "The Federal Effort Against Organized Crime," (Washington, D.C., April 1967).

United States House of Representatives, Hearings of the House Committee on Foreign Affairs, Subcommittee on International Security, (Washington, D.C., May 11, 1993).

United States House of Representatives, Hearings of the House Committee on Banking and Financial Services, Subcommittee on General Oversight and Investments, (Washington, D.C., October 22, 1997).

United States House of Representatives, Hearings of the House Committee on Banking and Financial Services, Subcommittee on Financial Institutions and Consumer Credit, (Washington, D.C., May 15, 1997).

United States House of Representatives, Hearings of the House Committee on Banking, Finance and Urban Affairs, Subcommittee on Financial Institutions Supervision, Regulation and Insurance, "Briefing on the 1970 Currency and Foreign Transactions Reporting Act," (Washington, D.C., March 1985).

United States House of Representatives, Hearings of the House Committee on Banking, Finance and Urban Affairs, Subcommittee on Financial Institutions Supervision, Regulation and Insurance, "The First National Bank of Boston," (Washington, D.C., March 1985).

United States House of Representatives, Hearings of the House Government Reform and Oversight Committee, National Security, International Affairs and Criminal Justice Subcommittee, (Washington, D.C., March 12, 1988).

United States House of Representatives, Hearings of the House Judiciary Subcommittee on Crime, July 24, 1997, (Washington, D.C., 1997).

United States House of Representatives, Various hearings of the House Appropriations Committee; Commerce, Justice, State and Judiciary Subcommittee, (Washington, D.C., 1997–1998).

United States House of Representatives, Various hearings of the House Appropriations Committee; Treasury, Postal Service and General Government Subcommittee, (Washington, D.C., 1997–1998).

United States House of Representatives, Various hearings of the House Banking and Financial Services Committee, General Oversight and Investigations Subcommittee, (Washington, D.C., 1997–1998).

United States House of Representatives, Various hearings of the House Government Reform and Oversight Committee; National Security, International Affairs, and Criminal Justice Subcommittee, (Washington, D.C., 1997–1998).

United States House of Representatives, Various hearings of the House International Relations Committee, (Washington, D.C., 1997–1998).

United States House of Representatives: the various Congressional websites for each Representative and Senator, for example, Senator Dianne Feinstein (R., Cal) Statement on the State Department Explanation of Mexico's Certification, March 10, 1997, appearing at *www.senate.gov/~feinstein/mexstmt2.html.*

United States Information Agency (USIA) federal government daily news service website at *http://usiahq.usis.usemb.se* (or at *www.usia.gov/current/news*).

United States Senate, Hearings of the Permanent Subcommittee on Investigations, Committee on Governmental Relations, "Drugs and Money Laundering in Panama," (Washington, D.C., 1988).

United States Senate, Hearings of the Senate Commerce Committee, Testimony of Under Secretary of Commerce William A. Reinsch, "Administration Encryption Policy," March 19, 1997 (website *www.fas.org/irp/congress/1997_hr*), Washington, D.C., 1997.

United States Senate, Hearings of the Subcommittee on Terrorism, Narcotics, and International Operations; Committee on Foreign Relations, "The BCCI Affair," (Washington, D.C., 1991, 1992).

United States Senate, Report of the Permanent Subcommittee on Investigations, Committee on Government Operations, "Final Report of the McClellan Subcommittee: Organized Crime and Illicit Traffic in Narcotics," (Washington, D.C., 1965).

United States Senate, Report of the Senate Committee on Governmental Affairs, Permanent Subcommittee on Investigations, "Domestic Money Laundering: Bank Secrecy Act Compliance and Enforcement," (Washington, D.C., December, 1986).

United States Senate, Various hearings of the Senate Banking, Housing, and Urban Affairs Committee; International Finance Subcommittee, (Washington, D.C., 1997–1998).

United States Senate, Various hearings of the Senate Foreign Relations Committee, (Washington, D.C., 1997–1998).

United States Senate, Various hearings of the Senate Governmental Affairs Committee, Permanent Investigations Subcommittee, (Washington, D.C., 1997–1998).

United States Senate, Various hearings of the Senate Judiciary Committee; Terrorism, Technology, and Government Information Subcommittee, (Washington, D.C., 1997–1998).

United States Sentencing Commission Guidelines website at *www.ussc.gov.*

Various online publications, news and press releases, updates, and background information, including those of the Internal Revenue Service (*www.treas.gov/irs/ci/media/*), Customs Service (*www.customs.treas.gov/hotnew/pressrel.*), the DEA (*www.usdoj.gov/dea/pubs*), and the OCC and OTS sites for money laundering at *www.occ.treas.gov/launder* and *www.ots.treas.gov/launder.*

Wall Street Journal Almanac, 1998, (Random House, 1997).

West Legal Publications, *Words and Phrases,* (West Publishing Co., 1961 and 1989).

Index